Revivals
of Religion

THE CHRISTIAN CLASSICS

REVIVALS OF RELIGION

By
Charles G. Finney

A 700 CLUB EDITION

CBN UNIVERSITY PRESS
VIRGINIA BEACH, VIRGINIA
1978

CONTENTS

PAGE

LECTURE I.—*WHAT A REVIVAL OF RELIGION IS.*

What a revival of religion is not—What it is—The agencies employed in promoting it 1

LECTURE II.—*WHEN A REVIVAL IS TO BE EXPECTED.*

When a revival is needed—The importance of a revival when it is needed—When a revival of religion may be expected .. 16

LECTURE III.—*HOW TO PROMOTE A REVIVAL.*

What it is to break up the fallow ground—How it is to be performed 32

LECTURE IV.—*PREVAILING PRAYER.*

What is effectual or prevailing prayer—Some of the most essential attributes of prevailing prayer—Some reasons why God requires this kind of prayer—That such prayer will avail much 45

LECTURE V.—*THE PRAYER OF FAITH.*

Faith an indispensable condition of prevailing prayer—What it is we are to believe when we pray—When we are bound to exercise this faith—This kind of faith in prayer always obtains the blessing sought—How we are to come into the state of mind in which we can exercise such faith—Objections answered 68

CONTENTS

PAGE

LECTURE VI.—*THE SPIRIT OF PRAYER.*

What Spirit is spoken of in the passage: "The Spirit also helpeth our infirmities"—What that Spirit does for us—Why He does what the text declares Him to do—How He accomplishes it—The degrees of His influences—How His influences are to be distinguished from the influences of evil spirits—Who have a right to expect His influences 86

LECTURE VII.—*ON BEING FILLED WITH THE SPIRIT.*

Individuals may have the Spirit of God—It is their duty to be filled with the Spirit—Why the Spirit is not obtained—The guilt of those who have not the Spirit of God—The consequences of having the Spirit.—The consequences that will follow not having the Spirit 106

LECTURE VIII.—*MEETINGS FOR PRAYER.*

The design of prayer meetings—The manner of conducting them—Several things that will defeat the design of holding them . 125

LECTURE IX.—*MEANS TO BE USED WITH SINNERS.*

On what particular points Christians are to testify for God—The manner in which they are to testify 143

CONTENTS

PAGE

LECTURE X.—*To Win Souls Requires Wisdom.*

How Christians should deal with *careless* sinners—How they should deal with *awakened* sinners, and with *convicted* sinners 160

LECTURE XI.—*A Wise Minister will be Successful.*

A right discharge of the duties of a minister requires great wisdom—The amount of success in the discharge of his duties (other things being equal) decides the amount of wisdom employed by him 180

LECTURE XII.—*How to Preach the Gospel.*

Several passages of Scripture ascribe conversion to man—This is consistent with other passages which ascribe conversion to God—Several important particulars in regard to preaching the Gospel 201

LECTURE XIII.—*How Churches Can Help Ministers.*

The importance of the co-operation of the Church in producing and carrying on a revival—Several things which Churches must do, if they would promote a revival and aid their ministers 232

CONTENTS

PAGE

LECTURE XIV.—*MEASURES TO PROMOTE REVIVALS.*

God has established no particular system of measures to be employed—Our present forms of public worship have been arrived at by a succession of new measures 260

LECTURE XV.—*HINDRANCES TO REVIVALS.*

A revival of religion is a great work—Several things which may put a stop to it—What must be done for the continuance of a revival 291

LECTURE XVI.—*THE NECESSITY AND EFFECT OF UNION.*

We are to be agreed in prayer—We are likewise to be agreed in everything that is essential to the blessing we seek 323

LECTURE XVII.—*FALSE COMFORTS FOR SINNERS.*

The necessity and design of instructing anxious sinners—Anxious sinners are always seeking comfort—The false comforts that are often administered 348

LECTURE XVIII.—*DIRECTIONS TO SINNERS.*

What is a proper direction to be given to sinners when they make inquiry for salvation—What is a proper answer to such inquiry—Several errors into which anxious sinners are apt to fall ... 378

CONTENTS

PAGE

LECTURE **XIX.**—*INSTRUCTIONS TO CONVERTS.*

Several things to be considered in regard to the hopes of young converts—Several things respecting their making a profession of religion—The importance of having correct instruction given to young converts—What should *not* be taught—What things are necessary to be taught 399

LECTURE **XX.**—*INSTRUCTIONS TO CONVERTS (continued).*

Other points on which young converts ought to be instructed—How young converts should be treated by the Church—Some of the evils resulting from defective instruction in the first stages of Christian experience 429

LECTURE **XXI.**—*THE BACKSLIDER IN HEART.*

What backsliding in heart is not—What it is—What are its evidences—What are its consequences—How to recover from such a state 452

LECTURE **XXII.**—*GROWTH IN GRACE.*

What grace is—What the injunction to "grow in grace" does *not* mean—What it *does* mean—Conditions of growth in grace—What is *not* proof of growth—What *is* proof—How to grow in grace 471

LECTURE I

WHAT A REVIVAL OF RELIGION IS

O Lord, revive Thy work in the midst of the years, in the midst of the years make known; in wrath remember mercy.—Hab. 3. 2.

It is supposed that the prophet Habakkuk was contemporary with Jeremiah, and that this prophecy was uttered in anticipation of the Babylonish captivity. Looking at the judgments which were speedily to come upon his nation, the soul of the prophet was wrought up to an agony, and he cried out in his distress: "O Lord, revive Thy work." As if he had said: "O Lord, grant that Thy judgments may not make Israel desolate. In the midst of these awful years let the judgments of God be made the means of reviving religion among us. In wrath remember mercy."

Religion is the work of man. It is something for man to do. It consists in obeying God. It is man's duty. It is true God induces him to do it. He influences him by His Spirit, because of his great wickedness and reluctance to obey. If it were not necessary for God to influence men, if men were disposed to obey God, there would be no occasion to pray: "O Lord, revive Thy work." The ground of necessity for such a prayer is that men are wholly indisposed to obey; and unless God interpose the influence of His Spirit, not a man on earth will ever obey the commands of God.

1

A "Revival of Religion" presupposes a declension. Almost all the religion in the world has been produced by revivals. God has found it necessary to take advantage of the excitability there is in mankind, to produce them to obey. Men are so sluggish, there are so many things to lead their minds off from religion and to oppose the influence of the Gospel, that it is necessary to raise an excitement among them, till the tide rises so high as to sweep away the opposing obstacles. They must be so aroused that they will break over these counteracting influences, before they will obey God.

Look back at the history of the Jews, and you will see that God used to maintain religion among them by special occasions, when there would be a great excitement, and people would turn to the Lord. And after they had been thus revived, it would be but a short time before there would be so many counteracting influences brought to bear upon them, that religion would decline, and keep on declining, till God could have time, so to speak, to convict them of sin by His Spirit, and rebuke them by His providence, and thus so gain the attention of the masses to the great subject of salvation, as to produce a widespread awakening. Then the counteracting causes would again operate, religion would decline, and the nation would be swept away in the vortex of luxury, idolatry, and pride.

There is so little *principle* in the Church, so little firmness and stability of purpose, that unless it is greatly excited, it will go back from the path of duty, and do nothing to promote the glory of God. The state of the world is still such, and probably will be till the millennium is fully come, that religion will be mainly promoted by means of revivals. How long and how often has the experiment been tried, to bring the Church to act steadily for God, without these periodical excitements! Many good men have supposed, and still suppose, that the best way to promote religion is to go along *uniformly,* and gather in the ungodly gradually, and without excitement. But however sound such reasoning may appear in the abstract, *facts* demonstrate its futility. If the Church were far enough advanced in knowledge, and had stability of principle enough to *keep awake,* such a course would do. But the Church is so little enlightened, and there are so many counteracting causes, that the Church will not go steadily to work without a special excitement. As the millennium advances, it is probable that these periodical excitements will be unknown. Then the Church will be enlightened, and the counteracting causes removed, and the entire Church will be in a state of habitual and steady obedience to God. Children will be trained up in the way they should go, and there will be no such torrents of worldliness, and fashion, and covetousness, to bear away the piety of the Church, as soon as the excitement of a revival is withdrawn.

It is very desirable that the Church should go on steadily in a course of obedience without these excitements. Our nervous system is so strung that any powerful excitement, if long continued, injures our health, and unfits us for duty. If religion is ever to have a pervading influence in the world, this spasmodic religion must be done away with. Indeed, it will then be uncalled for. Christians will not sleep the greater part of the time, and once in a while wake up, and rub their eyes, and bluster about, and vociferate a little while, and then go to sleep again. Then there will be no need that ministers should wear themselves out and kill themselves, by their efforts to roll back the flood of worldly influence that sets in upon the Church. But as yet the state of the Christian world is such, that to expect to promote religion without excitements is unphilosophical and absurd. The great political and other worldly excitements that agitate Christendom, are all unfriendly to religion, and divert the mind from the interests of the soul. Now, these excitements can only be counteracted by *religious* excitements. And until there is sufficient religious principle in the world to put down irreligious excitements, it is in vain to try to promote religion, except by counteracting excitements. This is true in philosophy, and it is a historical fact.

It is altogether improbable that religion will ever make progress among *heathen* nations except through the influence of revivals. The attempt is now in making to do it by education, and other cautious and gradual improvements. But so long as the laws of mind remain what they are, it cannot be done in this way. There must be excitement sufficient to wake up the dormant moral powers, and roll back the tide of degradation and sin. And precisely so far as our land approximates to heathenism, it is impossible for God or man to promote

3

religion in such a state of things but by powerful excitements. This is evident from the fact that this has always been the way in which God *has* done it. God does not create these excitements, and choose this method to promote religion, for nothing, or without reason. Men being so reluctant to obey God, will not act until they are excited. For instance, how many there are who know that they ought to be religious, but they are afraid that if they become pious they will be laughed at by their companions. Many are wedded to idols; others are procrastinating repentance until they are settled in life, or until they have secured some favourite worldly interest. Such persons never will give up their false shame, or relinquish their ambitious schemes, till they are so excited by a sense of quiet and danger they cannot hold back any longer.

These remarks are designated only as an introduction. I shall now proceed with the main design, to show:

I. What a revival of religion is not. II. What it is. And III. The agencies employed in promoting it.

I. *A REVIVAL IS NOT A MIRACLE.*

1. A miracle has been generally defined to be a Divine interference, setting aside, or suspending, the laws of nature. A revival is not a miracle in this sense. All the laws of matter and mind remain in force. They are neither suspended nor set aside in a revival.

2. A revival is not a miracle according to another definition of the term "miracle"—something above the powers of nature. There is nothing in religion beyond the ordinary powers of nature. It consists entirely in the *right exercise* of the powers of nature. It is just that, and nothing else. When mankind become religious, they are not *enabled* to put forth exertions which they were unable before to put forth. They only exert powers which they had before, in a different way, and use them for the glory of God.

3. A revival is not a miracle, nor dependent on a miracle, in any sense. It is a purely philosophical result of the right use of the constituted means—as much so as any other effect produced by the application of means. There may be a miracle among its antecedent causes, or there may not. The apostles employed miracles simply as a means by which they arrested

attention to their message, and established its Divine authority. But the miracle was not the revival. The miracle was one thing; the revival that followed it was quite another thing. The revivals in the apostles' days were connected with miracle, but they were not miracles.

I said that a revival is the result of the *right* use of the appropriate means. The means which God has enjoined for the production of a revival, doubtless have a natural tendency to produce a revival. Otherwise God would not have enjoined them. But means will not produce a revival, we all know, without the blessing of God. No more will grain, when it is sown, produce a crop without the blessing of God. It is impossible for us to say that there is not as direct an influence or agency from God, to produce a crop of grain, as there is to produce a revival. What are the laws of nature according to which it is supposed that grain yields a crop? They are nothing but the constituted manner of the operations of God. In the Bible, the Word of God is compared to grain, and preaching is compared to sowing the seed, and the results to the springing up and growth of the crop. A revival is as naturally a result of the use of the appropriate means as a crop is of the use of its appropriate means.

I wish this idea to be impressed on your minds, for there has long been an idea prevalent that promoting religion has something very peculiar in it, not to be judged of by the ordinary rules of cause and effect; in short, that there is no connection of the means with the result, and no tendency in the means to produce the effect. No doctrine is more dangerous than this to the prosperity of the Church, and nothing more absurd.

Suppose a man were to go and preach this doctrine among farmers, regarding their sowing of grain. Let him tell them that God is a Sovereign, and will give them a crop only when it pleases Him, and that for them to plough, and plant, and labour, as if they expected to raise a crop, is very wrong, that it amounts to taking the work out of the hands of God, that it is an interference with His Sovereignty, and that there is no connection between the means and the result on which they can depend. Suppose the farmers should believe such a doctrine? Why, they would starve the world to death.

Just such results would follow on the Church being persuaded that promoting religion is somehow so mysteriously a subject of Divine Sovereignty, that there is no natural connection between the means and the end. In fact, what *are* the results? Why, generation after generation has gone to hell, while the Church has been dreaming and waiting for God to save them without the use of the means. It has been the devil's most successful means of destroying souls! The connection is as clear in religion as it is when the farmer sows his grain.

There is one fact under the government of God worthy of universal notice and of everlasting remembrance; which is, that the most useful and important things are most easily and certainly obtained by the use of the appropriate means. This is evidently a principle in the Divine administration. Hence, all the *necessaries* of life are obtained with great *certainty* by the use of the simplest means. The luxuries are more difficult to obtain; the means to procure them are more intricate, and less certain in their results; while things absolutely hurtful and poisonous, such as alcohol and the like, are often obtained only by torturing nature and making use of a kind of internal sorcery to procure death-dealing abominations.

This principle holds true in moral government, and as spiritual blessings are of surpassing importance, we should expect their attainment to be connected with *great certainty* with the use of the appropriate means; and such we find to be the fact. And I fully believe that, could facts be known, it would be found that when the appointed means have been *rightly* used, spiritual blessings have been obtained with greater uniformity than temporal ones.

II. *WHAT A REVIVAL IS.*

It presupposes that the Church is sunk down in a back-slidden state, and a revival consists in the return of the Church from her backslidings, and in the conversion of sinners.

1. A revival always includes conviction of sin on the part of the church. Backslidden professors cannot wake up and begin right away in the service of God, without deep searchings of

heart. The fountains of sin need to be broken up. In a true revival, Christians are always brought under such conviction; they see their sins in such a light that often they find it impossible to maintain a hope of their acceptance with God. It does not always go to that extent, but there are always, in a genuine revival, deep convictions of sin, and often cases of abandoning all hope.

2. Backslidden Christians will be brought to repentance. A revival is nothing else than a new beginning of obedience to God. Just as in the case of a converted sinner, the first step is a deep repentance, a breaking down of heart, a getting down into the dust before God, with deep humility, and a forsaking of sin.

3. Christians will have their faith renewed. While they are in their backslidden state they are blind to the state of sinners. Their hearts are hard as marble. The truths of the Bible appear like a dream. They admit it to be all true; their conscience and their judgment assent to it; but their faith does not see it standing out in bold relief, in all the burning realities of eternity. But when they enter into a revival, they no longer see "men as trees, walking," but they see things in that strong light which will renew the love of God in their hearts. This will lead them to labour zealously to bring others to Him. They will feel grieved that others do not love God, when they love Him so much. And they will set themselves feelingly to persuade their neighbours to give Him their hearts. So their love to men will be renewed. They will be filled with a tender and burning love for souls. They will have a longing desire for the salvation of the whole world. They will be in an agony for individuals whom they want to have saved—their friends, relations, enemies. They will not only be urging them to give their hearts to God, but they will carry them to God in the arms of faith, and with strong crying and tears beseech God to have mercy on them, and save their souls from endless burnings.

4. A revival breaks the power of the world and of sin over Christians. It brings them to such vantage-ground that they get a fresh impulse towards heaven; they have a new foretaste of heaven, and new desires after union with God; thus the charm of the world is broken, and the power of sin overcome.

5. When the Churches are thus awakened and reformed, the

reformation and salvation of sinners will follow. Their hearts will be broken down and changed. Very often the most abandoned profligates are among the subjects. Harlots, and drunkards, and infidels, and all sorts of abandoned characters, are awakened and converted. The worst of human beings are softened and reclaimed, and made to appear as lovely specimens of the beauty of holiness.

III. THE AGENCIES EMPLOYED.

Ordinarily, there are employed in the work of conversion three agents and one instrument. The agents are God; some person who brings the truth to bear on the mind; and the sinner himself. The instrument is the truth. There are always two agents, God and the sinner, employed and active in every case of genuine conversion.

1. The agency of God is twofold: by His Providence and by His Spirit.

(a) By His providential government He so arranges events as to bring the sinner's mind and the truth in contact. He brings the sinner where the truth reaches his ears or his eyes. It is often interesting to trace the manner in which God arranges events so as to bring this about, and how He

---

[1]When, in 1832, Finney made his home in New York, where he had accepted the pastorate of the Second Free Presbyterian Church, an epidemic of cholera broke out, which was specially fatal in the district where he had gone to reside. One day he counted, from his own house, five hearses, drawn up at one time before as many doors. Next, he was himself smitten, and although he slowly recovered, his system received a severe shock. On his restoration to health he preached (in the theatre which was the meeting-place of his congregation) for twenty evenings, in addition to the Sabbath services. Undoubtedly the preaching was the chief agency, but the remembrance of the epidemic and the preacher's inevitable allusions thereto tended to the deepening of conviction. There were so many converts that another Church was speedily formed. Finney's aim throughout was not to fill his building with Christians from other places, but to gather in the ungodly. Ultimately (so widely did the work spread) he wrote: "When I left New York we had seven such Churches, where members were labouring to secure the salvation of souls."

sometimes makes everything seem to favour a revival. The state of the weather and of the public health[1] and other circumstances concur to make everything just right to favour the application of truth with the greatest possible efficacy. How He sometimes sends a minister along just at the time he is wanted! How He brings out a particular truth just at the particular time when the individual it is fitted to reach is in the way to hear!

(*b*) God's special agency by His Holy Spirit. Having direct access to the mind, and knowing infinitely well the whole history and state of each individual sinner, He employs that truth which is best adapted to his particular case, and then drives it home with Divine power. He gives it such vividness, strength, and power that the sinner quails, and throws down his weapons of rebellion, and turns to the Lord. Under His influence the truth burns its way like fire. He makes the truth stand out in such aspects that it crushes the proudest man down with the weight of a mountain. If men were *disposed* to obey God, the truth is given with sufficient clearness in the Bible; and from preaching they could learn all that is necessary for them to know. But because they are wholly *disinclined* to obey it, God makes it clear before their minds, and pours in upon their souls a blaze of convincing light which they cannot withstand; and they yield to it, obey God, and are saved.

2. The agency of men is commonly employed. Men are not mere *instruments* in the hands of God. Truth is the instrument. The preacher is a moral agent in the work: he acts; he is not a mere passive instrument; he is voluntary in promoting the conversion of sinners.

3. The agency of the sinner himself. The conversion of a sinner consists in his obeying the truth. It is therefore impossible it should take place without his agency, for it consists in *his* acting right. He is influenced to this by the agency of God and by the agency of men. Men act on their fellow-men, not only by language, but by their looks, their tears, their daily deportment. See that impenitent man, who has a pious wife. Her very looks, her tenderness, her solemn, compassionate dignity, softened and moulded into the image of Christ, are a sermon to him all the time. He has to turn his mind away, because it is such a reproach to him. He feels a

sermon ringing in his ears all day long.

Mankind are accustomed to read the countenances of their neighbours. Sinners often read the state of a Christian's mind in his eyes. If his eyes are full of levity, or worldly anxiety and contrivance, sinners read it. If they are full of the Spirit of God, sinners read it. The ungodly are often led to conviction simply by seeing the countenance of Christians.

An individual once went into a manufactory to see the machinery. His mind was solemn, as he had been where there was a revival. The people who laboured there all knew him by sight, and knew who he was. A young lady who was at work saw him, and whispered some foolish remark to her companion, and laughed. The person stopped and looked at her with a feeling of grief. She stopped; her thread broke—and she was so much agitated that she could not join it. She looked out at the window to compose herself, and then tried again; again and again she strove to recover her self-command. At length she sat down, overcome by her feelings. The person then approached and spoke with her; she soon manifested a deep sense of sin. The feeling spread through the establishment like fire, and in a few hours almost every person employed there was under conviction; so much so that the owner, though a worldly man, was astounded, and requested to have the works stopped and a prayer-meeting held; for he said it was a great deal more important to have these people converted than to have the works go on. And in a few days the owner and nearly all the persons employed in the establishment were hopefully converted. The eye of this individual, his solemn countenance, his compassionate feeling, rebuked the levity of the young woman, and brought her under conviction of sin; and probably in a great measure this whole revival followed from so small an incident.[1]

---

[1]The story is from Finney's own experience. The factory was "on the Oriskany Creek, a little above Whitesborough." The words of the gentleman who gave the order to close were: "Stop the mill and let the people attend to religion; for it is more important that our souls should be saved than that this factory should run." Accordingly the gates were closed, the factory stopped, and the meeting held forthwith. Finney's brother-in-law, who was superintendent of the factory, had invited the evangelist to the neighbourhood, and a

If Christians themselves have deep feeling on the subject of religion, they will produce deep feeling wherever they go. And if they are cold, or light and trifling, they inevitably destroy all deep feeling, even in awakened sinners.

I knew a case once of an individual who was very anxious, but one day I was grieved to find that her convictions seemed to be all gone. I asked her what she had been doing. She told me she had been spending the afternoon at a certain place, among some professors of religion—not thinking that it would dissipate her convictions to spend an afternoon with professors of religion! But they were trifling and vain people, and her convictions were lost. And no doubt those professors of religion, by their folly, destroyed a soul, for her convictions did not return.

The Church is required to use the means for the conversion of sinners. Sinners cannot properly be said to use the means for their own conversion. The Church uses the means. What sinners do is submit to the truth, or to resist it. It is a mistake of sinners, to think they are using means for their own conversion. The whole drift of a revival, and everything about it, is designed to present the truth *to* your mind, for your obedience or resistance.

REMARKS:

1. Revivals were formerly regarded as miracles. And it has been so by some even in our day. And others have ideas on the subject so loose and unsatisfactory, that if they would only *think,* they would see their absurdity. For a long time it was supposed by the Church that a revival was a miracle, an interposition of Divine power, with which they had nothing to do, and which they had no more agency in producing than they had in producing thunder, or a storm of hail, or an earthquake.

---

crowded meeting had been held the previous night in the village school-house. Most of the young people from the factory had been present, and many had come under deep conviction. When, therefore, Finney visited the factory next morning they needed only a word to lead them to immediate decision for Christ. In a pamphlet issued by the minister of the Presbyterian Church at Whitesborough it was stated that the converts in the district, during the revival, numbered three thousand.

It is only within a few years that ministers generally have supposed revivals were to be *promoted,* by the use of means designed and adapted specially to that object. It has been supposed that revivals came just as showers do, sometimes in one town, and sometimes in another, and that ministers and Churches could do nothing more to produce them than they could to make showers of rain come on their own town, when they were falling on a neighbouring town.

It used to be supposed that a revival would come "about once in fifteen years, when all would be converted that God intended to save," after which the Church must wait until another crop came forward on the stage of life. Finally, the time got shortened down to five years; it was supposed there might be a revival about as often as that!

I have heard a fact in relation to a pastor who entertained this supposition—that a revival might come about once in five years. There had been a revival in his congregation. The next year there was a revival in a neighbouring town, and he went there to preach, staying several days, till he became engrossed in the work. He returned home on a Saturday, and went into his study to prepare for the Sabbath. His soul was in agony. He thought how many adult persons there were in his congregation at enmity with God. He reasoned thus: "There are so many still unconverted; so many persons *die* yearly— such a portion of them unconverted; if a revival does not come under five years, so many adult heads of families will be lost." He put down his calculations on paper, and embodied them in his sermon for the next day, with his heart bleeding at the dreadful picture. As I understood it, he did not do this with any expectation of a revival; but he felt deeply, and poured out his heart to his people; and that sermon awakened *forty heads of families,* and a powerful revival followed; and so his theory about a revival once in five years was exploded.

Thus God has overthrown, generally, the theory that revivals are miracles.

2. Revivals have been greatly hindered by mistaken notions concerning the Sovereignty of God. Many people have supposed God's Sovereignty to be something very different from what it is. They have supposed it to be such an arbitrary disposal of events, and particularly of the gift of His Spirit, as

precluded a rational employment of means for promoting a revival. But there is no evidence from the Bible that God exercises any such sovereignty. There are no facts to prove it, but everything goes to show that God has connected means with the end, through all the departments of His government, in nature and in grace. There is no *natural* event in which His own agency is not concerned. He has not built the creation like a vast machine that will go on alone, without His further care. He has not retired from the universe, to let it work for itself. That is mere Deism. He exercises a universal superintendence and control. And yet every event in nature has been brought about by means. He administers neither providence nor grace with that sort of sovereignty that dispenses with the use of means. There is no more sovereignty in the one than in the other.

And yet some people are terribly alarmed at all direct efforts to promote a revival, and they cry out: "You are trying to get up a revival in your own strength. Take care, you are interfering with the Sovereignty of God. Better keep along in the usual course, and let God give a revival when He thinks it is best. God is a Sovereign, and it is very wrong for you to attempt to get up a revival, just because *you think* a revival is needed." This is just such preaching as the devil wants. And men cannot do the devil's work more effectually than by preaching up the Sovereignty of God as a reason why we should not put forth efforts to produce a revival.[1]

3. You see the error of those who are beginning to think that religion can be better promoted in the world without revivals, and who are disposed to give up all efforts to produce religious

---

[1]"Till a few years past," wrote Rev. Calvin Colton, M.A., in 1832, "this was the ordinary character of revivals of religion in America: Churches and Christians waited for them, as men are wont to wait for showers of rain, without ever imagining that any duty was incumbent on themselves as instruments. The common apology for indolence, which clothes itself with the sanctity of a resignation to the Divine will, has been too long employed. But it is now getting to be more generally understood that to wait God's time in this matter, is not to wait at all, and that sitting still, or standing still, is not the submission of piety, but an expression of the sloth and recklessness of unbelief" ("History and Character of American Revivals").

awakenings. Because there are evils arising in some instances out of great excitements on the subject of religion, they are of opinion that it is best to dispense with them altogether. This cannot, and must not be. True, there is danger of abuses. In cases of great *religious* as well as in other excitements, more or fewer incidental evils may be expected, of course. But this is no reason why revivals should be given up. The best things are always liable to abuses. Great and manifold evils have originated under (but not because of) the providential and moral governments of God. So in revivals of religion, it is found by experience, that in the present state of the world, religion cannot be promoted to any considerable extent without them. The evils which are sometimes complained of, when they are real, are accidental, and of small importance when compared with the amount of good produced by revivals. The sentiment should not be admitted by the Church for a moment, that revivals may be given up. It is fraught with all that is dangerous to the interests of Zion, is death to the cause of missions, and brings in its train the damnation of the world.[1]

Finally, I have not commenced this course of Lectures on Revivals to get up a curious theory of my own on the subject. I would not spend my time and strength merely to give instructions, to gratify curiosity, and furnish people with something to talk about. I have no idea of a preaching *about*

---

[1]That judicious work "Religion in the United States," by Rev. Robert Baird (an esteemed minister of the American Presbyterian Church) written for European readers, and published in 1840, gave, in a chapter on "Revivals of Religion"—in the preparation of which Mr. Baird enjoyed the co-operation of Dr. Goodrich, of Yale—both a record and a justification of revivals, and said of the typical scenes of a spiritual awakening: "What is there that can appeal more to all the sensibilities of a Christian heart?" God is *here* with the effusions of His Spirit! Who does not feel the thrill of joy, of hope, of confidence which pervades the heart of every spiritually-minded Christian? What can be more suited to revive the decaying graces of backsliders and to bring the whole Church to harmonious action? When the confidence thus inspired has been high and yet humble, resting on the mighty power of the Spirit, when has God failed to bestow a signal blessing?

revivals. It is not my design to preach so as to have you able to say at the close: "We *understand* all about revivals now," while you *do nothing*.

Will you follow the instructions I shall give you from the Word of God, and then put them in practice in your own lives? Will you bring them to bear upon your families, your acquaintance, neighbours, and through the city? Or will you spend the time in learning *about* revivals, and do nothing *for* them? I want you as fast as you learn anything on the subject of revivals, to put it in practice, and go to work and see if you cannot promote a revival among sinners here. If you will not do this, I wish you to let me know at the beginning, so that I need not waste my strength. You ought to decide *now* whether you will do this or not. You know that we call sinners to decide on the spot whether *they* will obey the Gospel. And we have no more authority to let *you* take time to deliberate whether you will obey God, than we have to let sinners do so. We call on you to unite now in a solemn pledge to God, that you will do your duty as fast as you learn what it is, and to pray that He will pour out His Spirit upon this Church and upon all the city.

LECTURE II

WHEN A REVIVAL IS TO BE EXPECTED

Wilt Thou not revive us again, that Thy people may rejoice in Thee?—Psa. 85. 6.

The Psalmist felt that God had been very favourable to the people, and while contemplating the goodness of the Lord in bringing them back from the land whither they had been carried away captive, and while looking at the prospects before them, he breaks out into a prayer for a revival of religion: "Wilt Thou not revive us again, that Thy people may rejoice in Thee?" Since God in His providence had re-established the ordinances of His house among them, he prays that there may be a revival of religion to crown the work.

In my first Lecture I attempted to show what a revival of religion is not, what a revival is, and the agencies to be employed in promoting it. The topics to which I now wish to call attention are: I. When a revival of religion is needed. II. The importance of a revival when it is needed. III. When a revival of religion may be expected.

I. *WHEN A REVIVAL OF RELIGION IS NEEDED.*

1. When there is a want of brotherly love and Christian confidence among professors of religion, then a revival is needed. Then there is a loud call for God to revive His work.

When Christians have sunk down into a low and backslidden state, they neither have, nor can have, the same love and confidence toward each other, as when they are all alive, and active, and living holy lives. God loves all men with the love of benevolence, but He does not feel the love of complacency toward any but those who live holy. Christians love each other with the love of complacency, only in proportion to their holiness. If Christian love is the love of the image of Christ in His people, then it can be exercised only where that image really or apparently exists. A person must reflect the image of Christ, and show the spirit of Christ before other Christians can love him with the love of complacency. It is in vain to call on Christians to love one another with the love of complacency, as Christians, when they are sunk down in stupidity. They see nothing in each other to produce this love. It is next to impossible that they should feel otherwise toward each other than they do toward sinners. Merely knowing that they belong to the Church, or seeing them occasionally at the Communion table, will not produce Christian love, unless they see the image of Christ.

2. When there are dissensions, and jealousies, and evil speakings among professors of religion, then there is a great need of a revival. These things show that Christians have got far from God, and it is time to think earnestly of a revival. Religion cannot prosper with such things in the Church, and nothing can put an end to them like a revival.

3. When there is a worldly spirit in the Church. It is manifest that the Church has sunk down into a low and back-slidden state, when you see Christians conform to the world in dress, equipage, and "parties," in seeking worldly amusements, and reading novels, and other books such as the world reads. It shows that they are far from God, and that there is a great need of a revival of religion.

4. When the Church finds its members falling into gross and scandalous sins, then it is time to awake and cry to God for a revival of religion. When such things are taking place as give the enemies of religion an occasion for reproach, it is time to ask of God: "What will become of Thy great Name?"

5. When there is a spirit of controversy in the Church or in the land, a revival is needful. The spirit of religion is not the

spirit of controversy. There can be no prosperity in religion where the spirit of controversy prevails.

6. When the wicked triumph over the Churches, and revile them, it is time to seek for a revival of religion.

7. When sinners are careless and stupid, it is time Christians should bestir themselves. It is as much their duty to awake as it is for the firemen to do so when a fire breaks out in the night in a great city. The Church ought to put out the fires of hell which are laying hold of the wicked. Sleep! Should the firemen sleep and let the whole city burn down, what would be thought of such firemen? And yet their guilt would not compare with the guilt of Christians who sleep while sinners around them are sinking stupidly into the fires of Hell.

II. *THE IMPORTANCE OF A REVIVAL IN SUCH CIRCUMSTANCES.*

1. A revival of religion is the only possible thing that can wipe away the reproach which covers the Church, and restore religion to the place it ought to have in the estimation of the public. Without a revival, this reproach will cover the Church more and more, until it is overwhelmed with universal contempt. You may do anything else you please, and you may change the aspects of society in some respects, but you will do no real good; you only make it worse without a revival of religion. You may go and build a splendid new house of worship, and line your seats with damask, put up a costly pulpit, and get a magnificent organ, and everything of that kind, but it does no good in reality. It rather does hurt. It misleads them as to the real nature of religion; and so far from converting them, it carries them farther away from salvation. Look wherever they have surrounded the altar of Christianity with splendour, and you will find that the impression produced is contrary to the true nature of religion. There must be a waking up of energy on the part of Christians, and an outpouring of God's Spirit, or the world will laugh at the Church.

2. Nothing else will restore Christian love and confidence among Church members. Nothing but a revival can restore it, and nothing else *ought* to restore it. There is no other way to wake up that love of Christians for one another which is sometimes felt, when they have such love as they cannot express. You cannot have such love without confidence; and you

cannot restore confidence without such evidence of piety as is seen in a revival. If a *minister* find he has lost in any degree the confidence of his people, he ought to labour for a revival as the only means of regaining their confidence. I do not mean that his *motive* in labouring for a revival should be merely to regain the confidence of his people, but that a revival through his instrumentality (and ordinarily nothing else) will restore to him the confidence of the praying part of his people. So if an elder or private member of the Church finds his brethren cold towards him, there is but one way to restore it. It is by being revived himself, and pouring out from his eyes and from his life the splendour of the image of Christ. This spirit will catch and spread in the Church; confidence will be renewed, and brotherly love prevail again.

3. At such a time a revival of religion is indispensable to avert the judgments of God from the Church. This would be a strange preaching if revivals were only miracles, and if the Church has not more agency in producing them than it has in producing a thunderstorm. We could not say to the Church: "Unless there is a revival you may expect judgments." The fact is, *Christians* are more to blame for not being revived, than *sinners* are for not being converted. And if they are not awakened, they may know assuredly that God will visit them with His judgments. How often God visited the Jewish Church with judgments because they would not repent and be revived at the call of His prophets! How often have we seen Churches, and even whole denominations, cursed with a curse, because they would not wake up and seek the Lord, and pray: "Wilt Thou not revive us again, that Thy people may rejoice in Thee?"

4. Nothing but a revival of religion can preserve such a Church from annihilation. A Church declining in this way cannot continue to exist without a revival. If it receives new members, they will, for the most part, be made up of ungodly persons. Without revivals there will not ordinarily be as many persons converted as will die off in a year. There have been Churches in this country where the members have died off, and, since there were no revivals to convert others in their place, the Church has "run out," and the organisation has been dissolved.

A minister told me he once laboured as a missionary in Virginia, on the ground where such a man as Samuel Davies once shone like a flaming torch;[1] and that Davies' Church was so reduced as to have but one male member, and he, if I remember right, was a coloured man. The Church had got proud, and was "run out." I have heard of a Church in Pennsylvania, that was formerly flourishing, but neglected revivals, and it became so reduced that the pastor had to send to a neighbouring Church for a ruling elder when he administered the Communion. (Why not, in such a case, let any member of the Church, male or

---

[1] The name of Samuel Davies is indissolubly associated with the history of revival in Virginia. While the "Great Awakening" in the north, under the preaching of the Tennents, Jonathan Edwards, George Whitefield, and many others had become general by the end of 1742, the revival in the south did not originate until 1743. In Virginia, the flickering flame of revival was fanned by a number of laymen, who experienced considerable opposition from cold formalists. Through the reading of Whitefield's sermons (procured through "a young gentleman from Scotland") by Samuel Morris, "many were convinced of their undone condition, and were constrained to seek deliverance with the greatest solicitude." A visit from the noted Rev. William Robinson (a graduate of the famous "Log College"—the forerunner of Princeton, which William Tennent, sen., had founded *circa* 1730) aroused the country. Among the Churches created through the revival, Samuel Davies ministered with intense devotion, and the work continued to make progress, in spite of the harassments of various authorities, until the commencement of the Revolutionary War. "Prior to the revival, some had been much stirred" (wrote Davies) "by reading some authors of the last (seventeenth) century, particularly Boston, Baxter, Flavel, and Bunyan." Morris had been much helped by " 'Luther on the Galatians,' Luther's 'Table Discourses,' and several pieces of honest Bunyan's." Davies not only ministered at seven meeting-houses, amid a scattered population, but preached frequently in adjacent counties, and gathered many converts far and near. Of a visit to his friend Henry, at Lunenburg, he wrote "the assemblies were numerous—though in the extremity of a cold winter—and unwearied in attending the Word. Oh, these were the happiest days that ever I saw!" He also evangelised among the coloured people, writing (1756) to Gillies: "My principal encouragement of late has been among the poor negro slaves; in the land of their slavery, they have been brought into the glorious liberty of the sons of God." (See Gillies' "Historical Collections," and Dr. F. G. Beardsley's "History of American Revivals.")

female, distribute the elements? Is it indispensable to have an elder?)

5. Nothing but a revival of religion can prevent the means of grace from doing a great injury to the ungodly. Without a revival they will grow harder and harder under preaching, and will experience a more horrible damnation than they would if they had never heard the Gospel. Your children and your friends will go down to a much more horrible fate in hell, in consequence of the means of grace, if there are no revivals to convert them to God. Better were it for them if there were no means of grace, no sanctuary, no Bible, no preaching, than to live and die where there is no revival. The Gospel is the savour of death unto death, if it is not made a savour of life unto life.

6. There is no other way in which a Church can be sanctified, grow in grace, and be fitted for heaven. What is "growing in grace"? Is it hearing someone and getting some new *notions* about religion? No; no such thing. The Christian who does this, and nothing more, is getting worse and worse, more and more hardened, and every week it is more difficult to rouse him up to duty.

III. *WHEN A REVIVAL MAY BE EXPECTED.*

1. When the providence of God indicates that a revival is at hand. The indications of God's providence are sometimes so plain as to amount to a revelation of His will. There is a conspiring of events to open the way, a preparation of circumstances to favour a revival, so that those who are looking out can see that a revival is at hand, just as plainly as if it had been revealed from heaven. Cases have occurred in this country where the providential manifestations were so plain that those who were careful observers felt no hesitation in saying that God was coming to pour out His Spirit and grant a revival. There are various ways for God so to indicate His will to a people; sometimes by giving them peculiar means, sometimes by peculiar and alarming events, sometimes by remarkably favouring the employment of means, or by the state of the public health.

2. When the wickedness of the wicked grieves and humbles and distresses Christians. Sometimes Christians do not seem to mind anything about the wickedness about them. Or, if they do

talk about it, it is in a cold, and callous, and unfeeling way, as if they despaired of a reformation: they are disposed to scold sinners—not to feel the compassion of the Son of God for them. But sometimes the conduct of the wicked drives Christians to prayer, breaks them down, and makes them sorrowful and tender-hearted, so that they can weep day and night, and instead of scolding the wicked they pray earnestly for them. Then you may expect a revival. Indeed, it is begun already.

Sometimes the wicked will get up an opposition to religion. And when this drives Christians to their knees in prayer to God, with strong cryings and tears, you may be certain there is going to be a revival. The prevalence of wickedness is no evidence at all that there is not going to be a revival. That is often God's time to work. When the enemy cometh in like a flood, the Spirit of the Lord lifts up a standard against him. Often the first indication of a revival is that the devil gets up something new in opposition. This will invariably have one of two effects. It will either drive Christians to God, or it will drive them farther away from God, to some carnal policy or other that will only make things worse. Frequently the most outrageous wickedness of the ungodly is followed by a revival. If Christians are made to feel that they have no hope but in God, and if they have sufficient feeling left to care for the honour of God and the salvation of the souls of the impenitent, there will certainly be a revival. Let hell boil over if it will, and spew out as many devils as there are stones in the pavement, if it only drives Christians to God in prayer—it cannot hinder a revival. Let Satan "get up a row," and sound his horn as loud as he pleases; if Christians will only be humbled and pray, they shall soon see God's naked arm in a revival of religion. I have known instances where a revival has broken in upon the ranks of the enemy, almost as suddenly as a clap of thunder, and scattered them, taken the ringleaders as trophies, and broken up their party in an instant.[1]

3. A revival may be expected when Christians have a spirit of prayer for a revival. That is, when they pray as if their hearts were set upon it. Sometimes Christians are not engaged in

---

[1]Finney would naturally feel strongly upon the subject. Prior to his own conversion some members of the Church which he attended

definite prayer for a *revival,* not even when they are warm in prayer. Their minds are upon something else; they are praying for something else—the salvation of the heathen and the like—and not for a revival among themselves. But when they feel the want of a revival, they pray for it; they feel for their own families and neighbourhoods; they pray for them as if they could not be denied. What constitutes a spirit of prayer? Is it many prayers and warm words? *No.* Prayer is the state of the heart. The spirit of prayer is a state of continual desire and anxiety of mind for the salvation of sinners. It is something that weighs them down. It is the same, so far as the philosophy of mind is concerned, as when a man is anxious for some worldly interest. A Christian who has this spirit of prayer feels anxious for souls. It is the subject of his thoughts all the time, and makes him look and act as if he had a load on his mind. He thinks of it by day, and dreams of it by night. This is properly "praying without ceasing." His prayers seem to flow from his heart liquid as water: "O Lord, revive Thy work." Sometimes this feeling is very deep; persons have been bowed down so that they could neither stand nor sit. I can name men in this State, of firm nerves, who stand high in character, who have been absolutely crushed with grief for the state of sinners. The feeling is not always so great as this, but such things are much more common than is supposed. In the great revivals in 1826, they were common.[1] This is by no means enthusiasm. It is just

---

had proposed to make him a special subject of prayer, but so hard did he appear that the pastor advised them otherwise, declaring: "I do not believe Finney will ever be converted." When, however, the news spread that Finney had become a Christian, so much excitement was created in Adams that, without any invitation being issued, the people flocked, next night, to the Church. Finney duly appeared, and told the story of the Lord's dealings with him (see footnote, p. 90). Then the pastor arose, confessing his error, with sorrow, and adding that when told of the conversion, in the earliest part of the day, he had retorted, "I do not believe it." It was a fact full of promise that from this meeting, the first which Finney addressed as a servant of Christ, a revival broke out which extended to various townships.

[1]The revivals of 1826 were perhaps as remarkable as any in Finney's experience. Striking evidences of the thoroughness and

what Paul felt when he said: "My little children, of whom I travail in birth." This travail of soul is that deep agony which persons feel when they lay hold on God for such a blessing, and will not let Him go till they receive it. I do not mean to be understood that it is essential to a spirit of prayer that the distress should be so great as this. But this deep, continual, earnest desire for the salvation of sinners is what constitutes a spirit of prayer for a revival.

When this feeling exists in a Church, unless the Spirit is grieved away by sin, there will infallibly be a revival of Christians generally, and it will involve the conversion of sinners to God. A clergyman once told me of a revival among his people, which commenced with a zealous and devoted woman in the Church. She became anxious about sinners, and gave herself to praying for them; she prayed, and her distress increased; and she finally came to her minister and talked with him, asking him to appoint an anxious inquirers' meeting, for she felt that one was needed. The minister put her off, for he felt nothing of any such need. The next week she came again, and besought him again to appoint such a meeting. She knew there would be somebody to come, for she felt as if God was going to pour out His Spirit. The minister once more put her off. And finally she said to him: "If you do not appoint the meeting I shall die, for there is certainly going to be a revival." The next Sabbath he appointed a meeting, and said that if there were any who wished to converse with him about the salvation of their souls, he would meet them on such an evening. He did not know of one, but when he went to the place, to his astonishment he found a large number of anxious inquirers. Now, do not you think that that woman knew there was going to be a revival? Call it what you please, a new revelation or an old revelation, or anything else. I say it was the Spirit of God that taught that praying woman there was going to be a revival. "The secret of the Lord" was with her, and she

---

effectiveness of the work were seen at Auburn, N. Y., where the opposition was so fierce that a number of unconverted members left and organised a new Church. About five years later Finney was again at Auburn—when these very men, apologising for their former conduct, invited him to their Church. He went, with the result that nearly all who had previously opposed him became converted.

knew it. She knew God had been in her heart, and filled it so full that she could contain no longer.

Sometimes ministers have had this distress about their congregations, so that they felt as if they could not live unless they saw a revival. Sometimes elders and deacons, or private members of the Church, men or women, have the spirit of prayer for a revival of religion, so that they will hold on and prevail with God, till He pours out His Spirit. The first ray of light that broke in upon the midnight which rested on the Churches in Oneida County, in the fall of 1825,[1] was from a woman in feeble health, who, I believe, had never been in a powerful revival. Her soul was exercised about sinners. She was in an agony for the land. She did not know what ailed her, but she kept praying more and more, till it seemed as if her agony would destroy her body. At length she became full of joy, and exclaimed: "God has come! God has come! There is no mistake about it, the work is begun, and is going all over the region." And sure enough the work began, and her family were all converted, and the work spread all over that part of the country. Now, do you think that woman was deceived? I tell you, no. She knew she had prevailed with God in prayer.

Generally there are but few professors of religion who know anything about this spirit of prayer which prevails with God. I have been amazed to see such accounts as are often published about revivals, as if the revival had come without any cause—

---

[1]In October, 1825, Finney was invited by his former pastor (Rev. G. W. Gale, who was now in cordial sympathy with him) to visit the town of Western, Oneida County, N. Y., at which place Mr. Gale was staying for reasons of health. Finney accordingly went, and the interest which was immediately created in the cold and pastorless Church was so deep that meetings were immediately arranged in the school-houses of the district—school-houses rather than churches being chosen, because the plain, colloquial "talk" of Finney so little resembled the sermonic style with which the people were familiar, that it was thought to be inappropriate to a church building. However, the spiritual results were so extraordinary that henceforward Finney was generallly regarded throughout the land as a chief apostle of revival. Regarding the character of his teaching he said: "The doctrine upon which I insisted, that the command to obey God implied the power to do so, created in some places con-

nobody knew why or wherefore.[1] I have sometimes inquired into such cases; when it had been given out that nobody knew anything about it until one Sabbath they saw by the faces of the congregation that God was there, or they saw it in their conference-room, or prayer-meeting, and were astonished at the mysterious Sovereignty of God in bringing in a revival without any apparent connection with means. Now mark me. Go and inquire among the obscure members of the Church and you will always find that somebody had been praying for a revival, and was expecting it—some man or woman had been agonising in prayer for the salvation of sinners, until the blessing was gained. It may have found the minister and the body of the Church fast asleep, and they would wake up all of a sudden, like a man just rubbing his eyes open, running round the room, pushing things over, and wondering where all the excitement comes from. But though few knew it, you may be sure there had been somebody on the watch-tower, constant in prayer till the blessing came. Generally, a revival is more or less extensive, as there are more or less persons who have the spirit of prayer.

4. Another sign that a revival may be expected is when the attention of ministers is especially directed to this particular object, and when their preaching and other efforts are aimed particularly at the conversion of sinners. Most of the time the labours of ministers are, it would seem, directed to other objects. They seem to preach and labour with no particular design to effect the *immediate* conversion of sinners, and then it need not be expected that there will be a revival till *somebody* makes particular efforts for this end. But when the attention of a minister is directed to the state of the families in his congregation, and when his heart is full of feeling of the necessity of a revival, and he puts forth the proper efforts for this end, then you may be prepared to expect a revival. As I

---

siderable opposition. It was said that I taught self-conversion. However, I persisted, and it was seen by ministers and Christians that God owned it as His truth, and blessed it to the salvation of thousands of souls."

[1]The Ulster awakening of 1859 furnishes an apt illustration of this truth. Undoubtedly the circumstances were peculiarly favour-

have explained, the connection between the right use of means for a revival, and a revival, is as philosophically sure as between the right use of means to raise grain, and a crop of wheat. I believe, in fact, it is more certain, and that there are fewer instances of failure. The effect is more certain to follow. Probably the law connecting cause and effect is more undeviating in spiritual than in natural things, and so there are fewer exceptions. The paramount importance of spiritual things makes it reasonable that it should be so.

Take the Bible, the nature of the case, and the history of the Church all together, and you will find fewer failures in the use of means for a revival than in farming or any other worldly business. In worldly affairs there are sometimes cases where counteracting causes annihilate all a man can do. In raising grain, for instance, there are cases which are beyond the control of man, such as drought, hard winter, worms, and so on. So in labouring to promote a revival, there may things occur to counteract it, something or another suddenly diverting the public attention from religion, which may baffle every effort. But I believe there are fewer such cases in the moral than in the natural world. I have seldom seen an individual fail when he used the means for promoting a revival in earnest, in the manner pointed out in the Word of God. I believe a man may enter on the work of promoting a revival with as reasonable an expectation of success as he can enter on any other work with an expectation of success—with the same expectation as the farmer has of a crop when he sows his grain. I have sometimes seen this tried and succeed under circumstances the most forbidding that can be conceived.

---

able; earnest preaching of sound doctrine had familiarised the people with at any rate a correct theory of the Gospel, and the news of the American revival of 1857 had created a spirit of expectancy. Nevertheless it was from a prayer-meeting of obscure and uninfluential young men that the revival—one of the most remarkable ever known in the British Isles—originated. The history of revivals shows again and again how humble believers have prevailed in prayer. "*Homines obscuri*" ("obscure men") was the sneering comment of Maitland of Lethington (debating with John Knox) upon a list of preachers. "*Dei tamen servi*" ("Servants of God, however"), replied Knox.

The great revival at Rochester[1] began under the most disadvantageous circumstances that could well be imagined. It seemed as though Satan had interposed every possible obstacle to a revival. The three Churches were at variance. One had no minister: one was divided and was about to dismiss its minister. An elder of the third Presbyterian Church had brought a charge against the pastor of the first Church. After the work began, one of the first things was, the great stone Church gave way and created a panic.[1] Then one of the Churches went on and dismissed their minister right in the midst of it. Many other things occurred, so that it seemed as if the devil were determined to divert public attention from the subject of religion. But there were a few remarkable cases of the spirit of prayer, which assured us that God was there, and we went on; and the more Satan opposed, the Spirit of the Lord lifted up the standard higher and higher, till finally a wave of salvation rolled over the place.

5. A revival of religion may be expected when Christians begin to confess their sins to one another. At other times they

---

[1]The reference is to the revival which had its origin in Finney's preaching at Rochester, N.Y., in 1830. The magnitude of the work attracted general attention in the United States, so that (says Finney) the very fame of it was an efficient instrument in the hands of the Spirit of God in promoting the greatest revival of religion that the country had seen for years. Long after, in conversation upon the subject, Dr. Lyman Beecher said to Finney (speaking of the revival in its widest aspect): "That was the greatest revival that the world has ever seen in so short a time. One hundred thousand persons were reported as having connected themselves with the Churches. It is unparalleled in the history of the Church."

[1]The building had been "settling" for some time, the ground being damp through its proximity to the canal. One of the timbers fell end downward and broke through the ceiling. The congregation fled and the minister, who was in the pulpit, vaulted almost over Finney and reached the street. "The rush," said Finney, "was terrific. Several leaped through a window into the canal. The interior of the building was strewn with apparel." Happily, though a number of people were injured, nobody was killed, nor was interest in the revival lessened, for the people thronged the other two meeting-places.

confess in a general manner, as if they are only half in earnest. They may do it in eloquent language, but it does not mean anything. But when there is an ingenuous breaking down, and a pouring out of the heart in confession of sin, the flood-gates will soon burst open, and salvation will flow over the place.

A revival may be expected whenever Christians are found wiling to make the sacrifices necessary to carry it on. They must be willing to sacrifice their feelings, their business, their time, to help forward the work. Ministers must be willing to lay out their strength, and to jeopard their health and life. They must be willing to offend the impenitent by plain and faithful dealing and perhaps offend many members of the Church who will not come up to the work. They must take a decided stand with the revival, be the consequences what they may. They must be prepared to go on with the work even though they should lose the affections of all the impenitent, and of all the cold part of the Church. The minister must be prepared, if it be the will of God, to be driven away from the place. He must be determined to go straight forward, and leave the entire event with God.

I knew a minister who had a young man labouring with him in a revival. The young man preached pretty plain truth and the wicked did not like him. They said: "We like *our* minister and we wish to have *him* preach." They finally said so much that the minister told the young man: "Such and such a person, who gives so much towards my support, says so-and-so; Mr. A. also says so, and Mr. B. likewise. They think it will break up the society if you continue to preach, and I think you had better not preach any more." The young man went away, but the Spirit of God immediately withdrew from the place and the revival stopped short. The minister, by yielding to the wicked desires of the ungodly, drive Him away, being afraid that the devil would drive *him* away from his people. So by undertaking to satisfy the devil he offended God. And God so ordered events that in a short time the minister had to leave his people after all. He undertook to go between the devil and God, and God dismissed him.

So the people, also, must be willing to have a revival, let the sacrifice be what it may. It will not do for them to say: "We are willing to attend so many meetings, but we cannot attend any more." Or: "We are willing to have a revival if it will not disturb our arrangements about our business, or prevent our making money." I tell you, such people will never have a revival till they are willing to do anything, and sacrifice anything, that God indicates to be their duty. Christian merchants must feel willing to lock up their stores for six months, if it is necessary to carry on a revival. I do not mean that any such thing is called for, or that it is their duty to do so. But if there should be such a state of feeling as to call for it, then it would be their duty and they ought to be willing to do it. They ought to be willing to do it at the call of God, for He can easily burn down their stores if they do not. In fact, I should not be sorry to see such a revival in New York, as would make every merchant in the city lock up his store till spring, and say that he had sold goods enough and would now give up his whole time to leading sinners to Christ.

7. A revival may be expected when ministers and professors are willing to have God promote it by whatsoever instruments He pleases. Sometimes ministers are not willing to have a revival unless *they* can have the management of it, or unless *their* agency can be conspicuous in promoting it. They wish to prescribe to God what He shall direct and bless, and what men He shall put forward. They will have no new measures. They cannot have any of this "new-light"[1] preaching, or of these *evangelists* that go about the country preaching! They have a good deal to say about God being a Sovereign, and that He will have revivals come in His own way and time. But then He must choose to have it just in their way or they will have nothing to do with it. Such men will sleep on until they are awakened by the judgment trumpet, without a revival, unless they are willing that God should come in His own way—unless they are willing to have anything or anybody employed that will do the most good.

8. Strictly I should say that when the foregoing things occur,

---

[1]By "new-light" Finney of course did not mean any new and strange doctrine; the allusion was to the charge that in his methods of calling upon people to repent immediately and to make public confession of Christ, he was "introducing new measures" (see footnote p. 210).

a revival, to some extent, already exists. In truth a revival should be *expected* whenever it is *needed*. If we need to be revived it is our duty to be revived. If it is duty it is possible, and we should set about being revived ourselves, and, relying on the promise of Christ to be with us in making disciples always and everywhere, we ought to labour to revive Christians and convert sinners, with a confident expectation of success. Therefore, whenever the Church needs reviving, it ought and may expect to be revived, and to see sinners converted to Christ. When those things are seen which are named under the foregoing heads, let Christians and ministers be encouraged and know that a good work is already begun. Follow it up.

REMARKS.

1. Brethren, you can tell from our subject, whether you need a revival or not, in your Church or in your city, and whether you are going to have one or not. Elders of the Church, men, women, any of you, and all of you—what do you say? Do you need a revival? Do you expect to have one? Have you any reason to expect one? You need not be in any mist about it, for you know, or can know if you will, whether you have any reason to look for a revival.

2. You see why you have not a revival. It is only because you do not want one. Because you are neither praying for it, nor feeling anxious for it, nor putting forth efforts for it. I appeal to your own consciences: Are you making these efforts now, to promote a revival? You know, brethren, what the truth is about it. Will you stand up and say that you have made efforts for a revival and have been disappointed—that you have cried to God: "Wilt Thou not revive us?" and that God would not do it?

3. Do you wish a revival? Will *you* have one? If God should ask you this moment, by an audible voice from heaven, "Do you want a revival?" would you dare to say: "Yes"? If He were to ask: "Are you willing to make the sacrifices?" would you answer: "Yes"? And if He said: "When shall it begin?" would you answer: "Let it begin to-night—let it begin here—let it begin in my heart NOW"? Would you dare to say so to God, if you should hear His voice to-night?

LECTURE III

HOW TO PROMOTE A REVIVAL

Break up your fallow ground: for it is time to seek the Lord, till He come and rain righteousness upon you.—Hos. 10. 12.

The Jews were a nation of farmers, and it is therefore a common thing in the Scriptures to refer for illustrations to their occupation, and to the scenes with which farmers and shepherds are familiar. The prophet Hosea addresses them as a nation of backsliders; he reproves them for their idolatry, and threatens them with the judgments of God. I have shown in my first Lecture what a revival is not, what it is, and what are the agencies to be employed in promoting it; and in my second, when it is needed, its importance, and when it may be expected. My design in this Lecture is to show how a revival is to be promoted.

A revival consists of two parts: as it respects the Church, and as it respects the ungodly. I shall speak on this occasion of a revival in the Church. Fallow ground is ground which has once been tilled, but which now lies waste, and needs to be broken up and mellowed, before it is suited to receive grain. I shall show, as it respects a revival in the Church: I. What it is to break up the fallow ground, in the sense of the text. II. How it is to be performed.

32

I. *WHAT IS IT TO BREAK UP THE FALLOW GROUND?*

To break up the fallow ground, is to *break up your hearts,* to prepare your minds to bring forth fruit unto God. The mind of man is often compared in the Bible to ground, and the Word of God to seed sown therein, the fruit representing the actions and affections of those who receive it. To break up the fallow ground, therefore, is to bring the mind into such a state that it is fitted to receive the Word of God. Sometimes your hearts get matted down, hard and dry, till there is no such thing as getting fruit from them till they are broken up, and mellowed down, and fitted to receive the Word. It is this softening of the heart, so as to make it feel the truth, which the prophet calls breaking up your fallow ground.

II. *HOW IS THE FALLOW GROUND TO BE BROKEN UP?*

It is not by any direct efforts to feel. People fall into a mistake on this subject, from not making the laws of mind the object of thought. There are great errors on the subject of the laws which govern the mind. People talk about religious feeling as if they could, by direct effort, call forth religious affection. But this is not the way the mind acts. No man can make himself feel in this way, merely by *trying* to feel. The feelings of the mind are not *directly* under our control. We cannot by willing, or by direct volition, call forth religious feelings. We might as well think to "call spirits from the vasty deep." They are purely involuntary states of mind. They naturally and necessarily exist in the mind under certain circumstances calculated to excite them. But they can be controlled *indirectly.* Otherwise there would be no moral character in our feelings, if there were not a way to control them. We cannot say: "Now I will feel so-and-so towards such an object." But we can command our *attention* to it, and look at it intently, till the proper feeling arises. Let a man who is away from his family bring them up before his mind, and will he not feel? But it is not by saying to himself: "Now I will feel deepy for my family." A man can direct his attention to any object, about which he ought to feel and wishes to feel, and in that way he will call into existence the proper emotions. Let a man call up his enemy before his mind, and his feelings of enmity will rise. So if a man thinks of God, and fastens his mind on any parts of God's character, he will feel—emotions will come up by the very laws of mind. If he is a friend of God, let him contemplate God as a gracious and holy Being, and he will have emotions of friendship kindled in his mind. If he is an enemy of God, only let him get the true character of God before his mind, and then his bitter enmity will rise against God, or he will break down and give his heart to God.

If you mean to break up the fallow ground of your hearts, and make your minds feel on the subject of religion, you must go to work just as you would to feel on any other subject. Instead of keeping your thoughts on everything else, and then imagining that by going to a few meetings you will get your feelings enlisted, go the common-sense way to work, as you would on any other subject. It is just as easy to make your minds feel on the subject of religion as it is on any other. God has put these states of mind under your control. If people were as unphilosophical about moving their limbs as they are about regulating their emotions, you would never have reached this meeting.

If you mean to break up the fallow ground of your hearts, you must begin by looking at your hearts: examine and note the state of your minds, and see where you are. Many never seem to think about this. They pay no attention to their own hearts, and never know whether they are doing well in religion or not; whether they are gaining ground or going back; whether they are fruitful, or lying waste. Now you must draw off your attention from other things, and look into this. Make a business of it. Do not be in a hurry. Examine thoroughly the state of your hearts, and see where you are: whether you are walking with God every day, or with the devil; whether you are serving God or serving the devil most; whether you are under the dominion of the prince of darkness, or of the Lord Jesus Christ.

To do all this, you must set yourself to work to consider your sins. You must examine yourselves. And by this I do not mean that you must stop and look directly within to see what is the present state of your feelings. This is the very way to put a stop to all feeling. That is just as absurd as it would be for a man to shut his eyes on the lamp, and try to turn his eyes inward to find whether there was any image painted on the retina. The man complains that he does not see anything! And why? Because he has turned his eyes away from the objects of sight. The truth is, our moral feelings are as much an object of consciousness as our senses. And the way to find them out is to go on acting, and employing our minds. Then we can tell our moral feelings by consciousness, just as I could tell my natural feelings by consciousness if I should put my hand in the fire.

Self-examination consists in looking at your lives, in considering your actions, in calling up the past, and learning its true character. Look back over your past history. Take up your individual sins one by one, and look at them. I do not mean that you should just cast a glance at your past life, and see that it has been full of sins, and then go to God and make a sort of general confession, and ask for pardon. That is not the way. You must take them up one by one. It will be a good thing to take a pen and paper, and as you go over them, and write them down as they occur to you. Go over them as carefully as a merchant goes over his books; and as often as a sin comes before your memory, add it to the list. General confessions of sin will never do. Your sins were committed *one by one*; and as far as you can come at them, they ought to be reviewed and repented of one by one. Now begin, and take up first what are commonly, but *improperly,* called Sins of Omission.

1. *Ingratitude.* Take this sin, for instance, and write down under that head all the instances you can remember wherein you have received favours from God for which you have never exercised gratitude. How many cases can you remember? Some remarkable providence, some wonderful turn of events, that saved you from ruin. Set down the instances of God's goodness to you when you were in sin, before your conversion, for which you have never been half thankful enough; and the numerous mercies you have received since. How long the catalogue of instances, where your ingratitude has been so black that you are forced to hide your face in confusion! Go on your knees and confess them one by one to God, and ask forgiveness. The very act of confession, by the laws of suggestion, will bring up others to your memory. Put down these. Go over them three or four times in this way, and see what an astonishing number of mercies there are for which you have never thanked God.

2. *Want of love to God.* Think how grieved and alarmed *you* would be if you discovered any flagging of affection for you in your wife, husband, or children; if you saw another engrossing their hearts, and thoughts, and time. Perhaps in such a case you would wellnigh die with a just and virtuous *jealousy.* Now, God calls Himself a jealous God; and have you not given your heart to other loves and infinitely offended Him?

3. *Neglect of the Bible.* Put down the cases when for perhaps weeks, or longer, God's Word was not a pleasure. Some people, indeed, read over whole chapters in such a way that they could not tell what they had been reading. If so, no wonder that your life is spent at random, and that your religion is such a miserable failure.

4. *Unbelief.* Recall the instances in which you have virtually charged the God of truth with lying, by your unbelief of His express promises and declarations. God has promised to give the Holy Spirit to them that ask Him. Now, have you believed this? Have you expected Him to answer? Have you not virtually said in your hearts, when you prayed for the Holy Spirit: "I do not believe that I shall receive"? If you have not believed nor expected to receive the blessing which God has expressly promised, you have charged Him with lying.

5. *Neglect of prayer.* Think of the times when you have neglected secret prayer, family prayer, and prayer-meetings; or have prayed in such a way as more grievously to offend God than to have omitted it altogether.

6. *Neglect of the means of grace.* When you have suffered trifling excuses to prevent your attending meetings, have neglected and poured contempt upon the means of salvation, merely from disrelish of spiritual duties.

7. *The manner in which you have performed those duties.* That is, with want of feeling and want of faith, in a worldly frame of mind, so that your words were nothing but the mere chattering of a wretch who did not deserve that God should feel the least care for him. When you have fallen down upon your knees and "said your prayers" in such an unfeeling and careless manner that if you had been put under oath five minutes after you could not have said for what you had been praying.

8. *Want of love for the souls of your fellow-men.* Look round

upon your friends and relatives, and remember how little compassion you have felt for them. You have stood by and seen them going right to hell, and it seems as though you did not care if they did go. How many days have there been, in which you did not make their condition the subject of a single fervent prayer, or evince an ardent desire for their salvation?

9. *Want of care for the heathen.* Perhaps you have not cared enough for them to attempt to learn their condition; perhaps not even to take a missionary magazine. Look at this, and see how much you really care for the heathen, and set down honestly the real amount of your feelings for them, and your desire for their salvation. Measure your desire for their salvation by the self-denial you practice, in giving of your substance to send them the Gospel. Do you deny yourself even the hurtful superfluities of life, such as tea, coffee, and tobacco? Do you retrench your style of living, and scruple not to subject yourself to any inconvenience to save them? Do you daily pray for them in private? Are you laying by something to put into the treasury of the Lord when you go up to pray? If you are not doing these things, and if your soul is not agonised for the poor benighted heathen, why are you such a hypocrite as to pretend to be a Christian? Why, your profession is an insult to Jesus Christ!

10. *Neglect of family duties.* Think how you have lived before your family, how you have prayed, what an example you have set before them. What direct efforts do you habitually make for their spiritual good? What duty have you *not* neglected?

11. *Neglect of social duties.*

12. *Neglect of watchfulness over your own life.* In how many instances you have hurried over your private duties, and have neither taken yourself to task, nor honestly made up your accounts with God; how often have you entirely neglected to watch your conduct, and, having been off your guard, have sinned before the world, and before the Church, and before God!

13. *Neglect to watch over your brethren.* How often have you broken your covenant that you would watch over them in the Lord! How little do you know or care about the state of their souls! And yet you are under a solemn oath to watch over

them. What have you done to make yourself acquainted with them? In how many of them have you interested yourself, to know their spiritual state? Go over the list, and wherever you find there has been a neglect, write it down. How many times have you seen your brethren growing cold in religion, and have not spoken to them about it? You have seen them beginning to neglect one duty after another, and you did not reprove them, in a brotherly way. You have seen them falling into sin, and you let them go on. And yet you pretend to love them. What a hypocrite! Would you see your wife or child going into disgrace, or into the fire, and hold your peace? No, you would not. What do you think of yourself, then, to pretend to love Christians, and to love Christ, while you can see them going into disgrace, and say nothing to them?

14. *Neglect of self-denial.* There are many professors who are willing to do almost anything in religion, that does not require self-denial. But when they are required to do anything that requires them to deny themselves—oh, that is too much! They think they are doing a great deal for God, and doing about as much as He ought in reason to ask, if they are only doing what they can do just as well as not; but they are not willing to deny themselves any comfort or convenience whatever for the sake of serving the Lord. They will not willingly suffer reproach for the name of Christ. Nor will they deny themselves the *luxuries* of life, to save a world from hell. So far are they from remembering that self-denial is a *condition of discipleship* that they do not know what self-denial is. They never have really denied themselves a riband or a pin for Christ and the Gospel. Oh, how soon such professors will be in hell! Some are giving of *their abundance,* and are giving much, and are ready to complain that others do not give more, when, in truth, they do not themselves give anything that they *need,* anything that they could enjoy if they kept it. They only give of their surplus wealth; and perhaps that poor woman who puts in her mite, has exercised more self-denial than they have in giving thousands.

From these we now turn to Sins of Commission.

1. *Worldly mindedness.* What has been the state of your heart in regard to your worldly possessions? Have you looked at them as really *yours*—as if you had a right to dispose of

them as your own, according to your own will? If you have, write that down. If you have loved property, and sought after it for its own sake, or to gratify lust or ambition, or a worldly spirit, or to lay it up for your families, you have sinned, and must repent.

2. *Pride.* Recollect all the instances you can, in which you have detected yourself in the exercise of pride. Vanity is a particular form of pride. How many times have you detected yourself in consulting vanity about your dress and appearance? How many times have you thought more, and taken more pains, and spent more time about decorating your body to go to Church, than you have about preparing your mind for the worship of God? You have gone caring more as to how you appeared outwardly in the sight of mortal man, than how your soul appeared in the sight of the heart-searching God. You have, in fact, set up yourself to be worshipped by them, rather than prepared to worship God yourself. You sought to divide the worship of God's house, to draw off the attention of God's people to look at your pretty appearance. It is in vain to pretend now, that you do not care anything about having people look at you. Be honest about it. Would you take all this pains about your looks if every person were blind?

3. *Envy.* Look at the cases in which you were envious of those whom you thought were above you in any respect. Or perhaps you have envied those who have been more talented or more useful than yourself. Have you not so envied some, that you have been pained to hear them praised? It has been more agreeable to you to dwell upon their faults than upon their virtues, upon their failures than upon their success. Be honest with yourself; and if you have harboured this spirit of hell, repent deeply before God, or He will never forgive you.

4. *Censoriousness.* Instances in which you have had a bitter spirit, and spoken of Christians in a manner devoid of charity and love; of charity, which requires you always to hope the best the case will admit, and to put the best construction upon any ambiguous conduct.

5. *Slander.* The times you have spoken behind people's backs of the faults, real or supposed, of members of the Church or others, unnecessarily, or without good reason. This is slander. You need not lie to be guilty of slander: to tell the

truth with the design to injure is to slander.

6. *Levity.* How often have you trifled before God as you would not have dired to trifle in the presence of an earthly sovereign? You have either been an atheist, and forgotten that there was a God, or have had less respect for Him, and His presence, than you would have had for an earthly judge.

7. *Lying.* Understand now what lying is. *Any* species of *designed* deception. If the deception be not designed, it is not *lying.* But if you design to make an impression contrary to the naked truth, you lie. Put down all those cases you can recollect. Do not call them by any soft name. God calls them LIES, and charges you with LYING, and you had better charge yourself correctly. How innumerable are the falsehoods perpetrated every day in business, and in social intercourse, by words, and looks, and actions, designed to make an impression on others, for selfish reasons that is contrary to the truth!

8. *Cheating.* Set down all the cases in which you have dealt with an individual, and done to him that which you would not like to have done to you. *That* is cheating. God has laid down a rule in the case: "All things whatsoever ye would that men should do to you, do ye even so to them." That is the rule. And if you have not done so you are a cheat. Mind, the rule is not that you should do "what you might reasonably expect them to do to you": for that is a rule which would admit of every degree of wickedness. But it is: "As ye WOULD they should do to you."

9. *Hypocrisy.* For instance, in your prayers and confessions to God. Set down the instances in which you have prayed for things you did not really want. And the evidence is, that when you have done praying, you could not tell for what you had prayed. How many times have you confessed sins that you did not mean to break off, and when you had no solemn purpose not to repeat them? Yes, have confessed sins when you knew you as much as expected to go and repeat them, as you expected to live.

10. *Robbing God.* Think of the instances in which you have misspent your time, squandering the hours which God gave you to serve Him and save souls, in vain amusements or foolish conversation, in reading novels or doing nothing; cases where you have misapplied your talents and powers of mind;

where you have squandered money on your lusts, or spent it for things which you did not need, and which did not contribute to your health, comfort, or usefulness. Perhaps some of you have laid out God's money for tobacco. I will not speak of intoxicating drink, for I presume there is no professor of religion here that would drink it, and I hope there is not one that uses that filthy poison, tobacco. Think of a professor of religion using God's money to poison himself with tobacco!

11. *Bad temper.* Perhaps you have abused your wife, or your children, or your family, or servants, or neighbours. Write it all down.

12. *Hindering others from being useful.* Perhaps you have weakened their influence by insinuations against them. You have not only robbed God of your own talents, but tied the hands of somebody else. What a wicked servant is he who not only loiters himself but hinders the rest! This is done sometimes by taking their time needlessly; sometimes by destroying Christian confidence in them. Thus you have played into the hands of Satan, and not only showed yourself an idle vagabond, but prevented others from working.

If you find you have committed a fault against an individual, and that individual is within your reach, go and confess it immediately, and get that out of the way. If the individual you have injured is too far off for you to go and see him, sit down and write him a letter and confess the injury. If you have defrauded anybody, send the money, the full amount and the interest.

Go thoroughly to work in all this. Go *now*. Do not put it off; that will only make the matter worse. Confess to God those sins that have been committed against God, and to man those sins that have been committed against man. Do not think of getting off by going round the stumbling-blocks. Take them up out of the way. In breaking up your fallow ground, you must remove every obstruction. Things may be left that you think little things, and you may wonder why you do not feel as you wish to feel in religion, when the reason is that your proud and carnal mind has covered up something which God required you to confess and remove. Break up all the ground and turn it over. Do not "*balk*" it, as the farmers say; do not turn aside for little difficulties; drive the plough right through them, beam deep, and turn the ground up, so that it may all be mellow and soft, and fit to receive the seed and bear fruit "an hundredfold."

When you have gone over your whole history in this way, thoroughly, if you will then go over the ground the second time, and give your solemn and fixed attention to it, you will find that the things you have put down will suggest other things of which you have been guilty, connected with them, or near them. Then go over it a third time, and you will recollect other things connected with these. And you will find in the end that you can remember an amount of history, and particular actions, even in this life, which you did not think you would remember in eternity. Unless you take up your sins in this way, and consider them in detail, one by one, you can form no idea of the amount of them. You should go over the list as thoroughly, and as carefully, and as solemnly, as you would if you were just preparing yourself for the Judgment.

As you go over the catalogue of your sins, be sure to resolve upon present and entire reformation. Wherever you find anything wrong, resolve at once, in the strength of God, to sin no more in that way. It will be of no benefit to examine yourself, unless you determine to amend in every particular that which you find wrong in heart, temper, or conduct.

If you find, as you go on with this duty, that your mind is still all dark, cast about you, and you will find there is some reason for the Spirit of God to depart from you. You have not been faithful and thorough. In the progress of such a work you have got to do violence to yourself and bring yourself as a rational being up to this work, with the Bible before you, and try your heart till you *do* feel. You need not expect that God will work a miracle for you to break up your fallow ground. It is to be done by means. Fasten your attention to the subject of your sins. You cannot look at your sins long and feeling deeply. Experience fully proves the benefit of going over our history in this way. Set yourself to find you can *pray*. You never will have the Spirit of God dwelling in you till you have unravelled this whole mystery of iniquity, and spread out your sins before God. Let there be this deep work of repentance and full confession, this breaking down before God, and you will have as much of the spirit of prayer as your body can bear up under. The reason why so few Christians know anything about the spirit of prayer is because they never would take the pains to examine themselves properly, and so never knew what it was to have their hearts all broken up in this way.

You see I have only begun to lay open this subject. I want to lay it out before you, in the course of these Lectures, so that if you will begin and go on to do as I say, the results will be just as certain as they are when a farmer breaks up a fallow field, and mellows it, and sows his grain. It will be so, if you will only begin in this way and hold it on till all your hardened and callous hearts break up.

REMARKS:

1. It will do no good to preach to you while you hearts are in this hardened, and wasted, and fallow state. The farmer might just as well sow his grain on the rock. It will bring forth no fruit. This is the reason why there are so many fruitless professors in the Church, and why there is so much outside machinery and so little deep-toned feeling. Look at the Sabbath-school, for instance, and see how much machinery there is and how little of the power of godliness. If you go on in this way the Word of God will continue to harden you, and you will grow worse and worse, just as the rain and snow on an old fallow field make the turf thicker and the clods stronger.

2. See why so much preaching is wasted, and worse than wasted. It is because the Church will not break up their fallow ground. A preacher may wear out his life, and do very little good, while there are so many "stony-ground" hearers, who have never had their fallow ground broken up. They are only half converted, and their religion is rather a change of opinion than a change of the feeling of their hearts. There is mechanical religion enough, but very little that looks like deep heart-work.

3. Professors of religion should never satisfy themselves, or expect a revival, just by starting out of their slumbers, and blustering about, and talking to sinners. They must get their fallow grounds broken up. It is utterly unphilosophical to think of getting engaged in religion in this way. If your fallow ground is broken up, then the way to get more feeling is to go out and see sinners on the road to hell, and talk to them, and guide inquiring souls, and you will get more feeling. You may

get into an *excitement* without this breaking up; you may show a kind of zeal, but it will not last long, and it will not take hold of sinners, unless your hearts are broken up. The reason is, that you go about it mechanically, and have not broken up your fallow ground.

4. And now, finally, will *you* break up *your* fallow ground? Will you enter upon the course now pointed out and persevere till you are thoroughly awake? If you fail here, if you do not do this, and get prepared, you can go no farther with me. I have gone with you as far as it is of any use to go until your fallow ground is broken up. Now, you must make thorough work upon this point, or all I have further to say will do you little good. Nay, it will only harden, and make you worse. If, when next Lecture-night arrives it finds you with unbroken hearts, you need not expect to be benefited by what I shall say. If you do not set about this work immediately I shall take it for granted that you do not mean to be revived, that you have forsaken your minister, and mean to let him go up to battle alone. If you do not do this, I charge you with having forsaken Christ, with refusing to repent and do your first works. But if you will be prepared to enter upon the work, I propose, God willing, in the next Lecture, to lead you into the work of saving sinners.

LECTURE IV

PREVAILING PRAYER

The effectual fervent prayer of a righteous man availeth much.—
Jas. 5. 16.

There are two kinds of means requisite to promote a revival: the one to influence men, the other to influence God. The truth is employed to influence men, and prayer to move God. When I speak of moving God, I do not mean that God's mind is changed by prayer, or that His disposition or character is changed. But prayer produces such a change *in us* as renders it consistent for God to do as it would not be consistent for Him to do otherwise. When a sinner repents, that state of feeling makes it proper for God to forgive him. God has always been ready to forgive him on that condition, so that when the sinner changes his feelings and repents, it requires no change of feeling in God to pardon him. It is the sinner's repentance that renders His forgiveness proper, and is the occasion of God's acting as he does. So when Christians offer effectual prayer, their state of feeling renders it proper for God to answer them. He was never unwilling to bestow his blessing—on the condition that they felt aright, and offered the right kind of prayer.

Prayer is an essential link in the chain of causes that lead to a revival, as much so as truth is. Some have zealously used truth to convert men, and laid very little stress on prayer. They have preached, and talked, and distributed tracts with great zeal, and then wondered that they had so little success. And the reason was, that they forgot to use the other branch of the means, effectual prayer. They overlooked the fact that truth, by itself, will never produce the effect, without the Spirit of God, and that the Spirit is given in answer to prayer.

Sometimes it happens that those who are the most engaged in employing truth are not the most engaged in prayer. This is always unhappy. For unless they have the spirit of prayer (or unless some one else has), the truth, by itself, will do nothing but harden men in impenitence. Probably in the Day of Judgment it will be found that nothing is ever done by the truth, used ever so zealously, unless there is a spirit of prayer somewhere in connection with the presentation of truth.

Others err in the reverse direction. Not that they lay too much stress on prayer. But they overlook the fact that prayer might be offered for ever, by itself, and nothing would be done. Because sinners are not converted by direct contact of the Holy Ghost, but by the truth, employed as a means. To expect the conversion of sinners by prayer alone, without the employment of truth, is to tempt God.

Our subject being Prevailing Prayer, I propose:—

I. To show what is effectual or prevailing prayer. II. To state some of the most essential attributes of prevailing prayer. III. To give some reasons why God requires this kind of prayer. IV. To show that such prayer will avail much.

I. *WHAT PREVAILING PRAYER IS.*

1. Effectual, prevailing prayer, does not consist in benevolent desires alone. Benevolent desires are doubtless pleasing to God. Such desires pervade heaven and are found in all *holy* things. But *they are not prayer.* Men may have these desires as the angels and glorified spirits have them. But this is not the effectual, prevailing prayer spoken of in the text. Prevailing prayer is something more than this.

2. Prevailing, or effectual prayer, is that prayer which attains the blessing that it seeks. It is that prayer which effectually moves God. The very idea of *effectual* prayer is that it effects its object.

II. *ESSENTIAL ATTRIBUTES OF PREVAILING PRAYER.*

I cannot detail in full all the things that go to make up prevailing prayer. But I will mention some things that are essential to it; some things which a person must do in order to prevail in prayer.

1. *He must pray for a definite object.* He need not expect to offer such prayer if he *prays at random,* without any distinct or definite object. I speak now of secret prayer. Many people go away into their rooms alone "to pray," simply because "they must say their prayers." The time has come when they are in the habit of going by themselves for prayer—in the morning, or at noon, or at whatever time of day it may be. But instead of having anything to say, any definite object before their mind, they fall down on their knees and pray for just what comes into their minds—for everything that floats in the imagination at the time, and when they have done they can hardly tell a word of what they have been praying for. This is not effectual prayer. What should we think of anybody who should try to move a Legislature so, and should say: "Now it is winter, and the Legislature is in session, and it is time to send up petitions," and should go up to the Legislature and petition at random, without any definite object? Do you think such petitions would move the Legislature?

A man must have some definite object before his mind. He cannot pray effectually for a variety of objects at once. The mind is so constituted that it cannot fasten its desires intensely upon many things at the same time. All the instances of effectual prayer recorded in the Bible are of this kind. Wherever you see that the blessing sought for in prayer was attained, you will find that the prayer which was offered was prayer for that definite object.

2. *Prayer, to be effectual, must be in accordance with the revealed will of God.* To pray for things contrary to the revealed will of God, is to tempt God. There are three ways in which God's will is revealed to men for their guidance in prayer.

(*a*) By express promises or predictions in the Bible, that He will give or do certain things; promises in regard to particular things, or in general terms, so that we may apply them to particular things. For instance, there is this promise: "What things soever ye desire when ye pray, believe that ye receive them, and ye shall have them" (Mark 11. 24).

(b) Sometimes God reveals His will by His Providence. When He makes it clear that such and such events are about to take place, it is as much a revelation as if He had written it in His Word. It would be impossible to reveal everything in the Bible. But God often makes it clear to those who have spiritual discernment that it is His will to grant such and such blessings.

(c) By His Spirit. When God's people are at a loss what to pray for, agreeable to His will, His Spirit often instructs them. Where there is no particular revelation, and Providence leaves it dark, and we know not what to pray for as we ought, we are expressly told that "the Spirit also helpeth our infirmities," and "the Spirit itself maketh intercession for us with groanings which cannot be uttered" (Rom. 8. 26). A great deal has been said on the subject of praying in faith for things not revealed. It is objected that this doctrine implies a new revelation. I answer that, new or old, it is the very revelation that Jehovah says He makes. It is just as plain here as it if were now revealed by a voice from heaven, that the Spirit of God helps the people of God to pray according to the will of God, when they themselves know not what they ought to pray for. "And He that searcheth the hearts knoweth what is the mind of the Spirit, because He maketh intercession for the saints according to the will of God" (Rom. 8. 27); and He leads Christians to pray for just those things, "with groanings which cannot be uttered." When neither the Word nor Providence enables them to decide, let them be "filled with the Spirit," as God commands them to be. He says: "Be filled with the Spirit" (Eph. 5. 18). And *He* will lead their minds to such things as God is willing to grant.

3. *To pray effectually you must pray with submission to the will of God.* Do not confound submission with indifference. No two things are more unlike. I once knew an individual come where there was a revival. He himself was cold, and did not enter into the spirit of it, and had not spirit of prayer; and when he heard the brethren pray as if they could not be denied, he was shocked at their boldness, and kept all the time insisting on the importance of praying with submission; when it was as plain as anything could be that he confounded

submission with indifference.

Again, do not confound submission in prayer with a general confidence that God will do what is right. It is proper to have this confidence that God will do right in all things. But this is a different thing from submission. What I mean by submission in prayer is, acquiescence in the revealed will of God. To submit to any *command* of God is to obey it. Submission to some supposable or possible, but secret, decree of God is not submission. To submit to any dispensation of Providence is impossible till it comes. For we never can know what the event is to be, till it takes place.

Take a case: David, when his child was sick, was distressed, and agonised in prayer, and refused to be comforted. He took it so much to heart that when the child died his servants were afraid to tell him. But as soon as he heard that the child was dead, he laid aside his grief, and arose, and asked for food, and ate and drank as usual. While the child was yet alive he did not know what was the will of God, and so he fasted and prayed, and said: "Who can tell whether God will be gracious to me, that my child may live"? He did not know but that his prayer, his agony, was the very thing on which it turned, whether the child was to live or not. He thought that if he humbled himself and entreated God, perhaps God would spare him this blow. But as soon as God's will appeared, and the child was dead, he bowed like a saint. he seemed not only to acquiesce, but actually to take a satisfaction in it. "I shall go to him, but he shall not return to me" (2 Sam. 12. 15-23). This was true submission. He reasoned correctly in the case. While he had no revelation of the will of God he did not know but that the child's recovery depended on his prayer. But when he had a revelation of the will of God he submitted. While the will of God is not known, to submit, without prayer, is tempting God. Perhaps, and for aught you know, the fact of your offering the right kind of prayer may be the thing on which the event turns. In the case of an impenitent friend, the very condition on which he is to be saved from hell may be the fervency and importunity of your prayer for that individual.

4. *Effectual prayer for an object implies a desire for that object commensurate with its importance.* If a person *truly* desires any blessing, his desires will bear some proportion to

the greatness of the blessing. The desires of the Lord Jesus Christ for the blessing He prayed for were amazingly strong, amounting even to agony. If the desire for an object is strong, and is a benevolent desire, and the thing is not contrary to the will and providence of God, the presumption is that it will be granted. There are two reasons for this presumption:

(a) From the general benevolence of God. If it is a desirable object; if, so far as we can see, it would be an act of benevolence in God to grant it, His general benevolence is presumptive evidence that He will grant it.

(b) If you find yourself exercised with benevolent desires for any object, there is a strong presumption that the Spirit of God is exciting these very desires, and stirring you up to pray for that object, so that it may be granted in answer to prayer. In such a case no degree of desire or importunity in prayer is improper. A Christian may come up, as it were, and take hold of the hand of God. See the case of Jacob, when he exclaimed, in an agony of desire: "I will not let Thee go, except Thou bless me" (Gen. 32. 26). Was God displeased with his boldness and importunity? Not at all; but He granted him the very thing he prayed for. So in the case of Moses. God said to him: "Let Me alone, that My wrath may wax hot against them, and that I may consume them; and I will make of thee a great nation" (Exod. 32. 10). What did Moses do? Did he stand aside and let God do as He said? No; his minds runs back to the Egyptians, and he thinks how they will triumph. "Wherefore should the Egyptians say, For mischief did He bring them out?" It seemed as if he took hold of the uplifted hand of God, to avert the blow. Did God rebuke him and tell him he had no business to interfere? No; it seemed as if He was unable to deny anything to such importunity, and so Moses stood in the gap, and prevailed with God.

Prevailing prayer is often offered in the present day, when Christians have been wrought up to such a pitch of importunity and such a *holy* boldness that afterwards when they looked back upon it, they were frightened and amazed at themselves, to think they should have dared to exercise such importunity with God. And yet these prayers have prevailed, and obtained the blessing. And many of these persons, with whom I am acquainted, are among the holiest persons I know in the world.

5. *Prayer, to be effectual, must be offered from right motives.* Prayer should not be selfish, but should be dictated by a supreme regard for the glory of God.[1] A great deal is offered from pure selfishness. Women sometimes pray for their husbands, that they may be converted, because, they say: "It would be so much more pleasant to have my husband go to Church with me," and all that. And they seem never to lift up their thoughts above self at all. They do not seem to think how their husbands are dishonouring God by their sins, nor how God would be glorified in their conversion. So it is very often with parents. They cannot bear to think that *their* children should be lost. They pray for them very earnestly indeed. But if you talk with them upon the subject they are very tender about it and tell you how good their children are—how they respect religion, and how they are, indeed, "almost Christians now"; and so they talk as if they were afraid you would hurt their children by simply telling them the truth. They do not think how such amiable and lovely children are dishonouring God by their sins; they are only thinking what a dreadful thing it will be for them to go to hell. Unless their thoughts rise higher than this, their prayers will never prevail with a holy God.

The temptation to selfish motives is so strong that there is reason to fear a great many parental prayers never rise above the yearnings of parental tenderness. And that is the reason why so many prayers are not answered and why so many pious, praying parents have ungodly children. Much of the prayer for the heathen world seems to be based on no higher principle than sympathy. Missionary agents and others are dwelling almost exclusively upon the six hundred millions of heathens going to hell, while little is said of their dishonouring God. This is a great evil, and until the Church learns to have higher motives for prayer and missionary effort than sympathy for the heathen, her prayers and efforts will never amount to much.

---

[1]Writing only a few months (in October, 1835) after the publication of these Lectures, George Müller, recording his own desire to demonstrate the faithfulness of God in answering prayer, declared that this was his primary reason for establishing his

6. *Prayer, to be effectual, must be by the intercession of the Spirit.* You never can expect to offer prayer according to the will of God without the Spirit. In the first two cases, it is not because Christians are unable to offer such prayer, where the will of God is revealed in His Word or indicated by His providence. They are able to do it, just as they are able to be holy. But the fact is, that they are so wicked that they never do offer such prayer, unless they are influenced by the Spirit of God. There must be a faith, such as is produced by the effectual operation of the Holy Ghost.

7. *It must be persevering prayer.* As a general thing, Christians who have backslidden and lost the spirit of prayer, will not get at once into the *habit* of persevering prayer. Their minds are not in a right state, and they cannot fix their thoughts so as to hold on till the blessing comes. If their minds were in that state in which they would persevere till the answer came, effectual prayer might be offered at once, as well as after praying ever so many times for an object. But they have to pray again and again, because their thoughts are so apt to wander away and are so easily diverted from the object.

Most Christians come up to prevailing prayer by a protracted process. Their minds gradually become filled with anxiety about an object, so that they will even go about their business sighing out their desires to God. Just as the mother whose child is sick goes round her house sighing as if her heart would break. And if she is a praying mother, her sighs are breathed out to God all the day long. If she goes out of the room where her child is, her mind is still on it; and if she is asleep, still her thoughts are on it, and she starts in her dreams, thinking that perhaps it may be dying. Her whole mind is

---

Orphan Houses: "I certainly did desire to be used of God, to benefit the bodies of poor children, and to seek, in other respects, to do them good for this life. I also particularly longed to be used of God in getting the dear orphans trained up in the fear of God; but still, the first object of the work was that God might be magnified by the fact that the orphans under my care are provided with all they need, only by prayer and faith, without any one being asked by me or my fellow-labourers, whereby it may be seen that God is FAITHFUL STILL, and HEARS PRAYER STILL" ("Narrative of some of the Lord's Dealings with George Muller").

absorbed in that sick child. This is the state of mind in which Christians offer prevailing prayer.

For what reason did Jacob wrestle all night in prayer with God? He knew that he had done his brother Esau a great injury, in getting away the birthright, a long time before. And now he was informed that his injured brother was coming to meet him with an armed force, altogether too powerful to contend with. And there was great reason to suppose that Esau was coming with a purpose of revenge. There were two reasons then why Jacob should be distressed. The first was that he had done this great injury and had never made any reparation. The other was that Esau was coming with a force sufficient to crush him. Now what does he do? He first arranges everything in the best manner he can to placate and meet his brother: sending his present first, then his property, then his family, putting those he loved most farthest behind. And by this time his mind was so exercised that he could not contain himself. He goes away alone over the brook and pours out his very soul in an agony of prayer all night. And just as the day was breaking, the Angel of the Covenant said: "Let me go"; and Jacob's whole being was, as it were, agonised at the thought of giving up, and he cried out: "I will not let Thee go, except Thou bless me." His soul was wrought up into an agony, and he obtained the blessing, but he always bore the marks of it, and showed that his body had been greatly affected by this mental struggle. This is prevailing prayer.

Now, do not deceive yourselves with thinking that you offer effectual prayer, unless you have this intense desire for the blessing. I do not believe in it. Prayer is not effectual unless it is offered up with an agony of desire. The apostle Paul speaks of it as a travail of the soul. Jesus Christ, when he was praying in the garden, was in such an agony that "His sweat was as it were great drops of blood falling down to the ground" (Luke 22. 44). I have never known a person sweat blood; but I have known a person pray till the blood started from his nose. And I have known persons pray till they were all wet with perspiration, in the coldest weather of winter. I have known persons pray for hours, till their strength was all exhausted with the agony of their minds. Such prayers prevailed with God.

This agony in prayer was prevalent in President Edwards'

day, in the revivals which then took place.[1] It was one of the great stumbling-blocks in those days to persons who were opposed to the revival, that people used to pray till their body was overpowered with their feelings. I will give a paragraph of what President Edwards says on the subject, to let you see that this is not a new thing in the Church, but has always prevailed wherever revivals prevailed with power. It is from his "Thoughts on Revivals":[1]

"We cannot determine that God shall never give any person so much of a discovery of Himself, not only as to weaken their bodies, but to take away their lives. It is supposed by very learned and judicious divines, that Moses' life was taken away after this manner, and this has also been supposed to be the case with some other saints.

"If God gives a great increase of discoveries of Himself and of love to Him, the benefit is infinitely greater than the calamity, though the life should presently after be taken away. . . .

---

[1]The awakening at Northampton, Mass., under the preaching of Jonathan Edwards, originated in a sense of profound concern regarding the frivolity of the young people. "Indeed" (wrote Edwards in his "Narrative of the Surprising Work of God"), "family government did too much fail in the town." But an astonishing change was at hand; he says, later on: "There was scarcely a single person in the town, either old or young, that was left unconcerned about the great things of the eternal world. Souls did, as it were, come by flocks to Jesus Christ. In the year 1735, the town seemed to be full of the presence of God. Strangers were wont to tell that the state of the town could not be conceived by those who had not seen it." This revival was the beginning of the spiritual movement in which Gilbert Tennent, "who preached with terrible power," and George Whitefield were mighty instruments of God. As in Britain, Whitefield had prodigious congregations; regarding the results at Philadelphia, Benjamin Franklin declared that it seemed "as if all the world were growing religious."

[1]To be precise: "Thoughts on the Revival of Religion in New England, A. D. 1740, and the Way in which it Ought to be Acknowledged and Promoted." A prefatory note (in the Worcester edition of President Edwards' works) said: "The gracious influences of the Holy Spirit with which Northampton was so abundantly

"There is one particular kind of exercise and concern of mind that many have been empowered by, that has been especially stumbling to some; and that is, the deep concern and distress that they have been in *for the souls of others*. I am sorry that any put us to the trouble of doing that which seems so needless, as defending such a thing as this. It seems like mere trifling in so plain a case, to enter into a formal and particular debate, in order to determine whether there be anything in the greatness and importance of the case that will answer and bear a proportion to the greatness of the concern that some have manifested. Men may be allowed, from no higher a principle than common ingenuousness and humanity, to be very deeply concerned, and greatly exercised in mind, at seeing others in great danger of no greater a calamity than drowning or being burned up in a house on fire. And if so, then doubtless it will be allowed to be equally reasonable, if they saw them in danger of a calamity ten times greater, to be still much more concerned: and so much more still, if the calamity were still vastly greater. And why, then, should it be thought unreasonable and looked upon with a very suspicious eye, as if it must come from some bad cause, when persons are extremely concerned at seeing others in very great danger of suffering the wrath of Almighty God to all eternity? And besides, it will doubtless be allowed that those that have very great degrees of the Spirit of God, that is, a spirit of love, may well be supposed to have vastly more of love and compassion to their fellow-creatures than those that are influenced only by common humanity.

"Why should it be thought strange that those that are full of the Spirit of Christ should be proportionally in their love to souls, like Christ?—who had so strong a love for them, and concern for them, as to be willing to drink the dregs of the cup of God's fury for them; and at the same time that He offered

---

enriched, were soon folllowed by an extensive revival all over the land. An extraordinary zeal was excited in many ministers. Zion put on her robes of salvation. Converts to Jesus were multiplied as the drops of the morning dew. Religion became almost the only subject of concern. The glorious work had its opposers. Mr. Edwards' design was to vindicate it as undoubtedly a work of God."

up His blood for souls, offered up also, as their High Priest, strong crying and tears, with an extreme agony, wherein the soul of Christ was, as it were, in travail for the souls of the elect; and, therefore in saving them He is said to 'see of the *travail* of His soul.' As such a spirit of love to, and concern for, souls was the spirit of Christ, so it is the spirit of the Church; and therefore the Church, in desiring and seeking that Christ might be brought forth in the world, and in the souls of men, is represented (Rev. 12. 1, 2) as 'a woman crying, travailing in birth, and pained to be delivered.' The spirit of those that have been in distress for the souls of others, so far as I can discern, seems not to be different from that of the apostle, who travailed for souls, and was ready to wish himself accursed from Christ for others (Rom. 9. 3).[1] Nor from that of the Psalmist (Psa. 119. 53): 'Horror hath taken hold upon me, because of the wicked that forsake Thy law.' And (ver. 136): 'Rivers of waters run down mine eyes, because they keep not Thy law.' Nor from that of the prophet Jeremiah (4. 19): 'My bowels, my bowels! I am pained at my very heart; my heart maketh a noise in me: I cannot hold my peace, because Thou hast heard, O my soul, the sound of the trumpet, the alarm of war.' And so chap. 9. 1, and 13. 17, and Isaiah 22. 4. We read of Mordecai, when he saw his people in danger of being destroyed with a temporal destruction (Esther 4. 1), that he 'rent his clothes, and put on sackcloth with ashes, and went out into the midst of the city, and cried with a loud and a bitter cry.' And why then should persons be thought to be distracted when they cannot forbear crying out at the consideration of the misery of those that are going to eternal destruction?"

I have quoted this to show that this thing was common in the great revivals of those days. It has always been so in all great revivals, and has been more or less common in proportion to the greatness, and extent, and depth of the

---

[1]Compare, too, the parallel passage in the Old Testament—the anguished cry of Moses: "Oh, this people have sinned a great sin . . . Yet now, if Thou wilt forgive their sin—; and if not, blot me, I pray Thee, out of Thy book" (Exod. 32. 31, 32); and the saying of Whitefield: "Let the name of George Whitefield perish, if God be not glorified!"

work. It was so in the great revivals in Scotland,[1] and multitudes used to be overpowered, and some almost died, by the depth of their agony.

8. *If you mean to pray effectually, you must pray a great deal.* It was said of the Apostle James that after he was dead it was found that his knees were callous, like a camel's knees, by praying so much. Ah, here was the secret of the success of those primitive ministers! They had callous knees!

9. *If you intend prayer to be effectual, you must offer it in the name of Christ.* You cannot come to God in your own name. You cannot plead your own merits. But you can come in a name that is always acceptable. You all know what it is to *use the name* of a man. If you should go to the bank with a draft or

---

[1] This would fitly apply to John Livingstone ("Livingstone of Shotts"), who spent the whole night prior to June 21, 1630, in prayer and conference, being designated to preach next day at the Kirk of Shotts. When alone in the fields, about eight o'clock in the morning, he began to steal away, in an agony of fear, when the overcoming power of the Spirit constrained him to return. He accordingly preached, as arranged; his text being Ezekiel 36. 25, 26. After he had been speaking for an hour and a half a few drops of rain decomposed the people, Livingstone, asking the people if they had any shelter from the storm of God's wrath, went on for another hour. There were about five hundred converted on the spot. It is an illustration of revival being linked to revival that at the great meeting at Kilsyth (of which place Livingstone was a native), on July 23, 1839, William Chalmers Burns, preaching on Psa. 110.3, retold the story of the Kirk of Shotts, and pressed immediate acceptance of Christ: "I felt my own soul moved in a manner so remarkable," said Burns, "that I was led, like Mr. Livingstone, to plead with the unconverted *instantly* to close with God's offer of mercy.... The power of the Lord's spirit became so mighty upon their souls as to carry all before it, like the 'rushing mighty wind' of Pentecost. Some were screaming out in agony; others—and among these strong men—fell to the ground as if they had been dead. I was obliged to give out a psalm, our voices being mingled with the mourning groans of many prisoners sighing for deliverance."

So also, prayer prevailed at Cambuslang, 1741-2, in the revival under William McCulloch and Whitefield. When Whitefield reached Cambuslang he immediately preached, on the braeside, to a vast congregation (on a Tuesday at noon). At six o'clock he preached

note, endorsed by John Jacob Astor,[1] that would be giving you his name, and you know you could get the money from the bank just as well as he could himself. Now, Jesus Christ gives you the use of His name. And when you pray in the name of Christ the meaning of it is, that you can prevail just as well as He could Himself, and receive just as much as God's well-beloved Son would if He were to pray Himself for the same things. But you must pray in faith.

10. *You cannot prevail in prayer without renouncing all your sins.* You must not only recall them to mind, and repent of them, but you must actually renounce them, and leave them off, and in the purpose of your heart renounce them all for ever.

11. *You must pray in faith.* You must expect to obtain the things for which you ask. You need not look for an answer to prayer, if you pray without any expectation of obtaining it. You are not to form such expectations without any reason for them. In the cases I have supposed, there is a reason for the expectation. In case the thing is revealed in God's Word, if you pray without an expectation of receiving the blessings, you just make God a liar. If the will of God is indicated by His

---

again, and a third time at nine. Then McCulloch took up the parable and preached till one in the morning, and still the people were unwilling to leave. So many were convicted, crying to God for mercy, that Whitefield described the scene as "a very field of battle." On the ensuing Communion Sunday, Whitefield preached to twenty thousand people; and again on the Monday, when, he said: "you might have seen thousands bathed in tears, some at the same time wringing their hands, others almost swooning, and others crying out and mourning over a pierced Saviour. It was like the Passover in Josiah's time." On the voyage from London to Scotland, prior to this campaign, Whitefield had "spent most of his time on board ship in secret prayer." (See Gledstone's ((George Whitefield, M. A., Field Preacher.")

[1]The most prominent man of his day in American commercial citcles. Having risen from a humble position in life to one of great wealth and influence, he may be said to have typified, not only strength and sagacity according to worldly standards, but, in the sense in which Finney refers to him, financial reliability and resource.

providence, you ought to depend on it, according to the clearness of the indication, so far as to expect the blessing if you pray for it. And if you are led by His Spirit to pray for certain things, you have as much reason to expect those things to be done as if God had revealed it in His Word.

But some say: "Will not this view of the leadings of the Spirit of God lead people into fanaticism?" I answer that I know not but many may deceive themselves in respect to this matter. Multitudes have deceived themselves in regard to all the other points of religion. And if some people should think they are led by the Spirit of God, when it is nothing but their own imagination, is that any reason why those who know that they are led by the Spirit should not follow the Spirit? Many people suppose themselves to be converted when they are not. Is that any reason why we should not cleave to the Lord Jesus Christ? Suppose some people are deceived in thinking they love God, is that any reason why the pious saint who knows he has the love of God shed abroad in his heart should not give vent to his feelings in songs of praise? Some may deceive themselves in thinking they are led by the Spirit of God. But there is no need of being deceived. If people follow impulses, it is their own fault. I do not want you to follow impulses. I want you to be sober-minded, and follow the sober, rational leadings of the Spirit of God. There *are those* who understand what I mean, and who know very well what it is to give themselves up to the Spirit of God in prayer.

III. *WHY GOD REQUIRES SUCH PRAYER.*

I will state some of the reasons why these things are essential to effectual prayer. Why does God require such prayer, such strong desires, such agonising supplications?

1. These strong desires strongly illustrate the strength of God's feelings. They are like the real feelings of God for impenitent sinners. When I have seen, as I sometimes have, the amazing strength of love for souls that has been felt by Christians, I have been wonderfully impressed with the amazing love of God, and His desires for their salvation. The case of a certain woman, of whom I have read, in a revival, made the greatest impression on my mind. She had such an unutterable compassion and love for souls, that she actually

panted for breath. What must be the strength of the desire which God feels, when His Spirit produces in Christians such amazing agony, such throes of soul, such *travail*—God has chosen the best word to express it: it is travail—travail of the soul.

I have seen a man of as much strength of intellect and muscle as any man in the community fall down prostrate, absolutely overpowered by his unutterable desires for sinners. I know this is a stumbling-block to many; and it always will be as long as there remain in the Church so many blind and stupid professors of religion. But I cannot doubt that these things are the work of the Spirit of God. Oh, that the whole Church could be so filled with the Spirit as to travail in prayer, till a nation should be born in a day!

It is said in the Word of God that "as soon as Zion *travailed,* she brought forth" (Isa. 66. 8). What does that mean? I asked a professor of religion this question once. He was taking exception to our ideas of effectual prayer, and I asked what he supposed was meant by Zion's travailing. "Oh," said he, "it means that as soon as the Church shall walk together in the fellowship of the Gospel, then it will be said that Zion *travels!* This walking together is called *travelling."* Not the same term, you see.

2. These strong desires that I have described are the natural results of great benevolence and clear views regarding the danger of sinners. It is perfectly reasonable that it should be so. If the women who are present should look up yonder and see a family burning to death in a fire, and hear their shrieks, and behold their agony, they would feel distressed, and it is very likely that many of them would faint away with agony. And nobody would wonder at it, or say they were fools or crazy to feel so much distressed at such an awful sight. It would be thought strange if there were not some expressions of powerful feeling. Why it is any wonder, then, if Christians should feel as I have described when they have clear views of the state of sinners, and the awful danger they are in? The fact is, that those individuals who never have felt so have never felt much real benevolence, and their piety must be of a very superficial character. I do not mean to judge harshly, or to speak unkindly, but I state it as a simple matter of fact; and

people may talk about it as they please, but I know such piety is superficial. This is not censoriousness, but plain truth.

People sometimes "wonder at Christians having such feelings." Wonder at what? Why, at the natural, and philosophical, and necessary results of deep piety towards God, and deep benevolence towards man, in view of the great danger they see sinners to be in.

3. The soul of a Christian, when it is thus burdened, must have relief. God rolls this weight upon the soul of a Christian, for the purpose of bringing him nearer to Himself. Christians are often so unbelieving that they will not exercise proper faith in God till He rolls this burden upon them so heavily that they cannot live under it, but must go to Him for relief. It is like the case of many a convicted sinner. God is willing to receive him at once, if he will come right to Him, with faith in Jesus Christ. But the sinner will not come. He hangs back, and struggles, and groans under the burden of his sins, and will not throw himself upon God, till his burden of conviction becomes so great that he can live no longer; and when he is driven to desperation, as it were, and feels as if he were ready to sink into hell, he makes a mighty plunge, and throws himself upon God's mercy as his only hope. It was his duty to come before. God had no delight in his distress, for its own sake.

So, when professors of religion get loaded down with the weight of souls, they often pray again and again, and yet the burden is not gone, nor their distress abated, because they have never thrown it all upon God in faith. But they cannot get rid of the burden. So long as their benevolence continues, it will remain and increase; and unless they resist and quench the Holy Ghost, they can get no relief, until, at length, when they are driven to extremity, they make a desperate effort, roll the burden upon the Lord Jesus Christ, and exercise a child-like confidence in Him. Then they feel relieved; then they feel as if the soul they were praying for would be saved. The burden is gone, and God seems in kindness to soothe the mind with a sweet assurance that the blessing will be granted. Often, after a Christian has had this struggle, this agony in prayer, and has obtained relief in this way, you will find the sweetest and most heavenly affections flow out—the soul rests sweetly and gloriously in God, and rejoices "with joy unspeakable and full of glory."

Do any of you think that there are no such things now in the experience of believers? If I had time, I could show you, from President Edwards and other approved writers, cases and descriptions just like this.[1] Do you ask why we never have such things here? I tell you it is not at all because you are so much wiser than Christians are in rural districts, or because you have so much more intelligence or more enlarged views of the nature of religion, or a more stable and well-regulated piety. I tell you, no; instead of priding yourselves in being free from such extravagances, you ought to hide your heads, because Christians in the city are so worldly, and have so much starch, and pride, and fashion, that they cannot *come down* to such spirituality as this. I wish it could be so. Oh, that there might be such a spirit in this city and in this Church! I know it would make a noise if we had such things done here. But I would not care for that. Let them say, if they please, that the folks in Chatham Chapel[2] are getting deranged. We need not be afraid

---

[1]Thus, it was said (by Robert Fleming) of Robert Bruce, the Scottish worthy, that, during his ministry in Edinburgh: "He shined as a great light through the whole land; the power and efficacy of the Spirit most sensibly accompanied the Word he preached. He was a terror to evildoers, and the authority of God did so appear upon him, with such a majesty in his countenance, as forced fear and respect from the greatest in the land, even those who were the most avowed haters of godliness. Yea, it was known what an awful impression King James had of him, and did once give him that testimony before many, that he judged Mr. Bruce was worthy of the half of his kingdom. . . . Mr. Bruce *was a great wrestler,* who had more than ordinary familiarity with God" ("The Fulfilling of the Scripture," Part I.).

[2]The old Chatham Street Theatre, New York, a haunt of blasphemy and vice, was purchased by a committee, which included Mr. Lewis Tappan, and other friends of Finney's. It was during the height of the great revival of 1831 (said Dr. T. L. Cuyler) that two gentlemen called on the lessee and proposed to buy his lease. "What for?" said he. "For a church," they replied. "A w-h-a-t?" he inquired, aghast. "A church," they reiterated. The astonished man broke into tears and exclaimed: "You may have it, and I will give you a thousand dollars towards it." At the close of a morning rehearsal,

of that, if we live near enough to God to enjoy His Spirit in the manner I have described.

4. These effects of the spirit of prayer upon the body are themselves no part of religion. It is only that the body is often so weak that the feelings of the soul overpower it. These bodily effects are not at all essential to prevailing prayer; but are only a natural or physical result of highly excited emotions of the mind. It is not at all unusual for the body to be weakened, and even overcome, by any powerful emotion of the mind, on other subjects besides religion. The doorkeeper of Congress, in the time of the Revolution, fell down dead on the reception of some highly cheering intelligence. I knew a woman in Rochester who was in a great agony of prayer for the conversion of her son-in-law. One morning he was at an anxious meeting, and she remained at home praying for him. At the close of the meeting he came home a convert, and she was so rejoiced that she fell down and died on the spot. It is no more strange that these effects should be produced by religion than by strong feeling on any other subject. It is not essential to prayer, but is the natural result of great efforts of the mind.

5. Doubtless one great reason why God requires the exercise of this agonising prayer is, that it forms such a bond of union between Christ and the Church. It creates such a sympathy between them. It is as if Christ came and poured the overflowings of His own benevolent heart into His people,

---

the beautiful hymn, "The Voice of Free Grace," was sung, and Mr. Tappan announced to the actors that there would be preaching that night upon that stage. When the house was consecrated to the service of God, Finney preached on, "Who is on the Lord's side?" The bar-room was changed into a prayer-room, and the first convert was an actor. For some years the building was used for revival meetings, Finney continuing to preach there until the erection of the Broadway Tabernacle. Dr. Cuyler related these particulars when, on a parallel occasion, during the revival of 1857-8, he conducted the inaugural meeting at Burton's Theatre. (See also "History of the Broadway Tabernacle," by Susan Hayes Ward, which says: "Mr. Finney's imprint upon the Church was clearly marked, so that no history of the Tabernacle could be written without taking into account the wonderful work and personality of that prince of revival preachers.")

and led them to sympathise and to co-operate with Him as they never do in any other way. They feel just as Christ feels— so full of compassion for sinners that they cannot contain themselves. Thus it is often with those ministers who are distinguished for their success in preaching to sinners; they often have such compassion, such overflowing desires for their salvation, that these are shown in their speaking, and their preaching, just as though Jesus Christ spoke through them. The words come from their lips fresh and warm, as if from the very heart of Christ. I do not mean that He dictates their words; but He excites the feelings that give utterance to them. Then you see a movement in the hearers, as if Christ Himself spoke through lips of clay.

6. This travailing in birth for souls creates also a remarkable bond of union between warm-hearted Christians and the young converts. Those who are converted appear very dear to the hearts that have had this spirit of prayer for them. The feeling is like that of a mother for her first-born. Paul expresses it beautifully when he says: "My little children!" His heart was warm and tender to them. "My little children, of whom I travail in birth *again*"—they had backslidden, and he has all the agonies of a parent over a wandering child—"I travail in birth again until Christ be formed in you" (Gal. 4. 19); "Christ, the hope of glory" (Col. 1. 27). In a revival, I have often noticed how those who had the spirit of prayer, loved the young converts. I know this is all so much algebra to those who have never felt it. But to those who have experienced the agony of wrestling, prevailing prayer, for the conversion of a soul, you may depent upon it, that that soul, after it is converted, appears as dear as a child is to the mother. He has agonised for it, received it in answer to prayer, and can present it before the Lord Jesus Christ, saying: "Behold, I and the children whom the Lord hath given me" (Isa. 8. 18. See also Heb. 2. 13).

7. Another reason why God requires this sort of prayer is, that it is the only way in which the Church can be properly prepared to receive great blessings without being injured by them. When the Church is thus prostrated in the dust before God, and is in the depth of agony in prayer, the blessing does them good. While at the same time, if they had received the

blessing without this deep prostration of soul, it would have puffed them up with pride. But as it is, it increases their holiness, their love, their humility.

IV. *SUCH PRAYER WILL AVAIL MUCH.*

The prophet Elijah mourned over the declensions of the house of Israel, and when he saw that no other means were likely to be effectual, to prevent a perpetual going away into idolatry, he prayed that the judgments of God might come upon the guilty nation. He prayed that it might not rain, and God shut up the heavens for three years and six months, till the people were driven to the last extremity. And when he sees that it is time to relent what does he do? See him go up to the mountain and bow down in prayer. He wished to be alone; and he told his servant to go seven times, while he was agonising in prayer. The *last* time, the servant told him that a little cloud had appeared, like a man's hand, and he instantly arose from his knees—the blessing was obtained. The time had come for the calamity to be turned back. "Ah, but," you say, "Elijah was a prophet." Now, do not make this objection. They made it in the apostle's days, and what does the apostle say? Why, he brought forward this very instance, and the fact that Elijah was a man of like passions with ourselves, as a case of prevailing prayer, and insisted that they should pray so too (I Kings 17. 1; 18. 41-5; Jas. 5. 17).

John Knox was a man famous for his power in prayer, so that Queen Mary of England used to say that she feared his prayers more than all the armies of Europe. And events showed that she had reason to do it. He used to be in such an agony for the deliverance of his country, that he could not sleep. He had a place in his garden where he used to go to pray. One night he and several friends were praying together, and as they prayed, Knox spoke and said that deliverance had come.[1]

---

[1]In his "Admonition to the Professors of God's Truth in England," Knox had written: "Thou hast brought to ruyne the palaces of tyrauntes. Thou hast been, O Lorde, a strong defence to the poore, a sure place of refuge to the afflicted in the tyme of his anguisshe. This no dout shall one day be the song of God's electe within the realme of England. Shortly shall the Lord come to the comforte of your heartes."

He could not tell what had happened, but he felt that something had taken place, for God had heard their prayers. What was it? Why, the next news they had was, that Mary was dead!

Take a fact which was related in my hearing by a minister. He said that in a certain town there had been no revival for many years; the Church was nearly extinct, the youth were all unconverted, and desolation reigned unbroken. There lived in a retired part of the town, an aged man, a blacksmith by trade, and of so stammering a tongue that it was painful to hear him speak. On one Friday, as he was at work in his shop, alone, his mind became greatly exercised about the state of the Church and of the impenitent. His agony became so great that he was induced to lay by his work, lock the shop door, and spend the afternoon in prayer.

He prevailed, and on the Sabbath called on the minister and desired him to appoint a "conference meeting." After some hesitation, the minister consented; observing however, that he feared but few would attend. He appointed it the same evening at a large private house. When evening came, more assembled than could be accommodated in the house. All were silent for a time, until one sinner broke out in tears, and said, if any one could pray, would he pray for *him?* Another followed, and another, and still another, until it was found that persons from every quarter of the town were under deep conviction. And what was remarkable was, that they all dated their conviction at the hour that the old man was praying in his shop. A powerful revival followed. Thus this old stammering man prevailed, and as a prince had power with God.

REMARKS.

1. A great deal of prayer is lost, and many people never prevail in prayer, because, when they have *desires* for particular blessings, they do not follow them up. They may have desires, benevolent and pure, which are excited by the Spirit of God; and when they have them, they should persevere in prayer, for if they turn off their attention, they will quench the Spirit. When you find these holy desires in your mind:

(*a*) Do not quench the Spirit; (*b*) Do not be diverted to other objects. Follow the leadings of the Spirit till you have offered that "effectual fervent prayer" that "availeth much" (Jas. 5. 16).

2. Without the spirit of prayer, ministers will do but little good. A minister need not expect much success unless he prays for it. *Sometimes* others may have the spirit of prayer and obtain a blessing on his labours. Generally, however, those preachers are the most successful who have most of the spirit of prayer themselves.

3. Not only must ministers have the spirit of prayer, but it is necessary that the Church should unite in offering that effectual fervent prayer which can prevail with God. "I will yet for this be inquired of by the house of Israel, to do it" (Ezek. 36. 37).

Now I have only to ask you, in regard to what I have set forth: "Will you do it?" Have you done what I said to you at the last Lecture? Have you gone over your sins, and confessed them, and got them all out of the way? Can you pray now? And will you join and offer prevailing prayer that the Spirit of God may come down here?

LECTURE V

THE PRAYER OF FAITH

Therefore I say unto you, What things soever ye desire when ye pray, believe that ye receive them, and ye shall have them.—Mark 11. 24.

These words have been by some supposed to refer exclusively to the faith of miracles. But there is not the least evidence of this. That the text was not designed by our Saviour to refer exclusively to the faith of miracles, is proved by the connection in which it stands. If you read the chapter, you will see that Christ and His apostles, as they returned from their place of retirement in the morning, faint and hungry, saw a fig-tree at a little distance. It looked very beautiful, and doubtless gave signs of having fruit on it; but when they came nigh, they found nothing on it but leaves. And Jesus said: "No man eat fruit of thee hereafter for ever. And His disciples heard it" (Mark 11. 14).

"And in the morning as they passed by, they saw the fig-tree dried up from the roots.

"And Peter calling to remembrance saith unto Him, Master, behold the fig-tree which Thou cursedst is withered away.

"And Jesus answering saith unto them, Have faith in God.

"For verily I say unto you, That whosoever shall say unto this mountain, Be thou removed, and be thou cast into the sea;

and shall not doubt in his heart, but shall believe that those things which he saith shall come to pass; he shall have whatsoever he saith" (20-23).

Then follow the words of the text: "Therefore I say unto you, What things soever ye desire when ye pray, believe that ye receive them, and ye shall have them."

Our Saviour was desirous of giving His disciples instructions respecting the nature and power of prayer, and the necessity of strong faith in God. He therefore stated a very strong case, a miracle—one so great as the removal of a mountain into the sea. And He tells them, that if they exercise a proper faith in God, they might do such things. But His remarks are not to be limited to faith merely in regard to working miracles, for he goes on to say:

"And when ye stand praying, forgive, if ye have ought against any: that your Father also which is in heaven may forgive you your trespasses. But if ye do not forgive, neither will your Father which is in heaven forgive your trespasses" (25, 26).

Does that relate to miracles? When you pray, you must forgive. Is that required only when a man wishes to work a miracle? There are many other promises in the Bible nearly related to this, and speaking nearly the same language, which have ben all disposed of in this way, as referring to the faith employed in miracles. Just as if the faith of miracles was something different from faith in God!

In my last Lecture I dwelt upon the subject of Prevailing Prayer; and you will recollect that I passed over the subject of *faith* in prayer very briefly, because I wished to reserve it for a separate discussion. The subject of the present Lecture, then, is The Prayer of Faith.

I propose to show: I. That faith is an indispensable condition of prevailing prayer. II. What it is that we are to believe when we pray. III. When we are bound to exercise this faith, or to believe that we shall receive the thing we ask for. IV. That this kind of faith in prayer always does obtain the blessing sought. I also propose, V., to explain how we are come into the state of mind in which we can exercise such faith; and, VI., to answer several objections, which are sometimes alleged against these views of prayer.

I. *FAITH AN INDISPENSABLE CONDITION.*

That this is so will not be seriously doubted. There is such a thing as offering benevolent desires, which are acceptable to God as such, that do not include the exercise of faith in regard to the actual reception of those blessings. But such desires are not prevailing prayer, the prayer of faith. God may see fit to grant the things desired, as an act of kindness and love, but it would not be properly in answer to prayer. I am speaking now of the kind of faith that *ensures* the blessing. Do not understand me as saying that there is nothing in prayer that is acceptable to God, or that even obtains the blessing sometimes, without *this* kind of faith. But I am speaking of the faith which secures the very blessing it seeks. To prove that faith is indispensable to prevailing prayer, it is only necessary to repeat what the apostle James expressly tells us: "If any of you lack wisdom, let him ask of God, that giveth to all men liberally, and upbraideth not; and it shall be given him. But let him ask in faith, nothing wavering. For he that wavereth, is like a wave of the sea driven with the wind and tossed" (Jas. 1. 5, 6).

II. *WHAT WE ARE TO BELIEVE WHEN WE PRAY.*

1. *We are to believe in the existence of God.* "He that cometh to God must believe that He *is*"—and in His willingness to answer prayer—"that He is, and that He is a rewarder of them that diligently seek Him" (Heb. 11. 6). There are many who believe in the existence of God, but do not believe in the efficacy of prayer. They profess to believe in God, but deny the necessity or influence of prayer.

2. *We are to believe that we shall recieve*—something—what? Not something, or anything, as it happens; but some particular thing we ask for. We are not to think that God is such a Being, that if we ask a fish He will give us a serpent; or if we ask bread, He will give us a stone. But he says: "*What things soever ye desire* when ye pray, believe that ye receive *them,* and ye shall have them." With respect to the faith of miracles, it is plain that the disciples were bound to believe they should receive just what they asked for—that the very thing itself should come to pass. That is what they were to believe. Now, what ought men to believe in regard to other

blessings? It is a mere loose idea, that if a man prays for a specific blessing, God will by some mysterious Sovereignty give something or other to him, or something to somebody else, somewhere? When a man prays for his children's conversion, is he to believe that either his children will be converted or somebody else's children—it is altogether uncertain which? No, this is utter nonsense, and highly dishonourable to God. We are to believe that we shall receive the *very things* that we ask for.

III. *WHEN ARE WE BOUND TO MAKE THIS PRAYER?*

When are we bound to believe that we shall have the very things we pray for? I answer: "When we have evidence of it." Faith must always have evidence. A man cannot believe a thing, unless he sees something which he supposes to be evidence. He is under no obligation to believe, and has no right to believe, a thing will be done, unless he has evidence. The kinds of evidence a man may have are the following:

1. Suppose that God has *especially promised* the thing. As, for instance, when God says He is more ready to give His Holy Spirit to them that *ask* Him, than parents are to give bread to their children. Here we are bound to believe that we shall receive it when we pray for it. You have no right to put an *if*, and say, "Lord, *if it be Thy will*, give us Thy Holy Spirit." This is to insult God. To put an *if* into God's promise, where God has put none, is tantamount to charging God with being insincere. It is like saying: "O God, if Thou art in earnest in making these promises, grant us the blessing we pray for."

I heard of a case where a young convert was the means of teaching a minister a solemn truth on the subject of prayer. She was from a very wicked family, but went to live at a minister's house. While there she was hopefully converted. One day she went to the minister's study while he was there— a thing she was not in the habit of doing; and he thought there must be something the matter with her. So he asked her to sit down, and kindly inquired into the state of her religion feelings. She then told him that she was distressed at the manner in which the older Church members prayed for the Spirit. They would pray for the Holy Spirit to come, and would seem to be very much in earnest, and plead the promises of

God, and then say: "O Lord, *if it be thy will,* grant us these blessings for Christ's sake." She thought that saying: "If it be Thy will," when God had expressly promised it, was questioning whether God was sincere in His promises. The minister tried to reason her out of it, and he succeeded in confounding her. But she was distressed and filled with grief, and said: "I cannot argue the point with you, sir, but it is impressed on my mind that it is wrong, and dishonouring to God." And. she went away, weeping with anguish. The minister saw she was not satisfied, and it led him to look at the matter again; and finally he saw that it was putting in an *if* where God had put none, but where He had revealed His will expressly; and he saw that it was an insult to God. Thereupon he went and told his people they were bound to believe that God was in earnest when He made them a promise. And the spirit of prayer came down upon that Church, and a most powerful revival followed.

2. Where there is a *general promise* in the Scriptures which you may reasonably apply to the particular case before you. If its real meaning includes the particular thing for which you pray, or if you can reasonably apply the principle of the promise to the case, there you have evidence. For instance, suppose it is a time when wickedness prevails greatly, and you are led to pray for God's interference. What promise have you? Why, this one: "When the enemy shall come in like a flood, the Spirit of the Lord shall lift up a standard against him." (Isa. 59. 19). Here you see a general promise, laying down a principle of God's administration, which you may apply to the case before you, as a warrant for exercising faith in prayer. And if the inquiry is made as to the *time* in which God will grant blessings in answer to prayer, you have this promise: "While they are yet speaking, I will hear" (Isa. 65. 24).

There are general promises and principles laid down in the Bible which Christians might make use of, if they would only *think.* Whenever you are in circumstances to which the promises or principles apply, there you are to use them. A parent finds this promise: "The mercy of the Lord is from everlasting to everlasting upon them that fear Him, and His righteousness unto children's children; to such as keep His covenant, and to those that remember His commandments to do them" (Psa. 103. 17, 18). Now, here is a promise made to those who possess a certain character. If any parent is conscious that this is his character, he has a rightful ground to apply it to himself and his family. If you are this character, you are bound to make use of this promise in prayer, and believe it, even to your children's children.

I could go from end of the Bible to the other, and produce an astonishing variety of texts that are applicable as promises; enough to prove, that in whatever circumstances a child of God may be placed, God has provided in the Bible some promise, either general or particular, which He can apply, that is precisely suited to his case. Many of God's promises are very broad, on purpose to cover much ground. What can be broader than the promise in our text: "What things soever ye desire when ye pray"? What praying Christian is there who has not been surprised at the length and breadth and fulness, of the promises of God, when the Spirit has applied them to his heart? Who that lives a life of prayer has not wondered at his own blindness, in not having before seen and felt the extent of meaning and richness of those promises, when viewed under the light of the Spirit of God? At such times he has been astonished at his own ignorance, and found the Spirit applying the promises and declarations of the Bible in a sense in which he had never before dreamed of their being applicable.

The manner in which the apostles applied the promises, the prophecies, and declarations of the Old Testament, places in a strong light the breadth of meaning, and fulness, and richess of the Word of God. He that walks in the light of God's countenance, and is filled with the Spirit of God as he ought to be, will often make an appropriation of promises to himself, and an application of them to his own circumstances, and the circumstances of those for whom he prays, that a blind professor of religion would never dream of making.

3. Where there is any *prophetic declaration* that the thing prayed for is agreeable to the will of God. When it is plain from prophecy that the event is certainly to come, you are bound to believe it, and to make it the ground for your special faith in prayer. If the time is not specified in the Bible, and there is no evidence from other sources, you are not bound to believe that it shall take place now, or immediately. But if the

time is specified, or if the time may be learned from the study of the prophecies, and it appears to have arrived, then Christians are under obligation to understand and apply it, by offering the prayer of faith. For instance, take the case of Daniel, in regard to the return of the Jews from captivity. What does he say? "I Daniel understood by books the number of the years, whereof the world of the Lord came to Jeremiah the prophet, that He would accomplish seventy years in the desolations of Jerusalem" (Dan. 9. 2). Here he learned from books; that is, he studied his Bible, and in that way understood that the length of the captivity was to be seventy years.

What does he do then? Does he sit down upon the promise, and say: "God has pledged Himself to put an end to the captivity in seventy years, and the time has expired, and there is no need of doing anything"? Oh, no. He says: "And I set my face unto the Lord God, to seek by prayer and supplications, with fasting, and sackcloth, and ashes" (v. 3). He set himself at once to pray that the thing might be accomplished. He prayed in faith. But what was he to believe? What he had learned from the prophecy. There are many prophecies yet unfulfilled, in the Bible, which Christians are bound to understand, as far as they are capable of understanding them, and then make them the basis of believing prayer. Do not think, as some seem to do, that because a thing is foretold in prophecy it is not necessary to pray for it, or that it will come whether Christians pray for it or not. God says, in regard to this very class of events, which are revealed in prophecy: "I will yet for this be inquired of by the house of Israel, to do it for them" (Ezek. 36. 37).

4. When the signs of the times, or the providence of God, indicate that *a particular blessing* is about to be bestowed, we are bound to believe it. The Lord Jesus Christ blamed the Jews, and called the hypocrites, because they did not understand the indications of Providence. They could understand the signs of the weather, and see when it was about to rain, and when it would be fair weather; but they could not see, from the signs of the times, that the time had come for the Messiah to appear, and build up the house of God. There are many professors of religion who are always stumbling and hanging back whenever anything is proposed to be done. They always say: "The time has not come—the time has not come"; when there

are others who pay attention to the signs of the times, and who have spiritual discernment to understand them. These pray in faith for the blessing, and it comes.

5. When the *Spirit of God is upon you,* and excites strong desires for any blessing, you are bound to pray for it in faith. You are bound to infer, from the fact that you find yourself drawn to desire such a thing while in the exercise of such holy affections as the Spirit of God produces, that these desires are the work of the Spirit. People are not apt to desire with the right kind of desires, unless they are excited by the Spirit of God. The apostle refers to these desires, excited by the Spirit, in his Epistle to the Romans, where he says: "Likewise the Spirit also helpeth our infirmities: for we know not what we should pray for as we ought: but the Spirit itself maketh intercession for us with groanings which cannot be uttered. And He that searcheth the hearts knoweth what is the mind of the Spirit, because He maketh intercession for the saints according to the will of God" (Rom. 8. 26, 27). Here, then, if you find yourself strongly drawn to desire a blessing, you are to understand it as an intimation that God is willing to bestow that particular blessing, and so you are bound to believe it. God does not trifle with His children. He does not go and excite in them a desire for one blessing, to turn them off with something else. But He excites the very desires He is willing to gratify. And when they feel such desires, they are bound to follow them out till they get the blessing.

IV. *THIS KIND OF FAITH ALWAYS OBTAINS THE OBJECT.*

The text is plain here, to show that you shall receive the very thing prayed for. It does not say: "Believe that ye shall recieve, and ye shall either have that or something else equivalent to it." To prove that this faith obtains the very blessing that is asked, I observe:

1. That otherwise we could never know whether our prayers were answered. We might continue praying and praying, long after the prayer was answered by some other blessing equivalent to the one for which we asked.

2. If we are not bound to expect the very thing we ask for, it must be that the Spirit of God deceives us. Why should He excite us to desire a certain blessing when He means to grant

something else?

3. What is the meaning of this passage: "If his son ask bread, will he give him a stone"? (Matt. 7. 9). Does not our Savior rebuke the idea that prayer may be answered by giving something else? What encouragement have we to pray for any thing in particular, if we are to ask for one thing and receive another? Suppose a Christian should pray for a revival here— he would be answered by a revival in China! Or he might pray for a revival, and God would send the cholera or an earthquake! All the history of the Church shows that when God answers prayer He gives His people the very thing for which their prayers are offered. God confers other blessings, on both saints and sinners, which they do not pray for at all. He sends His rain both upon the just and the unjust. But when He *answers prayer*, it is by doing what they ask Him to do. To be sure, He often *more* than answers prayer. He grants them not only what they ask, but often connects other blessings with it.

4. Perhaps a difficulty may be felt about the prayers of Jesus Christ. People may ask: "Did not He pray in the garden for the cup to be removed, and was His prayer answered?" I answer that this is no difficulty at all, for the prayer was answered. The cup He prayed to be delivered from was removed. This is what the apostle refers to when he says: "Who in the days of His flesh, when He had offered up prayers and supplications with strong crying and tears unto Him that was able to save Him from death, was heard in that He feared" (Heb. 5. 7).

Some have supposed that He was praying against the cross, and begging to be delivered from dying on the cross! Did Christ ever shrink from the cross? Never. He came into the world on purpose to die on the cross, and He never shrank from it. But He was afraid He should die in the garden before He came to the cross. The burden on His soul was so great, and produced such an agony that He felt as if He was at the point of dying. His soul was sorrowful even unto death. But the angel appeared unto Him, strengthening Him. He received the very thing for which He asked; as He says: "I knew that Thou hearest Me always" (John 11. 42).[1]

---

[1]In his "Systematic Theology" (see footnote, p.   ) Finney carefully elaborates this. With reference to Heb. 5. 7, he says: "To

But there is another case which is often brought up, that of the apostle Paul praying against the "thorn in the flesh." He says: "I besought the Lord thrice, that it might depart from me." And the Lord answered him: "My grace is sufficient for thee" (2 Cor. 12. 7-9). It is the opinion of Dr. Clarke and others, that Paul's prayer was answered in the very thing for which he prayed; that "the thorn in the flesh, the messenger of Satan," of which he speaks, was a false apostle who had distracted and perverted the Church at Corinth; that Paul prayed against his influence, the Lord answering him by the assurance: "My grace is sufficient for thee."[1]

But admitting that Paul's prayer was not answered by the granting of the particular thing for which he prayed, in order to make out this case as an exception to the prayer of faith, they are obliged to assume the very thing to be proved; and that is, that the apostle *prayed in faith*. There is no reason to suppose that Paul would always pray in faith, any more than any other Christian does. The very manner in which God answered him shows that it was not in faith. He virtually tells

---

what does this refer, if not to the death He feared in the Garden? He said, on that occasion: 'My soul is exceedingly sorrowful, even unto death.' He then offered up prayer with strong crying and tears, and was heard. To my mind, all the circumstances taken together make it very evident that Christ did not pray against the cross." Finney is not labouring, however, to maintain a special opinion regarding the Agony, but rather to declare the faithfulness of God in answering prayer; he continues: "Be that as it may, we are to remember that Christ expressly affirms that His Father always hears, that is, answers His prayers."

[1]The question of Paul's "stake in the flesh" has of course been the subject of fruitful conjecture. Whether it was some peculiar form of temptation—spiritual or carnal; some painful physical malady such as epilepsy or acute ophthalmia; or the opposition of some scornful Judaist or false apostle, we need not stay to discuss. It is sufficient to remark that after the arguments of centuries and the expression of widely differing views, from the Greek Fathers to Luther and Calvin, from Bede and Aquinas to Lightfoot, Alford, and other modern scholars, the matter is one upon which the several schools of opinion may agree to differ. In any case, Finney's main contention regarding the prayer of faith holds good.

him: "That thorn is necessary for your sanctification, and to keep you from being exalted above measure, I sent it upon you in love, and in faithfulness, and you have no business to pray that I should take it away. LET IT ALONE."

There is not only no evidence that Paul prayed in faith, but a strong presumption that he did not. From the record it is evident that he had nothing on which to repose faith. There was no express promise, no general promise that could be applicable—no providence of God, no prophecy, no teaching of the Spirit, that God would remove this thorn; but the presumption was that God would not remove it, since He had given it for a particular purpose. The prayer appears to have been selfish, praying against a mere personal influence. This was not any personal suffering that retarded his usefulness, but, on the contrary, it was given him to increase his usefulness by keeping him humble; and because on some account he found it inconvenient and mortifying, he set himself to pray out of his own heart, evidently *without being led to do so by the Spirit of God.* Could Paul pray in faith without being led by the Spirit of God, any more than any other man? And will any one undertake to say that the Spirit of God led him to pray that this might be removed, when God Himself had given it for a particular purpose, which purpose could be answered only as the "thorn" continued with him?

Why, then, is this made an exception to the general rule laid down in the text, that a man shall receive whatsoever he asks in faith? I was once amazed and grieved, at a public examination at a Theological Seminary, to hear them "darken counsel by words without knowledge" on this subject. This case of Paul, and that of Christ just adverted to, were both of them cited as instances to prove that the prayer of faith would not be answered in the particular thing for which they prayed. Now, to teach such sentiments as these, in or out of a Theological Seminary, is to trifle with the Word of God, and to break the power of the Christian ministry. Has it come to this, that our grave doctors in our seminaries are employed to instruct Zion's watchmen to believe and teach that it is not to be expected that the prayer of faith is to be answered in the granting of the object for which we pray? Oh, tell it not in Gath, nor let the sound readh Askelon! What is to become of the Church while such are the views of its gravest and most influential ministers? I would be neither unkind nor censorious, but, as one of the ministers of Jesus Christ, I feel bound to bear testimony against such a perversion of the Word of God.

5. It is evident that the prayer of faith will obtain the blessing, from the fact that our faith rests on evidence that to grant *that* thing is the will of God. Not evidence that something else will be granted, but that this particular thing will be. But how, then, can we have evidence that *this* thing will be granted, if *another* thing is to be granted? People often receive more than they pray for. Solomon prayed for wisdom, and God granted him riches and honour in addition. So, a wife sometimes prays for the conversion of her husband, and if she offers the prayer of faith, God may not only grant that blessing, but convert her child, and her whole family. Blessings seem sometimes to "hang together," so that if a Christian gains one he gets them all.

V. *HOW WE ARE TO COME INTO THIS STATE OF MIND.*

That is to say, the state of mind in which we can offer such prayer. People often ask: "How shall I offer such prayer? Shall I say: 'Now I will pray in faith for such and such blessings'?" No, the human mind is not moved in this way. You might just as well say: "Now I will call up a spirit from the bottomless pit."

1. You must first obtain *evidence* that God will bestow the blessing. How did Daniel make out to offer the prayer of faith? He searched the Scriptures. Now, you need not let your Bible lie on a shelf, and expect God to reveal His promises to you. "Search the Scriptures," and see where you can get either a general or special promise, or a prophecy, on which you can plant your feet. Go through your Bible, and you will find it full of such precious promises, which you may plead in faith.

A curious case occurred in one of the towns in the western part of the State of New York. There was a revival there. A certain clergyman came to visit the place, and heard a great deal said about the Prayer of Faith. He was staggered at what they said, for he had never regarded the subject in the light in which they did. He inquired about it of the minister that was labouring there. The minister requested him, in a kind spirit, to go home and take his Testament, look out the passages that refer to prayer, and go round to his most praying people and ask them how they understood these passages. He did so, going to his praying men and women, reading the passages, without note or comment, and asking what they thought. He found that their plain common sense had led them to understand these passages and to believe that they meant just what they say. This affected him; then, the fact of his presenting the promises before their minds awakened the spirit of prayer in them, and a revival followed.

I could name many individuals who have set themselves to examine the Bible on this subject, who, before they got half through with it, have been filled with the spirit of prayer. They found that God meant by His promises just what a plain, common-sense man would understand them to mean. I advise you to try it. You have Bibles; look them over, and whenever you find a promise that you can use, fasten it in your mind before you go on; and you will not get through the Book without finding out that God's promises mean just what they say.

2. Cherish the *good desires you have.* Christians very often lose their good desires by not attending to this; and then their prayers are mere words, without any desire or earnestness at all. The least longing of desire must be cherished. If your body were likely to freeze, and you had even the least spark of fire, how you would cherish it! So, if you have the least desire for a blessing, let it be ever so small, do not trifle it away. Do not lose good desires by levity, by censoriousness, by worldly-mindedness. Watch and pray.

3. *Entire consecration to God is indispensable to the prayer of faith.* You must live a holy life, and consecrate all to God—your time, talents, influence—all you have, and all you are, to be His entirely. Read the lives of pious men, and you will be struck with this fact, that they used to set apart times to renew their covenant, and dedicate themselves anew to God; and whenever they have done so, a blessing has always followed immediately. If I had President Edwards' works here, I could read passages showing how it was in his days.[1]

---

[1]"To promote a reformation, with respect to all sorts of duties among a professing people, one proper means, and that which is

4. *You must persevere.* You are not to pray for a thing once and then cease, and call that the prayer of faith. Look at Daniel. He prayed twenty-one days, and did not cease till he had obtained the blessing. He set his heart and his face unto the Lord, to seek by prayer and supplications, with fasting, and sackcloth, and ashes; and he held on three weeks, and then the answer came. And why did not it come before? God sent an Archangel to bear the message, but the devil hindered him all this time. See what Christ says in the Parable of the Unjust Judge, and the Parable of the Loaves. What does He teach us by them? Why, that God will grant answers to prayer when it is importunate. "Shall not God avenge His own elect, which *cry day and night unto Him?*" (Luke 18. 7).

5. If you would pray in faith, be sure to *walk every day with God.* If you do, He will tell you what to pray for. Be filled with His Spirit, and He will give you objects enough to pray for. He will give you as much of the spirit of prayer as you have strength of body to bear.

Said a good man to me: "Oh, I am dying for the want of strength to pray! My body is crushed, the world is on me, and how can I forbear praying?" I have known that man go to bed absolutely sick, for weakness and faintness, under the pressure. And I have known him pray as if he would do violence to Heaven, and then have seen the blessing come as plainly in answer to his prayer as if it were revealed, so that no person would doubt it any more than if God had spoken from heaven. Shall I tell you how he died? He prayed more and more; he used to take the map of the world before him, and pray, till he absolutely expired in his room, praying. Blessed man! He was the reproach of the ungodly, and of carnal, unbelieving professors; but he was the favourite of Heaven, and a prevailing prince in prayer.

VI. *OBJECTIONS BROUGHT AGAINST THIS DOCTRINE.*

1. "It leads to fantacism and amounts fo a new revelation." Why should this be a stumbling-block? They must have evidence to believe, before they can offer the prayer of faith. And if God should give other evidence besides the senses,

recommended by frequent Scripture examples, is their solemn, *public renewing their covenant with God.* And doubtless it would

where is the objection? True, there is a sense in which this is a new revelation; it is making known a thing by His Spirit. But it is the very revelation which God has promised to give. It is just the one we are to expect, if the Bible is true; that when we know not what we ought to pray for, according to the will of God, His Spirit helps our infirmities, and teaches us. Shall we deny the teaching of the Spirit?

2. It is often asked: "Is it our duty to offer the prayer of faith for the salvation of all men?" I answer: "No," for that is not a thing according to the will of God. It is directly contrary to His revealed will. We have no evidence that all will be saved. We should feel benevolently to all, and, in itself considered, desire their salvation. But God has revealed that many of the human race shall be damned, and it cannot be a duty to *believe* that all shall be saved, in the face of a revelation to the contrary. In Christ's prayer in John 17, He expressly said: "I pray not for the world, but for those Thou hast given me" (*v.* 9).

3. But some ask: "If we were to offer this prayer for all men, would not all be saved?" I answer: "Yes, and so they would be saved, if they would all repent. But they will not."

4. But you ask: "For whom are we to pray this prayer? We want to know in what cases, for what persons, and places, and at what times, we are to make the prayer of faith." I answer, as I have already answered: "When you have evidence—from promises, or prophecies, or providences, or the leadings of the Spirit—that God will do the things for which you pray."

5. "How is it that so many prayers of pious parents for their children are not answered? Did you not say there was a promise which pious parents may apply to their children? Why is it, then, that so many pious, praying parents have had impenitent children, who have died in their sins?" Grant that it is so, what does it prove? "Let God be true, but every man a liar" (Rom. 3. 4). Which shall we believe, that God's promise has failed or that these parents did not do their duty? Perhaps they did not believe the promise, or did not believe that there

---

greatly tend to promote this work in the land, if the congregations of God's people could generally be brought to this."—Jonathan Edwards, "Thoughts on the Revival in New England, 1740." Part 5—"What Ought to be Done to Promote this Work?"

was any such thing as the prayer of faith. Wherever you find a professor who does not believe in any such prayer, you find, as a general thing, that he has children and domestics yet in their sins.

6. "Will not these views lead to fanaticism? Will not many people think they are offering the prayer of faith when they are not?" That is the same objection that Unitarians make against the doctrine of regeneration—that many people think they have been born again when they have not. It is an argument against all spiritual religion whatever. Some think they have it when they have not, and are fanatics. But there are those who *know* what the prayer of faith is, just as there are those who know what spiritual experience is, though it may stumble cold-hearted professors who know it not. Even ministers often lay themselves open to the rebuke which Christ gave to Nicodemus: "Art thou a master in Israel, and knowest not these things?" (John 3. 10).

REMARKS.

1. Persons who have not known by experience what the prayer of faith is, have great reason to doubt their own piety. This is by no means uncharitable. Let them examine themselves. It is to be feared that they understand prayer as little as Nicodemus did the New Birth. They have not walked with God, and you cannot describe it to them, any more than you can describe a beautiful painting to a blind man.

2. There is reason to believe that millions are in hell because professors have not offered the prayer of faith. When they had promises under their eye, they have not had faith enough to use them. The signs of the times, and the indications of Providence, were favourable, perhaps, and the Spirit of God prompted desires for their salvation. There was evidence enough that God was ready to grant a blessing, and if professors had only prayed in faith, God would have granted it; but He turned it away, because they could not discern the signs of the times.

3. You say: "This leaves the Church under a great load of guilt." True, it does so; and no doubt multitudes will stand up before God, covered all over with the blood of souls that have been lost through their want of faith. The promises of God,

accumulated in their Bibles, will stare them in the face, and weigh them down to hell.

4. Many professors of religion live so far from God, that to talk to them about the prayer of faith, is all unintelligible. Very often the greatest offence possible to them, is to preach about this kind of prayer.

5. I now want to ask professors a few questions. Do you know what it is to pray in faith? Did you ever pray in this way? Have you ever prayed till your mind was assured the blessing would come—till you felt that rest in God, that confidence, as if you saw God come down from heaven to give it to you? If not, you ought to examine your foundation. How can you live without praying in faith? How do you live in view of your children, while you have no assurance whatever that they will be converted? One would think you would go deranged. I knew a father who was a good man, but had erroneous views respecting the prayer of faith; and his whole family of children were grown up, without one of them being converted. At length his son sickened, and seemed about to die. The father prayed, but the son grew worse, and seemed sinking into the grave without hope. The father prayed, till his anguish was unutterable. He went at last and prayed (there seemed no prospect of his son surviving) so that he poured out his soul as if he would not be denied, till at length he got an assurance that his son would not only live but be converted, and that not only this one, but his whole family would be converted to God. He came into the house, and told his family his son would not die. They were astonished at him. "I tell you," said he, "he will not die. And no child of mine will ever die in his sins." That man's children were all converted, years ago.

What do you think of that? Was that fanticism? If you believe so, it is because you know nothing about the matter. Do you pray so? Do you live in such a manner that you can offer such prayer for your children? I know that the children of professors may sometimes be converted in answer to the prayers of somebody else. But ought you to live so? Dare you trust to the prayers of others, when God calls *you* to sustain this important relation to your children?

Finally; see what combined effort is made to dispose of the Bible. The wicked are for throwing away the threatenings of the Bible, and the Church the promises. And what is there left? Between them, they leave the Bible a blank. I ask it in love: "What is our Bible good for, if we do not lay hold of its precious promises, and use them as the ground of our faith when we pray for the blessing of God?" You had better send your Bibles to the heathen, where they will do some good, if you are not going to believe and use them. I have no evidence that there is much of this prayer now in this Church, or in this city. And what will become of them? What will become of your children?—your neighbours?—the wicked?

THE SPIRIT OF PRAYER

Likewise the Spirit also helpeth our infirmities: for we know not what we should pray for as we ought: but the Spirit itself maketh intercession for us with groanings which cannot be uttered. And He that searcheth the hearts knoweth what is the mind of the Spirit, because He maketh intercession for the saints according to the will of God.—Rom. 8. 26, 27.

My last Lecture but one was on the subject of Effectual Prayer; in which I observed that one of the most important attributes of effectual or prevailing prayer is FAITH. This was so extensive a subject that I reserved it for a separate discussion. And accordingly my last Lecture was on the subject of Faith in Prayer, or as it is termed, the Prayer of Faith. It was my intention to discuss the subject in a single Lecture. But as I was under the necessity of condensing so much on some points, it occurred to me, and was mentioned by others, that there might be some questions which people would ask, that ought to be answered more fully, especially as the subject is one on which there is so much darkness. One grand design in preaching is to exhibit the truth in such a way as to answer the questions which would naturally arise in the minds of those who read the Bible with attention, and who want to know what it means, so that they can put it in practice. In explaining the text, I propose to show: I. What Spirit is here spoken of:

"The Spirit also helpeth our infirmities." II. What that Spirit does for us. III. Why He does what the text declares Him to do. IV. How He accomplishes it. V. The degree in which He influences the minds of those who are under His influence. VI. How His influences are to be distinguished from the influences of evil spirits, or from the suggestions of our own minds. VII. How we are to obtain this agency of the Holy Spirit. VIII. Who have a right to expect to enjoy His influences in this matter—or for whom the Spirit does the things spoken of in the text.

I. *WHAT SPIRIT IS SPOKEN OF.*

Some have supposed that the Spirit spoken of in the text means our own spirit—our own mind. But a little attention to the text will show plainly that this is not the meaning. "The Spirit helpeth our infirmities" would then read, "Our own spirit helpeth the infirmities of our own spirit"—and "Our own spirit maketh intercession for our own spirit." You can make no sense of it on that supposition. It is evident from the manner in which the text is introduced that the Spirit referred to is the Holy Ghost. "For if ye live after the flesh, ye shall die: but if ye through the Spirit do mortify the deeds of the body, ye shall live. For as many as are led by the Spirit of God, they are the sons of God. For ye have not received the spirit of bondage again to fear; but ye have received the spirit of adoption, whereby we cry, Abba, Father. The Spirit itself beareth witness with our spirit, that we are the children of God" (Rom. 8. 13-16). And the text is plainly speaking of the same Spirit.

II. *WHAT THE SPIRIT DOES.*

He intercedes for the saints. "He maketh intercession for us," and "helpeth our infirmities," when "we know not what to pray for as we ought." He helps Christians to pray "according to the will of God," or for the things that God desires them to pray for.

III. *WHY IS THE HOLY SPIRIT THUS EMPLOYED?*

Because of our ignorance. Because we know not what we should pray for as we ought. We are so ignorant both of the will of God, revealed in the Bible, and of His unrevealed will, as we ought to learn it from His providence. Mankind are vastly ignorant both of the promises and prophecies of the Bible, and blind to the providence of God. And they are still more in the dark about those points of which God has said nothing but through the leadings of His Spirit. I have named these four sources of evidence on which to ground faith in prayer—promises, prophecies, providences, and the Holy Spirit. When all other means fails of leading us to the knowledge of what we ought to pray for, the Spirit does it.

IV. *HOW DOES HE MAKE INTERCESSION?*

In what mode does He operate, so as to help our infirmities?

1. Not by superseding the use of our faculties. It is not by praying for us, while we do nothing. He prays for us by exciting our faculties. Not that He immediately suggests to us words, or guides our language. But He enlightens our minds, and makes the truth take hold of our souls. He leads us to consider the state of the Church, and the condition of sinners around us. The *manner* in which He brings the truth before the mind, and keeps it there till it produces its effect, we cannot tell. But we can know as much as this—that He leads us to a deep consideration of the state of things; and the result of this, the natural and philosophical result, is, deep feeling. When the Spirit brings the truth before a man's mind there is only one way in which he can keep from deep feeling. That is, by turning away his thoughts, and leading his mind to think of other things. Sinners, when the Spirit of God brings the truth before them, must feel. They feel wrong, as long as they remain impenitent. So, if a man is a Christian, and the Holy Spirit brings the subject into warm contact with his heart, it is just as impossible he should not feel as it is that your hand should not feel if you put it into the fire. If the Spirit of God leads a man to dwell on things calculated to excite over-powering feelings regarding the salvation of souls, and he is not excited thereby, it proves that he has no love for souls, nothing of the Spirit of Christ, and knows nothing about Christian experience.

2. The Spirit makes the Christian feel the value of souls and the guilt and danger of sinners in their present condition. It is amazing how dark and stupid Christians often are about this. Even Christian parents let their children go right down to hell

before their eyes, and scarcely seem to exercise a single feeling, or put forth an effort to save them. And why? Because they are so blind to what hell is, so unbelieving about the Bible, so ignorant of the precious promises which God has made to faithful parents. They grieve the Spirit of God away—and it is in vain to make them pray for their children, while the Spirit of God is away from them.

3. He leads Christians to understand and apply the promises of Scripture. It is wonderful that in no age have Christians been able fully to apply the promises of Scripture to the events of life, as they go along. This is not because the promises themselves are obscure. But there has always been a wonderful disposition to overlook the Scriptures, as a source of light respecting the passing events of life. How astonished the apostles were at Christ's application of so many prophecies to Himself! They seemed to be continually ready to exclaim: "Astonishing! Can it be so? We never understood it before!" Who, that has witnessed the manner in which the apostles, influenced and inspired by the Holy Ghost, applied passages of the Old Testament to Gospel times, has not been amazed at the richness of meaning which they found in the Scriptures? So it has been with many a Christian; while deeply engaged in prayer he has seen that passages of Scripture are appropriate which he never thought of before as having any such application.

I once knew an individual who was in great spiritual darkness. He had retired for prayer, resolved that he would not desist till he had found the Lord. He kneeled down and tried to pray. All was dark, and he could not pray. He rose from his knees, and stood awhile; but he could not give it up, for he had promised that he would not let the sun go down before he had given himself to God. He knelt again; but was all dark, and his heart was as hard as before. He was nearly in despair, and said in agony: "I have grieved the Spirit of God away, and there is no promise for me. I am shut out from the presence of God." But his resolution was formed not to give over, and again he knelt down. He had said but a few words when this passage came into his mind, as fresh as if he had just read it: "Ye shall seek Me, and find Me, when ye shall search for Me with all your heart" (Jer. 29. 13). He saw that though this promise was in the Old Testament, and addressed to the Jews, it was still as applicable to him as to them. And it broke his heart, like the hammer of the Lord, in a moment. And he prayed, and rose up happy in God.[1]

Thus it often happens when professors of religion are praying for their children. Sometimes they pray, and are in darkness and doubt, feeling as if there were no foundation for faith, and no special promises for the children of believers. But while they have been pleading, God has shown them the full meaning of some promise, and their soul has rested on it as on His mighty arm. I once heard of a widow who was greatly exercised about her children, till this passage was brought powerfully to her mind: "Thy fatherless children, I will preserve them alive; and let thy widows trust in Me" (Jer. 49. 11). She saw it had an extended meaning, and she was enabled

---

[1]In this pathetic passage, Finney, adopting the Pauline "I knew a man" (2 Cor. 12. 2), gives the story of his own conversion. It was at Adams, N. Y., where he was studying law. He had been asked (in the prayer-meeting which he attended at the Presbyterian Church): "Do you not wish us to pray for you?" His rejoinder was characteristic, if irritable: "I do not see that it will do any good, for you are continually asking, but you do not receive. You have been praying for a revival of religion ever since I have been in Adams, and yet you have it not." Nevertheless, continuing his study of the Bible, he came under deepening conviction, realising that "salvation, instead of being a thing to be wrought out by my own works, was a thing to be found entirely in the Lord Jesus Christ, who presented Himself as my God and my Saviour." As he walked along the street an inward voice seemed to demand of him: "Will you accept it now, to-day?" and his reply was: "Yes, I will accept it to-day, or I will die in the attempt." Instead of proceeding to his studies he made his way into a wood near the village, and crept between some fallen trees, to pray. There, as he afterwards said: "God gave me many other promises" (in addition to the text quoted from Jeremiah), "especially some most precious promises respecting our Lord Jesus Christ. I seized hold of them." His perturbed mind became "most wonderfully calm and peaceful"; indeed, as he walked back towards Adams "so perfectly quiet was my mind that it seemed as if all nature listened." He had gone to the woods immediately after an early breakfast, and now it was dinner-time, yet it appeared to him that he had been absent but a little time.

to lay hold of it, as it were, with her hands. She prevailed in prayer, and her children were converted. The Holy Spirit was sent into the world by the Saviour to guide *His people,* and instruct them, and bring things to their remembrance, as well as to convince the world of sin.

4. The Spirit leads Christians to desire and pray for things of which nothing is specifically said in the Word of God. Take the case of an individual. That God is willing to save is a general truth. So it is a general truth that He is willing to answer prayer. But how shall I know the will of God respecting that individual—whether I can pray in faith according to the will of God for the conversion and salvation of that individual, or not? Here the agency of the Spirit comes in to lead the minds of God's people to pray for those individuals, and at those times, when God is prepared to bless them. When we know not what to pray for, the Holy Spirit leads the mind to dwell on some object, to consider its situation, to realise its value, and to feel for it, and pray, and "travail in birth," till the person is converted. This sort of experience, I know, is less common in cities than it is in some parts of the country, because of the infinite number of things which in cities divert the attention and grieve the Spirit.

I have had much opportunity to know how it has been in some districts. I was acquainted with an individual who used to keep a list of persons for whom he was especially concerned; and I have had the opportunity to know a multitude of persons, for whom he became thus interested, who were immediately converted.[1] I have seen him pray for persons on his list when he was literally in an agony for them; and have sometimes known him call on some other person to help him pray for such-a-one. I have known his mind to fasten thus on an individual of hardened, abandoned character, and who

---

[1]This worthy man was Rev. Daniel Nash, generally known as "Father" Nash, who, after "a terrible overhauling of his spiritual experience," emerged from a cold and backslidden condition and went out to labour for souls—often at Finney's meetings—full of the power of prayer. He prayed daily—very often, indeed, many times a day—for those whom he was led to place upon his list. The incident of the tavern-keeper's conversion occurred at Evans' Mills, and the confession which he made was described by Finney as "one

could not be reached in any ordinary way. In a town in a north part of this State, where there was a revival, there was a certain individual who was a most violent and outrageous opposer. He kept a tavern, and used to delight in swearing at a desperate rate, whenever there were Christians within hearing, on purpose to hurt their feelings. He was so bad that one man said he believed he should have to sell his place, or give it away, and move out of town, for he could not live near a man who swore so. This good man of whom I was speaking passed through the town, and, hearing of the case, was very much grieved and distressed for the individual. He took him on his praying list. The case weighed on his mind when he was asleep and when he was awake. He kept thinking about the ungodly man, and praying for him for days. And, the first we knew of it, the tavern-keeper came into a meeting, got up and confessed his sins, and poured out his soul. His bar-room immediately became the place where they held prayer-meetings. In this manner the Spirit of God leads individual Christians to pray for things which they would not pray for, unless they were led by the Spirit; and thus they pray for things "according to the will of God."

Great evil has been done by saying that this kind of influence amounts to a new revelation. Many people will be so afraid of it, if they hear it called a new revelation, that they will not stop to inquire what it means, or whether the Scriptures teach it or not. The plain truth of the matter is, that the Spirit leads a man to pray; and if God leads a man to pray for an individual, the inference from the Bible is, that God designs to save that individual. If we find, by comparing our state of mind with the Bible, that we are *led by the Spirit* to pray for an individual, we have good evidence to believe that God is prepared to bless him.

---

of the most heartbroken I ever heard. It seemed to cover the whole ground of his treatment of God, of Christians, of the revival, and of everything good." In remarkable contrast was the case of a railing infidel who, in the midst of his opposition, was smitten with apoplexy. A physician assured him that he had not long to live, and that if he had anything to say he must say it at once. He had only time and strength enough to stammer out one sentence; it was: "Don't let Finney pray over my corpse."

5. By giving to Christians a spiritual discernment respecting the movements and developments of Providence. Devoted, praying Christians often see these things so clearly, and look so far ahead, as greatly to stumble others. They sometimes almost seem to prophesy. No doubt persons may be deluded, and sometimes are, by leaning to their own understanding when they think they are led by the Spirit. But there is no doubt that a Christian may be made to discern clearly the signs of the times, so as to understand, by Providence, what to expect, and thus to pray for it in faith. Thus they are often led to expect a revival, and to pray for it in faith, when nobody else can see the least signs of it.

There was a woman in New Jersey, in a place where there had been a revival. She was very positive there was going to be another. She wanted to have "conference meetings" appointed. But the minister and elders saw nothing to encourage it, and would do nothing. She saw they were blind, and so she went forward, and got a carpenter to make seats for her, for she said she would have meetings in her own house; there was certainly going to be a revival. She had scarcely opened her doors for meetings, before the Spirit of God came down with great power, and these sleepy Church members found themselves surrounded all at once with convicted sinners. They could only say: "Surely the Lord is in this place; and we knew it not" (Gen. 28. 16). The reason why such persons as this praying woman understand the indication of God's will is not because of the superior wisdom that is in them, but because the Spirit of God leads them to see the signs of the times. And this, not by revelation; but they are led to see that converging of providences to a single point, which produces in them a confident expectation of a certain result.

V. *THE DEGREE OF INFLUENCE.*

In what degree are we to expect the Spirit of God to affect the minds of believers? The text says: "The Spirit maketh intercession with groanings that cannot be uttered." The meaning of this I understand to be, that the Spirit excites desires too great to be uttered except by groans—making the soul too full to utter its feelings by words, so that the person can only groan them out to God, who understands the language of the heart.

VI. Distinguishing the Influences.

How are we to know whether it is the Spirit of God that influences our minds, or not?

1. Now by feeling that some external influence or agency is applied to us. We are not to expect to feel our minds in direct physical contact with God. If such a thing can be, we know of no way in which it can be made sensible. We know that we exercise our minds freely, and that our thoughts are exercised on something that excites our feelings. But we are not to expect a miracle to be wrought, as if we were led by the hand, sensibly, or like something whispered in the ear, or any miraculous manifestation of the will of God.

Individuals often grieve the Spirit away, because they do not harbour Him and cherish His influences. Sinners often do this ignorantly. They suppose that if they were under conviction by the Spirit, they should have such-and-such mysterious feelings—a shock would come upon them which they could not mistake. Many Christians are so ignorant of the Spirit's influences, and have thought so little about having his assistance in prayer, that when they have such influences they do not know it, and so do not yield to them, and cherish them. We are sensible of nothing in the case, only the movement of our own minds. There is nothing else that *can* be felt. We are merely sensible that our thoughts are intensely employed on a certain subject.

Christians are often unnecessarily misled and distressed on this point, for fear they have not the Spirit of God. They feel intensely, but they know not what makes them feel. They are distressed about sinners; but should they not be distressed, when they think of their condition? They keep thinking about them all the time, and why should they not be distressed? Now the truth is, that the very fact that you are *thinking* upon them is evidence that the Spirit of God is leading you. Do you not know that the greater part of the time these things do not affect you so? The greater part of the time you do not think much about the case of sinners. You know their salvation is always equally important. But at other times, even when you are quite at leisure, your mind is entirely dark, and vacant of any feeling for them. But now, although you may be busy about other things, you think, you pray, and feel intensely for them, even while you are about business that at other times would occupy all your thoughts. Now, almost every thought you have is: "God have mercy upon them!" Why is this? Why, their case is placed in a strong light before your mind. Do you ask what it is that leads your mind to exercise benevolent feelings for sinners, and to agonise in prayer for them? What can it be but the Spirit of God? There are no devils that would lead you so. If your feelings are truly benevolent, you are to consider it as the Holy Spirit leading you to pray for things according to the will of God.

2. "Try the spirits" by the Bible. People are sometimes led away by strange fantasies and crazy impulses. If you compare them faithfully with the Bible, you never need to be led astray. You can always know whether your feelings are produced by the Spirit's influences, by comparing your desires with the spirit and temper of religion, as described in the Bible. The Bible commands you to "try the spirits." "Beloved, believe not every spirit, but try the spirits whether they are of God" (I John 4. 1).

VII. *HOW SHALL WE GET THIS INFLUENCE OF THE SPIRIT?*
1. It must be sought by fervent, believing prayer. Christ says: "If ye then, being evil, know how to give good gifts unto your children; how much more shall your heavenly Father give the Holy Spirit to them that ask Him?" (Luke 11. 13). Does any one say, I have prayed for it, and it does not come? It is because you do not pray aright. "Ye ask, and receive not, because ye ask amiss, that ye may consume it upon your lusts" (Jas. 4. 3).[1] You do not pray from right motives. A professor of religion, and a principal member in a Church, once asked a minister what he thought of his case; he had been praying week after week for

---

[1] The gifted but profligate Brownlow North (afterwards so mightily used of God in the 1859 revival) once asked the godly Duchess of Gordon: "Duchess, what should a man do who has often prayed to God and never been answered?" The Duchess quietly made reply in the words of the text quoted by Finney. "Whereat," wrote the Duchess, "his countenance changed; he became very greatly moved, was very quiet during the evening, and thanked me ere he left."

the Spirit, and had not found any benefit. The minister asked: what was his motive in praying? He replied that "he wanted to be happy." He knew those who had the Spirit were happy, and he wanted to enjoy his mind as they did. Why the devil himself might pray so! That is mere selfishness. The man, when this was shown him, at first turned away in anger. He was con-vinced he was a hypocrite, and that his prayers were all selfish, dictated only by a desire for his own happiness.[1] David prayed that God would uphold him by His free Spirit, that he might teach transgressors and turn sinners to God. A Christian should pray for the Spirit that he may be the more useful and glorify God more; not that he himself may be more happy. This man saw clearly where he had been in error, and he was converted. Perhaps many here have been making just the same mistake. You ought to examine and see if your prayers are not tinctured with selfishness.

2. Use the means adapted to stir up your minds on the subject, and to keep your attention fixed there. If a man prays for the Spirit, and then diverts his mind to other objects; if he uses no other means, but goes away to worldly objects, he tempts God, he swings loose from his object, and it would be a miracle if he should get what he prays for. How is a sinner to get conviction? Why, by thinking of his sins. That is the way for a Christian to obtain deep feeling—by thinking upon the object. God is not going to pour these things on you without any effort of your own. You must cherish the slightest impressions. Take the Bible, and go over the passages that show the condition and prospects of the world. Look at the world, look at your children, and your neighbours, and see

---

[1]This is another incident from one of Finney's own campaigns, that at Brownville, N. Y., to which place he had received an urgent invitation. The gentleman referred to was Finney's host for the time being, and was the most intimate friend of the minister of the Church. Although at first annoyed by Finney's faithful dealing on the subject, he subsequently said: "What you said forced the conviction upon me that I had never been converted, that I had never had any higher motive than a mere selfish desire for my own happiness." And from the time of this experience he was a changed man.

their condition while they remain in sin; then, persevere in prayer and effort till you obtain the blessing of the Spirit of God to dwell in you. This was the way, doubtless, that Dr. Watts came to have the feelings which he has described in his hymn:

> My thoughts on awful subjects dwell,
> Damnation and the dead;
> What horrors seize the guilty soul
> Upon a dying bed!

Look, as it were, through a telescope that will bring it up near to you; look into hell, and hear them groan; then turn the glass upwards and look into heaven, and see the saints there, in their white robes, with their harps in their hands, and hear them sing the song of redeeming love; and ask yourself: "Is it possible that I should prevail with God to elevate the sinner there?" Do this, and if you are not a wicked man, and a stranger to God, you will soon have as much of the spirit of prayer as your body can sustain.

3. You must watch unto prayer. You must keep a look-out, and see if God grants the blessing when you ask Him. People sometimes pray, and never look to see if the prayer is granted. Be careful also, not to grieve the Spirit of God. Confess and forsake your sins. God will never lead you as one of His hidden ones, and let you into His secrets, unless you confess and forsake your sins. Be not always confessing and never forsaking, but confess and forsake too. Make redress wherever you have committed an injury. You cannot expect to get the spirit of prayer first, and repentance afterwards. You cannot fight it through so. Professors of religion, who are proud and unyielding, and justify themselves, never will force God to dwell with them.

4. Aim to obey perfectly the written law. In other words, have no fellowship with sin. Aim at being entirely above the world; "Be ye therefore perfect, even as your Father which is in heaven is perfect" (Matt. 5. 48). If you sin at all, let it be your daily grief. The man who does not aim at this, means to live in sin. Such a man need not expect God's blessing, for he is not sincere in desiring to keep all His commandments.

VIII. *FOR WHOM DOES THE SPIRIT INTERCEDE?*

The answer is that "He maketh intercession for the saints," for all saints, for any who are saints.

REMARKS.

1. Why do you suppose it is that so little stress is laid on the influences of the Spirit in prayer, when so much is said about His influences in conversion? Many people are amazingly afraid the Spirit's influences will be left out. They lay great stress on the Spirit's influences in converting sinners. But how little is said, how little is printed, about His influence in prayer! How little complaining there is that people do not make enough of the Spirit's influence in leading Christians to pray according to the will of God! Let it never be forgotten that no Christian ever prays aright, unless led by the Spirit. He has natural power to pray, and so far as the will of God is revealed, is able to do it; but he never does, unless the Spirit of God influences him; just as sinners are able to repent, but never do, unless influenced by the Spirit.

2. This subject lays open the foundation of the difficulty felt by many persons on the subject of the Prayer of Faith. They object to the idea that faith in prayer is a belief that we shall receive the very things for which we ask, and insist that there can be no foundation or evidence upon which to rest such a belief.

In a sermon upon this subject a writer brings forward this difficulty, and presents it in its full strength. "I have," says he, "no evidence that the thing prayed for will be granted, *until* I have prayed in faith; because, praying in faith is the condition upon which it is promised. And, of course, I cannot claim the promise, until I have fulfilled the condition. Now, if the condition is, that I am to believe I shall receive the very blessing for which I ask, it is evident that the promise is given upon the performance of an *impossible* condition, and is, of course, a mere nullity. The promise would amount to just this: You shall have whatsoever you ask, upon the condition that you first believe that you shall receive it. Now I must fulfil the condition before I can claim the promise. But I can have no evidence that I shall receive it until I have believed that I shall receive it. This reduces me to the necessity of believing that I shall receive it, *before* I have any evidence that I shall receive it—which is impossible."

The whole force of this objection arises out of the fact that the *Spirit's influences* are entirely overlooked, which He exerts in leading an individual to the exercise of faith. It has been supposed that the passage in Mark 11. 22-24, with other kindred promises on the subject of the Prayer of Faith, relate exclusively to miracles. But suppose this were true. I would ask: "What were the apostles to believe, when they prayed for a miracle? Were they to believe that the precise miracle would be performed for which they prayed?" It is evident that they were. In the verses just alluded to, Christ says: "For verily I say unto you, that whosoever shall say unto this mountain, Be thou removed, and be thou cast into the sea; and shall not doubt in his heart, but *shall believe that those things which he saith shall come to pass;* he shall have whatsoever he saith. Therefore I say unto you, What things soever ye desire when ye pray, *believe that ye receive them,* and ye shall have them." Here it is evident, that the thing to be believed, and which they were not to doubt in their heart, was that they should have the very blessing for which they prayed. Now the objection above stated, lies in all its force against this kind of faith, when praying for the performance of a miracle. If it be impossible to believe this in praying for any other blessing, it was equally so in praying for a miracle. I might ask: "Could an apostle believe that the miracle would be wrought, before he had fulfilled the condition, inasmuch as the condition was, that he should believe that he should receive that for which he prayed?" Either the promise is a nullity and a deception, or there is a possibility of performing the condition.

Now, as I have said, the whole difficulty lies in the fact that the Spirit's influences are entirely overlooked, and that that faith which is of the operation of God, is left out of the question. If the objection is good against praying for any object, it is as good against praying in faith for the performance of a miracle. The fact is, that the Spirit of God could give evidence, on which to believe that any particular miracle would be granted; could lead the mind to a firm reliance upon God, and trust that the blessing sought would be obtained. And so at the present day He can give the same assurance, in praying for any blessing that we need.

Praying is the same thing, whether you pray for the conversion of a soul, or for a miracle. Faith is the same thing in the one case as in the other; it only terminates on a different object; in the one case on the conversion of a soul, and in the other on the performance of a miracle. Nor is faith exercised in the one more than in the other without reference to a promise; and a *general* promise may with the same propriety be applied to the conversion of a soul as to the performance of a miracle. And it is equally true in the one case as the other, that no man ever prays in faith without being influenced by the Spirit of God. And if the Spirit could lead the mind of an apostle to exercise faith in regard to a miracle, He can lead the mind of another Christian to exercise faith in regard to receiving any other blessing, by a reference to the same general promise.

Should any one ask: "When are we *under an obligation* to believe that we shall receive *the blessing* for which we ask?" I answer—

(*a*) When there is a particular promise, specifying the particular blessing: as where we pray for the Holy Spirit. This blessing is particularly named in the promise, and here we have evidence, and we are bound to believe, whether we have any Divine influence or not: just as sinners are bound to repent whether the Spirit strives with them or not, their obligation resting not upon the Spirit's influences, but upon the powers of moral agency which they possess; upon their ability to do their duty. And while it is true that not one of them ever will repent without the influences of the Spirit, still they have power to do so, and are under obligation to do so whether the Spirit strives with them or not. So with the Christian. He is bound to believe where he has evidence. And although he never does believe, even where he has an express promise, without the Spirit of God, yet his obligation to do so rests upon his ability, and not upon the Divine influence.

(*b*) Where God makes a revelation by His providence, we are bound to believe in proportion to the clearness of the providential indication.

(*c*) So where there is a prophecy, we are bound also to believe. But in neither of these cases *do we,* in fact, believe, without the Spirit of God.

But where there is neither promise, providence, nor prophecy, on which we are to repose our faith, we are under no obligation to believe, unless, as I have shown in this discourse, *the Spirit* gives us evidence, by creating desires, and by leading us to pray for a particular object. In the case of those promises of a general nature, where we are honestly at a loss to know in what *particular* cases to apply them, it may be considered rather as our privilege than as our duty, in many instances, to apply them to particular cases; but whenever the Spirit of God leads us to apply them to a particular object, then it becomes *our duty* so to apply them. In this case, God explains His own promise, and shows how He designed it should be applied. Our obligation, then, to make this application, and to believe in reference to this particular object, remains in full force.

3. Some have supposed that Paul prayed in faith for the removal of the thorn in the flesh, and that it was not granted. But they cannot prove that Paul *prayed in faith*. The presumption is all on the other side, as I have shown in a former Lecture. He had neither promise, nor prophecy, nor providence, nor the Spirit of God, to lead him to believe. The whole objection goes on the ground that the apostle might pray in faith without being led by the Spirit. This is truly a short method of disposing of the Spirit's influences in prayer. Certainly, to assume that he prayed in faith, is to assume, either that he prayed in faith without being led by the Spirit, or that the Spirit of God led him to pray for that which was not according to the will of God.

I have dwelt the more on this subject, because I want to have it made so plain that you will be careful not to grieve the Spirit. I want you to have high ideas of the Holy Ghost, and to feel that nothing good will be done without His influences. No praying or preaching will be of any avail without Him. If Jesus Christ were to come down here and preach to sinners, not one would be converted without the Spirit. Be careful, then, not to grieve Him away, by slighting or neglecting His heavenly influences when He invites you to pray.

4. In praying for an object, it is necessary to persevere till you obtain it. Oh, with what eagerness Christians sometimes pursue a sinner in their prayers, when the Spirit of God has

fixed their desires on him! No miser pursues gold with so fixed a determination.

5. The fear of being led by impulses has done great injury, by not being duly considered. A person's mind *may be* led by an *ignis fatuus*. But we do wrong if we let the fear of impulses lead us to resist the *good* impulses of the Holy Ghost. No wonder Christians have not the spirit of prayer, if they are unwilling to take the trouble to distinguish; but will reject or resist all impulses, and all leadings of invisible agents. A great deal has been said on the subject of fanaticism, that is very unguarded, and that causes many minds to reject the leadings of the Spirit of God. "As many as are led by the Spirit of God, they are the sons of God" (Rom. 8. 14). And it is our duty to "try the spirits whether they are of God" (I John 4. 1). We should insist on a close scrutiny, and an accurate discrimination. There *must* be such a thing as being led by the Spirit. And when we are convinced it is of God, we should be sure to follow—follow on, with full confidence that He will not lead us wrong.

6. We see from this subject the absurdity of using set forms of prayer. The very idea of using a form rejects, *of course,* the leadings of the Spirit. Nothing is more calculated to destroy the spirit of prayer, and entirely to darken and confuse the mind, as to what constitutes prayer, than to use forms. Forms of prayer are not only absurd in themselves, but they are the very device of the devil to destroy the spirit and break the power of prayer. It is of no use to say the form is a good one. Prayer does not consist in words. And it matters not what the words are if the heart is not led by the Spirit of God. If the desire is not enkindled, the thoughts directed, and the whole current of feeling produced and led by the Spirit of God, it is not prayer. And set forms are, of all things, best calculated to keep an individual from praying as he ought.

7. The subject furnishes a test of character. "The Spirit maketh intercession"—for whom? For the saints. Those who are saints are thus exercised. If you are saints you know by experience what it is to be thus exercised; or, if you do not, it is because you have grieved the Spirit of God so that He will not lead you. You live in such a manner that this Holy Comforter will not dwell with you, nor give you the spirit of prayer. If this is so, you must repent. Do not stop to settle whether you are a

Christian or not, but repent, as if you never had repented. Do your first works. Do not take it for granted that you are a Christian, but go, like a humble sinner, and pour out your heart unto the Lord. You never can have the spirit of prayer in any other way.

8. It is important to understand this subject:—

(*a*) In order to be useful. Without this spirit there can be no such sympathy between God and you, that you can either walk with God or work with God. You need to have a strong beating of your heart with His, or you need not expect to be greatly useful.

(*b*) As being important to your sanctification. Without such a spirit you will not be sanctified, nor will you understand the Bible, and therefore you will not know how to apply it to your case. I want you to feel the importance of having God with you all the time. If you live as you ought, He says He will come unto you, and make His abode with you, and sup with you, and you with Him.

9. If people know not the spirit of prayer, they are very apt to be unbelieving in regard to the results of prayer. They do not see what takes place, or do not see the connection, or do not see the evidence. They are not expecting spiritual blessings. When sinners are convicted, they conclude that such are merely frightened by terrible preaching. And when people are converted, they feel no confidence, saying: "We will see how they turn out."

10. Those who have the spirit of prayer know when the blessing comes. It was just so when Jesus Christ appeared. Those ungodly doctors did not know Him. Why? Because they were not praying for the redemption of Israel. But Simeon and Anna knew Him. How was that? Mark what they said, how they prayed, and how they lived. They were praying in faith, and so they were not surprised when He came (Luke 2. 25-38). So it is with the Christians of whom I speak. If sinners are convicted or converted, they are not surprised at it. They are expecting just such things. They know God when He comes, because they are looking out for His visits.

11. There are three classes of persons in the Church who are liable to error, or have left the truth out of view, on this subject.

(*a*) Those who place great reliance on prayer, and use no other means. They are alarmed at any special means, and talk about your "getting up a revival."

(*b*) Over against these are those who use means, and pray, but never think about the influences of the Spirit in prayer. They talk about prayer for the Spirit, and feel the importance of the Spirit in the conversion of sinners, but do not realise the importance of the Spirit in prayer. And their prayers are all cold talk, nothing that anybody can feel, or that can take hold of God.

(*c*) Those who have certain strange notions about the Sovereignty of God, and are waiting for God to convert the world without prayer or means.

There must be in the Church a deeper sense of the need of the spirit of prayer. The fact is, that, *generally,* those who use means most assiduously, and make the most strenuous efforts for the salvation of men, and who have the most correct notions of the manner in which means should be used for converting sinners, also pray most for the Spirit of God, and wrestle most with God for His blessing. And what is the result? Let facts speak, and say whether these persons do or do not pray, and whether the Spirit of God does not testify to their prayers, and follow their labours with His power.

12. Nothing will produce an excitement and opposition so quickly as the spirit of prayer. If any person should feel burdened with the case of sinners, so as to groan in his prayer, some become nervous, and he is visited at once with rebuke and opposition! From my soul I abhor all affectation of feeling where none exists, and all attempts to work one's self up into feeling, by groans. But I feel bound to defend the position, that there is such a thing as being in a state of mind in which there is but one way to keep from groaning; and that is, by resisting the Holy Ghost. I was once present where this subject was discussed. It was said that "groaning ought to be discountenanced." The question was asked, in reply: Whether God cannot produce such a state of feeling, that to abstain from groaning is impossible? The answer was: "Yes, but He never does." Then the apostle Paul was egregiously deceived when he wrote about groanings that cannot be uttered. Edwards was deceived when he wrote his book upon revivals. Revivals are

all in the dark. Now, no man who reviews the history of the Church will adopt such a sentiment. I do not like this attempt to shut out, or stifle, or keep down, or limit, the spirit of prayer. I would sooner cut off my right hand than rebuke the spirit of prayer, as I have heard of its being done by saying: "Do not let me hear any more groaning!"

I hardly know where to end this subject. I should like to discuss it a month, indeed, till the whole Church could understand it, so as to pray the prayer of faith. Beloved, I want to ask you: Do you believe all this? Or do you wonder that I should talk so? Perhaps some of you have had some glimpses of these things. Now, will you give yourselves up to prayer, and live so as to have the spirit of Prayer, and have the Spirit with you all the time? Oh, for a praying Church! I once knew a minister who had a revival fourteen winters in succession. I did not know how to account for it, till I saw one of his members get up in a prayer-meeting and make a confession. "Brethren," said he, "I have been long in the habit of praying every Saturday night till after midnight, for the descent of the Holy Ghost among us. And now, brethren," and he began to weep, "I confess that I have neglected it for two or three weeks." The secret was out. That minister had a praying Church. Brethren, in my present state of health, I find it impossible to pray as much as I have been in the habit of doing, and yet continue to preach. It overcomes my strength. Now, shall I give myself up to prayer, and stop preaching? That will not do. Now, will not you, who are in health, throw yourselves to prayer, till God shall pour out His blessing upon us?

LECTURE VII

ON BEING FILLED WITH THE SPIRIT

Be filled with the Spirit.—Eph. 5. 18.

Several of my Lectures have been on the subject of Prayer, and the importance of having the spirit of prayer—of the intercession of the Holy Ghost. Whenever the necessity and importance of the Spirit's influences are held forth, there can be no doubt that persons are in danger of abusing the doctrine, and perverting it to their own injury. For instance: when you tell sinners that without the Holy Spirit they never will repent, they are very liable to pervert the truth, and understand by it that they *cannot* repent, and therefore are under no obligation to do it until they feel the Spirit. It is often difficult to make them see that all the "cannot" consists in their unwillingness, and not in their inability. So again, when we tell Christians that they need the Spirit's aid in prayer, they are very apt to think they are under no obligation to pray the prayer of faith until they feel the influences of the Spirit. They overlook their obligation to pray the prayer of faith until they feel the influences of the Spirit. They overlook their obligation to be filled with the Spirit, and wait for the spirit of prayer to come upon them without asking, and thus they tempt God.

Before we come to consider the other department of means

for promoting a revival—that is, *the means to be used with sinners*—I wish to show that, if you live without the Spirit, you are without excuse. Obligation to perform duty never rests on the condition that we shall have the influence of the Spirit, but on the powers of moral agency. We, as moral agents, have the power to obey God, and are perfectly bound to obey; and the reason that we do not is, that we are unwilling. The influences of the Spirit are wholly a matter of grace. If they were indispensable to *enable* us to perform duty, the bestowment of them would not be a gracious act, but a mere matter of common justice. Sinners are not bound to repent because they have the Spirit's influence, or because they can obtain it, but because they are moral agents, and have the powers which God requires them to exercise. So in the case of Christians. They are not bound to pray in faith because they have the Spirit (except in those cases where His influences in begetting the desire constitute the evidence that it is God's will to grant the object of desire), but because they have evidence. They are not bound to pray in faith at all, except when they have evidence as the foundation of their faith. They must have evidence from promises, or principles, or prophecy, or providence. And where they have evidence independent of His influences, they are bound to exercise faith, whether they have the Spirit's influence or not. They are bound to see the evidence, and to believe. The Spirit is given, not to enable them to see or believe, but because without the Spirit they *will not* look, or feel, or act, as they ought. I purpose to show, from the text: I. That Christians may be filled with the Spirit of God. II. That it is their duty to be filled with the Spirit. III. Why they are not filled with the Spirit. IV. The guilt of those who have not the Spirit of God, to lead their minds in duty and prayer. V. The consequence that will follow if they are filled with the Spirit. VI. The consequences if they are not.

I. *YOU MAY HAVE THE SPIRIT.*

Not because it is a matter of justice for God to give you His Spirit, but because He has promised to give His Spirit to those that ask. "If ye then, being evil, know how to give good gifts unto your children: *how much more* shall your heavenly Father give the Holy Spirit to them that ask Him?" (Luke 11. 13.) If you ask for the Holy Spirit, God has promised to answer.

But again, God has *commanded* you to have the Spirit. He says in the text: "Be filled with the Spirit." When God commands us to do a thing, it is the highest possible evidence that we can do it. For God to command is equivalent to an oath that we can do it. He has no right to command, unless we have power to obey. There is no stopping short of the conclusion that God is tyrannical, if He commands that which is impracticable.

II. *IT IS YOUR DUTY TO BE FILLED WITH THE SPIRIT.*

1. It is your duty because you have a promise of it.

2. Because God has commanded it.

3. It is essential to your own growth in grace that you should be filled with the Spirit.

4. It is as important as it is that you should be sanctified.

5. It is as necessary as it is that you should be useful and do good in the world.

6. If you do not have the Spirit of God in you, you will dishonour God, disgrace the Church, and be lost.

III. *WHY MANY DO NOT HAVE THE SPIRIT.*

There are some, even professors of religion, who will say: "I do not know anything about all this; I never had any such experience; either it is not true, or I am all wrong." No doubt you are all wrong, if you know *nothing* about the influence of the Spirit. I want to present you with a few of the reasons that may prevent you from being filled with the Spirit.

1. It may be that you live a hypocritical life. Your prayers are not earnest and sincere. Not only is your religion a mere outside show, without any heart, but you are insincere in your intercourse with others. Thus you do many things to grieve the Spirit, so that He cannot dwell with you.

A minister was once boarding in a certain family, and the lady of the house was constantly complaining that she did not "enjoy" religion, and nothing seemed to help her. One day some ladies called to see her, and, protesting that she was very much offended because they had not called before, she pressed them to stay and spend the day, and declared she *could not* consent to let them go. They excused themselves, and left the house; and as soon as they were gone she told her servant that she wondered these people had so little sense as to be always troubling her and taking up her time! The minister heard it, and immediately rebuked her, and told her she ought to see why she did not "enjoy" religion. It was because she was in the daily habit of insincerity that amounted to downright lying. And the Spirit of Truth could not dwell in such a heart.

2. Others have so much levity that the Spirit will not dwell with them. The Spirit of God is solemn, and serious, and will not dwell with those who give way to thoughtless levity.

3. Others are so proud that they cannot have the Spirit. They are so fond of dress, high life, equipage, fashion, &c., that it is no wonder they are not filled with the Spirit. And yet such persons will pretend to be at a loss to know why it is that they do not "enjoy" religion!

4. Some are so worldly-minded, love property so well, and are trying so hard to get rich, that they cannot have the Spirit. How can He dwell with them when all their thoughts are on the world, and all their powers absorbed in procuring wealth? And when they get money they are pained if pressed by conscience to do something with it for the conversion of the world. They show how much they love the world in all their intercourse with others. Little things show it. They will screw down a poor man, who is doing a little piece of work for them, to the lowest penny. If they are dealing on a large scale, very likely they will be liberal and fair, because it is for their advantage. But if it is a person they care about—a labourer, or a mechanic, or a servant—they will grind him down to the last fraction, no matter what the work is really worth; and they actually pretend to make it a matter of conscience, that they cannot possibly give any more. Now, they would be ashamed to deal so with people of their own rank, because it would be known and injury their reputation; but God knows it, and has it all written down, that they are covetous and unfair in their dealings, and will not do right, only when it is for their interest. Now, how can such professors have the Spirit of God? It is impossible.

There are multitudes of such things, by which the Spirit of God is grieved. People call them "little" sins, but God will not call them little. I was struck with this thought, when I saw a little notice in *The Evangelist*. The publishers stated that they had many thousands of dollars in the hands of subscribers, which sums were justly due, but that it would cost them as much as it was worth to send an agent to collect the money. I suppose it is so with other religious papers, that subscribers either put the publisher to the trouble and expense of sending an agent to collect his due, or else they cheat him out of it. There is, doubtless, a large amount of money held back in this way by professors of religion, just because it is in such small sums, or because they are so far off that they cannot be sued. And yet these people will pray, and appear very pious, and wonder why they do not "enjoy" religion, and have the Spirit of God! It is this looseness of moral principle, this want of conscience about little matters, that grieves away the Holy Ghost.

5. Others do not *fully* confess and *forsake* their sins, and so cannot enjoy the Spirit's presence. They will confess their sins in general terms, perhaps, and are ready always to acknowledge that they are sinners. Or they will confess partially some particular sins. But they do it reservedly, proudly, guardedly, as if they were afraid they should say a little more than is necessary; that is, when they confess to men. They do it in a way which shows that, instead of bursting forth from an ingenuous heart, the confession is *wrung* from them, by conscience gripping them. If they have injured any one, they will make a *partial* recantation, which is hard-hearted, cruel, and hypocritical, and then they will ask: "Now, brother, are you satisfied?" We know that it is very difficult for a person who has been wronged to say, in such a case, that he is not satisfied, even if the confession is cold and heartless. But I tell you, God is not satisfied. He knows whether you have gone to the full length of honest confession, and taken all the blame that belongs to you. If your confessions have been constrained and wrung from you, do you suppose you can cheat God? "He that covereth his sins shall not prosper: but whoso confesseth and forsaketh them shall have mercy" (Prov. 28. 13). "He that humbleth himself shall be exalted" (Luke 14. 11). Unless you come quite down, and confess your sins honestly, and remunerate where you have done injury, you have no right to expect the spirit of prayer.

6. Others are neglecting some known duty, and that is the reason why they have not the Spirit. One does not pray in his family, though he knows he ought to do so, and yet he is trying to get the spirit of prayer! There is many a young man who feels in his heart he ought to prepare for the ministry, but who has not the spirit of prayer because he has some worldly object in view which prevents his devoting himself to the work. He has known his duty, refuses to do it, and yet is praying for direction from the Spirit of God! He cannot have it.

Another has neglected to make a profession of religion. He knows his duty, but he refuses to join the Church. He once had the spirit of prayer, but, neglecting his duty, he grieved the Spirit away. And now he thinks, if he could once more enjoy the light of God's countenance, and have his evidences renewed, he would do his duty, and join the Church. And so he is trying to bring God over to his terms, to grant him His presence. He need not expect it. You will live and die in darkness, unless you are willing *first* to do your duty, *before* God manifests Himself as reconciled to you. It is in vain to say, you will come forward if God will *first* show you the light of His countenance. He never will do it as long as you live; He will let you die without it, if you refuse to do your duty.

I have known women who felt that they ought to talk to their unconverted husbands, and pray with them; but they neglected it, and so they got into the dark. They knew their duty and refused to do it; they "went round it," and there they lost the spirit of prayer.

If you have neglected any known duty, and thus lost the spirit of prayer, you must yield first. God has a controversy with you; you have refused obedience to God, and you must retract. You may have forgotten it, but God has not, and you must set yourself to recall it to mind and repent. God never will yield or grant you His Spirit, till you repent. Had I an omniscient eye now, I could call the names of the individuals in this congregation, who have neglected some known duty, or committed some sin, that they have not repented of, and now they are praying for the spirit of prayer, but they cannot succeed in obtaining it.

To illustrate this I will relate a case. A good man—an elder in the western part of this State, had been a long time an earnest Christian, and he used to talk to the sleepy Church with which he was connected. Presently the Church grew offended and got out of patience, so that many told him they wished he would let them alone, and that they did not think he could do them any good. He took them at their word, and they all "went to sleep" together, remaining so two or three years. Then a minister came among them, and a revival commenced; but this elder seemed to have lost his spirituality. He who used to be forward in a good work now held back. Everybody thought it was unaccountable. Finally, as he was going home one night, the truth of his situation flashed upon his mind, and, for a few minutes, he went into absolute despair. At length his thoughts were directed back to that sinful resolution to let the Church alone in her sins. He felt that no language could describe the blackness of that sin. He realised at that moment what it was to be lost, and to find that God had a controversy with him. He saw that it was a bad spirit which had led him to that weak resolution; the same that caused Moses to say: "Ye rebels" (Num. 20. 10). He humbled himself on the spot, and God poured out His Spirit on him. Perhaps some of you are just in this situation. You have said something provoking or unkind to some person. Perhaps it was peevishness to a servant who was a Christian. Or perhaps it was speaking censoriously of a minister or some other person. Perhaps you have been angry because your opinions have not been taken, or your dignity has been encroached upon. Search thoroughly, and see if you cannot find out the sin. Perhaps you have forgotten it. But God has not forgotten it, and never will forgive your unchristian conduct until you repent. God cannot overlook it. What good would it do to forgive while the sin is rankling in your heart?

7. Perhaps you have resisted the Spirit of God. Perhaps you are in the *habit* of resisting the Spirit. You resist conviction. In preaching, when something has been said that reached your case, your heart has risen up against it. Many are willing to hear plain and searching preaching, so long as they can apply it all to other people; a misanthropic spirit makes them take a satisfaction in hearing others searched and rebuked; but, if the truth touches *them,* the directly cry out that the preaching is "personal" and "abusive." Is this your case?

8. The fact is that you do not, *on the whole,* desire the Spirit.

This is true in every case in which you do not have the Spirit. Let me not be mistaken here. I want that you should carefully discriminate. Nothing is more common than for people to desire a thing on some accounts, which they do not choose *on the whole*. A person may see, in a shop window, an article which he desires to purchase; accordingly he goes in and asks the price, and thinks of it a little, yet on the whole concludes not to purchase it. He desires the article, but does not like the price, or does not like to be at the expense, so that, upon the whole, he prefers not to purchase it. So, persons may on some accounts desire the Spirit of God; from a regard to the comfort and joy of heart which He brings. If you know what it is by former experience to commune with God, and how sweet it is to dissolve in penitence and to be filled with the Spirit, you cannot but desire a return of those joys. And you may set yourself to pray earnestly for it, and to pray for a revival of religion. But, on the whole, you are unwilling it should come. You have so much to do that you cannot attend to it. Or it will require so many sacrifices that you cannot bear to have it. There are some things you are not willing to give up. You find that if you wish to have the Spirit of God dwell with you, you must lead a different life; you must give up the world; you must make sacrifices; you must break off from your worldly associates, and make confession of your sins. And so, on the whole, you do not wish to have the Spirit come, unless He will consent to dwell with you and let you live as you please. But that He will never do.

9. Perhaps you do not pray for the Spirit; or you pray and use no other means, or pray and do not act consistently with your prayers. Or you use means calculated to resist them. Or you ask, and as soon as He comes and begins to affect your mind, you grieve Him right away, and will not walk with Him.

IV. *THE GREAT GUILT OF NOT HAVING THE SPIRIT.*

1. Your guilt is just as great as the authority of God is great, which commands you: "Be filled with the Spirit. God commands it, and it is just as much a disobedience of God's commands, as it would be to swear profanely, or steal, or commit adultery, or break the Sabbath. Think of that. And yet are many people who do not blame themselves at all for not

having the Spirit. They even think themselves quite pious Christians, because they go to prayer-meetings, and partake of the sacrament, and all that, though they live year after year without the Spirit of God. Now you see that the same God who says: "Do not get drunk," says also: "Be filled with the Spirit."

You all say, if a man is a habitual murderer, or a thief, he is no Christian. Why? Because he lives in habitual disobedience to God. So, if he swears, you have no charity for him. You will not allow him to plead that his heart is right, and that words are nothing; that God does not care anything about words. You would think it outrageous to have such a man in the Church, or to have a company of such people pretend to call themselves a Christian Church. And yet they are not a whit more absolutely living in disobedience to God than you are, who live without the spirit of prayer and without the presence of God.

2. Your guilt is equal to all the good you might do if you were possessed by the Spirit of God in as great a measure as it is your duty to be, and as you might be. You, elders of this Church, how much good might you do if you had the Spirit! And you, Sunday-school teachers how much good you might do; and you, Church members, too, if you were filled with the Spirit you might do vast good, infinite good. Well, your guilt is just as great. Here is a blessing promised, and you can have it by doing your duty. You are entirely responsible to the Church and to God for all this good that you might do. A man is responsible for all the good he can do.

3. Your guilt is further measured by all the evil which you do in consequence of not having the Spirit. You are a dishonour to religion. You are a stumbling-block to the Church, and to the world; and your guilt is enhanced by all the various influences you exert. And it will prove so in the Day of Judgment.

V. THE CONSEQUENCES OF HAVING THE SPIRIT.

1. You will be called eccentric; and probably you will deserve it. Probably you will really be eccentric. I never knew a person who was filled with the Spirit that was not called eccentric. And the reason is that such people are unlike other folk. There is therefore the best of reasons why such persons should appear eccentric. They act under different influences, take different views, are moved by different motives, led by a

different spirit. You are to expect such remarks. How often I have heard the remark respecting such-and-such persons: "He is a good man—but he is rather eccentric." I have sometimes asked for the particulars; in what does this eccentricity consist? I hear the catalogue, and it amounts to this, to be "eccentric." There is such a thing as affected eccentricity. Horrible! But there is such a thing as being to so deeply imbued with the Spirit of God that you must and will act so as to appear strange and eccentric, to those who cannot understand the reasons of your conduct.

2. If you have much of the Spirit of God, it is not unlikely you will be thought deranged, by many. We judge men to be deranged when they act differently from what we think to be according to prudence and common sense, and when they come to conclusions for which we can see no good reasons. Paul was accused of being deranged by those who did not understand the views of things under which he acted. No doubt Festus thought the man was crazy, that "much learning had made him mad." But Paul said: "I am not mad, most noble Festus" (Acts 26. 24, 25). His conduct was so strange, so novel, that Festus thought it must be insanity. But the truth simply was, he saw the subject so clearly that he threw his whole soul into it. Festus and the rest were entirely in the dark in respect to the motive by which he was actuated. This is by no means uncommon. Multitudes have appeared, to those who had no spirituality, as if they were deranged. Yet *they* saw good reasons for doing as they did. God was leading their minds to act in such a way that those who were not spiritual could not see the reasons. You must make up your mind to this, and so much the more, as you live the more above the world and walk with God.

3. If you have the Spirit of God, you must expect to feel great distress in view of the condition of the Church and of the world. Some spiritual epicures ask for the Spirit because they think He will make them so perfectly happy. Some people think that spiritual Christians are always free from sorrow. There never was a greater mistake. Read your Bibles, and see how the prophets and apostles were always groaning and distressed, in view of the state of the Church and of the world. The apostle Paul says he was "always bearing about in the

body the dying of the Lord Jesus" (2 Cor. 4. 10). "I protest," says he, "I die daily" (1 Cor. 15. 31). You will know what it is to sympathise with the Lord Jesus Christ, and be baptized with the baptism that He was baptized with. Oh, how He agonised in view of the state of sinners! How He travailed in soul for their salvation? The more you have of His spirit, the more clearly will you see the state of sinners, and the more deeply you will be distressed about them. Many times you will feel as if you could not live in view of their situation; your distress will be unutterable.

4. You will be often grieved with the state of the ministry. Some years since I met a woman belonging to one of the Churches in this city. I inquired of her the state of religion here. She seemed unwilling to say much about it, made some general remarks, and then choked, and her eyes filled, and she said: "Oh, our minister's mind seems to be very dark!" Spiritual Christians often feel like this, and often weep over it. I have seen much of it, having often found Christians who wept and groaned in secret, to see the darkness in the minds of ministers in regard to religion, the earthliness, and fear of man; but they dared not speak of it lest they should be denounced and threatened, and perhaps turned out of the Church. I do not say these things censoriously, to reproach my brethren, but because they are true. And ministers ought to know that nothing is more common than for spritual Christians to feel burdened and distressed at the state of the ministry. I would not wake up any wrong feelings towards ministers, but it is time it should be known that Christians do often get spiritual views of things, and their souls are kindled up, and then they find that their minister does not enter into their feelings, that he is far below the standard of what he ought to be, and in spirituality is far below some of the members of his Church.

This is one of the most prominent and deeply-to-be-deplored evils of the present day. The *piety* of the ministry, though *real,* is so superficial, in many instances, that the spiritual people of the Church feel that ministers do not, cannot, sympathise with them. The preaching does not meet their wants; it does not feed them. The ministers have not depth enough of religions experience to know how to search and wake up the Church; how to help those under temptation, to support the weak, to direct the strong. When a minister has gone with a Church as far as his experience in spiritual exercises goes, there he stops; and until he has a renewed experience, until he is reconverted, his heart broken up afresh, and he set forward in the Divine life and Christian experience, he will help them no more. He may preach sound doctrine, and so may an unconverted minister; but, after all, his preaching will want that searching pungency, that practical bearing, that unction which alone will reach the case of a spiritually-minded Christian. It is a fact over which the Church is groaning, that the piety of young men suffers so much in the course of their education, that when they enter the ministry, however much intellectual furniture they may possess, they are in a state of *spiritual babyhood.* They want nursing; they need rather to be fed, than to undertake to feed the Church of God.

5. If you have much of the Spirit of God, you must make up your mind to have much opposition, both in the Church and the world. Very likely the leading men in the Church will oppose you. There has always been opposition in the Church. So it was when Christ was on earth. If you are far above their state of feeling, Church members will oppose you. If any man will live godly in Christ Jesus, he must expect persecution (2 Tim. 3. 12). Often the elders and even the minister will oppose you, if you are filled with the Spirit of God.

6. You must expect very frequent and agonising conflicts with Satan. Satan has very little trouble with those Christians who are not spiritual, but lukewarm, and slothful, and worldlyminded. And such do not understand what is said about spiritual conficts. Perhaps they will smile when such things are mentioned. And so the devil lets them alone. They do not disturb him, nor he them. But spiritual Christians, he understands very well, are doing him a vast injury, and therefore he sets himself against them. Such Christians often have terrible conficts. They have temptations that they never thought of before: blasphemous thoughts, atheism, suggestions to do deeds of wickedness, to destroy their own lives, and the like. And if you are spiritual, you may expect these terrible conficts.

7. You will have greater conflicts with yourself than you

ever thought of. You will sometimes find your own corruptions making strange headway against the Spirit. "The flesh lusteth against the Spirit, and the Spirit against the flesh" (Gal. 5. 17). Such a Christian is often thrown into consternation at the power of his own corruptions. One of the Commodores in the United States Navy was, as I have been told, a spiritual man; his pastor told me he had known that man lie on the floor and groan a great part of the night, in conflict with his own corruptions, and to cry to God, in agony, that He would break the power of the temptation. It seemed as if the devil was determined to ruin him, and his own heart, for the time being, was almost in league with the devil.

8. But, you will have peace with God. If the Church, and sinners, and the devil, oppose you, there will be One with whom you will have peace. Let you who are called to these trials, and conflicts, and temptations, and who groan, and pray, and weep, and break your hearts, remember this consideration: your peace, so far as your feelings towards God are concerned, will flow like a river.

9. You will likewise have peace of conscience, if you are led by the Spirit. You will not be constantly goaded and kept on the rack by a guilty conscience. Your conscience will be calm and quiet, unruffled as the summer's lake.

10. If filled with the Spirit, you will be useful. You cannot help being useful. Even if you were sick and unable to go out of your room, or to converse, and saw nobody, you would be ten times more useful than a hundred of those common sort of Christians who have no spirituality. To give you an idea of this, I will relate an anecdote. A pious man in the western part of this State, was suffering from consumption. He was a poor man, and was ill for years. An unconverted merchant in the place, who had a kind heart, used to send him now and then some things for his comfort, or for his family. He felt grateful for the kindness, but could make no return, as he wanted to do. At length he determined that the best return he could make would be to pray for the man's salvation. So he began to pray, and his soul kindled, and he got hold of God. No revival was taking place there, but, by and by, to the astonishment of everybody, this merchant came right out on the Lord's side. The fire kindled all over the place; a poweful revival followed,

and multitudes were converted.

This poor man lingered in this way for several years, and died. After his death, I visited the place, and his widow put into my hands his diary. Among other entries was this: "I am acquainted with about thirty ministers and Churches." He then went on to set apart certain hours in the day and week to pray for each of these ministers and Churches, and also certain seasons for praying for different missionary stations. Then followed, under different dates, such facts as these: "To-day I have been enabled to offer what I call the prayer of faith for the outpouring of the Spirit on——Church, and I trust in God there will soon be a revival there." Under another date he had written: "I have to-day been able to offer what I call the prayer of faith for —— Church, and trust there will soon be a revival there." Thus he had gone over a great number of Churches, recording the fact that he had prayed for them in faith that a revival might soon prevail among them.

Of the missionary stations, if I recollect right, he mentioned in particular one at Ceylon. I believe the last place mentioned in his dairy, for which he offered the prayer of faith, was the place in which he lived. Not long after, the revival commenced, and went over the region of the country, nearly, I believe, if not quite, in the order in which the places had been mentioned in his diary; and in due time news came from Ceylon that there was a revival of religion there. The revival in his own town did not commence till after his death. Its commencement was at the time when his widow put into my hands the documents to which I have referred. She told me that he was so exercised in prayer during his sickness, that she often feared he would "pray himself to death." The revival was exceedingly great and powerful in all the region, and the fact that it was about to prevail had not been hidden from this servant of the Lord. According to His Word, "the secret of the Lord is with them that fear Him" (Psa. 25. 14). Thus, this man, too feeble in body to go out of his house, was yet more useful to the world and the Church of God than all the heartless professors in the country. Standing between God and the desolations of Zion, and pouring out his heart in believing prayer, "as a prince he had power with God and with men, and prevailed" (Gen. 32. 28).

11. If you are filled with the Spirit, you will not find yourselves distressed, and galled, and worried, when people speak against you. When I find people irritated and fretting at any little thing that touches them, I am sure they have not the Spirit of Christ. Jesus Christ could have everything said against Him that malice could invent, and yet not be in the least disturbed by it. If you mean to be meek under persecution, and exemplify the temper of the Saviour, and honour religion in this way, you need to be filled with the Spirit.

12. You will be wise in using means for the conversion of sinners. If the Spirit of God is in you, He will lead you to use means wisely, in a way adapted to the end, and to avoid doing hurt.[1] No man who is not filled with the Spirit of God is fit to be employed in directing the measures adopted in a revival. His hands will be "all thumbs," unable to take hold, and he will act as if he had not common sense. But a man who is led by the Spirit of God will know how to *time* his measures aright, and how to apportion Divine truth so as to make it tell to the best advantage.

13. You will be calm under affliction; not thrown into confusion or consternation when you see the storm coming over you. People around will be astonished at your calmness

---

[1] A remarkable instance of Divine leading in the choice of a subject and the management of a meeting which occured in Finney's experience, aptly illustrates his point. In the outskirts of Antwerp, N. Y., where no religious services were usually held, he preached on the escape of Lot from Sodom. It so happened that the place was commonly called "Sodom," and the one pious man of the neighbourhood (who had invited Finney) was known as "Lot." Finney was entirely unaware of this, but the people, imagining him to have chosen the subject deliberately, in order to reproach them, were full of fury. In the end, however, there was an extraordinary breakdown, under the influence of the Spirit. Penitent sinners began to fall upon their knees in every direction, crying to God for mercy. "If I had had a sword in each hand, I could not have cut them down so fast as they fell," said Finney. The meeting continued all night, and in the morning (the building being required for school purposes) was adjourned to a private house, Finney renewing his labours in the afternoon. Years after, a minister who called upon him in order to give a donation of a hundred dollars to Oberlin College, proved to be one of the converts from that school-house meeting.

and cheerfulness under heavy trials, not knowing the inward supports of those who are filled with the Spirit.

14. You will be resigned in death; you will always feel prepared to die, and not afraid to die; and after death you will be proportionately more happy for ever in heaven.

VI. *THE CONSEQUENCES OF NOT BEING FILLED WITH THE SPIRIT.*

1. You will often doubt, in such a case, and reasonably so, whether you are a Christian. You will have doubts, and you ought to have them, for the sons of God are led by the Spirit of God, and if you are not led by the Spirit, what reason have you to think that you are a son? You will try to make a little evidence go a great way to bolster up your hopes; but you cannot do it, unless your conscience is seared as with a hot iron. You cannot help being plunged often into painful doubt about your state (Rom. 8. 9; 2 Cor. 13. 5).

2. You will always be unsettled in your views about the prayer of faith. The prayer of faith is something so spiritual, so much a matter of experience and not of speculation, that unless you are spiritual yourselves you will not understand it fully. You may talk a great deal about the prayer of faith, and for the time get thoroughly convinced regarding it. But you will never feel so settled on it as to retain the same position of mind concerning it, and in a little while you will be all uncertainty again. I knew a curious instance in a brother minster. He told me: "When I have the Spirit of God and enjoy His presence, I believe firmly in the prayer of faith; but when I have Him not, I find myself doubting whether there is any such thing, and my mind is full of objections." I know, from my own experience, what this is, and when I hear persons raising objections to that view of prayer which I have presented in these Lectures, I understand very well what their difficulty is, and have often found it impossible to satisfy their minds, while they are so far from God; when, at the same time, they would understand it themselves without argument, whenever they experienced it.

3. If you have not the Spirit, you will be very apt to stumble at those who have. You will doubt the propriety of their conduct. If they seem to feel a good deal more than yourself,

you will be likely to call it "animal feeling." You will perhaps doubt their sincerity when they say they have such feelings. You will say: "I don't know what to make of Brother Such-a-one; he seems to be very pious, but I do not understand him, I think he has a great deal of animal feeling." Thus you will be trying to censure them, for the purpose of justifying yourself.

4. You will be had in reputation with the impenitent, and with carnal professors. They will praise you, as "a rational, orthodox, consistent Christian." You will be just in the frame of mind to walk with them, because you are agreed.

5. You will be much troubled with fears about fanticism. Whenever there are revivals, you will see in them "a strong tendency to fanaticism," and will be full of fears and anxiety.

6. You will be much disturbed by the measures that are used in revivals. If any measures are adopted, that are decided and direct, you will think they are all "new," and will stumble at them just in proportion to your want of spirituality. You do not see their appropriateness. You will stand and cavil at the measures, because you are so blind that you cannot see their adaptedness, while all heaven is rejoicing in them as the means of saving souls.[1]

7. You will be a reproach to religion. The impenitent will sometimes praise you because you are so much like them-selves, and sometimes laugh about you because you are

---

[1]The objections commonly urged against revivals, by cold and worldly professors and by jealous minds, appear not only from generation to generation, but from country to country. Thus, McCheyne, writing of the revival at Dundee (in reply to an inquiry instituted by the Presbytery of Aberdeen, in 1840), said: "I have been fully convinced that the outpouring of the Holy Spirit at the Kirk of Shotts, and again, a century after, at Cambuslang, &c., in Scotland, and under the ministry of President Edwards in America, was attended by the very same appearances as the work in our own day. Indeed, so completely do they agree, both in their nature and in the circumstances that attended them, that I have not heard a single objection brought against it in former time, and that has not been most scripturally and triumphantly removed by Mr. [James] Robe [of Kilsyth] in his 'Narrative' ["of the Extraordinary Work of the Spirit of God at Kilsyth, and other Congregations in the Neighbourhood, 1742"], and by President Edwards in his invaluable 'Thoughts on the Revival of Religion in New England.' "

such a hypocrite.

8. You will know but little about the Bible.

9. If you die without the Spirit, you will fall into hell. There can be no doubt about this. Without the Spirit you will never be prepared for heaven.

REMARKS.

1. Christians are as guilty for not having the Spirit, as sinners are for not repenting.

2. They are even more so. As they have more light, they are so much the more guilty.

3. All beings have a right to complain of Christians who have not the Spirit. You are not doing work for God, and He has a right to complain. He has placed His Spirit at your disposal, and if you have not the Spirit, God has a right to look to you and to hold you responsible for all the good you might otherwise do. You are sinning against all heaven, for you ought to be adding to the happy ranks of the redeemed. Sinners, the Church, and ministers, all have a right to complain.

4. You are an obstacle in the way of the work of the Lord. It is in vain for a minister to try to work over your head. Ministers often groan and struggle, and wear themselves out in vain, trying to do good where there is a people who live so that they do not have the Spirit of God. If the Spirit is poured out at any time, the Church will grieve Him right away. Thus, you may tie the hands and break the heart of your minister, and break him down, and perhaps kill him, because you will not be filled with the Spirit.

5. You see the reason why Christians need the Spirit, and the degree of their dependence upon Him.

6. Do not tempt God by "waiting" for His Spirit, while using no means to procure His presence.

7. If you mean to have the Spirit, you must be childlike, and yield to His influences—just as yielding as air. If He is drawing you to prayer, you must quit everything to yield to His gentle strivings. No doubt you have sometimes felt a desire to pray for some object, and you have put it off and resisted, until God left you. If you wish Him to remain, you must yield to His softest leadings, watch to learn what He would have you do, and yield yourself up to His guidance.

8. Chrsitians ought to be willing to make any sacrifice to enjoy the presence of the Spirit. Said a woman in high life (a professor of religion): "I must either give up hearing such-and-such a minister [naming him] preach, or I must give up my gay company." She gave up the preaching and stayed away. How different from another case—that of a woman in the same rank of life—who heard the same minister preach, and went home resolved to abandon her gay and worldly manner of life. She changed her whole mode of dress, of equipage, of living, and of conversation; so that her gay and worldly friends were soon willing to leave her to the enjoyment of communion with God, and free to spend her time in doing good.

9. You see from this, that it must be very difficult for those in fashionable life to go to heaven. What a calamity to be in such circles! Who can enjoy the presence of God in them?

10. See how crazy those are who are scrambling to get up to these circles, enlarging their houses, changing their style of living, their dress, and their furniture. It is like climbing up to the mast-head to be thrown off into the ocean. To enjoy God, you must come down, not go up there. God is not there, among all the starch and flattery of high life.

11. Many professors of religion are as ignorant of spirituality as Nicodemus was of the New Birth. They are ignorant, and I fear unconverted. If anybody talks to them about the spirit of prayer, it is all algebra to them. The case of such professors is awful. How different was the character of the apostles! Read the history of *their* lives, read *their* letters, and you will see that they were always spiritual, and walked daily with God. But now how little is there of such religion! "When the Son of Man cometh, shall He find faith on the earth?" (Luke 18. 18.) Set some of these professors to work in a revival, and they do not know what to do, for they have no energy, no skill, and make no impression. When will professors of religion set themselves to work, filled with the Spirit? If I could see this Church filled with the Spirit, I would ask nothing more to move this whole mighty mass of minds around us. Not two weeks would pass before the revival would spread all over this city.

Lecture VIII

MEETINGS FOR PRAYER

Again I say unto you, That if two of you shall agree on earth as touching anything that they shall ask, it shall be done for them of My Father which is in heaven.—Matt. 18. 19.

Hitherto, in treating of the subject of PRAYER, I have confined my remarks to secret prayer. I am now to speak of social prayer, or prayer offered in company, where two or more are united in praying. Such meetings have been common from the time of Christ, and it is probable that God's people have always been in the habit of making united supplication, whenever they had the privilege. The propriety of the practice will not be questioned here. I need not dwell now on the duty of social prayer. Nor is it my design to discuss the question, whether any two Christians agreeing to ask any blessing, will be sure to obtain it. My object is to make some remarks on Meetings for Prayer, noting: I. The design of prayer-meetings. II. The manner of conducting them. III. Several things that will defeat the design of holding them.

I. *THE DESIGN OF PRAYER-MEETINGS.*

1. One design of assembling several persons together for united prayer, is to *promote union* among Christians. Nothing tends more to cement the hearts of Christians than praying

together. Never do they love one another so well as when they witness the outpouring of each other's hearts in prayer. Their spirituality begets a feeling of union and confidence, highly important to the prosperity of the Church. It is doubtful whether Christians can ever be otherwise than united, if they are in the habit of really praying together. And where they have had hard feelings and differences among themselves, these ard all done away by uniting in prayer. The great object is gained, if you can bring them *really to unite* in prayer; if this can be done, the difficulties vanish.

2. To *extend the spirit of prayer.* God has so constituted us, and such is the economy of His grace, that we are sympathetic beings, and communicate our feelings to one another. A minister, for instance, will often, as it were, breathe his own feelings into his congregation. The Spirit of God that inspires his soul, makes use of his *feelings* to influence his hearers, just as much as He makes use of the words he preaches. So He makes use of the feelings of Christians. Nothing is more calculated to beget a prayer than to unite in social prayer with one who has the spirit himself; unless this one should be so far ahead that his prayer will repel the rest. His prayer will awaken them, if they are not *so far* behind as to revolt at it and resist it. If they are anywhere near the standard of his feelings, his spirit will kindle, and burn, and spread all around. One individual who obtains the spirit of prayer will often arouse a whole Church, and extend the same spirit through the whole, so that a general revival follows.

3. Another grand design of social prayer, is *to move God.* Not that it changes the mind and feelings of God. When we speak of "moving" God, as I have said in a former Lecture, we do not mean that prayer alters the will of God. But when the right kind of prayer is offered by Christians, they are in such a state of mind that it becomes proper for God to bestow a blessing. They are then prepared to receive it, and He gives because He is always the same, and always ready and happy to show mercy. When Christians are united, and praying as they ought, God opens the windows of heaven, and pours out His blessing till there is not room to receive it. (Mal. 3. 10).[1]

---

[1]"When God has something very great to accomplish for His Church," says Jonathan Edwards, "it is His will that there should

4. Another important design of prayer-meetings is the *conviction and conversion of sinners*. When properly conducted, they are eminently calculated to produce this effect. Sinners are apt to be solemn when they hear Christians pray. Where there is a spirit of prayer, sinners must feel. An ungodly man (a universalist) once said respecting a certain minister: "I can bear his preaching very well; but when he prays, I feel awfully—as if God were coming down upon me." Sinners are often convicted by hearing prayer. A young man of distinguished talents said, concerning a certain minister to whom, before his conversion, he had been very much opposed: "As soon as he began to pray, I began to be convicted; and if he had continued to pray much longer, I should not have been able to hold myself back from Christ." Just as soon as Christians begin to pray as they ought, sinners then know that they pray, and begin to feel awfully. They do not understand what spirituality is, because they have no experience of it. But when such prayer is offered, they know there is something in it; they know God is in it, and it brings them near to God; it makes them feel awfully solemn, and they cannot bear it. And not only is it calculated to impress the minds of sinners, but when Christians pray in faith, the Spirit of God is poured out, and sinners are melted down and converted on the spot.

II. *THE MANNER OF CONDUCTING PRAYER-MEETINGS.*

1. It is often well to open a prayer-meeting by *reading a short portion* of the Word of God; especially if the person who

---

precede it, the extraordinary prayers of His people; as is manifest by Ezek. 36, 37, together with the context. And it is revealed that when God is about to accomplish great things for His Church, He will begin by remarkable pouring out the spirit of grace and supplication (Zech. 12. 10). If we are not to expect that the devil should go out of a particular person, that is, under a bodily possession, without extraordinary prayer, or *prayer and fasting;* how much less should we expect to have him cast out of the land and the world without it! I should think the people of God in this land would be in the way of their duty to do three times as much at fasting and prayer as they do" ("Thoughts on the Revival," Part 5). Finney was much influenced by the writings of Edwards. He first read them in the house of Dr. Aiken (of Utica), who said that Finney "often spoke of them with rapture."

takes the lead of the meeting, can call to mind any portion that will be applicable to the object or occasion, and that is impressive, and to the point. If he has no passage that is applicable, he had better not read any at all. Do not drag in the word of God to make up part of the meeting as a mere matter of form. This is an insult to God. It is not well to read any more than is applicable to the subject before the meeting or the occasion. Some people think it always necessary to read a whole chapter, though it may be ever so long, and have a variety of subjects. It is just as impressive and judicious to read a whole chapter as it would be for a minister to take a whole chapter for his text, when his object was to make some particular truth bear on the minds of his audience. The design of a prayer-meeting should be to bring Christians to the point, to pray for a definite object. Wandering over a large field hinders and destroys this design.

2. It is proper that the person who leads should make some short and appropriate remarks, calculated to explain the nature of prayer, and the encouragements we have to pray, and to *bring the object to be prayed for* directly before the minds of the people.

A man can no more pray without having his thoughts concentrated than he can do anything else. The person leading should therefore see to this, by bringing up before their minds the object for which they came to pray. If they came to pray for *any* object, he can do this. And if they did not, they had better go home. It is of no use to stay there and mock God by pretending to pray when they have nothing on earth to pray for.

After stating the object, he should bring up some promise or some principle, as the ground of encouragement to expect an answer to their prayers. If there is any indication of Providence, or any promise, or any principle in the Divine government, that affords a ground of faith, let him call it to mind, and not let them be talking out of their own hearts at random, without knowing any solid reason for expecting an answer. One reason why prayer-meetings mostly accomplish so little, is because there is so little common sense exercised about them. Instead of looking round for some solid footing on which to repose their faith, people come together and pour forth *words,* and neither know nor care whether they are any reason to expect an answer. If they are going to pray about anything concerning which there can be any doubt or any mistake, in regard to the ground of faith, they should be shown the reason there is for believing that their prayers will be heard and answered. It is easy to see that, unless something like this is done, three-fourths of them will have no idea of what they are doing, or of the ground on which they should expect to receive what they pray for.

3. In *calling on persons to pray* it is always desirable to let things take their own course, wherever it is safe. If it can be left so with safety, let those pray who are most inclined to pray. It sometimes happens that even those who are ordinarily the most spiritual, and most proper to be called on, are not, at the time, in a suitable frame; they may be cold and worldly, and only freeze the meeting. But if you let those pray who desire to pray, you avoid this. But often this cannot be done with safety, especially in large cities, where a prayer-meeting might be liable to be interrupted by those who have no business to pray; some fanatic or crazy person, some hypocrite or enemy, who would only make a noise. In most places, however, the course may be taken with perfect safety. Give up the meeting to the Spirit of God. Those who desire to pray, let them pray. If the leader sees anything that needs to be set right, let him remark, freely and kindly, and put it right, and then go on again. Only he should be careful to *time* his remarks, so as not to interrupt the flow of feeling, or to chill the meeting, or to turn the thoughts of the people from the proper subject.

4. If it is necessary to name the individuals who are to pray, it is best to call *first* on those who are *most spiritual;* and, if you do not know who they are, then choose those whom you would naturally suppose to be most "alive." If they pray at the outset, they will be likely to spread the spirit of prayer through the meeting, and elevate the tone of the whole. Otherwise, if you call on those who are cold and lifeless, they will be likely to diffuse a chill. The only hope of having an efficient prayer-meeting is when at least a part of the Church is spiritual, and infuses its spirit into the rest. This is the very reason why it is often best to let things take their course, for then those who have the most feeling are apt to pray first, and give character

REVIVALS OF RELIGION

to the meeting.

5. The prayers should always *be very short*. When individuals suffer themselves to pray long they forget that they are only the mouth of the congregation, and that the congregation cannot be expected to sympathise with them, so as to feel united in prayer, if they are long and tedious, and go all around the world, and pray for everything they can think of. Commonly, those who pray long in a meeting do so, not because they *have* the spirit of prayer, but because they *have not*. Some men will spin out a long prayer in telling God who and what He is, or they pray out a whole system of divinity. Some preach; others exhort the people—till everybody wishes they would stop, and God wishes so, too, most undoubtedly. They should keep to the point, and pray for what they came to pray for, and not follow the imagination of their own foolish hearts all over the universe.

6. Each one should pray for *some one object*. It is well for every individual to have one object for prayer; two or more may pray for the same thing, or each for a separate object. If the meeting is convened to pray for some specific thing, let them all pray for that. If its object is more general, let them select their subjects, according as they feel interested. If one feels particularly disposed to pray for the Church, let him do it. If the next feels disposed to pray for the Church, he may do so, too. Perhaps the next will feel inclined to pray for sinners; let him do it, and as soon as he has got through *let him stop*. Whenever a man has deep feelings, he always feels on some particular point, and if he prays about that, he will speak out of the abundance of his heart, and then he will naturally stop when he is done.

7. If, in the progress of the meeting, it becomes necessary to *change the object* of prayer, let the leader state the fact, and explain it in a few words. If the object is to pray for the Church, or for backsliders, or sinners, or the heathen, let him state it plainly, and then turn it over and hold it up before them, till he brings them to think and feel deeply before they pray. Then he should state to them the grounds on which they may repose their faith in regard to obtaining the blessings for which they pray, if any such statement is needed, and so lead them right up to the Throne, and let them take hold of the hand of God. This

is according to the philosophy of the mind. People always do it for themselves when they pray in secret, if they really mean to pray to any purpose. And so it should be in prayer-meetings.

8. It is important that *the time should be fully occupied,* so as not to leave long seasons of silence, which make a bad impression, and chill the meeting. I know that sometimes Churches have seasons of silent prayer. But in those cases they should be specially requested to pray in silence, so that all may know why they are silent. This often has a most powerful effect, where a few moments are spent by a whole congregation in silence, while all lift up their thoughts to God. This is very different from having long intervals of silence because there is nobody to pray. Every one feels that such a silence is like the cold damp of death over the meeting.

9. It is exceedingly important that he who leads the meeting should press sinners who may be present to *immediate repentance.* He should earnest urge the Christians who are present, to pray in such a way as to make sinners feel that they are expected to repent immediately. This tends to inspire Christians with compassion and love for souls. The remarks made to sinners are often like pouring fire upon the hearts of Christians, to awaken them to prayer and effort for the conversion of the unsaved. Let them see and feel the guilt and danger of sinners right among them, and then they will pray.

III. *THINGS WHICH MAY DEFEAT THE PRAYER-MEETING.*

1. When there is an unhappy *want of confidence* in the leader, there is no hope of any good. Whatever may be the cause, whether he is to blame or not, the very fact that *he* leads the meeting will cast a damp over it, and prevent all good. I have witnessed it in Churches, where there was some offensive elder or deacon (perhaps justly deemed offensive; perhaps not) set to lead, and the meeting would die under his influence. If there is a want of confidence in regard to his piety, or in his ability, or in his judgment, or in anything connected with the meeting, everything he says or does will fall to the ground. The same thing often takes place where the Church has lost confidence in the minister.

2. Where the leader *lacks spirituality,* there will be a dryness and coldness in his remarks and prayers; everything will

indicate his want of unction, and his whole influence will be the very reverse of what it ought to be. I have known Churches where a prayer-meeting could not be sustained, and the reason was not obvious, but those who understood the state of things knew that the leader was so notorious for his want of spirituality that he would inevitably freeze a prayer-meeting to death. In many Churches the elders are so far from being spiritual men that they always freeze a prayer-meeting. And at the same time they are often amazingly jealous for their dignity, and cannot bear to have anybody else lead the meeting. If any member that is spiritual takes the lead, they will take him to task for it, saying: "Why, you are not an elder; you ought not to lead a prayer-meeting in the presence of an elder!" And thus they stand in the way, while the whole Church is suffering under their blighting influence.

A man who knows he is not in a spiritual frame of mind has no business to conduct a prayer-meeting—he will kill it. There are two reasons: First, he will have *no spiritual discernment,* and will know neither what to do, nor when to do it. A person who is spiritual can see the movements of Providence, and can feel the Spirit of God, and understand what He is leading them to pray for, so as to time his subjects, and take advantage of the state of feeling among Christians. He will not overthrow all the feeling in a meeting by introducing things that are incongruous or ill-timed. He has spiritual discernment to understand the leadings of the Spirit, and His workings on those who pray; and to follow on as the Spirit leads. Suppose an individual leads who is not spiritual, that there are two or three prayers, and the spirit of prayer arises, but the leader, having no spiritual discernment to see it, makes some remarks on another point, or reads a piece out of some book that is as far from the feeling of the meeting as the North Pole! What they are called to pray for may be just as evident to the praying people present as if the Son of God Himself had come into the meeting and named the subject; but the leader will overthrow it all, because he is so stupid that he does not know the indications of the meeting.

And then, if the leader is not spiritual, he will very likely be *dull and dry* in his remarks, and in all his exercises. He will give out a long hymn in a dreamy manner, and then read a long passage of Scripture, in a tone so cold that he will spread a wintry pall over the meeting, and it will be dull, as long as his cold heart is placed in front of the whole thing.

3. A want of *suitable talents* in the leader. If he is wanting in the talents which are fitted to make a meeting useful, if he can say nothing, or if his remarks are so out of the way as to produce levity or contempt, or if they have nothing in them that will impress the mind, or are not guided by good sense, or are not appropriate, he will injure the meeting. A man may be pious, but so weak that his prayers do not edify, but rather disgust. When this is so, he had better keep silence.

4. Sometimes the benefit of a prayer-meeting is defeated by a *bad spirit* in the leader. For instance, where there is a revival, and great opposition, if a leader gets up in a prayer-meeting and speaks of instances of opposition, and comments upon them, and thus diverts the meeting away from the object, he knows not what spirit he is of. Its effect is always ruinous to a prayer-meeting. Let a minister in a revival come out and preach against the opposition, and he will infallibly destroy the revival, and turn the hearts of Christians away from their proper object. Let the man who is set to lead the Church be careful to guard his own spirit, lest he should mislead the Church, and diffuse a wrong temper. The same will be true, *if any one* who is called upon to speak or pray, introduces in his remarks or prayers anything controversial, impertinent, unreasonable, unscriptural, ridiculous, or irrelevant. Any of these things will quench the tender breathings of the spirit of prayer, and destroy the meeting.

5. Persons *coming late* to the meeting. This is a very great hindrance. When people have begun to pray, and their attention is fixed, and they have shut their eyes and closed their ears, to keep out everything from their minds, in the midst of a prayer somebody will come bolting in and walk through the room. Some will look up, and all have their minds interrupted for the moment. They they all get fixed again, and another comes in, and so on. I suppose the devil would not care how many Christians went to a prayer-meeting, if they would only go after the meeting had begun. He would be glad to have ever so many go "scattering along" in such a way, dodging in very piously and distractingly.

6. When persons make *cold prayers* and cold confessions of sins, they are such to quench the spirit of prayer. When the influences of the Spirit are enjoyed, in the midst of the warm expressions that are flowing forth, let an individual come in who is cold, and pour out his cold breath like the damp of death, and it will make every Christian who has any feeling want to get out of the meeting.

7. In some places it is common to begin a prayer-meeting by reading *a long portion* of Scripture. Then the deacon or elder gives out a long hymn. Next, they sing it. Then he prays a long prayer, praying for the Jews, and the fulness of the Gentiles, and many other objects that have nothing to do with the occasion of the meeting. After that perhaps he reads a long extract from some book or magazine. Then they have another long hymn and another long prayer, and then they go home.

I once heard an elder say that a Church had kept up a prayer-meeting so many years, and yet had experienced no revival. The truth was, that the officers of the Church had been accustomed to carry on the meetings in just such a dignified way, and their dignity would not allow anything to be altered. No wonder there was no revival! Such prayer-meetings are enough to hinder a revival.[1] And if every so many revivals should commence, the prayer-meeting would destroy them.

---

[1] This illustration accords with Finney's story of the prayer-meeting which began the revival at Western, N. Y. Expecting to be at the place for one afternoon only, while on a visit, Finney accepted an invitation to be present. He was particularly shocked by the coldness of the elder who was leading, and who gave "a long prayer, or exhortation, or narrative," in which he told the Lord how many years they had been holding the meeting and that no answer had been given to their prayers. They were about to close, when an elder asked Finney to "make a remark." In response, the visitor proceeded to dissect their prayers, and to ask them, if they intended to mock God by implying that all the blame of what had been passing was to be ascribed to His Sovereignty? All were angry; some were about to leave forthwith; but Finney went on, and suddenly the leading elder burst into tears, and, falling on his knees, admitted the entire justice of the searching words. A general breaking-down ensued. They wept and confessed for an hour; and a revival began, which extended throughout the district.

There was a prayer-meeting once in this city, as I have been told, where there appeared to be some feeling, and some one very reasonably proposed that they should have two or three prayers in succession, without rising from their knees. One dignified man present opposed it, and said that they never had done so, and he hoped there would be no innovations! He did not approve of innovations. That was the last of the revival! Such persons have their prayer-meetings stereotyped, and are determined not to turn out of their track, whether they receive blessing or not. To allow any such thing would be "a new measure," and they never like "new measures"!

8. A *great deal of singing* often injures a prayer-meeting. The *agonising spirit of prayer* does not lead people to sing. There is a time for everything; a time to sing, and a time to pray. But if I know what it is to *travail in birth* for souls, Christians never feel less like singing than when they have the spirit of prayer for sinners.

When singing is introduced in a prayer-meeting, the hymns should be short, and so selected as to bring out something solemn; some striking words, such as the Judgment Hymn, and others calculated to produce an effect on sinners; or something that will produce a deep impression on the minds of Christians; but not that joyful kind of singing that makes everybody feel comfortable, and turns off the mind from the object of the prayer-meeting.

I once heard a celebrated organist produce a remarkable effect in a protracted meeting. The organ was a powerful one, and the double bass pipes were like unto thunder. The hymn was given out that had these lines:

> See the storm of vengeance gathering
> O'er the path you dare to tread;
> Hear the awful thunder rolling,
> Loud and louder o'er your head.

When he came to these words, we first heard the distant roar of thunder, then it grew nearer and louder, till at the word "louder," there was a crash that seemed almost to overpower the congregation. Such things in their proper place do good. But common singing dissipates feeling. It should always be such as will not take away feeling, but deepen it.

Often a prayer-meeting is injured by calling on the young converts to sing joyful hymns. This is highly improper in a prayer-meeting. It is no time for them to let feeling flow away in joyful singing, while so many sinners around them, and their own former companions, are going down to hell. A revival is often put down by the Church and the minister giving themselves up to singing with young converts. Thus, by stopping to rejoice when they ought to feel more and more deeply for sinners, they grieve away the Spirit of God, and they soon find that the agony and travail of soul are gone.

9. Introducing *subjects of controversy* into prayer will defeat a prayer-meeting. Nothing of a controversial nature should be introduced into prayer, unless it is the object of the meeting to *settle that thing*. Otherwise, let Christians come together in their prayer-meetings, on the broad ground of offering united prayer for a common object. And let controversies be settled somewhere else.

10. Great pains should be taken, both by the leader and others, to *watch narrowly the leadings of the Spirit of God.* Let them not quench the Spirit for the sake of praying according to the regular custom. Avoid everything calculated to divert attention away from the object. All affectation of feeling should be particularly guarded against. If there is an affectation of feeling, most commonly others see and feel that it *is* affectation, not reality. At any rate, the Spirit of God knows it, and will be grieved. On the other hand, all resistance to the Spirit will equally destroy the meeting. Not infrequently it happens that there are some so cold that they would call it fantaticism, and perhaps display opposition.

11. If individuals *refuse to pray when they are called upon,* it injures a prayer-meeting. There are some people who always pretend they have no gift. Women sometimes refuse to take their turn in prayer, and pretend they have not ability to pray. But if any one else should say so, they would be offended! Suppose they should learn that any other person had made such a remark as this: "Do not ask her to pray, she cannot pray, she has not talent enough": would they like it? So with a man who pretends he has no gift; let any one else report that "he has not talent enough to make a decent prayer," and see if he will like it. The pretence is not sincere; it is all a sham.

Some say they cannot pray in their families; they have no gift. But a person could not offend one of them more than to say: "He cannot pray a decent prayer before his own family." The retort would be: "Why, So-and-so talks as if he thought nobody else had any gifts but himself." People are not apt to have such a low opinion of themselves. I have often seen the curse of God follow such professors. They have no excuse. God will take none. The man has got a tongue to talk to his neighbours, and he can talk to God if he has any heart for it. You will see their children unconverted: their son has a curse; their daughter—tongue cannot tell. God says He will pour out His fury on the families that call not on His name. I could mention a host of facts to show that God MARKS with His disapprobation and curse those who refuse to pray when they ought. Until professors of religion will repent of this sin, and take up this cross (if they choose to call praying "a cross"), they need not expect a blessing.

12. Prayer-meetings are often *too long*. They should always be dismissed while Christians have feeling, and not be spun out until all feeling is exhausted, and the spirit of prayer is gone.

13. *Heartless confessions* injure a meeting. People confess their sins but do not forsake them. Every week they will make the same confession. Why, they have no intention to forsake their sins! It shows plainly that they do not mean to reform. All their religion consists in these confessions. Instead of getting a blessing from God thereby they will get only a curse.

14. Injury is also done when Christians spend all the time in *praying for themselves*. They should have done this in their own homes. When they come to a prayer-meeting, they should be prepared to offer effectual intercessions for others. If Christians pray at home as they ought, they will feel like praying for sinners. If, however, their private prayers are exclusively for themselves, they will not get the spirit of prayer. I have known men shut themselves up for days to pray for themselves, and never get any life, because their prayers were all selfish. But if such people will just forget themselves, and throw their hearts abroad, and pray for others, it will wake up such a feeling, that they will be able to pour forth their hearts in prayer. And then they can go to work for souls. I

knew an individual in a revival, who shut himself up for seventeen days, and prayed as if he would have God come to his terms; but it would not do, and therefore he went out to work, and immediately he had the Spirit of God in his soul. It is well for Christians to pray for themselves, and confess their sins, and then throw their hearts abroad, till they feel as they ought.

15. Prayer-meetings are often defeated by the *want of appropriate remarks*. The things are not said which are calculated to lead them to pray. Perhaps the leader has not prepared himself; or perhaps he has not the requisite talents to lead the Church out in prayer, or he does not lead their minds to dwell on the appropriate topics of prayer.

16. It is a hindrance, when individuals who are *justly obnoxious* are forward in speaking and praying. Such persons are sometimes very much set upon taking part. They say it is their duty to get up and testify for God on all occasions. They will say, they know they are not able to edify the Church, but nobody else can do *their* duty, and they wish to testify. Perhaps the only place they ever did testify *for God* was in a prayer-meeting; their lives, out of the meeting, testify *against* God. They had better keep still.

17. When persons take part whose *illiteracy is so pronounced* as to cause disgust among people of taste and intelligence, attention is diverted. I do not mean to imply that it is necessary that a person should have a liberal education, in order to lead in prayer. All persons of common education, especially if they are in the habit of praying, can lead in prayer, if they have the spirit of prayer. But there are some persons who use expressions so absurd and illiterate as to disgust every intelligent mind. The feeling of disgust is an involuntary thing, and when a disgusting object is before the mind, the feeling is irresistible. Piety will not keep a person from feeling it. The only way is to take away the object. Such persons may feel grieved at not being called upon to take part, but it is better that they should be kindly told the reason, than that the prayer-meeting should be regularly injured, and rendered ridiculous.

18. A *want of union* in prayer mars the meeting; that is, when one leads, but the others do not follow, for they are

thinking of something else. Their hearts do not unite, do not say: "Amen." It is as bad as if one person should make a petition and another remonstrate against it. It is as though one asks God to do a thing, and the others ask Him not to do it, or to do something else.

19. *Neglect of secret prayer* is yet another hindrance. Christians who do not pray in secret cannot unite with power in a prayer-meeting, and cannot have the spirit of prayer.

REMARKS.

1. A badly-conducted prayer-meeting often does more hurt than good. In many Churches, the general manner of conducting prayer-meetings is such that Christians have not the least idea of the design or the power of such meetings. It is such as tends to keep down rather than to promote pious feeling and the spirit of prayer.

2. A prayer-meeting is an index to the state of religion in a Church.[1] If the prayer-meeting is neglected, or the spirit of prayer is not manifested, you know of course that religion is in a low condition. Let me go into the prayer-meeting, and I can always see the state of religion which prevails in the Church.

3. Every minister ought to know that if the prayer-meetings are neglected, all his labours are in vain. Unless he can get Christians to attend the prayer-meetings, all else that he can do will not improve the state of religion.

4. A great responsibility rests on him who leads a prayer-meeting. If the meeting be not what it ought to be, if it does not elevate the state of religion, he should go seriously to work and see what is the matter, and get the spirit of prayer, and prepare himself to make such remarks as are calculated to do good and set things right. A leader has no business to lead prayer-meetings, if he is not prepared, both in head and heart, to do this.

---

[1]Writing upon the relation of prayer to revival, Dr. Porter, of Andover, Mass., in his "Letters on Revivals" (addressed, in 1832, to the Revival Association in the Theological Seminary, Andover, and dealing specifically with the Revivals in America which prevailed about the beginning of the nineteenth century) said: "Prayer-meetings were often found more directly conducive to the spirit of

5. Prayer-meetings are the most difficult meetings to sustain—as, indeed, they ought to be. They are so spiritual that unless the leader be peculiarly prepared, both in heart and mind, they will dwindle. It is in vain for the leader to complain that members of the Church do not attend. In nine cases out of ten it is the leader's fault that they do not attend. If he felt as he ought, they would find the meeting so interesting that they would attend as a matter of course. If he is so cold, and dull, and lacking in spirituality, as to freeze everything, no wonder people do not come to the meeting. Church officers often complain and scold because people do not come to the prayer-meeting, when the truth is, they themselves are so cold that they freeze to death everybody who does come.

6. Prayer-meetings are most important meetings for the Church. It is highly important for Christians to sustain the prayer-meetings, in order to (*a*) promote union, (*b*) increase brotherly love, (*c*) cultivate Christian confidence, (*d*) promote their own growth in grace, and (*e*) cherish and advance spirituality.

7. Prayer-meetings should be so numerous in the Church, and be so arranged, as to exercise the gifts of every member— man or woman. Every one should have the opportunity to

---

revivals, than conferences. Their whole tendency was, to humble Christians, and lead them to look away from every other reliance, to God alone. When a Church, mourning the absence of Divine influence, was brought to bow down before God, with fasting and sackcloth and supplication, then there was reason to hope that deliverance was at hand. I say 'with fasting'; for lightly as this religious ordinance is regarded by man, experience demonstrates its adaptedness to give intensity to special prayer." Dr. Porter cited, in this connection, the narrative of the revival at Newark, N. J., which says: "A Society was formed, to meet on Sabbath morning, and to spend an hour previous to engaging in public worship, in prayer to God for His blessing on the Word. They styled themselves 'The Aaron and Hur Society,' as supporting the hands of their minister." "Just such a Sabbath morning meeting," added Dr. Porter, "was attended by the Church of which I was pastor, and the practice I suppose to have been somewhat extensive amid the prevalence of revivals, and certainly with a direct tendency to *promote* their prevalence."

pray, and to express the feelings of his heart. The sectional prayer-meetings are designed to do this. And if they are too large to allow of it, let them be divided, so as to bring the entire mass into the work, to exercise all gifts, and diffuse union, confidence, and brotherly love, through the whole.

8. It is important that impenitent sinners should attend prayer-meetings. If none come of their own accord, go out and invite them. Christians ought to take great pains to induce their impenitent friends and neighbours to come to prayer-meetings. They can pray better for impenitent sinners when they have them right before their eyes. I have known women's prayer-meetings exclude sinners from the meetings. And the reason was, they were so proud that they were ashamed to pray before sinners. What a spirit! Such prayers will do no good. They insult God. You have not done enough, by any means, when you have gone to the prayer-meeting yourself. You cannot pray if you have invited no sinner to go. If all the members have neglected their duty so, and have gone to the prayer-meeting, and taken no sinners along with them, no subjects for prayer—what have they come for?

9. The great object of all the means of grace is to aim directly at the conversion of sinners. You should pray that they may be converted *there*. Do not pray that they may be merely awakened and convicted, but that they may be converted on the spot. No one should either pray or make any remarks, as if he expected a single sinner would go away without giving his heart to God. You should all make the impression on his mind, that NOW he must submit. And if you do this, while you are yet speaking God will hear.

If Christians made it manifest that they had really set their hearts on the conversion of sinners, and were bent upon it, and prayed as they ought, there would rarely be a prayer-meeting held without souls being converted; and sometimes every sinner in the room. That is the very time, if ever, that sinners *should* be converted in answer to those prayers. I do not doubt but that you may have sinners converted in every sectional prayer-meeting, if you do your duty. Take them there, take your families, your friends, or your neighbours there with that design; give them the proper instruction, if they need instruction, and pray for them as you ought, and you will save their souls. Rely upon it, if you do your duty, in a right manner, God will not keep back His blessing, but the work will be done.

LECTURE IX

MEANS TO BE USED WITH SINNERS

Ye are My witnesses, saith the Lord, and My servant whom I have
chosen.—Isa. 43. 10.

In the text it is affirmed of the children of God, that they are
His witnesses. In several preceding Lectures I have been
dwelling on the subject of prayer, or on that department of
means for the promotion of a revival, which is intended to
move God to pour out His Spirit. I am now to commence the
other department, dealing with the *means to be used for the
conviction and conversion of sinners*.

It is true, in general, that persons are affected by the subject
of religion in proportion to their conviction of its truth.
Inattention to religion is the great reason why so little is felt
concerning it. No being can look at the great truths of religion,
as truths, and not feel deeply concerning them. The devil
cannot. He believes and trembles. Angels in heaven feel, in
view of these things. God feels! An intellectual *conviction* of
truth is always accompanied with feeling of some kind.

One grand design of God in leaving Christians in the world
after their conversion is that they may be *witnesses for God*. It
is that they may call the attention of the thoughtless multitude
to the subject, and make them see the difference in the
character and destiny of those who believe the Gospel and

those who reject it. This inattention is the grand difficulty in the way of promoting religion. And what the Spirit of God does is to awaken the attention of men to the subject of their sin and the plan of salvation. Miracles have sometimes been employed to arrest the attention of sinners, and in this way miracles may become instrumental in conversion—although conversion is not itself a miracle, nor do miracles themselves ever convert anybody. They may be the means of awakening. Miracles are not always effectual even in that. And if continued or made common, they would soon lose their power. What is wanted in the world is something that can be a sort of omnipresent miracle, able not only to arrest attention but to fix it, and keep the mind in warm contact with the truth, till it yields.

Hence we see why God has scattered His children everywhere, in families and among the nations. He never would suffer them to be altogether in one place, however agreeable it might be to their feelings. He wishes them scattered. When the Church at Jerusalem herded together, neglecting to go forth as Christ had commanded, to spread the Gospel all over the world, God let loose a persecution upon them and scattered them abroad, and then they "went everywhere preaching the Word" (Acts 8. 4).

In examining the text, I purpose to inquire: I. On what particular points Christians are to testify for God. II. The manner in which they are to testify.

I. ON WHAT POINTS ARE CHRISTIANS TO TESTIFY?

Generally, they are to testify to the truth of the Bible. They are competent witnesses to this, for they have experience of its truth. The experimental Christian has no more need of external evidence to prove the truth of the Bible to his mind, then he has to prove his own existence. The whole plan of salvation is so fully spread out and settled in his conviction, that to undertake to reason him out of his belief in the Bible would be a thing as impracticable as to reason him out of the belief in his own existence. Men have tried to awaken a doubt of the existence of the material world, but they cannot succeed. No man can doubt the existence of the material world. To doubt it is against his own consciousness. You may use arguments that he cannot answer, and may puzzle and perplex him, and shut his mouth; he may be no logician or philosopher, and may not be able to detect your fallacies. But, what he knows, he knows.

So it is in religion. The Christian is conscious that the Bible is true. The veriest child in religion knows by his experience the truth of the Bible. He may hear objections from infidels, that he never thought of, and that he cannot answer, and he may be confounded; but he cannot be driven from his ground. He will say: "I cannot answer you, but I know the Bible is true." It is as if a man should look in a mirror, and say: "That is my face." The question is put to him: "How do you know it is your face?" "Why," he replies, "by its looks." So when a Christian sees himself drawn and pictured forth in the Bible, he sees the likeness to be so exact, that he knows it is true.

More particularly, Christians are to testify to: 1. The immortality of the soul. This is clearly revealed in the Bible.

2. The vanity and unsatisfying nature of all earthly goods.

3. The satisfying nature and glorious sufficiency of religion.

4. The guilt and danger of sinners. On this point they can speak from experience as well as from the Word of God. They have seen their own sins, and they understand more of the nature of sin, and the guilt and danger of sinners.

5. The reality of hell, as a place of eternal punishment for the wicked.

6. The love of Christ for sinners.

7. The necessity of a holy life, if we think of ever getting to heaven.

8. The necessity of self-denial, and of living above the world.

9. The necessity of meekness, heavenly-mindedness, humility, and integrity.

10. The necessity of an entire renovation of character and life, for all who would enter heaven.

These are the subjects on which they are to be witnesses for God. And they are bound to testify in such a way as to constrain men to believe the truth.

II. *HOW ARE THEY TO TESTIFY?*

By *precept and example.* On every proper occasion by their

lips, but mainly by their lives. Christians have no right to be silent with their lips; they should "reprove, rebuke, exhort with all longsuffering and doctrine" (2 Tim. 4. 2). But their main influence as sitnesses is by their example.

They are required to be witnesses in this way, because example teaches with so much greater force than precept. This is universally known. "Actions speak louder than words." But where both precept and example are brought to bear, the greatest amount of influence is brought to bear upon the mind. As to the manner in which they are to testify; the way in which they should bear witness to the truth of the points specified; in general—they should live in thier daily walk and conversation, as if they believed the Bible.

1. As if they believed the soul to the immortal, and as if they believed that death was not the termination of their existence, but the entrance into an unchanging state. They ought to live so as to make this impression upon all around them. It is easy to see that precept without example will do no good. All the arguments in the world will not convince mankind that you really believe this, unless you live as if you believe it. Your reasoning may be unanswerable, but if you do not live accordingly, your practice will defeat your arguments. They will say you are an ingenious sophist, or an acute reasoner, and perhaps admit that they cannot answer you; but then they will say: it is evident that your reasoning is all false, and that you know it is all false, because your life contradicts your theory. Or they will say that, if it is true, you do not believe it, at any rate. And so all the influence of your testimony goes to the other side.

2. Against the vanity and unsatisfying nature of the things of this world. The failure to testify in this is the great stumbling-block in the way of mankind. Here the testimony of God's children is needed more than anywhere else. Men are so struck with the objects of sense, and so constantly occupied with them, that they are very apt to shut out eternity from their minds. A small object that is held close to the eye, may shut out the distant ocean. So the things of the world, that are near, appear so magnified in their minds, that they overlook everything else. One important design in keeping Christians in the world is, to teach people on this point, *practically*. But

suppose professors of religion teach the vanity of earthly things by precept, and contradict it in practice? Suppose the women are just as fond of dress, and just as particular in observing all the fashions, and the men as eager to have fine houses and equipages, as the people of the world; who does not see that it would be quite ridiculous for them to testify with their lips, that this world is all vanity, and its joys unsatisfying and empty? People feel the absurdity, and this shuts up the lips of Christians. They are ashamed to speak to their neighbours, while they cumber themselves with these gewgaws, because their daily conduct testifies, to everybody, the very reverse. How it would look for certain Church members, men or women, to go about among the common people, and talk to them about the vanity of the world! Who would believe what they said?

3. To the satisfying nature of religion. Christians are bound to show, by their conduct, that *they are* actually satisfied with the enjoyments of religion, without the pomps and vanities of the world; that the joys of religion and communion with God keep them above the world. They are to manifest that this world is not their home. Their profession is, that heaven is a reality and that they expect to dwell there for ever. But suppose they contradict this by their conduct, and live in such a way as to prove that they cannot be happy unless they have a full share of the fashion and show of the world; and that as for going to heaven, they would much rather remain on earth than die and go there! What does the world think when it sees a professor of religion just as much afraid to die as an infidel? Such Christians perjure themselves—they swear to a lie, since their testimony amounts to this, that there is nothing in religion for which a person can afford to live above the world.

4. Regarding the guilt and danger of sinners. Christians are bound to warn sinners of their awful condition, and exhort them to flee from the wrath to come, and lay hold on everlasting life. But who does not know that *the manner* of doing this is everything? Sinners are often struck under conviction by the very manner of doing a thing. There was a man once very much opposed to a certain preacher. On being asked to specify some reason, he replied: "I cannot bear to hear him, for he says the word 'HELL' in such a way that it rings in

my ears for a long time afterwards." He was displeased with the very thing that constituted the power of speaking that word. The manner may be such as to convey an idea directly opposite to the meaning of the words. A man may tell you that your house is on fire in such a way as to make directly the opposite impression, and you will take it for granted that it is not *your* house that is on fire. The watchman might cry out: "Fire! fire!" in such a way that everybody would think he was either drunk or talking in his sleep.

Go to a sinner, and talk about him about his guilt and danger; and if in your manner you make an impression that does not correspond, you in effect bear testimony the other way, and tell him he is in no danger. If the sinner believes at all that he is in danger of hell, it is wholly on other grounds than your saying so. If you live in such a way as to show that you do not feel compassion for sinners around you; if you show no tenderness, by your eyes, your features, your voice; if your manner is not solemn and earnest, how can they believe you are sincere?

Woman, suppose you tell your unconverted husband, in an easy, laughing way: "My dear, I believe you are going to hell"; will he believe you? If your life is gay and trifling, you show that you either do not believe there is a hell, or that you wish to have him go there, and are trying to keep off every serious impression from his mind. Have you children that are unconverted? Suppose you never say anything to them about religion, or when you talk to them it is in a cold, hard, dry way, conveying the impression that you have no feeling in the matter; do you suppose they believe you? They do not see the same coldness in you in regard to other things. They are in the habit of seeing all the mother in your eye, and in the tones of your voice, your emphasis, and the like, and feeling the warmth of a mother's heart as it flows out from your lips on all that concerns them. If, then, when you talk to them on the subject of religion, you are cold and trifling, can they suppose that you believe it? If your deportment holds up before your child this careless, heartless, prayerless spirit, and then you talk to him about the importance of religion, the child will go away and laugh, to think you should try to persuade him there is a hell.

5. To the love of Christ. You are to bear witness to the reality of the love of Christ, by the regard you show for His precepts, His honour, His kingdom. You should act as if you believed that He died for the sins of the whole world, and as if you blamed sinners for rejecting His great salvation. This is the only legitimate way in which you can impress sinners with the love of Christ. Christians, instead of this, often live so as to make the impression on sinners that Christ is so compassionate that they have very little to fear from Him. I have been amazed to see how a certain class of professors want ministers to be always preaching about the *love* of Christ. If a minister urges Christians to be holy, and to labour for Christ, they call it "legal" preaching. They say they want to hear the Gospel. Well, suppose you present the love of Christ. How will they bear testimony in their lives? How will they show that they believe it? Why, by conformity to the world they will testify, point-blank, that they do not believe a word of it, and that they care nothing at all for the love of Christ, only to have it for a cloak, that they can talk about it, and so cover up their sins. They have no sympathy with His compassion, and no belief in it as a reality, and no concern for the feelings of Christ, which fill His mind when He sees the condition of sinners.

6. To the necessity of holiness in order to enter heaven. It will not do to depend on talking about this. They must live holy. The idea has so long prevailed that we "cannot be perfect here," that many professors do not so much as seriously aim at a sinless life. They cannot honestly say that they even so much as really meant to live without sin. They drift along before the tide, in a loose, sinful, unhappy, and abominable manner, at which, doubtless, the devil laughs, because it is, of all others, the surest way to hell.

7. To the necessity of self-denial, humility, and heavenly-mindedness. Christians ought to show, by their own example, what the religious walk is which is expected of men. That is the most powerful preaching, after all, and the most likely to have influence on the impenitent, which shows them the great difference between themselves and Christians. Many people seem to think they can make men fall in with religion best by bringing religion down to their standard. As if the nearer you bring religion to the world, the more likely the world will be to

embrace it. Now all this is as wide as the poles are asunder
from the true philosophy about making Christians. But it is
always the policy of carnal professors. And they think they are
displaying wonderful sagacity, and prudence, by taking so
much pains not to scare people at the mighty strictness and
holiness of the Gospel. They argue that if you exhibit religion
to mankind as requiring such a great change in their manner of
life, such innovations upon their habits, such a separation
from their old associates, why, you will drive them all away.
This seems plausible at first sight. But it is not true. Let
professors live in this lax and easy way, and sinners asy: "Why,
I do not see but I am about right, or at least so near right that it
is impossible God should send me to hell only for the
difference between me and these professors. It is true, they do
a little more than I do; they go to the Communion-table, and
pray in their families, and a few suchlike little things, but these
details cannot make any such great difference as between
heaven and hell." No, the true way is, to exhibit religion and
the world in strong contrast, or you[1] can never make sinners
feel the necessity of a change. Until the necessity of this
fundamental change is embodied and held forth in strong
light, by example, how can you make men believe they are
going to be sent to hell if they are not wholly transformed in
heart and life?

This is not only true in philosophy, but it has been proved by
the history of the world. Now, I was reading a letter from a
missionary in the East, who writes to this effect: that "a

---

[1]   It is characteristic of Finney that he is always gravitating to the
second person singular; from "they" to "you." It was part of his
method of preaching, and we have to remember the great fact which
underlies all his teaching, that he was the life-long apostle of vital
truth as against dead orthodoxy. It was a complaint against him, in
his early days (in the Evans' Mills revival, for example) that he "let
down the dignity of the pulpit, talking like a lawyer at the bar." He
says: "They used to complain...that I talked to the people in a
colloquial manner, that I said 'you' instead of preaching about
'sinners.' " However, Finney soon found a reply: "I said: 'Show me
the fruits of your ministry, and if they so far exceed mine as to give
evidence that you have found a more excellent way, I will adopt your
views.' "

missionary must be able to rank with the English nobility, and so recommended his religion to the *respect* of the natives." He must get away up above them, so as to show a superiority, and thus impress them with respect! Is this the way to convert the world? You can no more convert the world in this way than by blowing a ram's horn. What did the Jesuits do? They went about among the people in the daily practice of self-denial, teaching, and preaching, and praying, and labouring; mingling with every caste and grade, and bringing down their instructions to the capacity of every individual. In that way their religion spread over the vast empire in Japan. I am not saying anything in regard to the religion they taught. I speak only of their following the true policy of missions, by showing, by their lives, a wide contrast with a worldly spirit. If Christians attempt to accommodate religion to the worldliness of men, they render the salvation of the world impossible. How can you make people believe that self-denial and separation from the world are necessary, unless you practise them?

8. Again, they are to testify by meekness, humility, and heavenly-mindedness. The people of God should always show a temper like the Son of God, who, when He was reviled, reviled not again. If a professor of religion is irritable, ready to resent an injury, to fly in a passion, and to take the same measures as the world does to get redress, by going to law and the like—how is he to make people believe there is any reality in a change of heart! He cannot recommend religion while he has such a spirit.

If you are in the habit of resenting injurious conduct; if you do not bear it meekly, and put the best construction upon it, you contradict the Gospel. Some people always show a bad spirit, ever ready to put the worst construction upon what is done, and to take fire at any little thing. This shows a great want of that charity which "beareth all things, believeth all things, hopeth all things, endureth all things" (1 Cor. 13. 7). But if a man always shows meekness under injuries, it will confound gainsaying. Nothing makes so solemn an impression upon sinners, and bears down with such tremendous weight on their consciences, as to see a Christian, truly Christ-like, bearing affronts and injuries with the meekness of a lamb.

It cuts like a two-edged sword.

I will mention a case to illustrate this. A young man abused a minister to his face, and reviled him in an unprecedented manner. The minister possessed his soul in patience, and spoke mildly in reply, telling him the truth pointedly, but yet in a very kind manner. This only made him the more angry, and at length he went away in a rage, declaring that he was "not going to stay and bear this vituperation," as if it were the minister, instead of himself, that had been scolding. The sinner went away, but with the arrows of the Almighty in his heart; and in less than half an hour he followed the minister to his lodgings in intolerable agony, wept, begged forgiveness, and broke down before God, and yielded up his heart to Christ. This calm and mild manner was more overwhelming to him than a thousand arguments. Now, if that minister had been thrown off his guard, and answered harshly, no doubt he would have ruined the soul of that young man. How many of you have defeated every future effort you may make with your impenitent friends or neighbours, in some such way as this? On some occasion you have shown yourself so irascible that you have sealed up your own lips, and laid a stumbling-block over which that sinner will stumble into hell. If you have done it in any instance, do not sleep till you have done all you can to retrieve the mischief.

9. Finally, they are to testify to the necessity for entire honesty in a Christian. Oh, what a field opens here for remark! It extends to all the departments of life. Christians need to show the strictest regard to integrity in every department of business, and in all their intercourse with their fellow-men. If every Christian would pay a scrupulous regard to honesty, and always be conscientious to do exactly right, it would make a powerful impression, on the minds of people, of the reality of religious principle.

A lady was once buying some eggs in a store, and the clerk made a miscount and gave her one more than the number. She saw it at the time, but said nothing, and after she got home it troubled her. Feeling that she had acted wrongly, she went back to the young man and confessed it, and paid the difference. The impression of her conscientious integrity went to his heart like a sword. It was a great sin in her in concealing the miscount, because the temptation was so small; for if she would cheat him out of an egg, it showed that she would cheat him out of his whole store, if she could do it without being found out. But her prompt and humble confession showed an honest conscience.

I am happy to say, there are some men who conduct their business on this principle of integrity. The wicked hate them for it, railing against them, and vociferating in bar-rooms that they will never buy goods of such-and-such individuals; that such a hyprocrite shall never touch a dollar of their money, and all that; and then they will go right away and buy of them, because they know they will be honestly dealt with. Suppose that all Christians could be equally trusted: what would be the consequence? Christians would run away with the business of the city. The Christians would soon do the business of the world. The great argument which some professed Christians urge, that if they do not do business upon the common principle, of stating one price and taking another, they cannot compete with men of the world, is all false—false in philosophy, false in history. Only make it your invariable rule to do right, and do business upon principle, and you control the market. The ungodly will be obliged to conform to your standard. It is perfectly in the power of Christians to regulate the commerce of the world, if they will only themselves maintain perfect integrity.

Again, if Christians will do the same in *politics* they will sway the destinies of nations, without involving themselves at all in the base and corrupting strife of parties. Only let Christians generally determine to vote for no man who is not an honest man, and a man of pure morals; only let it be known that Christians are united in this, whatever may be their difference in political sentiments, and no man would be put up for election who was not such a character. In three years it would be talked about in taverns, and published in newspapers, when any man set up as a candidate for office: "What a good man he is—how moral—how pious!" and the like. And any political party would no more set up a known Sabbath-breaker, or a gambler, or a profane swearer, or a rum-seller, as their candidate for office, than they would set up the devil himself for President of the United States. The carnal policy of many professors, who undertake to correct politics by such means as wicked men employ, and who are determined to vote with a party, let the candidate be ever so profligate, is all wrong—wrong in principle, contrary to philosophy and common sense, and ruinous to the best interests of mankind. The dishonesty of the Church is cursing the world. I am not going to preach a political sermon; but I want to show you that if you mean to impress men favourably to your religion by your lives, you must be honest, strictly honest, in business, politics, and everything you do. What do you suppose those ungodly politicians, who know themselves to be playing a dishonest game in carrying an election, think of your religion, when they see you uniting with them? They know you are a hypocrite!

REMARKS.

1. It is unreasonable for professors of religion to wonder at the thoughtlessness of sinners. Everything considered, the carelessness of sinners is not wonderful. We are affected by testimony, and only by that testimony which is received by our minds. Sinners are so taken up with business, pleasure, and the things of the world, that they will not examine the Bible to find what religion is. Their feelings are excited only on worldly subjects, because these only are brought into warm contact with their minds. The things of the world make, therefore, a strong impression. But there is so little to make an impression on their minds in respect to eternity, and to bring religion home to them, that they do not feel on the subject. If they examined the subject, they would feel. But they do not examine it, nor think upon it, nor care for it. And they never will, unless God's witnesses rise up and testify. But inasmuch as the great body of Christians so live, as, by their conduct, to testify *on the other side*, how can we expect that sinners will feel rightly upon the subject? Nearly all the testimony and all the influence that comes to their minds tends to make them feel the other way. God has left His cause here before the human race, and left His witnesses to testify in His behalf; and, behold, they turn round and testify the other way! It is any wonder that sinners are careless?

2. We see why it is that preaching does so little good; and how it is that so many sinners get Gospel-hardened. Sinners

that live under the Gospel are often supposed to be Gospel-hardened; but only let the Church wake up and act consistently, and they will feel. If the Church were to live one week as if they believed the Bible, sinners would melt down before them. Suppose I were a lawyer, and should go into court and spread out my client's case. The issue is joined; I make my statements, tell what I expect to prove, and then call my witnesses. The first witness takes his oath, and then rises up and contradicts me to my face. What good will all my pleading do? I might address the jury for a month, and be as eloquent as Cicero; but so long as my witnesses contradict me, all my pleading will do no good. Just so it is with a minister who is preaching in the midst of a cold, stupid, and God-dishonouring Church. In vain does he hold up to view the great truths of religion, when every member of the Church is ready to witness that he lies. Why, in such a Church, the very manner of the people in going out of the aisles contradicts the sermon. They press out as cheerful and as easy, bowing to one another, and whispering together, as if nothing were the matter. If the devil should come in and see the state of things, he would think he could not better the business for his interest.

Yet there are ministers who will go on in this way for years, preaching to a people who, by their lives, contradict every word that is said. And these ministers think it their duty to do so. Duty! For a minister to preach to a Church that is undoing all his work, contradicting all his testimony, and that will not alter! No. Let him shake off the dust from his feet for a testimony, and go to the heathen, or to new settlements. The man is wasting his energies, and wearing out his life, and just rocking the cradle for a sleepy Church, which is testifying to sinners that there is no danger. Their whole lives are a practical assertion that the Bible is not true. Shall ministers continue to wear themselves out so? Probably not less than ninety-nine-hundredths of the preaching in this country is lost, because it is contradicted by the Church. Not one truth in a hundred, that is preached, takes effect, because the lives of the professors declare that it is not so.

3. It is evident that the standard of Christian living must be raised, or the world will never be converted. If we had, scattered all over the world, a minister to every five hundred

souls, and every child in a Sabbath-school, and every young person in a Bible-class, you might have all the machinery you want; but, if the Church members should contradict the truth by their lives, no revival would be produced.

They never will have a revival in any place while the whole Church in effect testifies against the minister. Often it is the case that where there is the most preaching, there is the least religion, because the Church contradicts the preaching. I never knew means fail of a revival where Christians live consistently. One of the first things is to raise the standard of religion, so as to embody the truth of the Gospel in the sight of all men. Unless ministers can get their people to wake up, and act as if religion were true, and back their testimony by their lives, in vain will be the attempt to promote a revival.[1]

Many Churches are depending on their minister to do everything. When he preaches, they will say: "What a great sermon that was! He is an excellent minister. Such preaching must do good. We shall have a revival soon, no doubt." And all the while they are contradicting the preaching by their lives. I tell you, if they are depending on preaching alone to carry on the work, they must fail. Let an apostle rise from the dead, or an angel come down from heaven and preach, without the Church to witness for God, and it would have no effect. The

---

[1]   Among the many friends whom Dr. A. J. Gordon, of Boston, had among the negroes, was a certain ebony sage known as Brother Moses, a deacon of the "coloured" mission attached to Dr. Gordon's Church. Moses was both whole-hearted and shrewd, and Dr. Gordon loved to repeat his remarks for the benefit of the whites. Thus, Moses once rebuked the "coloured" meeting, saying: "Didn't de Lord tell you dat youse to be de salt ob de earth? Well, when I sees how much time some ob you gibs to fairs an' festibals, an' den you can't come to de prayer-meetin' because youse so busy, I sez, if ever you was de Lord's true salt, youse lost your flavour, en if you don't look out you'll be cast out en trodden underfoot ob men. . .Christians is de salt ob de world, an' dey is put into de world to preserve it from corruption. But some's got de idee, dat you mus' bring corruption into de Church, so's to preserve de salt, as dough de Gospel is goin' to die out unless it's sugared an' seasoned wid carnal 'musements. Dat's de pop'lar notion. But I kicks agin it, sah!" ("Adoniram Judson Gordon," by his son, Ernest B. Gordon).

novelty might produce a certain kind of interest for a time, but as soon as the novelty was gone, the preaching would have no saving effect, while contradicted by the witnesses.

4. Every Christian makes an impression by his conduct, and witnesses either for one side or the other. His looks, dress, whole demeanour, make a constant impression on one side or the other. He cannot help testifying for or against religion. He is either gathering with Christ, or scattering abroad. At every step you tread on chords that will vibrate to all eternity. Every time you move, you touch keys whose sound will re-echo all over the hills and dales of heaven, and through all the dark caverns and vaults of hell. Every movement of your lives, you are exerting a tremendous influence that will tell on the immortal interests of souls all around you. Are you asleep, while all your conduct is exerting such an influence?

Are you going to walk in the street? Take care how you dress. What is that on your head? What does that gaudy ribbon, and those ornaments upon your dress, say to every one who meets you? They make the impression that you wish to be thought pretty. Take care! You might just as well write on your clothes: *"No truth in religion!"* They say: *"Give me dress; Give me fashion; Give me flattery, and I am happy!."* The world understands this testimony as you walk the streets. You are living "epistles, known and read of all men" (2 Cor. 3. 2). If you show pride, levity, bad temper, it is like tearing open the wounds of the Saviour. How Christ might weep to see professors of religion going about hanging up His cause to contempt at the corners of streets. Only let the "women adorn themselves in modest apparel, with shamefacedness and sobriety; not with broidered hair, or gold, or pearls, or costly array; but (which becometh women professing godliness) with good works" (1 Tim. 2. 9, 10); only let them act consistently, and their conduct will tell on the world—heaven will rejoice and hell groan at their influence. But oh! Let them display vanity; try to be pretty; bow down to the goddess of fashion; fill their ears with ornaments, and their fingers with rings: let them put feathers in their hats and clasps upon their arms, lace themselves up till they can hardly breathe; let them put on their "round tires like the moon," "walking and mincing as they go" (Isa. 3. 18, 16), and their influence is reversed: heaven puts on the robes of mourning, and hell may hold a jubilee!

5. It is easy to see why revivals do not prevail in a great city. How can they? Just look at God's witnesses, and see what they are testifying to! They seem to be agreed together to tempt the Spirit of the Lord, and to lie to the Holy Ghost! They make their vows to God, to consecrate themselves wholly to Him, then they go bowing down at the shrine of fashion—and next they wonder why there are no revivals! It would be more than a miracle to have a revival under such circumstances. How can a revival prevail here? Do you suppose I have such a vain imagination of my own ability, as to think I can promote a revival by my preaching, merely, while you live on as you do? Do you not know that so far as your influence goes, many of you are right in the way of a revival? Your spirit and deportment produce an influence on the world against religion. How shall the world believe religion, when the witnesses are not agreed among themselves? You contradict yourselves; you contradict one another; you contradict your minister; and the sum of the whole testimony is, there is no need of being pious.

Do you believe the things I have been preaching are true, or are they the ravings of a disturbed mind? If they are true, do you recognise the fact that they have reference to YOU? You say, perhaps: "I wish some of the rich Churches could hear it!" But I am not preaching to them; I am preaching to you. My responsibility is to you, and my fruits must come from you. Now, are you contradicting it? What is the testimony on the leaf of the record that is now sealed for the Judgment, concerning this day? Have you manifested a sympathy with the Son of God, when His heart is bleeding in view of the desolations of Zion? Have your children, your clerks, your servants seen it to be so? Have they seen a solemnity on your countenance, and tears in your eyes, in view of perishing souls?

Finally, I remark that God and all moral beings have great reason to complain of this false testimony. There is ground to complain that God's witnesses turn and testify point-blank against Him. They declare by their conduct that there is no truth in the Gospel. Heaven might weep and hell rejoice to see this. Oh, how guilty! Here you are, going to the Judgment, red all over with blood. Sinners are to meet you there; those who have seen how you live, many of them already dead, and many others whom you will never see again upon earth. What an influence you have exerted! Perhaps hundreds of souls will meet you in the Judgment Day and curse you (if they are allowed to speak) for leading them to hell, by practically denying the truth of the Gospel. What will become of this city, and of the world, when the Church is united in practically testifying that God is a liar? They testify by their lives, that if they make a profession and live a moral life, that is religion enough. Oh, what a doctrine of devils is that! It is enough to ruin the whole human race!

Lecture X

TO WIN SOULS REQUIRES WISDOM

He that winneth souls is wise.—Prov. 11.30.

The most common definition of wisdom is, that it is the choice of the best end and the selection of the most appropriate means for the accomplishment of that end. "He that winneth souls," God says, "is wise." The object of this Lecture is to direct Christians in the use of means for accomplishing their infinitely desirable end, the salvation of souls. I shall confine my attention to the private efforts of individuals for the conversion and salvation of men. On another occasion, perhaps, I shall use the same text in speaking of what is wise in the public preaching of the Gospel, and the labours of ministers. In giving some directions to aid private Christians in this work, I propose to show Christians: I. How they should deal with *careless* sinners. II. How they should deal with *awakened* sinners. III. How they should deal with *convicted* sinners.

I. *DEALING WITH CARELESS SINNERS.*

1. In regard to the *time*. It is important that you should select a proper *time* to try to make a serious impression on the mind of a careless sinner. For if you fail of selecting the most proper time, very probably you will be defeated. True, you may

say that it is your duty at all times to warn sinners, and try to awaken them to think of their souls. And so it is; yet if you do not pay due regard to the time and opportunity, your hope of success may be very doubtful.

(*a*) It is desirable, if possible, to address a person who is careless, *when he is disengaged from other employments*. In proportion as his attention is taken up with something else, it will be difficult to awaken him to religion. People who are careless and indifferent to religion are often offended, rather than benefited, by being called off from important and lawful business. For instance, a minister perhaps goes to visit the family of a merchant, or mechanic, or farmer, and finds the man absorbed in his business; perhaps he calls him off from his work when it is urgent, and the man is uneasy and irritable, and feels as if it were an intrusion. In such a case, there is little room to expect any good. Notwithstanding it is true that religion is infinitely more important than all his worldly business, and he ought to postpone everything to the salvation of his soul, yet he does not feel it; for if he did, he would no longer be a careless sinner; and therefore he regards it as unjustifiable, and gets offended. You must take him as you find him, a careless, impenitent sinner, and deal with him accordingly. He is absorbed in other things, and very apt to be offended, if you select such a time to call his attention to religion.

(*b*) It is important to take a person, if possible, at a time when he is *not strongly excited with any other subject*. Otherwise he will be in an unfit frame to be addressed on the subject of religion. In proportion to the strength of that excitement would be the probability that you would do no good. You may possibly reach him. Persons have had their inds arrested and turned to religion in the midst of a powerful excitement on other subjects. But it is not likely.

(*c*) Be sure that the person is *perfectly sober*. It used to be more common than it is now for people to drink spirits every day, and become more or less intoxicated. Precisely in proportion as they are so, they are rendered unfit to be approached on the subject of religion. If they have been drinking beer, or cider, or wine, so that you can smell their breath, you may know there is but little chance of producing any lasting effect on them. I have had professors of religion bring to me persons whom they supposed were under conviction (people in liquor are very fond of talking upon religion); but as soon as I came near enough to smell the breath of such persons, I have asked: "Why do you bring this drunken man to me?" "Why," they have replied, "he is not drunk, he has only been drinking a little." Well, that little has made him a little drunk! The cases are exceedingly rare where a person has been truly convicted, who had any intoxicating liquor in him.

(d) If possible, where you wish to converse with a man on the subject of salvation, take him *when he is in a good temper*. If you find him out of humour, very probably he will get angry and abuse you. Better let him alone for that time, or you will be likely to quench the Spirit. It is possible you may be able to talk in such a way as to cool his temper, but it is not likely. The truth is, men hate God; and though their hatred be dormant, it is easily excited; and if you bring God fully before their minds when they are already excited with anger, it will be so much the easier to arouse their enmity to open violence.

(e) If possible, always take an opportunity to converse with careless sinners when they are *alone*. Most men are too proud to be conversed with freely respecting themselves in the presence of others, even their own family. A man in such circumstances will brace up all his powers to defend himself, while, if he were alone, he would melt down under the truth. He will resist the truth, or try to laugh it off, for fear that, if he should manifest any feeling, somebody will go and report that he is thinking seriously about religion.

In visiting families, instead of calling all the family together at the same time to be talked to, the better way is to see them all, *one at a time*. There was a case of this kind. Several young ladies, of a proud, gay, and fashionable character, lived together in a fashionable family. Two men were strongly desirous to get the subject of religion before them, but were at a loss how to accomplish it, for fear the ladies would combine to resist every serious impression. At length they took this course: they called and sent up their card to one of the young ladies by name. She came down, and they conversed with her on the subject of her salvation, and, as she was alone, she not only treated them politely, but seemed to receive the truth with seriousness. A day or two after they called, in like manner, on another; and then on another; and so on, till they had conversed with every one separately. In a little time the ladies were all, I believe, hopefully converted.[1] The impression made on one was followed up with the others; so that one was not left to exert a bad influence over the rest.

There was a pious woman who kept a boarding-house for young gentlemen; she had twenty-one or two of them in her house, and at length she became very anxious for their salvation. She made it a subject of prayer, but saw no seriousness among them. At length she saw that there must be something done besides praying, and yet she did not know what to do. One morning, after breakfast, as the rest were retiring, she asked one of them to stop a few minutes. She took him aside, and conversed with him tenderly on the subject of religion, and prayed with him. She followed up the impression made, and pretty soon he was hopefully converted. Then she spoke to another, and so on, taking one at a time, and letting none of the rest know what was going on, so as not to alarm them, till all these young men were converted to God. Now, if she had brought the subject before the whole of them together,

---

[1] A story from the life of D. L. Moody furnishes an apt companion to the incidents related in this chapter. There was a class of girls, in the Mission Sunday School at Chicago, who were particularly careless and frivolous. Their teacher fell incurably ill, and when Moody proceeded to supply his vacant place the girls laughed in his face. That week the teacher called upon Moody, saying: "I am going home to die; I am greatly troubled because I have never led any of my class to Christ." Moody sympathetically proposed that the class should all be visited in turn, and he volunteered to accompany the teacher. Accordingly, the two went to each house, in a carriage. This continued for ten days, and at length all were not only visited but converted. They met for a prayer-meeting, and the dying teacher, who was to leave next day, sat in the midst, and read John 14. The whole class prayed, one by one. Previous to this Moody's ambition had been to become a successful merchant, but, as he afterwards said: "That meeting kindled a fire in my soul, that has never gone out" ("The Life of Dwight L. Moody," by his son, W. R. Moody).

very likely they would have turned it all into ridicule; or perhaps they would have been offended and left the house, and then she could have had no further influence over them. But taking one alone, and treating him respectfully and kindly, he had no such motive for resistance as arises out of the presence of others.

(*f*) Try to seize an opportunity to converse with a careless sinner, *when the events of Providence seem to favour your design*. If any particular event should occur, calculated to make a serious impression, be sure to improve the occasion faithfully.

(*g*) Seize the *earliest opportunity* to converse with those around you who are careless. Do not put it off from day to day, thinking a better opportunity will come. You must *seek* an opportunity, and if none offers, *make* one. Appoint a time or place, and get an interview with your friend or neighbour, where you can speak to him freely. Send him a note; go to him on purpose; make it look like a matter of business—as if you were in earnest in endeavouring to promote his soul's salvation. Then he will feel that it is a matter of importance, at least in your eyes. Follow it up till you succeed, or become convinced that, for the time, nothing more can be done.

(*h*) If you have any feeling for a particular individual, take an opportunity to converse with that individual *while this feeling continues*. If it is a truly benevolent feeling, you have reason to believe the Spirit of God is moving you to desire the salvation of his soul, and that God is ready to bless your efforts for his conversion. In such a case, make it the subject of special and importunate prayer, and seek an early opportunity to pour out all your heart to him, and bring him to Christ.

2. In regard to the *manner* of doing all this:

(*a*) When you approach a careless individual, be sure to treat him *kindly*. *Let him see* that you address him, not becuase you seek a quarrel with him, but because you love his soul, and desire his best good in time and eternity. If you are harsh and overbearing in your manner, you will probably offend him, and drive him farther off from the way of life.

(*b*) Be *solemn*. Avoid all lightness of manner or language. Levity will produce anything but a right impression. You ought to feel that you are engaged in a very solemn work, which is going to affect the character of your friend or neighbour, and probably determine his destiny for eternity. Who could trifle and use levity in such circumstances, if his heart were sincere?

(c) Be *respectful.* Some seem to suppose it necessary to be abrupt, and rude, and coarse, in their intercourse with the careless and impenitent. No mistake can be greater. The apostle Peter has given us a better rule on the subject, where he says: "Be pitiful, be courteous: not rendering evil for evil, or railing for railing: but contrariwise blessing" (I Pet. 3. 8,9). A rude and coarse style of address is only calculated to create an unfavourable opinion both of yourself and of your religion.

(d) Be sure to be *very plain.* Do not suffer yourself to cover up any circumstance of the person's character, and his relations to God. Lay it all open, not for the purpose of offending or wounding him, but because it is necessary. Before you can cure a wound, you must probe it to the bottom. Keep back none of the truth, but let it come out plainly before him.

(e) Be sure to *address his conscience.* Unless you address the conscience pointedly, you get no hold of the mind at all.

(f) Bring the *great and fundamental truths* to bear upon the person's mind. Sinners are very apt to run off upon some pretext, or some subordinate point, especially one of sectarianism. For instance, if the man is a Presbyterian, he will try to turn the conversation on the points of difference between Presbyterians and Methodists. Or he will fall foul of "old school" divinity. Do not talk with him on any such point. Tell him the present business is to save his soul, and not to settle controverted questions in theology. Hold him to the great fundamental points, by which he must be saved or lost.

(g) Be *very patient.* If he has a real difficulty in his mind, be very patient till you find out what it is, and then clear it up. If what he alleges is a mere cavil, make him see that it is a cavil. Do not try to answer it by argument, but show him that he is not sincere in advancing it. It is not worth while to spend your time in arguing against a cavil; make him feel that he is committing sin to plead it, and thus enlist his conscience on your side.

(h) Be careful to *guard your own spirit.* There are many people who have not good temper enough to converse with

those who are much opposed to religion. And such a person wants no better triumph then to see you angry. He will go away exulting because he has "made one of these saints mad."

(i) If the sinner is inclined to entrench himself against God, be careful *not to take his part in anything*. If he says he cannot do his duty, do not take sides with him, or say anything to countenance his falsehood; do not tell him he cannot, or help him to maintain himself in the controversy against his Maker. Sometimes a careless sinner will commence finding fault with Christians; do not take his part, do not side with him against Christians. Just tell him he has not their sins to answer for: he had better see to his own concerns. If you agree with him, he feels that he has you on his side. Show him that it is a wicked and censorious spirit that prompts him to make these remarks, and not a regard for the honour of the religion or the laws of Jesus Christ.

(j) Bring up the individual's *particular sins*. Talking in general terms against sin will produce no results. You must make a man feel that you mean *him*. A minister who cannot make his hearers feel that he means them, cannot expect to accomplish much. Some people are very careful to avoid mentioning the particular sins of which they know the individual to be guilty, for fear of hurting his feelings. This is wrong. If you know his history, bring up his particular sins, kindly, but plainly; not to give offense, but to awaken conscience, and give full force to the truth.

(k) It is generally *best to be short*, and not spin out what we have to say. Get the attention as soon as you can to the very point; say a few things and press them home, and bring the matter to an issue. If possible, get them to repent and give themselves to Christ at the time. This is the proper issue. Carefully avoid making an impression that you do not wish them to repent NOW.

(l) If possible, when you can converse with sinners, be sure to *pray* with them. If you converse with them, and leave them without praying, you leave your work undone.

II. *THE MANNER OF DEALING WITH AWAKENED SINNERS.*

Be careful to distinguish between an awakened sinner, and

one who is under conviction. When you find a person who feels a little on the subject of religion, do not take it for granted that he is *convicted of sin*, and thus omit to use means to show him his sin. Persons are oftened *awakened* by some providential circumstance; as sickness, thunderstorm, pestilence, death in the family, disappointment, or the like; or directly by the Spirit of God; so that their ears are open, and they are ready to hear on the subject of religion with attention and seriousness, and some feeling. If you find a person awakened, no matter by what means, lose no time to pour in light upon his mind. Do not be afraid, but show him the breadth of the Divine law, and the exceeding strictness of its precepts. Make him see how it condemns his thoughts and life. Search out his heart, find what is there, and bring it up before his mind, as far as you can. If possible, melt him down on the spot. When once you have got a sinner's attention, very often his conviction and conversion are the work of a few moments. You can sometimes do more in five minutes, than in years—or a whole lifetime—while he is careless or indifferent.

I have been amazed at the conduct of those cruel parents, and other heads of families, who will let an awakened sinner be in their families for days and weeks, and not say a word to him on the subject. They say: "If the Spirit of God has begun a work in him, He will certainly carry it on!" Perhaps the person is anxious to converse, and puts himself in the way of Christians, as often as possible, expecting they will converse with him, and they do not say a word. Amazing! Such a person ought to be looked out immediately, as soon as he is awakened, and a blaze of light be poured into his mind without delay. Wherever you have reason to believe that a person within your reach is awakened, do not sleep till you have poured in the light upon his mind, and have tried to bring him to immediate repentance. Then is the time to press the subject with effect.

In revivals, I have often seen Christians who were constantly on the look-out to see if any persons appeared to be awakened; as soon as they saw any one begin to manifest feeling under preaching they would mark him, and (as soon as the meeting was over) invite him to a room, and converse and pray with him—if possible not leaving him till he was converted.

A remarkable case of this kind occurred in a town at the West. A merchant came to the place from a distance, to buy goods. It was a time of powerful revival, but he was determined to keep out of its influence; and so he would not go to any meeting at all. At length he found everybody so much engaged in religion that it met him at every turn; and he got vexed, and vowed that he would go home. There was so much religion there, he said, that he could do no business, and would not stay. Accordingly he booked his seat for the coach, which was to leave at four o'clock the next morning. As he spoke of going away, a gentleman belonging to the house, who was one of the young converts, asked him if he would not go to a meeting once before he left town. He finally consented, and went to the meeting. The sermon took hold of his mind, but not with sufficient power to bring him into the Kingdom. He returned to his lodgings, and called the landlord to bring his bill. The landlord, who had himself recently experienced religion, saw that he was agitated. He accordingly spoke to him on the subject of religion, and the man burst into tears. The landlord immediately called in three or four young converts, and they prayed, and exhorted him; and at four o'clock in the morning, when the coach called, he went on his way *rejoicing in God!* When he got home he called his family together, confessed to them his past sins, avowed his determination to live differently, and prayed with them for the first time. It was so unexpected that it was soon noised abroad; people began to inquire, and a revival broke out in the place. Now, suppose these Christians had done as some do, been careless, and let the man go off, slightly impressed? It is not probable he ever could have been saved. Such opportunities are often lost for ever, when once the favourable moment is passed.

III. *THE MANNER OF DEALING WITH WITH CONVICTED SINNERS.*

By a *convicted* sinner, I mean one who feels himself condemned by the law of God, as a guilty sinner. He has so much instruction as to understand something of the extent of God's law, and he sees and feels his guilty state, and knows what his remedy is. To deal with these often requires great wisdom.

1. When a person is *convicted*, but not *converted*, and remains in an anxious state, there is generally some specific reason for it. In such cases it does no good to exhort him to repent, or to explain the law to him. He knows all that; he understands these general points; but still he does not repent. There must be some particular difficulty to overcome. You may preach, and pray, and exhort, till doomsday, and not gain anything.

You must, then, set yourself to inquire what is that particular difficulty. A physician, when he is called to a patient, and finds him sick with a particular disease, first administers the general remedies that are applicable to that disease. If they produce no effect, and the disease still continues, he must examine the case, and learn the constitution of the individual, and his habits, diet, manner of living, &c., and see what the matter is that the medicine does not take effect. So it is with the case of a sinner convicted but not converted. If your ordinary instructions and exhortations fail, there must be a difficulty. The particular difficulty is often known to the individual himself, though he keeps it concealed. Sometimes, however, it is something that has escaped even his own observation.

(*a*) Sometimes the individual has some idol, something which he loves more than God, which prevents him from giving himself up. You must search out and see what it is that he will not give up. Perhaps it is wealth; perhaps some earthly friend; perhaps gay dress or gay company, or some favourite amusement. At any rate, there is something on which his heart is so set that he will not yield to God.

(*b*) Perhaps he has done an injury to some individual that calls for redress, and he is unwilling to confess it, or to make a just recompense. Now, until he will confess and forsake this sin, he can find no mercy. If he has injured the person in property or character, or has abused him, he must make it up. Tell him frankly that there is no hope for him till he is willing to confess it, and to do what is right.

(*c*) Sometimes there is some *particular sin* which he will not forsake. He pretends it is only a small one; or tries to persuade himself it is no sin at all. No matter how small it is, he can never get into the Kingdom of God till he gives it up.

Sometimes an individual has seen it to be a sin to use tobacco, and he can never find true peace till he gives it up. Perhaps he is looking upon it as a small sin. But God knows nothing about small sins in such a case. What is the sin? It is injuring your health, and setting a bad example; and you are taking God's money (which you are bound to employ in His service) and spending it for tobacco. What would a merchant say if he found one of his clerks in the habit of going to the money drawer, and taking money enough to keep him in cigars? Would he call it a small offense? No; he would say the clerk deserved to be sent to the State prison. I mention this particular sin, because I have found it to be one of the things to which men who are convicted will hold on, although they know it to be wrong, and then wonder why they do not find peace.

(*d*) See if there is some work of *restitution* which he is bound to do. Perhaps he has defrauded somebody in trade, or taken some unfair advantage, contrary to the golden rule of doing as you would be done by, and is unwilling to make satisfaction. This is a very common sin among merchants and men of business. I have known many melancholy instances, where men have grieved away the Spirit of God, or else have been driven wellnigh to absolute despair, because they were unwilling to give satisfaction where they have done such things. Now it is plain that such persons never can have forgiveness until they make restitution.

(*e*) They may have *entrenched* themselves somewhere, and fortified their minds in regard to some particular point, which they are determined not to yield. For instance, they may have taken strong ground that they will not do a particular thing. I knew a man who was determined not to go into a certain grove to pray. Several other persons during the revival had gone into the grove, and there, by prayer and meditation, given themselves to God. His own clerk had been converted there. The lawyer himself was awakened, but he was determined that he would not go into that grove. He had powerful convictions, and went on for weeks in this way, with no relief. He tried to make God believe that it was not pride that kept him from Christ; and so, when he was going home from meeting he would kneel down in the street and pray. And not only that, but he would look round for a mud-puddle in the street, in which he might kneel, to show that he was not proud. He once prayed *all night* in his parlour—but he would not go into the grove. His distress was so great, and he was so wroth with God, that he was strongly tempted to make away with himself, and actually threw away his knife for fear he should cut his throat. At length he concluded he would go into the grove and pray; and as soon as he got there he was converted, and poured out his full heart to God.[1]

So, individuals are sometimes entrenched in a determination that they will not go to a particular meeting (perhaps the inquiry meeting, or some prayer-meeting); or they will not have a certain person to pray with them; or they will not take a particular seat, such as the "anxious seat." They say they can be converted just as well without yielding this point, for religion does not consist in going to a particular meeting, or taking a particular attitude in prayer, or a particular seat. This is true; but by taking this ground they *make* it the material point. And so long as they are entrenched there, and determined to bring God to their terms, they never can be converted. Sinners will often yield anything else, and do anything else, and do anything in the world, but yield the point upon which they have taken a stand against God. They cannot be humbled, until they yield this point, whatever it is. And if, without yielding, they get a hope, it will be a false hope.

(*f*) Perhaps he has a prejudice against some one (a member of the Church, perhaps), on account of some faithful dealing with his soul; and he hangs on this, and will never be converted till he gives it up. Whatever it be, you should search

---

[1] This was Mr. Benjamin Wright, in whose office Finney studied law, "his own clerk" being, of course, Finney himself. "I have a parlour to pray in," said the lawyer; "I am not going into the woods." However, he gave in; and a young man who happened to overhear him in the wood came to Finney, in the village, crying: "Squire Wright is converted! I heard some one shouting very loudly, and I saw Squire Wright pacing to and fro and singing as loudly as he could sing; and every few moments he would stop and clap his hands with his full strength, and shout: 'I will rejoice in the God of my salvation!'" Presently the lawyer came into his office, crying: "I've got it! I've got it!" From that time he took a decided stand for God.

it out, and tell him the truth, plainly and faithfully.

(g) He may feel ill-will towards some one, or be angry, and cherish strong feelings of resentment, which prevent him from obtaining mercy from God. "And when ye stand praying, forgive, if ye have ought against any: that your Father also which is in heaven may forgive you your trespasses. But if ye do not forgive, neither will your Father which is in heaven forgive your trespasses" (Mark II. 25,26).

(h) Perhaps he entertains some errors in doctrine, or some wrong notions representing the *thing to be done*, or the way of doing it, which may be keeping him out of the Kingdom. Perhaps he is waiting for God to do something to him before he submits—in fact, is waiting for God to do for him what God has required the sinner to do himself.

He may be waiting for more conviction. People often do not know what conviction is, and think they are not under conviction when in fact they are under powerful conviction. They often think nothing is conviction unless they have great fears of hell. But the fact is, individuals often have strong convictions, who have very little fear of hell. Show them what is the truth, and let them see that they have no need to wait.

Perhaps he may be waiting for certain feelings, which he has heard somebody else had before obtaining mercy. This is very common in revivals where some one of the first converts has told of remarkable experiences. Others who are awakened are very apt to think they must wait for just such feelings. I knew a young man thus awakened; his companion had been converted in a remarkable way, and this one was waiting for just such feelings. He said he was "using the means, and praying for them," but he finally found that he was a Christian, although he had not been through the course of feeling which he expected.

Sinners often lay out a plan of what they expect to feel, and how they expect to be converted, and in fact lay out the work for God, determined that they will go in that path or not at all. Tell them this is all wrong; they must not lay out any such path beforehand, but let God lead them as He sees to be the best. God always leads the blind by a way they know not. There never was a sinner brought into the Kingdom through such a course of feeling as he expected. Very often they are amazed to find that they are in, and have had no such exercises as they expected.

It is very common for persons to be waiting to be made subjects of prayer, or for some other particular means to be used, or to see if they cannot make themselves better. They are so wicked, they say, that they cannot come to Christ. They want to try, by humiliation, and suffering, and prayer, to fit themselves to come. You will have to hunt them out of all these refuges. It is astonishing into how many corners they will often run before they will go to Christ. I have known persons almost deranged for the want of a little correct instruction.

Sometimes such people think their sins are too great to be forgiven, or that they have grieved the Spirit of God away, when that Spirit is all the while convicting them. They pretend that their sins are greater than Christ's mercy, thus actually insulting the Lord Jesus.

Sometimes sinners get the idea that they are given up of God, and that now they cannot be saved. It is often very difficult to beat persons off from this ground. Many of the most distressing cases I have met with have been of this character.

In a place where I was labouring in a revival, one day before the meeting commenced, I heard a low, moaning, distressing, unearthly noise. I looked and saw several women gathered round the person who made it. They said she was a woman in despair. She had been a long time in that state. Her husband was a drunkard. He had brought her to the meeting-place, and had gone himself to the tavern. I conversed with her, saw her state, and realised that it was very difficult to reach her case. As I was going to commence the meeting she said she must go out, for she could not bear to hear praying or singing. I told her she must not go, and asked the ladies to detain her, if necessary, by force. I felt that, if the devil had hold of her, God was stronger than the devil, and could deliver her. The meeting began, and she made some noise at first. But presently she looked up. The subject was chosen with special reference to her case, and as it proceeded her attention was gained, her eyes were fixed—I never shall forget how she looked—her eyes and mouth open, her head up—and how she almost rose from her seat as the truth poured in upon her mind. Finally, as the truth knocked away every foundation on which her despair had rested, she shrieked out, put her head down, and sat perfectly still till the meeting was over. I went to her, and found her perfectly calm and happy in God. I saw her long afterwards, and she still remained in that state of rest. Thus Providence led her where she never expected to be, and compelled her to hear instruction adapted to her case. You may often do incalculable good by finding out precisely where the difficulty lies, and then bringing the truth to bear on that point.

Sometimes persons will strenuously maintain that they have committed the unpardonable sin. When they get that idea into their minds, they will turn everything you say against themselves. In some such cases, it is a good way to take them on their own ground, and reason with them in this way: "Suppose you have committed the unpardonable sin, what them? It is reasonable that you should submit to God, and be sorry for your sins, and break off from them, and do all the good you can, even if God will not forgive you. Even if you go to hell, you ought to do this." Press this thought until you find they understand and consent to it.

It is common for persons in such cases to keep their eyes on themselves; they will shut themselves up, and keep looking at their own darkness, instead of looking away to Christ. Now, if you can take their minds off from themselves, and get them to think of Christ, you may draw them away from brooding over their own present feelings, and get them to lay hold on the hope set before them in the Gospel.

2. Be careful, in conversing with convicted sinners, not to make any *compromise* with them on any point where they have a difficulty. If you do, they will be sure to take advantage of it, and thus get a false hope. Convicted sinners often get into a difficulty, in regard to giving up some darling sin, or yielding some point where conscience and the Holy Ghost are at war with them. And if they come across an individual who will yield the point, they feel better, and are happy, and think they are converted. The young man who came to Christ was of this character. He had one difficulty, and Jesus Christ knew just what it was. He knew he loved his money; and instead of compromising the matter and thus trying to comfort him, he

just put His finger on the very place and told him: "Go and sell that thou hast, and give to the poor, and come and follow Me" (Matt. 19. 21). What was the effect? Why, the young man "went away sorrowful." Very likely, if Christ had told him to do anything else, he would have felt relieved, and would have got a hope; would have professed himself a disciple, joined the Church, and gone to hell.

People are often amazingly anxious to make a compromise. They will ask such questions as this: Whether you do not think a person may be a Christian, and yet do such-and-such things? Or: If he may be a Christian and not do such-and-such things? Now, do not yield an inch to any such questions. The questions themselves may often show you the very point that is labouring in their minds. They will show you that it is pride, or love of the world, or something of the kind, which is preventing them from becoming Christians.

Be careful to make thorough work on this point—the love of the world. I believe there have been more false hopes built on wrong instructions here, than in any other way. I once heard a Doctor of Divinity trying to persuade his hearers to give up the world; but he told them: "If you will only give it up, God will give it right back to you. He is willing that you should enjoy the world."[1] Miserable! God never gives back the world to a Christian, in the same sense that He requires a convicted sinner to give it up. He requires us to give up the *ownership* of everything to Him, so that we shall never again for a moment

---

[1]   The incident occurred in a meeting for inquirers, held in the basement of Dr. Lyman Beecher's Church, at Boston, during a campaign conducted by Finney, at various churches, in which "searching" sermons had first astonished and repulsed, and then attracted, the people. Finney felt that Dr. Beecher did not discriminate as to the sense in which they were to give their possessions, and the sense in which the Lord would allow them to retain such. In a courteous way, but so as to correct the impression, Finney told the inquirers that, while God did not require them to relinquish their houses and businesses, and never to have possession of them again, He did require that these things were not theirs but His; that His claim was absolute, and that they were never to think that they had a right to use their time, strength, substance, or influence, as though it were their own and not God's.

consider it *as our own*. A man must not think he has a right to
judge for himself how much of his property he shall lay out for
God. One man thinks he may spend seven thousand dollars a
year to support his family; he has a right to do it, because he
has the means of his own. Another thinks he may lay up fifty
or a hundred thousand dollars. One man said, the other day,
that he had promised he never would give any of his property
to educate young men for the ministry; so, when he is applied
to, he just answers: "I have said I never will give to any such
object, and I never will." Man! did Jesus Christ ever tell you to
act so with *His money?* Has he laid down any such rule?
Remember, it is His money you are talking about, and if He
wants it to educate ministers, you withhold it at your peril.
Such a man has yet to learn the first principle of religion, that
he is not his own, and that the money which he "possesses" is
Jesus Christ's.

Here is the great reason why the Church is so full of false
hopes. Men have been left to suppose they could be Christians
while holding on to their money. And this has served as a clog
to every enterprise. It is an undoubted fact, that the Church has
funds enough to supply the world with Bibles, and tracts, and
missionaries, immediately. But the truth is, that professors of
religion do not believe that "the earth is the Lord's, and the
fulness thereof." Every man supposes he has a right to decide
what appropriation he shall make of his own money. And they
have no idea that Jesus Christ shall dictate to them on the
subject.

Be sure to deal thoroughly on this point. The Church is now
filled up with hypocrites, because people were never made to
see that unless they made an entire consecration of all to
Christ—all their time, all their talents, all their influence—
they would never get to heaven. Many think they can be
Christians, and yet dream along through life, and use all their
time and property for themselves, only giving a little now and
then, just to save appearances, and when they can do it with
perfect convenience. But it is a sad mistake, and they will find
it so, if they do not employ their energies for God. And when
they die, instead of finding heaven at the end of the path they
are pursuing, they will find hell there.

In dealing with a convicted sinner, be sure to drive him away from every refuge, and not leave him an inch of ground to stand on so long as he resists God. This need not take a long time to do. When the Spirit of God is at work striving with a sinner, it is easy to drive him from his refuges. You will find the truth will be like a hammer, crushing wherever it strikes. Make clean work with it, so that he shall give up all for God.

Make the sinner see clearly the nature and extent of the Divine law, and press the *main question* of entire submission to God. Bear down on that point as soon as you have made him clearly understand what you aim at, and do not turn off upon anything else.

Be careful, in illustrating the subject, not to mislead the mind so as to leave the impression that a selfish submission will answer, or a selfish acceptance of the Atonement, or a selfish giving up to Christ and receiving Him, as if a man were making a good bargain, giving up his sins, and receiving salvation in *exchange*. This is mere barter, and not submission to God. Leave no ground in your explanations or illustrations, for such a view of the matter. Man's selfish heart will eagerly seize such a view of religion, if it be presented, and very likely close in with it, and thus get a false hope.

REMARKS.

1. Make it an object of *constant study, and of daily reflection and prayer*, to learn how to deal with sinners so as to promote their conversion. It is the great business on earth of every Christian, to save souls. People often complain that they do not know how to take hold of this matter. Why, the reason is plain enough; they have never studied it. They have never taken the proper pains to qualify themselves for the work. If people made it no more a matter of attention and thought to qualify themselves for their worldly business, than they do to save souls, how do you think they would succeed? Now, if you are thus neglecting the main business of life, what are you living for? If you do not make it a matter of study, how you may most successfully act in building up the Kingdom of Christ, you are acting a very wicked and absurd part as a Christian.

2. Many professors of religion do *more harm than good*, when they attempt to talk to impenitent sinners. They have so little knowledge and skill, that their remarks rather divert

attention than increase it.

3. Be careful to find the *point where the Spirit of God is pressing* a sinner, and press the same point in all your remarks. If you divert his attention from that, you will be in great danger of destroying his convictions. Take pains to learn the state of his mind, what he is thinking of, how he feels, and what he feels most deeply upon, and then press that chief point thoroughly. Do not divert his mind by talking about anything else. Do not fear to press that point for fear of driving him to distraction. Some people fear to press a point to which the mind is tremblingly alive, lest they should injure the mind, notwithstanding that the Spirit of God is evidently debating that very point with the sinner. This is an attempt to be wiser than God. You should clear up the point, throw the light of truth all around it, and bring the soul to yield, and then the mind will be at rest.

4. Great evils have arisen, and many false hopes have been created, by not *discriminating between an awakened, and a convicted, sinner*. For the want of this, persons who are only awakened are immediately pressed to submit—"you must repent," "submit to God"—when they are in fact neither convinced of their guilt, nor instructed so far as even to know what submission means. This is one way in which revivals have been greatly injured—by indiscriminate exhortations to repent, unaccompanied by proper instruction.

5. Anxious sinners are to be regarded as being in a very *solemn and critical state*. They have, in fact, come to a turning-point. It is a time when their destiny is likely to be settled for ever. Christians ought to feel deeply for them. In many respects their circumstances are more solemn than those of the Judgment. *Here* their destiny is *settled*. The Judgment Day reveals it. And the particular time when it is done is when the *Spirit is striving with them*. Christians should remember their awful responsibility at such times. The physician, if he knows anything of his duty, sometimes feels himself under a very solemn responsibility. His patient is in a critical state, where a little error will destroy life, and hangs quivering between life and death. If such responsibility should be felt in relation to the body, what awful responsibility should be felt in relation to the soul, when it is seen to hang trembling on a point, and its

destiny is now to be decided. One false impression, one indiscreet remark, one sentence misunderstood, a slight diversion of mind, may *wear* him the wrong way, and his soul be lost. Never was an angel employed in a more solemn work, than that of dealing with sinners who are under conviction. How solemnly and carefully then should Christians walk, how wisely and skilfully work, if they do not wish to be the means of the loss of a soul!

Finally, if there is a sinner in this house, let me say to him: "Abandon all your excuses. You have been told to-night that they are all in vain. This very hour may seal your eternal destiny. Will you submit to God to-night—NOW?"

LECTURE XI

A WISE MINISTER WILL BE SUCCESSFUL

He that winneth souls is wise.—Prov. 11. 30.

I lectured last, from the same text, on the methods of dealing with sinners by "private" Christians. My object at this time is to take up the more public means of grace, with particular reference to the Duties of *Ministers*.

As I observed in my last Lecture, wisdom is the choice and pursuit of the best end by the most appropriate means. The great end for which the Christian ministry is appointed, is to glorify God in the salvation of souls. In speaking on this subject I propose to show: I. That a right discharge of the duties of a minister requires great wisdom. II. That the amount of success in the discharge of his duties (*other things being equal*) decides the amount of wisdom employed by him in the exercise of his office.

I. *THE RIGHT DISCHARGE OF MINISTERIAL DUTY.*

A right discharge of the duties of a minister requires great wisdom: 1. On account of the *opposition* it encounters. The very end for which the ministry is appointed is one against which is arrayed the most powerful opposition of sinners themselves. If men were willing to receive the Gospel, and there were nothing needed to be done but to tell the story of Redemption, a child might convey the news. But men are opposed to the Gospel. They are opposed to their own salvation, *in this way*. Their opposition is often violent and determined. I once saw a maniac who had formed designs against his own life, and he would exercise the utmost sagacity and cunning to effect his purpose. He would be so artful as to make his keepers believe he had no such design, that he had given it all up; he would appear mild and sober, but the instant the keeper was off his guard he would lay hands on himself. So, sinners often exercise great cunning in evading all the efforts that are made to save them. In order to meet this dreadful cunning, and overcome it, so as to save men, ministers need a great amount of wisdom.

2. The *particular means* appointed to be employed in the work, show the necessity of great wisdom in ministers. If men were converted by an act of physical omnipotence, creating some new taste, or something like that, and if sanctification were nothing but the same physical omnipotence rooting out the remaining roots of sin from the soul, it would not require so much sagacity and skill to win souls. Nor would there then be any meaning in the text. But the truth is that regeneration and santification are to be effected by moral means—by argument, and not by force. There never was, and never will be, any one saved by anything but truth as the means. Truth is the outward means, the outward motive, presented first by man and then by the Holy Spirit. Take into view the opposition of the sinner himself, and you see that nothing, after all, short of the wisdom of God and the moral power of the Holy Spirit, can break down this opposition, and bring him to submit. Still, the means are to be used by men—means adapted to the end, and skilfully used. God has provided that the work of conversion and sanctification shall in all cases be done by means of that kind of truth, applied in that connection and relation, which is fitted to produce such a result.

3. He has the *powers of earth and hell to overcome*, and that calls for wisdom. The devil is constantly at work, trying to prevent the success of ministers, labouring to divert attention from the subject of religion, and to get the sinner away from God and lead him down to hell. The whole framework of

society, almost, is hostile to religion. Nearly all the influences which surround a man, from his cradle to his grave, are calculated to defeat the design of the ministry. Does not a minister, then, need great wisdom to conflict with the powers of darkness and the whole influence of the world, in addition to the sinner's own opposition?

4. The same is seen from the *infinite importance* of the end itself. The end of the ministry is the salvation of the soul. When we consider the importance of the end, and the difficulties of the work, who will not say with the apostle: "Who is sufficient for these things?" (2 Cor. 2. 16.)

5. He must understand *how to wake up* the professing Christians, and thus prevent them from hindering the conversion of sinners. This is often the most difficult part of a minister's work, and requires more wisdom and patience than anything else. Indeed, to do this successfully, is a most rare qualification in the Christian ministry. It is a point where almost all ministers fail. They know not how to wake up the Church, and raise the tone of piety to a high standard, and thus clear the way for the work of conversion. Many ministers can preach to sinners very well, but gain little success, while the counteracting influence of the Church resists it all, and they have not skill enough to remove the difficulty. There is only here and there a minister in the country who knows how to probe the Church when it is in a cold, backslidden state, so as effectually to awaken the members and *keep them awake*. The members of the Church sin against such light, that when they become cold it is very difficult to rouse them up. They have a form of piety which wards off the truth, while at the same time it is just that kind of piety which has no power or efficiency. Such professors are the most difficult individuals to arouse from their slumbers. I do not mean that they are always more wicked than the impenitent. They are often employed about the machinery of religion, and pass for very good Christians, but they are of no use in a revival.

I know ministers are sometimes amazed to hear it said that Churches are not awake. No wonder such ministers do not know how to wake a sleeping Church. There was a young licentiate heard Brother Foote the other day, in this city, pouring out truth, and trying to waken up the Churches; and he knew so little about it that he thought Mr. Foote was abusing the Churches. So perfectly blind was he that he really thought the Churches in New York were all awake on the subject of religion. So, some years ago, there was a great controversy and opposition raised, because so much was said about the Churches being asleep. It was all truth, yet many ministers knew nothing about it, and were astonished to hear such things said. When it has come to this, that *ministers* do not know when the Church is asleep, no wonder we have revivals! I was invited once to preach at a certain place. I asked the minister what was the state of the Church. "Oh," said he, "to a man they are awake." I was delighted at the idea of labouring in such a Church, for it was a sight I had never yet witnessed, to see every single member awake in a revival. But when I got there I found them sleepy and cold, and I doubt whether one of them was awake.

Here is the great difficulty in keeping up revivals, to keep the Church thoroughly awake and engaged. It is one thing for members to get up in their sleep and bluster about and run over each other; and a widely different thing for them to have their eyes open, and their senses about them, and be wide awake, so as to know how to work for Christ.

6. He must know how *to set the Church to work, when it is awake*. If a minister attempts to go to work singly, calculating to do it all himself, it is like attempting to roll a great stone up a hill, alone. The Church can do much to help forward a revival. Churches have sometimes had powerful revivals without any minister. But when a minister has a Church that is awake, and knows how to set his people to work, and how to sit at the helm, and guide them, he may feel strong, and oftentimes may find that they do more than he does himself in the conversion of sinners.

7. In order to be successful, a minister needs great wisdom to know *how to keep the Church to the work*. Often the Church seems just like an assembly of children. You set children to work, and they appear to be all occupied, but as soon as your back is turned, they will stop and go to play. The great difficulty in *containing* a revival, lies here. And to meet it requires great wisdom. To know how to break them down again, when their hearts get lifted up because they have had

such a great revival; to wake them up afresh when their zeal begins to flag; to keep their hearts full of zeal for the work; these are some of the most difficult things in the world. Yet if a minister would be successful in winning souls, he must know when they first begin to get proud, or to lose the spirit of prayer; when to probe them, and how to search them; in fact, how to keep the Church in the field, gathering the harvest of the Lord.

8. He must *understand the Gospel*. But you will ask: "Do not all ministers understand the Gospel?" I answer that they certainly do not all understand it alike, for they do not all preach alike.

9. He must know how to *divide* it, so as to bring forward the particular truths, in that order, and at such times, as will be calculated to produce a given result. A minister should understand the philosophy of the human mind, so as to know how to plan and arrange his labours wisely. Truth, when brought to bear upon the mind, is in itself calculated to produce corresponding feelings. The minister must know what feelings he wishes to produce, and how to bring to bear such truth as is calculated to produce those feelings. He must know how to present truth which is calculated to humble Christians, or to make them feel for sinners; or to awaken sinners, or to convert them.

Often, when sinners are awakened, the ground is lost for want of wisdom in following up the blow. Perhaps a rousing sermon is preached, Christians are moved, and sinners begin to feel, and yet, the next Sabbath, something will be brought forward that has no connection with the state of feeling in the congregation, and that is not calculated to lead the mind on to the exercise of repentance, faith, or love. It shows how important it is that a minister should understand how to produce a given impression, at what time it may and should be done, and by what truth, and how to follow it up till the sinner is broken down and brought in.

A great many good sermons that are preached, are lost for the want of a little wisdom on this point. They are good sermons, and calculated, if well timed, to do great good; but they have so little connection with the actual state of feeling in the congregation, that it would be more than a miracle if they should produce a revival. A minister may preach in this random way till he has preached himself to death, and never produce any great results. He may convert here and there a scattered soul; but he will not move the mass of the congregation unless he knows how to follow up his impressions—so to execute a general plan of operations as to carry on the work when it is begun. He must not only be able to blow the trumpet so loud as to start the sinner up from his lethargy, but when he is awakened, he must lead him by the shortest way to Jesus Christ; and not, as soon as sinners are roused by a sermon, immediately begin to preach about some remote subject that has no tendency to carry on the work.

10. To reach *different classes of sinners successfully* requires great wisdom on the part of a minister. For instance, a sermon on a particular subject may impress a particular class of persons among his hearers. Perhaps they will begin to look serious, or to talk about it, or to cavil about it. Now, if the minister is wise, he will know how to observe those indications, and to follow right on, with sermons adapted to this class, until he leads them into the Kingdom of God. Then, let him go back and take another class, find out where they are hid, break down their refuges, and follow them up, til he leads them, also, into the Kingdom. He should thus beat about every bush where sinners hide themselves, as the voice of God followed Adam in the garden: "ADAM, WHERE ART THOU?" till one class of hearers after another is brought in, and so the whole community converted. Now, a minister must be very wise to do this. It never will be done till a minister sets himself to hunt out and bring in every class of sinners in his congregation—the old and young, male and female, rich and poor.[1]

---

[1] Finney, in his revival campaigns, consistently urged the principle of "hunting out" classes and individuals. At Troy, N.Y., he held a sort of "prayer progress" through the town. "We had," said Finney, "a prayer-meeting from house to house, daily, at eleven o'clock." The spirit of soul-winning was strong. "At one of the meetings, Mr. S——, cashier of a bank, was so pressed with the spirit of prayer that when the meeting was dismissed, he was unable to rise from his knees. He remained, and writhed and groaned in agony, and said, 'Pray for Mr. ——,' who was president of the bank

11. A minister needs great wisdom to get sinners away from their *present* refuge of lies, *without forming new hiding-places* for them. I once sat under the ministry of a man who had contracted a great alarm about heresies, and was constantly employed in confuting them. And he used to bring up heresies that his people had never heard of. He got his ideas chiefly from books, and mingled very little among the people to know what they thought. And the result of his labours often was, that the people would be taken with the heresy, more than with the argument against it. The novelty of the error attracted their attention so much that they forgot the answer. And in that way he gave many of his people new objections against religion, such as they had never thought of before. If a man does not mingle enough with mankind to know how people think *nowadays*, he cannot expect to be wise to meet their objections and difficulties.

I have heard a great deal of preaching against Universalists, that did more harm than good, because the preachers did not understand how Universalists of the present day reason. When ministers undertake to oppose a present heresy, they ought to know what it actually is, at present. It is of no use to misrepresent a man's doctrines to his face, and then try to reason him out of them. He will say to you: "That man cannot argue with me on fair grounds; he has to misrepresent my doctrines in order to confute me." Great harm is done in this way. Ministers do not intend to misrepresent their opponents; but the effect of it is, that the poor miserable creatures who hold these errors go to hell because ministers do not take care to inform themselves what are their real errors. I mention this to show how much wisdom a minister must have to meet the cases that occur.

12. Ministers ought to know *what measures* are best calculated to aid in accomplishing the great end of their office,

---

where Mr. S—— was cashier. This president was a wealthy unconverted man. The praying people knelt down and wrestled in prayer. As soon as the mind of Mr. S—— was so relieved that we could go home, we all retired; and soon after the president of the bank expressed a hope in Christ. He had not, I believe, attended any meetings, and it was not known that he was concerned about salvation" (See Finney's "Memoirs").

the salvation of souls. Some measures are plainly necessary. By measures, I mean the things which should be done to secure the attention of the people, and bring them to listen to the truth. Erecting buildings for worship, visiting from house to house, &c., are "measures," the object of which is to get the attention of people to the Gospel. Much wisdom is requisite to devise and carry forward all the various measures that are adapted to favour the success of the Gospel.

What do politicians do? They get up meetings, circulate handbills and pamphlets, blaze away in the newspapers, send ships about the streets on wheels with flags and sailors, send conveyances all over the town, with handbills, to bring people up to the polls—all to gain attention to their cause, and elect their candidate. All these are their "measures," and for their *end* they are wisely calculated. The object is to get up an excitement, and bring the people out. They know that unless there can be an excitement it is in vain to push their end. I do not mean to say that their measures are pious, or right, but only that they are wise, in the sense that they are the appropriate application of means to the end.

The object of the ministry is to get all the people to feel that the devil has no right to rule this world, but that they ought all to give themselves to God, and "vote in" the Lord Jesus Christ as the Governor of the universe. Now, what shall be done? What measures shall we take? Says one: "Be sure and have nothing that is new." Strange! The object of our measure is to gain attention, and you *must have* something new. As sure as the effect of a measure becomes stereotyped, it ceases to give attention, and then you must try something new. You need not make innovations in everything. But whenever the state of things is such that anything *more* is needed, it must be something *new*, otherwise it will fail. A minister should never introduce innovations that are not called for. If he does, they will embarrass him. He cannot alter the Gospel; that remains the same. But new measures are necessary, from time to time, to awaken attention, and bring the Gospel to bear upon the public mind. And a minister ought to know how to introduce new things, so as to create the least possible resistance or reaction. Mankind are fond of *form* in religion. They love to have their religious duties stereotyped, so as to leave them at ease; and they are therefore inclined to resist any new movement designed to rouse them up to action and feeling. Hence it is all-important to introduce new things wisely, so as not to give needless occasion for resistance.

13. Not a little wisdom is sometimes needed by a minister to know *when to put a stop to new measures*. When a measure has novelty enough to secure attention to the truth, ordinarily no other new measure should be introduced. You have secured the great object of novelty. Anything more will be in danger of diverting the public mind away from the great object, and fixing it on the measures themselves. And then, if you introduce novelties when they are not called for, you will go over so large a field that, by and by, when you really want something new, you will have nothing else to introduce, without doing something that will give too great a shock to the public mind. The Bible has laid down no specific course of measures for the promotion of revivals of religion, but has left it to ministers to adopt such as are wisely calculated to secure the end. And the more sparing we are of our new things, the longer we can use them, to keep public attention awake to the great subject of religion. By a wise course this may undoubtedly be done for a long series of years, until our *present* measures will, by and by, have sufficient novelty in them again to attract and fix public attention. And so we shall never want for something *new*.

14. A minister, to win souls, must know how to deal with *careless*, with *awakened*, and with *anxious* sinners, so as to lead them right to Christ in the shortest and most direct way. It is amazing to see how many ministers there are who do not know how to deal with sinners, or what to say to them in various states of mind. A good woman in Albany told me, that when she was under concern she went to her minister, and asked him to tell her what she must do to get relief. He said that God had not given him much experience on the subject, and advised her to go to a certain deacon, who perhaps could tell her what to do. The truth was, he did not know what to say to a sinner under conviction, although there was nothing peculiar in her case. Now, if you think this minister a rare case, you are quite deceived. There are many ministers who do not know what to say to sinners.

A minister once appointed an anxious meeting, which he duly attended, but instead of going round to speak to the individuals, he began to ask them the catechism question: "Wherein doth Christ execute the office of a priest?" About as much in point to a great many of their minds as anything else.[1]

I know a minister who held an anxious meeting, and went to attend it with a *written discourse*, which he had prepared for the occasion. This was just as wise as it would be if a physician, going out to visit his patients, should sit down at leisure and write all the prescriptions beforehand. A minister needs to know the state of mind of individuals, before he can know what truth it will be proper and useful to administer. I say these things, not because I love to do it, but because truth and the object before me, require them to be said. And such instances as I have mentioned are by no means rare.

A minister should know how to apply truth to all the situations in which he may find dying sinners going down to hell. He should know how to preach, how to pray, how to conduct prayer-meetings, and how to use all the means for bringing the truth of God to bear upon the kingdom of darkness. Does not this require wisdom? And who is sufficient for these things?

II. *SUCCESS PROPORTIONATE TO WISDOM.*

The amount of a minister's success in winning souls (*other things being equal*) invariably decides the amount of wisdom he has exercised in the discharge of his office.

1. This is plainly asserted in the text. "He that winneth souls is wise." That is, if a man wins souls, *he does* skilfully

---

[1]   Finney's objection, of course, is not to the question itself (No. 25 in the Shorter Catechism), but to the inappropriateness of putting a question on doctrine—however sound the prescribed answer might be—to an assembly of people who were ready to be led immediately into saving faith in Christ; and who had come together, in an anxious state of soul, for that specific purpose and for no other. *Afterwards*, indeed, and with a lively faith, they might give the Catechism answer that "Christ executeth the office of a priest in His once offering up of Himself a sacrifice to satisfy Divine justice, and reconcile us to God; and in making continual intercession for us."

adapt means to the end, which is, to exercise wisdom. He is the more wise, by how much the greater is the number of sinners that he saves. A blockhead may, indeed, now and then, stumble on such truth, or such a manner of exhibiting it, as to save a soul. It would be a wonder indeed if any minister did not sometimes have something in his sermons that would meet the case of some individual. But the amount of wisdom is to be decided, other things being equal, by the *number* of cases in which he is successful in converting sinners.

Take the case of a physician. The greatest quack may now and then stumble upon a remarkable cure, and so get his name up with the ignorant. But sober and judicious people judge of the skill of a physician by the *uniformity* of his success in overcoming disease, the variety of diseases he can manage, and the number of cases in which he is successful in saving his patients. The most skilful saves the most. This is common sense. It is the truth. And it is just as true in regard to success in saving souls, and true in just the same sense.

2. This principle is not only asserted in the text, but it is a *matter of fact*, a historical truth, that "He that winneth souls is wise." He has actually employed means adapted to the end, in such a way as to secure the end.

3. Success in saving souls is evidence that a man *understands the Gospel*, and understands human nature; that he knows how to adapt means to his end; that he has common sense, and that kind of tact, that practical discernment, to know how to get at people. And if his success is extensive, it shows that he knows how to deal, in a great variety of circumstances, with a great variety of characters, who are all the enemies of God, and to bring them to Christ. To do this requires great wisdom. And the minister who does it shows that he is wise.

4. Success in winning souls shows that a minister not only knows how to labour wisely for that end, but also that he *knows where his dependence is*. Fears are often expressed respecting those ministers who are aiming most directly and earnestly at the conversion of sinners. People say: "Why, this man is going to work in his own strength; one would imagine he thinks he can convert souls himself." How often has the event showed that the man knew very well what he was about,

and knew where his strength was, too. He went to work to convert sinners so earnestly, just as if he could do it all himself; but that was the very way he should do. He *ought* to reason with sinners and plead with them, as faithfully and as fully as if he did not expect any interposition of the Spirit of God. But whenever a man does this successfully, it shows that, after all, he knows he must depend for success upon the Spirit of God alone.

There are many who feel an objection against this subject, arising out of the view they have taken of the ministry of Jesus Christ. They ask us: "What will you say of the ministry of Jesus Christ—was not He wise?" I answer: "Yes, infinitely wise." But in regard to His alleged "want of success" in the conversion of sinners you will observe the following things:

(*a*) That His ministry was vastly more successful than is generally supposed. We read in one of the sacred writers, that after His resurrection and before His ascension, "He was seen of above five hundred brethren at once" (I Cor 15. 6). If so many as five hundred brethren were found assembled together at one place, we judge that there must have been a vast number of them scattered over the country.

(*b*) Another circumstance to be observed is that His public ministry was *very short*, less than three years.

(*c*) Consider, too, the peculiar *design* of His ministry. His main object was to make Atonement for the sins of the world. It was not aimed so much at promoting revivals. The "dispensation of the Spirit" was not yet given. He did not preach the Gospel so fully as His apostles did afterwards. The prejudices of the people were so fixed and violent that they would not bear it. That He did not, is plain from the fact that even His apostles, who were constantly with Him, did not understand the Atonement. They did not get the idea that He was going to die; and consequently, when they heard that He was actually dead, they were driven to despair, and thought the thing was all gone by, and their hopes blown to the winds. The fact was that He had another object in view, to which everything else was made to yield; and the perverted state of the public mind, and the obstinate prejudices prevailing, showed why results were not seen any more in the conversion of sinners. The state of public opinion was such that they finally murdered Him for what He did preach.

Many ministers who have little or no success are hiding themselves behind the ministry of Jesus Christ, as if He were an unsuccessful preacher. Whereas, in fact, He was eminently successful, considering the circumstances in which He laboured. This is the last place, in all the world, where a minister who has no success should think of hiding himself.

REMARKS.

1. A minister may be *very learned and yet not wise*. There are many ministers possessed of great learning; they understand all the sciences, physical, moral, and theological; they may know the dead languages, and possess all learning, and yet not be *wise* in relation to the great end about which they are chiefly employed. Facts clearly demonstrate this. "He that *winneth souls* is wise."

2. An unsuccessful minister may be pious as well as learned, and yet not wise. It is unfair to infer that because a minister is unsuccessful, therefore he is a hypocrite. There may be something defective in his education, or in his mode of viewing a subject, or of exhibiting it, or such a want of *common sense*, as will defeat his labours, and prevent his success in winning souls, while he himself may be saved, "yet so as by fire."

3. A minister may be *very wise*, though he is *not learned*. He may not understand the dead languages, or theology in its common acceptation; and yet he may know just what a minister of the Gospel wants most to know, without knowing many other things. A learned minister, and a wise minister, are different things. Facts in the history of the Church in all ages prove this. It is very common for Churches, when looking out for a minister, to aim at getting a very learned man. Do not understand me to disparage learning. The more learned the better, if he is also wise in the great matter he is employed about. If a minister knows how to win souls, the more learning he has the better. But if he has any other kind of learning, and *not this*, he will infallibly fail of achieving that which should be the end of his ministry.

4. Want of success in a minister (*other things being equal*) proves (*a*) that he never was called to preach, but has taken it

up out of his head; or *(b)* that he was badly educated, and was never taught the very things he needs most to know; or *(c)* if he was called to preach, and knows how to do his duty, he is too indolent and too wicked to do it.

5. Those are the *best educated ministers* who win the most souls. Ministers are sometimes looked down upon, and called very ignorant, because they do not know the sciences and languages; although they are very far from being ignorant of the *great thing* for which the ministry is appointed. This is wrong. Learning is important, and always useful. But after all, a minister may know how to win souls to Christ, *without great* learning; and he has the best education *for a minister*, who can win the most souls to Christ.

6. There is evidently a great defect in the present mode of educating ministers. This is a SOLEMN FACT, to which the attention of the whole Church should be distinctly called, that the great mass of young ministers who are educated accomplish very little.

When young men come out of the seminaries, are they fit to go into a revival? Look at a place where there has been a revival in progress, and a minister is wanted. Let them send to a theological seminary for a minister. Will he enter into the work, and sustain it, and carry it on? Seldom. Like David with Saul's armour, he comes in with such a load of theological trumpery, that he knows not what to do. Leave him there for two weeks, and the revival is at an end. The Churches know and feel *that the greater part* of these young men do not know how to do anything that needs to be done for a revival, and the complaint is made that the young ministers are so far behind the Church. You may send all over the United States, to theological seminaries, and find *but few* young ministers fitted to carry forward the work. What a state of things!

There is a great defect in educating ministers. Education ought to be such, as to prepare young men for *the peculiar work to which they are destined*. But instead of this, they are educated for anything else. The grand mistake is this: that the mind is directed too much to irrelevant matters; it is carried over too wide a field, so that attention is diverted from the main thing and the young men get cold in religion. When, therefore, they get through their course, instead of being fitted for their work, they are *unfitted* for it. Under a pretence of disciplining the mind, attention is in fact scattered, so that when the young men come to their work, they are awkward, and know not how to take hold, or how to act, to win souls. This is not universally the case, but too often it is so.

It is common for people to talk loudly and largely about "an educated ministry." God forbid that I should say a word against an educated ministry! But what do we mean by an education for the ministry? Do we mean that they should be so educated, as to be fitted for the work? If they are so educated, the more education the better. Let education be of the right kind, teaching a young man the things he needs to know, and not the very things he does *not* need to know. Let them be educated *for the work*. Do not let education be such, that when young men come out, after spending six, eight, or ten years in study, they are not worth half as much as they were before they went. I have known young men come out after what they call "a thorough course," who could not manage a prayer-meeting, so as to make it profitable or interesting. An elder of a Church in a neighbouring city, informed me of a case in point. A young man, before he went to the seminary, had laboured as a layman with them, conducting their prayer-meetings, and been exceedingly useful among them. After he had been to the seminary, they sent for him and desired his help; but, oh, how changed! He was so completely transformed, that he made no impression; the members soon began to complain that they would "die" under his influences; and he left, because he was not prepared for the work.

It is common for those ministers who have been to the seminaries, and are now useful, to affirm that their course of studies there did them little or no good, and that they had to *unlearn* what they had there learned, before they could effect much. I do not say this censoriously, but it is a solemn fact, and in love I must say it.

Suppose you were going to make a man a surgeon in the navy. Instead of sending him to the medical school, to learn surgery, would you send him to the nautical school, to learn navigation? In this way, you might qualify him to navigate a ship, but he is no surgeon. Ministers should be educated to know what the Bible is, and what the human mind is, and how to bring the one to bear on the other. They should be brought into contact with mind, and made familiar with all the aspects of society. They should have the Bible in one hand, and the map of the human mind in the other, and know how to use the truth for the salvation of men.

7. A *want of common sense* often defeats the ends of the Christian ministry. There are many good men in the ministry, who have learning, and talents of a certain sort, but they have no common sense to win souls.

8. We see one great defect in our theological schools. Young men are confined to books, and shut out from intercourse with the *common people*, or contact with the common mind. Hence they are not familiar with the mode in which common people think. This accounts for the fact that some plain men, who have been brought up to business, and are acquainted with human nature, are ten times better qualified to win souls than those who are educated on the present principle, and are in fact ten times as well acquainted with the proper business of the ministry. These are called "educated men." This is a grand mistake. They are not learned in science, but they are learned in the very things which they need to know *as ministers*. They are not ignorant ministers, for they know exactly how to reach the mind with truth. They are better furnished *for their work*, than if they had all the machinery of the schools.

I wish to be understood. I do not say, that I would not have a young man go to school. Nor would I discourage him from going over the field of science. The more the better, if together with it he learns also *the things* that the minister needs to know, in order to win souls—if he understands his Bible, and understands human nature, and knows how to bring the truth to bear, and how to guide and manage minds, and to lead them away from sin and lead them to God.

9. The success of any measure designed to promote a revival of religion, demonstrates its wisdom; with the following exceptions:

(*a*) A measure may be introduced *for effect*, to produce excitement, and be such that when it is looked back upon afterwards, it will seem nonsensical, and appear to have been a mere trick. In that case, it will react, and its introduction will have done more harm than good.

(b) Measures may be introduced, and the revival be very powerful, and the success be attributed to the *measures*, when in fact, it was other things which made the revival powerful, and these very measures may have been a hindrance. The prayers of Christians, and the preaching, and other things, may have been so well calculated to carry on the work, that it has succeeded *in spite* of these measures.

But when the blessing evidently follows the introduction of the *measure itself*, the proof is unanswerable, that the measure is wise. It is profane to say that such a measure will do more harm than good. God knows about that. His object is, to do the *greatest amount* of good possible. And of course He will not add His blessing to a measure that will do some good, because it will be at the expense of a greater good. But He never will bless a pernicious proceeding. There is no such thing as *deceiving* God in the matter. He knows whether a given measure is, on the whole, wise or not. He may bless a course of labours notwithstanding some unwise or injurious measures. But if He blesses the *measure itself*, it is rebuking God to pronounce it unwise. He who undertakes to do this, let him look to the matter.

10. It is evident that much fault has been found with measures which have been *pre-eminently and continually* blessed of God for the promotion of revivals. If a measure is *continually or usually* blessed, let the man who thinks he is wiser than God, call it in question. TAKE CARE how you find fault with God!

11. Christians should *pray for ministers*. Brethren, if you felt how much ministers need wisdom to perform the duties of their great office with success, and how insufficient they are of themselves, you would pray for them a great deal more than you do; that is, if you cared anything for the success of their labours. People often find fault with ministers, when they do not pray for them. Brethren, this is tempting God; for you ought not to expect any better ministers, unless you pray for them. And you ought not to expect a blessing on the labours of your minister, or to have your families converted by his preaching, when you do not pray for him. And so for others, for the waste places, and the heathen: instead of praying all the

time, only that God would send out *more* labourers, you have need also to pray that God would make ministers *wise to win souls*, and that those He sends out may be *properly* educated, so that they shall be scribes well instructed in the kingdom of God.

12. Those *laymen* in the Church who know how to win souls are to be counted wise. They should not be called "ignorant laymen"; and those Church members who do not know how to convert sinners, and who cannot win souls, should not be called wise—*as Christians*. They are not wise Christians; only "he that winneth souls is wise." They may be learned in politics, in all sciences, or they may be skilled in the management of business, or other things, and they may look down on those who win souls, as nothing but plain, simple-hearted and ignorant men. If any of you are inclined to do this, and to undervalue those who win souls, as being not so wise and cunning as you are, you deceive yourselves. They may not know some things which you know; but they know those things which a Christian is *most concerned* to know, and which you do not.

It may be illustrated by the case of a minister who goes to sea. He may be learned in science, but he knows not how to sail a ship. And he begins to ask the sailors about this thing and that, and what this rope is for, and the like. "Why," say the sailors, "these are not *ropes*, we have only one rope in a ship; these are the rigging; the man talks like a fool." And so this learned man becomes a laughing-stock, perhaps, to the sailors, because he does not know how to sail a ship. But if he were to tell them one half of what he knows about science, perhaps they would think him a conjurer, to know so much. So, learned students may understand their Latin very well, and may laugh at the humble Christian, and call him ignorant, although he may know how to win more souls than five hundred of them.

I was once distressed and grieved at hearing a minister bearing down upon a young preacher, who had been converted under remarkable circumstances, and who was licensed to preach without having pursued a regular course of study. This minister, who was never, or at least very rarely, known to convert a soul, bore down upon the young man in a very lordly, censorious manner, depreciating him because he had not had the advantage of a liberal education—when, in fact, he was instrumental in converting more souls than any five hundred ministers like the one who criticised him.

I would say nothing to undervalue, or lead any to undervalue, a thorough education for ministers. But I do not call that a *thorough education*, which they receive in our colleges and seminaries. It does not fit them for *their work*. I appeal to all experience, whether our young men in seminaries are thoroughly educated for the purpose of winning souls. DO THEY DO IT? Everybody knows they do not. Look at the reports of the Home Missionary Society. If I recollect right, in 1830, the number of conversions in connection with the labours of the missionaries of that society did not exceed five to each missionary. I believe the number has increased since, but is still exceedingly small to what it would have been had they been fitted, by a right course of training, for their work. I do not say this to reproach them, for, from my heart, I pity them; and I pity the Church for being under the necessity of supporting ministers so trained, or of having none at all. They are the best men the Missionary Society can obtain.

I suppose I shall be reproached for saying this. But it is too true and too painful to be concealed. Those fathers who have the training of our young ministers are good men, but they are ancient men, men of another age and stamp from what is needed in these days, when the Church and world are rising to new thought and action. Those dear fathers will not, I suppose, see with me in this; and will perhaps think hardly of me for saying it; but it is the cause of Christ. Some of them are getting back toward second childhood, and ought to resign, and give place to younger men, who are not rendered physically incapable, by age, of keeping pace with the onward movements of the Church. And here I would say, that to my own mind it appears evident, that unless our theological professors preach a good deal, mingle much with the Church, and sympathise with her in all her movements, it is morally, if not naturally, impossible, that they should succeed in training young men to the spirit of the age. It is a shame and a sin, that theological professors, who preach but seldom, who are withdrawn from the active duties of the ministry, should sit in their studies and write their letters, advisory or dictatorial, to ministers and Churches who are in the field, and who are in circumstances to judge what needs to be done. The men who spend all, or at least a portion, of their time in the active duties of the ministry, are the only men who are able to judge of what is expedient or inexpedient, prudent or imprudent, as to measures, from time to time. It is as dangerous and ridiculous for our theological professors, who are withdrawn from the field of conflict, to be allowed to dictate, in regard to the measures and movements of the Church, as it would be for a general to sit in his bedchamber and attempt to order a battle.[1]

Two ministers were one day conversing about another minister, whose labours were greatly blessed—in the conversion of some thousands of souls. One of them said: "That man ought not to preach any more; he should stop and go to —— (a theological seminary which he named), and proceed through a regular course of study." He said the man had "a good mind, and if he were thoroughly educated, he might be very useful." The other replied: "Do you think he would be more useful for going to that seminary? I challenge you to show by facts that any are more useful who have been

---

[1] In view of Finney's obvious energy in defending revivals as against a certain school of ministers, it should be explained that he was by no means without justification. For example, in the volume of Lectures by Dr. Sprague, of Albany, upon the same topic— "Revivals of Religion"—there had appeared a number of added communications, received (in response to Dr. Sprague's invitation) from leading ministers and theological professors. These contained, in addition to a great deal of sound sense and encouraging intelligence from worthy and distinguished men, reflections calculated to imply a general condemnation of methods and causes championed by Finney—*e.g.*, camp meetings, "anxious seats," public prayer by women, and lay preaching. The "holding-up of special neighbourhoods as subjects of public prayer on account of their special wickedness" was considered to be objectionably personal; and another "excess" warmly criticised was that several women, on realising that they were converted, actually began to pray aloud for their respective husbands! Dr. Sprague was a friend and supporter of Dr. Nettleton, who had visited Albany specifically to oppose Finney while the latter was actively engaged in a revival at Troy, near by. (See footnote, p. 210, and Dr. Bennet Tyler's "Memoir" of Nettleton.)

there. No, sir, the fact is, that since this man has been in the ministry, he has been instrumental in converting more souls than all the young men who have come from that seminary in the time."

Finally: I wish to ask, who among you can lay any claim to the possession of this Divine wisdom? Who among you, laymen? Who among, ministers? Can any of you? Can I? Are we at work, wisely, to win souls? Or are we trying to make ourselves believe that success is no criterion of wisdom? *It is* a criterion. It is a safe criterion for every minister to try himself by. The amount of his success, *other things being equal*, measures the amount of wisdom he has exercised in the discharge of his office.

How few of you have ever had wisdom enough to convert so much as a single sinner? Do not say: "I cannot convert sinners. How can I convert sinners? God alone can convert sinners." Look at the text: "He that winneth souls is wise," and do not think you can escape the sentence. It is true that God converts sinners. But there is a sense, too, in which ministers convert them. And you have something to do; something which, if you do it wisely, will ensure the conversion of sinners in proportion to the wisdom employed. If you never have done this, it is high time to think about yourselves, and see whether you have wisdom enough to save even your own souls.

Men! Women! You are bound to be wise in winning souls. Perhaps already souls have perished, because you have not put forth the wisdom which you might, in saving them. The city is going to hell. Yes, the world is going to hell, and must go on, till the Church finds out what to do, to win souls. Politicians are wise. The children of this world are wise; they know what to do to accomplish their ends, while we are prosing about, not knowing what to do, or where to take hold of the work, and sinners are going to hell.

HOW TO PREACH THE GOSPEL

He that winneth souls is wise.—Prov. 11. 30.

One of the last remarks in my last Lecture was this, that the text ascribes conversion to men. Winning souls is converting men. I now design to show that: I. Several passages of Scripture ascribe conversion to men; and that: II. This is consistent with other passages which ascribe conversion to God. III. I also purpose to discuss several further particulars which are deemed important, in regard to the preaching of the Gospel, and which show that great practical wisdom is necessary to win souls to Christ.

I. THE BIBLE ASCRIBES CONVERSION TO MEN.

There are many passages which represent the conversion of sinners as the work of men. In Daniel 12. 3 it is said: "They that be wise shall shine as the brightness of the firmament; and they that turn many to righteousness as the stars for ever and ever." Here the work is ascribed to men. So also in I Cor. 4. 15: "Though ye have ten thousand instructors in Christ, yet have ye not many fathers: for in Christ Jesus I have begotten you through the Gospel." Here the apostle explicitly tells the Corinthians that he made them Christians, with the Gospel, or truth, which he preached. Again, in James 5. 19, 20, we are taught the same thing. "Brethren, if any of you do err from the truth, and one convert him; let him know, that he which converteth the sinner from the error of his way shall save a soul from death, and shall hide a multitude of sins." I might quote many other passages, equally explicit. But these are sufficient abundantly to establish the fact, that the Bible does actually ascribe conversion to men.

II. THE BIBLE ASCRIBES CONVERSION TO GOD.

Here let me remark that to my mind it often appears very strange that men should ever suppose there was an inconsistency here, or that they should ever have overlooked the plain common sense of the matter. How easy it is to see that there is a sense in which *God* converts them, and another sense in which *men* convert them.

The Scriptures ascribe conversion to four different agencies—to *men,* to *God*, to the *truth*, and to the *sinner himself*. The passages which ascribe it to the truth are the largest class. That men should ever have overlooked this distinction, and should have regarded conversion as a work performed exclusively by God, is surprising. So it is that any difficulty should ever have been felt on the subject, or that people should ever have professed themselves unable to reconcile these several classes of passages.

The Bible speaks on this subject, precisely as we speak on common subjects. There is a man who has been very ill. How natural it is for him to say to his physician: "That man saved my life." Does he mean to say that the physician saved his life without reference to God? Certainly not, unless he is an infidel. God made the physician, and He made the medicine too. And it never can be shown but that the agency of God is just as truly concerned in making the medicine take effect to save life, as it is in making the truth take effect to save a soul. To affirm the contrary is downright atheism. It is true, then, that the physician saved him; and it is also true that God saved him. It is equally true that the medicine saved his life, and also that he saved his own life by taking the medicine; for the medicine would have done no good if he had not taken it.

In the conversion of a sinner, it is true that God gives the truth efficiency to turn the sinner to God. He is an active, voluntary, powerful agent, in changing the mind. But the one who brings the truth to the sinner's notice is also an agent. We are apt to speak of ministers and other men as only *instruments* in converting sinners. This is not exactly correct. Man is something more than an instrument. Truth is the mere unconscious instrument. But man is more: he is a voluntary, responsible agent in the business. In a sermon, I have illustrated this idea by the case of an individual standing on the banks of Niagara.

"Suppose yourself to be standing on the banks of the Falls of Niagara. As you stand upon the verge of the precipice, you behold a man, lost in deep reverie, approaching its verge, unconscious of his danger. He approaches nearer and nearer, until he actually lifts his foot to take the final step that shall plunge him in destruction. At this moment, you lift your warning voice above the roar of the foaming waters, and cry out: 'Stop!' The voice pierces his ear, and breaks the charm that binds him; he turns instantly upon his heel; all pale and aghast he retires, quivering, from the verge of death. He reels and almost swoons with horror; turns, and walks slowly to the hotel; you follow him; the manifest agitation in his countenance calls numbers around him; and on your approach he points to you, and says: 'That man saved my life.' Here he ascribes the work to you; and certainly there is a sense in which you had saved him. But, on being further questioned, he says: 'Stop!' How that word rings in my ears. Oh, that was to me the word of life!' Here he ascribes it to the *word* that aroused him, and caused him to turn.

"But on conversing still further, he says: 'Had I not turned at that instant, I should have been a dead man.' Here he speaks of it (and truly) as his own act. But you directly hear him say: 'Oh, the mercy of God! If God had not interposed, I should have been lost!' Now, the only defect in this illustration is this: In the case supposed, the only interference on the part of God was a *providential* one; and the only sense in which the saving of the man's life is ascribed to Him, is in a providential sense. But in the conversion of a sinner there is something more than the providence of God employed; for here, not only does the providence of God so order it, that the preacher cries: 'Stop!' but the Spirit of God urges the truth home upon him with such tremendous power as to induce him to turn."

Not only does the minister cry: "Stop!" but through the living voice of the preacher, the Spirit cries: "Stop!" The preacher cries: "Turn ye, why will ye die?" The Spirit sends the expostulation home with such power that the sinner turns. Now, in speaking of this change, it is perfectly proper to say, that the Spirit turned him; just as you would say of a man who had persuaded another to change his mind on the subject of politics, that he had converted him, and brought him over. It is also proper to say that the truth converted him; as, in a case when the political sentiments of a man were changed by a certain argument, we should say that argument brought him over. So, also, with perfect propriety, may we ascribe the change to the preacher, or to him who had presented the motives; just as he would say of a lawyer who had prevailed in his argument with a jury: "He has won his case; he has converted the jury." It is also with the same propriety ascribed to the individual himself whose heart is changed; we should say that he has changed his mind, he has come over, he has repented. Now it is strictly true, and true in the most absolute and highest sense; the act is his own act, the turning is his own turning, while God by the truth has induced him to turn; still it is strictly true that he has turned, and has done it himself. Thus you see the sense in which it is the work of God; and also the sense in which it is the sinner's own work.

The Spirit of God, by the truth, influences the sinner to change, and in this sense is the efficient Cause of the change. But the sinner actually changes, and is therefore himself, in the most proper sense, the author of the change. There are some, who, on reading their Bibles, fasten their eyes on those passages that ascribe the work of the Spirit of God, and seem to overlook those which ascribe it to man, and speak of it as the sinner's own act. When they have quoted Scripture to prove it is the work of God, they seem to think they have proved that it is that in which man is passive, and that it can in no sense be the work of man.

Some time ago a tract was written, the title of which was, "Regeneration, the Effect of Divine Power." The writer goes on to prove that the work is wrought by the Spirit of God; and there he stops. Now it had been just as true, just as philosophical, and just as scriptural, if he had said that conversion was the work of man. It is easy to prove that it is the work of God, in the sense in which I have explained it. The writer, therefore, tells the truth, so far as he goes; but he has told only half the truth. For while there is a sense in which it is the work of God, as he has shown, there is also a sense in which it is the work of man, as we have just seen. The very title to this tract is a stumbling-block. It tells the truth, but it does not tell the whole truth. And a tract might be written upon this proposition that "*Conversion, or regeneration, is the work of man*"; which would be just as true, just as Scriptural, and just as philosophical, as the one to which I have alluded. Thus the writer, in his zeal to recognise and honour God as concerned in this work, by leaving out the fact that a change of heart is the sinner's *own act*, has left the sinner strongly entrenched, with his weapons in his rebellious hands, stoutly resisting the claims of his Maker, and waiting passively for God to make him a new heart. Thus you see the consistency between the requirement of the text, and the declared fact that God is the author of the new heart. God commands you to make you a new heart, expects you to do it; and, if ever it is done, you must do it.

And let me tell you, sinner, if you do not do it you will go to hell; and to all eternity you will feel that you *deserved* to be sent there for not having done it.

III. *GOSPEL PREACHING AND SOUL WINNING.*

I shall now advert to several important particulars growing out of this subject, as connected with preaching the Gospel, and which show that great practical wisdom is indispensable to win souls to Christ.

1. In regard to the *matter of preaching*. (*a*) First, all preaching should be *practical*. The proper end of all doctrine is practice. Anything brought forward as doctrine, which cannot be made use of as practical, is not preaching the Gospel. There is none of that sort of preaching in the Bible. That is all practical. "All Scripture is given by inspiration of God, and is profitable for doctrine, for reproof, for correction, for instruction in righteousness: that the man of God may be perfect, thoroughly furnished unto all good works" (2 Tim. 3.

16, 17). A vast deal of preaching in the present day, as well as in past ages, is called *doctrinal*, as opposed to *practical* preaching. The very idea of making this distinction is a device of the devil. And a more abominable device Satan himself never devised. You sometimes hear certain men talk a wonderful deal about the necessity of "indoctrinating the people." By which they mean something different from practical preaching; teaching them certain doctrines, as abstract truths, without any particular reference to practice. And I have known a minister in the midst of a revival, while surrounded with anxious sinners, leave off labouring to convert souls, for the purpose of "indoctrinating" the young converts, for fear somebody else should indoctrinate them before him. And there the revival stops! Either his doctrine was not true, or it was not preached in the right way. To preach doctrines in an abstract way, and not in reference to practice, is absurd. God always brings in doctrine to regulate practice. To bring forward doctrinal views for any other object is not only nonsense; it is wicked.

Some people are opposed to *doctrinal* preaching. If they have been used to hear doctrines preached in a cold, abstract way, no wonder they are opposed to it. They ought to be opposed to such preaching. But what can a man preach, who preaches no doctrine? If he preaches no doctrine, he preaches no Gospel. And if he does not preach it in a practical way, he does not preach the Gospel. All preaching should be doctrinal, and all preaching should be practical. The very design of doctrine is to regulate practice. Any preaching that has not this tendency is not the Gospel. A loose, exhortatory style of preaching may affect the passions, and may produce excitement, but will never sufficiently instruct the people to secure sound conversions. On the other hand, preaching doctrine in an abstract manner may fill the head with *notions*, but will never sanctify the heart or life.

(*b*) Preaching should be *direct*. The Gospel should be preached *to* men, and not *about* them. The minister must address his hearers. He must preach *to* them *about themselves*, and not leave the impression that he is preaching to them about others. He will never do them any good, further than he succeeds in convincing each individual that *he* is the person in question. Many preachers seem very much afraid of making the impression that they mean anybody in particular. They are preaching against certain *sins*—not that these have anything to do with the *sinner*; they would by no means speak as if they supposed any of *their hearers* were guilty of these abominable practices. Now this is anything but preaching the Gospel. Thus did not the prophets, nor Christ, nor the apostles. Nor do these ministers do this, who are successful in winning souls to Christ.

(*c*) Another very important thing to be regarded in preaching is, that the minister should *hunt after sinners* and Christians, wherever they may have entrenched themselves in inaction. It is not the design of preaching to make men easy and quiet, but to make them ACT. It is not the design, in calling in a physician, to have him give opiates, and so cover up the disease and let it run on till it works death; but to search out the disease wherever it may be hidden, and to remove it. So, if a professor of religion has backslidden, and is full of doubts and fears, it is not the minister's duty to quiet him in his sins, and comfort him, but to hunt him out of his errors and backslidings, and to show him just where he stands, and what it is that makes him full of doubts and fears.

A minister ought to know the religious opinions of every sinner in his congregation. Indeed, a minister in the country is inexcusable if he does not. He has no excuse for not knowing the religious views of all his congregation, and of all that may come under his influence. How otherwise can he preach to them? How can he know how to bring forth things new and old, and adapt truth to their case? How can he hunt them out unless he knows where they hide themselves? He may ring changes on a few fundamental doctrines—Repentance and Faith, and Faith and Repentance—till the Day of Judgment, and never make any impression on many minds. Every sinner has some hiding-place, some entrenchment, where he lingers. He is in possession of some darling LIE, with which he is quieting himself. Let the minister find it out, and get it away, either in the pulpit or in private, or the man will go to hell in his sins, and his blood will be found on the minister's skirts.

(*d*) Another important thing to observe is, that a minister should dwell most on those particular points which are most needed. I will explain what I mean.

Sometimes he may find a people who have been led to place great reliance on their own resolutions. They think they can consult their own convenience, and by-and-by they will repent, when they are ready, without any concern about the Spirit of God. Let him take up these notions, and show that they are entirely contrary to the Scriptures. Let him show that if the Spirit of God is grieved away, by and by, when it shall be convenient for the sinner to repent, he will have no inclination. The minister who finds these errors prevailing, should expose them. He should hunt them out, and understand just how they are held, and then preach the class of truths which show the fallacy, the folly, and the danger of these notions.

So, on the other hand, he may find a people who have such views of Election and Sovereignty, as to think they have nothing to do but to wait for "the moving of the waters." Let him go right over against them, urge upon them their ability to obey God, show them their obligation and duty, and press them with that until he brings them to submit and be saved. They have got behind a perverted view of these doctrines, and there is no way to drive them out of the hiding-place, but to set them right *on these points*. Wherever a sinner is entrenched, unless you pour light upon him *there*, you will never move him. It is of no use to press him with those truths which he admits, however plainly they may in fact contradict his wrong notions. *He supposes* them to be perfectly consistent, and does not see the inconsistency, and therefore it will not move him, or bring him to repentance.

I have been informed of a minister in New England, who was settled in a congregation which had long enjoyed little else than Arminian preaching, and the congregation themselves were chiefly Arminians. Well, this minister, in his preaching, strongly insisted on the opposite points, Election, Divine Sovereignty, Predestination, etc. The consequence was, as might have been expected where this was done with ability, that there was a powerful revival. Some time afterwards this same minister was called to labour in another field, in this State, where the people were all on the other side, and strongly tinctured with Antinomianism. They had got such perverted views of Election and Divine Sovereignty, that they were continually saying they had no power to do anything, but must wait God's time. Now, what does the minister do, but immediately go to preaching the doctrine of Election. And when he was asked how he could think of preaching the doctrine of Election so much to that people, when it was the very thing that lulled them to a deeper slumber, he replied: "Why, that is the very class of truths by which I had such a great revival in ——"; not considering the difference in the views of the people. You must take things as they are; find out where sinners lie, pour in truth upon them *there*, and START THEM OUT from their refuges of lies. It is of vast importance that a minister should find out where the congregation is, and preach accordingly.

I have been in many places in times of revival, and I have never been able to employ precisely the same course of preaching in one as in another. Some are entrenched behind one refuge, and some behind another. In one place, Christians will need to be instructed; in another, sinners. In one place, one set of truths; in another, another set. A minister must find out where people are, and preach accordingly. I believe this is the experience of all preachers who are called to labour from field to field.

(*e*) If a minister means to promote a revival, he should be very careful *not to introduce controversy*. He will grieve away the Spirit of God. In this way, probably, more revivals are put down than in any other. Look back upon the history of the Church from the beginning, and you will see that *ministers* are generally responsible for grieving away the Spirit and causing declensions by controversy. It is the ministers who bring forward controversial subjects for discussion, and by and by they get very zealous on the subject, and then get the Church into a controversial spirit, and so the Spirit of God is grieved away.

If I had time to go over the history of the Church from the days of the apostles, I could show that all the controversies that have taken place, and all the great declensions in religion, too, are chargeable upon ministers. I believe the ministers of the present day are responsible for the present state of the Church, and it will be seen to be true at the judgment. Who does not know that ministers have been crying out "Heresy," and "New Measures," and talking about the "Evils of Revivals," until they have got the Church all in confusion?[1] Oh, God, have mercy on ministers! They talk about their days of fasting and prayer, but are these the men to call on *others* to fast and pray? They ought to fast and pray themselves. It is time that ministers should assemble together, and fast and pray over the evils of controversy, for they have caused it. The Church itself

---

[1] Without stirring over much in the dust of dead controversy, it seems necessary to say for the elucidation of this and other passages (particularly in Lecture XIV.) that Finney had been tremendously attacked by Dr. Asahel Nettleton, Dr. Lyman Beecher, and others, on the ground of introducing "new measures." A charge against Finney, personally, was that "he rebuked, not only open transgressors, but professors of religion and ministers of the Gospel." Of the revival meetings, the complaint was that "fanaticism was promoted," by such measures as praying for persons by name, encouraging women to pray and exhort in promiscuous assemblies, and calling upon persons to "come to the 'anxious seat,' or to rise up in the public assembly to signify that they had given their hearts to God." It seems difficult to realise that a Convention of ministers was actually called, practically to confound Finney. Moreover, in the Convention an endeavour was made to silence those who had been engaged in the revivals, on the ground that they would be "prejudiced" witnesses; but the attempt failed. The Convention was a signal example of "much ado about nothing." The editor of the biography of Dr. Lyman Beecher subsequently declared that "a careful perusal of the minutes of the Convention has satisfied us that there was no radical difference." To which just remark Finney afterwards added that had no false reports been listened to by Dr. Nettleton, no Convention would have been thought of. Later, Dr. Beecher himself invited Finney to Boston. Throughout the hostility, Finney remained calm and confident. When certain college professors and others had come into concerted opposition to his work, in 1826, he experienced a solemn realisation of Divine support: "I shook from head to foot, under a full sense of the nearness of God. Never in my life was I so awed and humbled before God. God assured me that no opposition should prevail." It only remains to add that Dr. Nettleton (for a tender esteem) himself figures prominently in the annals of American revival, particularly in connection with such notable awakenings as those at Saratoga Springs and Nassau, in 1820.

would never get into a controversial spirit, unless led into it by ministers. The body of Church members are always averse to controversy, and would keep out of it, only they are dragged into it by ministers. When Christians are revived they are not inclined to meddle with controversy, either to read or hear it. But they may be told of such and such "damnable heresies" that are afloat, till they get their feelings enlisted in controversy, and then farewell to the revival. If a minister, in preaching, finds it necessary to discuss particular points about which Christians differ in opinion, let him BY ALL MEANS avoid a controversial *spirit and manner* of doing it.[1]

(*f*) The Gospel should be preached in *those proportions*, that *the whole Gospel* may be brought before the minds of the people, and produce its proper influence. If too much stress is laid on one class of truths, the Christian character will not have its due proportions. Its symmetry will not be perfect. If that class of truths be almost exclusively dwelt upon, that requires great exertion of intellect, without being brought home to the heart and conscience, it will be found that the Church will be indoctrinated *in those views*, but will not be awake, and active, and efficient in the promotion of religion. If, on the other hand, the preaching be loose, indefinite, exhortatory, and highly impassioned, the Church will be like a ship with too much sail for her ballast. It will be in danger of being swept away by a tempest of feeling, being carried away with every wind of doctrine. If Election and Sovereignty are *too much* preached, there will be Antinomianism in the Church, and sinners will hide themselves behind the delusion that they can do nothing. If, on the other hand, doctrines of ability and obligation be too prominent, they will produce Arminianism, and sinners will be blustering and self-confident.

When I entered the ministry, there had been so much said about Election and Sovereignty, that I found it was the universal hiding-place, both of sinners and of Christians, that they could not do anything, or could not obey the Gospel. And wherever I went, I found it indispensable to demolish these refuges of lies. And a revival would in no way have been

---

[1] In a note to the edition of 1868, Finney wrote of these remarks: "This was said with pain, in 1833-4."

produced or carried on, but by dwelling on that class of truths, which hold up man's ability, and obligation, and responsibility.

It was not so in the days when President Edwards and Whitefield laboured. Then, the Churches in New England had enjoyed little else than Arminian preaching, and were all resting in themselves and their own strength. These bold and devoted servants of God came out and declared those particular doctrines of grace, Divine Sovereignty and Election, and they were greatly blessed. They did not dwell on these doctrines exclusively, but they preached them very fully. The consequence was that because *in those circumstances* revivals followed from such preaching, the ministers who followed *continued to preach these doctrines almost exclusively*. And they dwelt on them so long that the Church and the world got entrenched behind them, waiting for God to come and do what He required *them* to do; and so revivals ceased for many years.

Now, and for years past, ministers have been engaged in hunting them out from these refuges. And here it is all-important for the ministers of this day to bear in mind that if they dwell exclusively on Ability and Obligation, they will get their hearers back on the old Arminian ground, and then they will cease to promote revivals. Here are ministers who have preached a great deal of truth, and have had great revivals, under God. Now, let it be known and remarked, that the reason is, they have hunted sinners out from their hiding-places. But if they continue to dwell on the same class of truths till sinners hide themselves behind such preaching, another class of truths must be preached. And then if they do not change their mode, another pall will hang over the Church, until another class of ministers shall arise and hunt sinners out of those new retreats.

A right view of both classes of truths, Election and Free-agency, will do no hurt. They are eminently calculated to convert sinners and strengthen saints. It is a perverted view that chills the heart of the Church, and closes the eyes of sinners in sleep. If I had time, I would remark on the manner in which I have sometimes heard the doctrines of Divine Sovereignty, Election, and Ability preached. They have been exhibited in irreconcilable contradiction, the one against the other. Such exhibitions are anything but the Gospel, and are calculated to make a sinner feel anything rather than his responsibility to God.

By preaching truth in proper proportions, I do not mean mingling all things together in the same sermon, in such a way that sinners will not see their connection or consistency. A minister once asked another: "Why do you not preach the doctrine of Election?" "Because," said the other, "I find sinners here are entrenched behind *Inability*." The first then said he once knew a minister who used to preach Election in the forenoon and Repentance in the afternoon. But, bringing things together that confound the sinner's mind, and overwhelm him with a fog of metaphysics, is not wise preaching. When talking of Election, the preacher is not talking of the sinner's duty. It has no relation to the sinner's duty. Election belongs to the government of God. It is a part of the exceeding richness of the grace of God. It shows the love of God—not the duty of the sinner. And to bring Election and Repentance together in this way is diverting the sinner's mind away from his duty. It has been customary, in many places, for a long time, to bring the doctrine of Election into every sermon. Sinners have been commanded to repent, and told that they could not repent, in the same sermon. A great deal of ingenuity has been exercised in endeavouring to reconcile a sinner's "inability" with his obligation to obey God. Election, Predestination, Free-agency, Inability, and Duty, have all been thrown together in one promiscuous jumble. And, with regard to many sermons, it has been too true, as has been objected, that ministers have preached: "You can and you cannot, you shall and you shall not, you will and you will not, and you will be lost if you do not!" Such a mixture of truth and error, of light and darkness, has confounded the congregation, and been the fruitful source of Universalism and every species of infidelity and error.

(*g*) It is of great importance that the sinner should be made to *feel his guilt*, and not left to the impression that he is *unfortunate*. I think this is a very prevalent fault, particularly in books on the subject. They are calculated to make the sinner think more of his sorrows than of his sins, and feel that his state is rather *unfortunate* than *criminal*. Perhaps most of you have seen a lovely little book, recently published, entitled

"Todd's Lectures to Children." It is exquisitely fine, and happy in some of its illustrations of truth. But it has one very serious fault. Many of its illustrations, I may say most of them, are not calculated to make a correct impression respecting the *guilt* of sinners, or to make them feel how much they have been to *blame*. This is very unfortunate. If the writer had guarded his illustrations on this point, so as to make them impress sinners with a sense of their *guilt*, I do not see how a child could have read through that book and not have been converted. Multitudes of the books written for children, and for adults too, within the last twenty years, have run into this mistake to an alarming degree. They are not calculated to make the sinner condemn himself. Until you can do this, the Gospel will never take effect.

(*h*) A prime object with the preacher must be to make *present obligation felt*. I have talked, I suppose, with many thousands of anxious sinners. And I have found that they had *never before felt* the pressure of present obligation. The impression is not commonly made by ministers in their preaching that sinners are expected to repent NOW. And if ministers suppose they make this impression, they deceive themselves. Most commonly any other impression is made upon the minds of sinners by the preacher than that they are expected *now* to submit. But what sort of a Gospel is this? Does God authorise such an impression? Is this according to the preaching of Jesus Christ? Does the Holy Spirit, when striving with the sinner, make the impression upon his mind that he is not expected to obey now? Was any such impression produced by the preaching of the apostles? How does it happen that so many ministers now preach, so as, in fact, to make an impression on their hearers that they are not expected to repent now? Until the sinner's conscience is reached on this subject, you preach to him in vain. And until ministers learn how to preach so as to make *the right* impression, the world never can be converted. Oh, to what an alarming extent does the impression now prevail among the impenitent, that they are not expected to repent *now*, but must wait God's time!

(*i*) Sinners ought to be made to feel that they have *something* to do, and that is, *to repent*; that it is something which *no other* being can do for them, neither God nor man; and something which *they can* do, and do *now*. Religion is something to *do*, not something to *wait for*. And they must do it now, or they are in danger of eternal death.

(*j*) Ministers should never rest satisfied, until they have ANNIHILATED every excuse of sinners. The plea of "inability" is the worst of excuses. It slanders God so, charging Him with infinite tyranny, in commanding men to do that which they have no power to do. Make the sinner see and feel that this is the very nature of his excuse. Make the sinner see that *all* pleas in excuse for not submitting to God, are acts of rebellion against Him. Tear away the last LIE which he grasps in his hand, and make him feel that he is absolutely condemned before God.

(*k*) Sinners should be made to feel that if they *now* grieve away the Spirit of God, it is very probable that they will be *lost for ever*. There is infinite danger of this. They should be made to understand *why* they are dependent on the Spirit, and that it is not because they *cannot* do what God commands, but because they are *unwilling*. They are so unwilling that it is just as certain they will not repent without the Holy Ghost, as if they were now in hell, or as if they were actually able. They are so opposed and so unwilling, that they never will repent in the world, unless God sends His Holy Spirit upon them.

Show them, too, that a sinner under the Gospel, who hears the truth preached, if converted at all, is generally converted young; and if not converted while young, he is commonly given up of God. Where the truth is preached, sinners are either Gospel-hardened or converted. I know some old sinners are converted, but they are rather exceptions, and by no means common.

2. I wish to make a few remarks on the *manner of preaching*.

(*a*) It should be *conversational*. Preaching, to be understood, should be colloquial in style. A minister must preach just as he would talk, if he wishes fully to be understood. Nothing is more calculated to make a sinner feel that religion is some mysterious thing that he cannot understand than this formal, lofty style of speaking which is so generally employed in the pulpit. The minister ought to do as the lawyer does when he wants to make a jury understand him perfectly. He uses a style perfectly colloquial. This lofty, swelling style will do no good. The Gospel will never produce any great effects until ministers *talk* to their hearers, in the pulpit, as they talk in private conversation.

(*b*) It must be in the *language of common life*. Not only should it be colloquial in its style, but the *words* should be such as are in common use. Otherwise they will not be understood. In the New Testament you will observe that Jesus Christ invariably uses words of the most common kind. The language of the Gospel is the plainest, simplest, and most easily understood of any language in the world.

For a minister to neglect this principle is *wicked*. Some ministers use language that is purely *technical* in preaching. They think to avoid the mischief by explaining the meaning fully at the outset; but this will not answer. It will not effect the object in making the people understand what he means. If he should use a word that is not in common use and that people do not understand, his explanation may be very full, but the difficulty is that people will forget his explanations, and then his words are so much Greek to them. Or if he uses a word in common use, but employs it in an *un*common sense, giving his special explanations, it is no better; for the people will soon forget his special explanations, and then the impression actually conveyed to their minds will be according to their *common* understanding of the word. And thus he will never convey the right idea to his congregation. It is amazing how many men of thinking minds there are in congregations, who do not understand the most common technical expressions employed by ministers, such as regeneration, sanctification, etc.

Use words that can be perfectly understood. Do not, for fear of appearing unlearned, use language which the people do not understand. The apostle says: "If I know not the meaning . . . he that speaketh shall be a barbarian unto me" (I Cor. 14. 11). And: "If the trumpet give an uncertain sound, who shall prepare himself to the battle?" (v. 8). In the apostle's days there were some preachers who were marvellously proud of displaying their command of language, and showing off the variety of tongues they could speak, which the common people could not understand. The apostle rebukes this spirit sharply, and says: "I had rather speak five words with my understanding, that by my voice I might teach others also, than ten thousand words in an unknown tongue" (v. 19).

I have sometimes heard ministers preach, even when there was a revival, when I have wondered what that part of the congregation would do, who had no dictionary. So many phrases were brought in, manifestly to adorn the discourse, rather than to instruct the people, that I have felt as if I wanted to tell the man: "Sit down, and do not confound the people's minds with your *barbarian* preaching, that they cannot understand."

(*c*) Preaching should be *parabolical*. That is, illustrations should be constantly used, drawn from incidents, real or supposed. Jesus Christ constantly illustrated His instructions in this way. He would either advance a principle and then illustrate it by a parable—that is, a short story of some event, real or imaginary—or else He would bring out the principle *in* the parable. There are millions of facts that can be used to advantage, and yet very few ministers dare to use them, for fear somebody will reproach them. "Oh," says somebody, "he actually tells stories!" Tells stories! Why, that is the way Jesus Christ preached. And it is the only way to preach. Facts, real or supposed, should be used to show the truth. Truths not illustrated, are generally just as much calculated to convert sinners as a mathematical demonstration. Is it always to be so? Shall it always be a matter of reproach, when ministers follow the example of Jesus Christ in *illustrating* truths by facts? Let them still do it, however much the foolish reproach them as story-telling ministers! They have Jesus Christ and common sense on their side.

(*d*) The illustrations should be drawn *from common life*, and the common business of society. I once heard a minister illustrate his ideas by the manner in which merchants transact business. Another minister who was present made some remarks to him afterwards. He objected to this illustration particularly, because, he said, it was too familiar, and was "letting down the dignity of the pulpit." He said all illustrations in preaching should be drawn from ancient history, or from an elevated source, that would keep up the dignity of the pulpit. Dignity indeed! Just the language of the devil. He rejoices in it. Why, the object of an illustration is to make people *see the truth*, not to bolster up pulpit dignity.

A minister whose heart is in the work does not use an illustration in order to make people stare, but to make them see the truth. If he brought forward his illustrations from ancient history, it could not make the people *see*; it would not illustrate anything. The novelty of the thing might awaken their attention, but they would lose the truth itself. For if the illustration itself be a novelty, the attention will be directed to this fact as a matter of history, and the *truth itself*, which it was designed to illustrate, will be lost sight of. The illustration should, if possible, be a matter of common occurrence, and the *more* common the occurrence the more sure it will be not to fix attention upon *itself*, but to serve as a *medium through which* the truth is conveyed.

The Saviour always illustrated His instructions by things that were taking place among the people to whom He preached, and with which their minds were familiar. He descended often very far below what is now supposed to be essential to support the dignity of the pulpit. He talked about hens and chickens, and children in market places, and sheep and lambs, and shepherds and farmers, and husbandmen and merchants. And when He talked about kings (as in the marriage of the King's son, and the nobleman that went into a far country to receive a Kingdom), He made reference to historical facts that were well known among the people at the time. The illustration should always be drawn from things so common that the illustration itself will not attract attention away from the subject, but that people may see, *through it*, the truth illustrated.

(*e*) Preaching should be *repetitious*. If a minister wishes to preach with effect, he must not be afraid of repeating whatever he may see is not perfectly understood by his hearers. Here is the evil of using a written sermon. The preacher preaches right along just as he has written it down, and cannot observe whether he is understood or not. If he should interrupt his reading, and attempt to catch the countenances of his audience, and to explain where he sees they do not understand, he grows confused. If a minister has his eyes on the people to whom he is preaching, he can commonly tell by their looks whether they understand him. If he sees that they do not understand any particular point, let him stop and illustrate it; and if they do not understand one illustration, let him give another, and make it clear to their minds before he goes on. But those who write their sermons go right on, in a regular consecutive train, just as in an essay or a book, failing, through want of repetition, to make the audience fully comprehend their points.

During a conversation with one of the first advocates in America, he expressed the view that when preachers experience difficulty in making themselves understood, it arises from the fact that they do not repeat their points sufficiently. Said he: "In addressing a jury, I always expect that whatever I wish to impress upon their minds, I shall have to repeat at least twice; and often I repeat it three or four times, and even as many times as there are jurymen before me. Otherwise, I do not carry their minds with me, so that they can feel the force of what comes afterwards." If a jury, under oath, called to decide on the common affairs of this world, cannot apprehend an argument, unless there is so much repetition, how is it to be expected that men will understand the preaching of the Gospel without it?

In like manner the minister ought to turn an important thought over and over before his audience, till even the children understand it perfectly. Do not say that so much repetition will create disgust in cultivated minds. It will not disgust. This is not what disgusts thinking men. They are not weary of the efforts a minister makes to be understood. The fact is, the more simple a minister's illustrations are, and the more plain he makes everything, the more men of mind are interested. I know, in fact, that men of the first minds often get ideas they never had before, from illustrations which were designed to bring the Gospel down to the comprehension of a child. Such men are commonly so occupied with the affairs of this world, that they do not *think* much on the subject of religion, and they therefore need the plainest preaching, and they will like it.

(f) A minister should always feel *deeply upon his subject*, and then he will suit the action to the word, and the word to the action, so as to make the full impression which the truth is calculated to make. He should be in solemn earnest in what he says. I heard a most judicious criticism on this subject: "How important it is that a minister should feel what he says. Then his actions will, of course, correspond to his words. If he undertakes to *make* gestures, his arms may go like a windmill, and yet make no impression." It is said to require the utmost stretch of art on the stage for the actors to make their hearers feel. The design of elocution is to teach this skill. But if a man *feels* his subject fully, he will *naturally* do it. He will *naturally* do the very thing that elocution laboriously teaches. See any common man in the streets who is earnest in talking; see with what force he gestures.[1] See a woman or a child in earnest—how natural! To gesture with their hands is as natural as it is to move their tongue and lips: it is the perfection of eloquence.[2]

No wonder that a great deal of preaching produces so little effect. Gestures are of more importance than is generally supposed. Mere words will never express the full meaning of

---

[1]"When I talked to plain people," wrote Wesley, of his early experiences, "I observed that they gasped and stared. This quickly obliged me to alter my style and adopt the language of those I spoke to. And yet there is a dignity in this simplicity which is not disagreeable to those of the highest rank." As to an effective manner in preaching, it is related of Wesley (by Tyerman), that, walking near Billingsgate Market with a friend, he stopped to watch two women who were quarrelling furiously. "Pray, sir, let us go," said his friend, "I cannot endure it." "Stay," replied Wesley, as he looked at the viragoes, "stay, and *learn how to preach!*"

[2]In the earliest years of his ministry, Finney "was commonly obliged to preach without any preparation whatever, except what I got in prayer. I depended on the occasion and the Holy Spirit to suggest the text and then to open up the subject to my mind." Later, he would prepare a "skeleton." His analytical mind and legal training always stood him in good stead. His style was colloquial and simple. He was never in the predicament of worthy "Father" Taylor, of Boston, who, in preaching to his usual congregation of seamen, when he found himself "tied up" in a series of clauses, happily escaped by remarking: "I have lost sight of the nominative case, but, my dear brethren, one thing I know, that I am bound for the Kingdom of Heaven." It is not to be supposed that Finney, if colloquial, was ordinary; his manner, arguments, earnestness and

the Gospel. The *manner* of saying it is almost everything. I once heard a remark made, respecting a young minister's preaching, which was instructive. (He was uneducated, in the common sense of the term, but well educated to win souls.) It was said of him: "The manner in which he comes in, and sits in the pulpit, and rises to speak, is a sermon of itself. It shows that he has something to say that is important and solemn." That man's manner of saying some things I have known to move the feelings of a whole congregation, when the same things said in a prosy way would have produced no effect at all.

A fact which was stated upon this subject by one of the most distinguished professors of elocution in the United States, ought to impress ministers. (The man was an unbeliever.) He said: "I have been fourteen years employed in teaching elocution to ministers, and I know they do not believe the Christian religion. Whether the Bible is true or not, I know these ministers do not believe it. I can demonstrate that they do not. The perfection of my art is to teach them to speak naturally on this subject. I go to their studies, and converse with them, and they speak eloquently. I say to them: 'Gentlemen, if you will preach naturally, just as you speak on any other subject in which you are interested, you do not need to be taught. That is just what I am trying to teach you. I hear you talk on other subjects with admirable force and eloquence. Then I see you go into the pulpit, and you speak and act as if you do not believe what you are saying.' I have told them, again, and again, to talk in the pulpit as they naturally talk to me. Yet I cannot *make* them do it; and so I know they do not believe the Christian religion."

I have mentioned this to show how universal it is, that men will gesture right, if they feel right. The only thing in the way of ministers being natural speakers is, that they do not DEEPLY FEEL. How can they be natural in elocution, when they do not feel?

---

tears, dominated his audiences. During his visit to England, in 1860, *The Revival* (No. 34) said of the meetings at Bolton (Lancs.): "The breathless attention, the murmured prayer and response and the falling tear have shown not less the preacher's power over his audience than their earnest sympathy with his message."

(g) A minister should aim to *convert his congregation*. But, you will ask: Does not all preaching aim at this? No. A minister always has *some* aim in preaching, but most sermons were never aimed at converting sinners. And if sinners were converted under them, the preacher himself would be amazed. I once heard a story bearing on this point. There were two young ministers who had entered the ministry at the same time. One of them had great success in converting sinners; the other, none. The latter inquired of the other, one day, what was the reason of this difference. "Why," replied his friend, "the reason is, that I *aim at* a different end from you in preaching. My object is to convert sinners, but you aim at no such thing; and then you put it down to the Sovereignty of God that you do not produce the same effect, when you never aim at it. Take one of my sermons and preach it, and see what the effect will be." The man did so, and preached the sermon, and it did produce effect. He was frightened when sinners began to weep; and when one came to him after meeting to ask what he should do, the minister apologised to him, and said: "I did not aim to wound you, I am sorry if I have hurt your feelings!" Oh, horrible!

(h) A minister must *anticipate the objections* of sinners, and answer them. What does the lawyer do, when pleading before a jury? (Oh, how differently from human causes is the cause of Jesus Christ pleaded!) It was remarked by a lawyer, that the cause of Jesus Christ had the fewest able advocates of any cause in the world. And I partly believe it. Does not a lawyer go along in his argument in a regular train, explaining anything that is obscure, and anticipating the arguments of his antagonist? If he did not, he would lose his case, to a certainty. But ministers often leave one difficulty and another untouched. Sinners who hear them feel a difficulty, and never know how to remove it, and perhaps the minister never takes the trouble to know that such a difficulty exists. Yet he wonders why his congregation is not converted, and why there is no revival. How can he wonder at it, when he has never hunted up the difficulties and objections that sinners feel, and removed them?

(i) If a minister means to preach the Gospel with effect, he must be sure *not to be monotonous*. If he preaches in a monotonous way, he will preach the people to sleep. Any monotonous sound, great or small, if continued, disposes people to sleep. The Falls of Niagara, the roaring of the ocean, or any sound ever so great or small, has this effect naturally on the nervous system. And a minister cannot be monotonous in preaching, if he feels what he says.

(*j*) A minister should address the feelings enough to secure attention, and then *deal with the conscience*, and probe to the quick. Appeals to the feelings alone will never convert sinners. If the preacher deals too much in these, he may get up an excitement, and have wave after wave of feeling flow over the congregation, and people may be carried away as with a flood, and rest in false hopes. The only way to secure *sound* conversions, is to deal faithfully with the conscience. If attention flags at any time, appeal to the feelings again, and rouse it up; but do your *work* with conscience.

(*k*) If he can, it is desirable that a minister should *learn the effect* of one sermon, before he preaches another. What would be thought of the physician who should give medicine to his patient, and then give it again and again, without trying to learn the effect of the first? A minister never will be able to deal with sinners as he ought, till he can find out whether his instruction has been received and understood, and whether the difficulties in sinners' minds are cleared away, and their path open to the Saviour, so that they need not go on stumbling and stumbling till their souls are lost.

REMARKS.

1. We see why so few of the *leading minds* in many communities are converted.

Until the late revivals, professional men were rarely reached by preaching, and they were almost all infidels at heart. People almost understood the Bible to warrant the idea that they could not be converted. The reason is obvious. The Gospel had not been commended to the conscience of such men. Ministers had not *reasoned* so as to make that class of mind see the truth of the Gospel, and feel its power; consequently such persons had come to regard religion as something unworthy of their notice.

Of late years, however, the case is altered, and in some

places there have been more of this class of persons converted, in proportion to their numbers, than of any other. That is because they were made to understand the claims of the Gospel. The preacher grappled with their minds, and showed them the reasonableness of religion. And when this is done, it is found that this class of mind is more easily converted than any other. They have so much better capacity to receive an argument, and are so much more in the habit of yielding to the force of reason, that as soon as the Gospel gets a fair hold of their minds, it breaks them right down, and melts them down at the feet of Christ.

2. Before the Gospel takes general effect, we must have a class of *extempore* preachers, for the following reasons:

(*a*) No set of men can stand the labour of writing sermons and doing all the preaching which will be requisite.

(*b*) Written sermons are not calculated to produce the requisite effect. Such preaching does not present the truth in right shape.

(*c*) It is impossible for a man who writes his sermons to arrange his matter, and turn and choose his thoughts, so as to produce the same effect as when he addresses the people directly, and makes them feel that he means *them*. Writing sermons had its origin in times of political difficulty. The practice was unknown in the apostles' days. No doubt written sermons have done a great deal of good, but they can never give to the Gospel its great power.

Perhaps many ministers have been so long trained in the use of notes, that they had better not throw them away. Perhaps they would make bad work without them. The difficulty would not be for want of mind, but from wrong training. The bad habit is begun with the school-boy, who is called to "speak his piece." Instead of being set to express his own thoughts and feelings in his own language, and in his own natural manner, such as Nature herself prompts, he is made to commit another person's writing to memory, and then he *mouths* it out in a stiff and formal way. And so when he goes to college, and to the seminary, instead of being trained to extempore speaking, he is set to write his piece, and commit it to memory.

I would pursue the opposite course from the beginning. I would give him a subject, and let him first *think*, and then *speak* his thoughts. Perhaps he will make mistakes. Very well, that is to be expected in a beginner. But he will learn. Suppose he is not eloquent, at first. Very well, he can improve. And he is in the very way to improve. This kind of training alone will raise up a class of ministers who can convert the world.

But it is objected to extemporaneous preaching, that if ministers do not *write*, they will not *think*. This objection will have weight with those men whose habit has always been to write down their thoughts. But to a man of different habit, it will have no weight at all.

The mechanical labour of writing is really a hindrance to close and rapid thought. It is true that some extempore preachers have not been men of thought. But so it is true that many men who write sermons are not men of thought. A man whose habits have always been such, that he has thought only when he has put his mind on the end of his pen, will, of course, if he lays aside his pen, at first find it difficult to think; and if he attempts to preach without writing, will, until his habits are thoroughly changed, find it difficult to throw into his sermons the same amount of thought, as if he conformed to his old habit of writing. But it should be remembered that this is only on account of his having been *trained* to write, and having always habituated himself to it. It is the training and habit that render it so difficult for him to think without writing. Will anybody pretend to say that lawyers are not men of thought? That their arguments before a court and jury are not profound and well digested? And yet every one knows that they do not write their speeches.

I have heard much of this objection to extempore preaching ever since I entered the ministry. It was often said to me then, in answer to my views of *extempore* preaching, that ministers who preached extemporaneously would not *instruct* the Churches, that there would be a great deal of *sameness* in their preaching, and they would soon become insipid and repetitious for want of thought. But every year's experience has ripened the conviction on my mind, that the *reverse* of this objection is true. The man who writes least, may, if he pleases, *think most*,[1] and will say what he does think in a manner that will be better understood than if it were written; and that, just in the proportion that he lays aside the labour of writing, his body will be left free to exercise, and his mind to vigorous and consecutive *thought*.

The great reason why it is supposed that *extempore* preachers more frequently repeat the same thoughts in their preaching, is because what they say is, in a general way, more perfectly remembered by the congregation, than if it had been read. I have often known preachers who could repeat their written sermons once in a few months, without the fact being recognised by the congregation. But the *manner* in which extempore sermons are generally delivered is so much more impressive, that the thoughts cannot in general be soon repeated without being remembered. We shall never have a set of men in our halls of legislation, in our courts of justice, and in our pulpits, who are powerful and overwhelming speakers, and can carry the world before them, till our system of education teaches them to *think*, closely, rapidly, consecutively, and till all their habits of speaking in the schools are extemporaneous. The very style of communicating thought, in what is commonly called a good style of writing, is not calculated to leave a deep impression. It is not laconic, direct, pertinent. It is not the language of nature.

In delivering a sermon in this essay style of writing, it is impossible that nearly all the fire of meaning, and power of geture, and looks, and attitude, and emphasis, should not be

---

[1]Finney, therefore, is not to be taken as discounting *preparation* for preaching. In considering his arguments we have to remember that his indignation was aroused by the prevalence of the "literary essay" style, with its deadening effects. On the general question of extemporising we may recall the words of G. W. Hervey: "We are often told that the reading of sermons is unfriendly to revivals. But Payson, Davies, and Edwards were revivalists, of whom the last-named (and most successful) always read from his MS. without a single gesture. Luther, Latimer, Baxter, and Chalmers were at once readers and revivalists." After all, the vital difference is between spiritual life and spiritual death. "Melted by the glorious things which the Word reveals," said Dr. Candlish, "we speak to men who have hearts to feel, if only the heart can be reached."

lost. We can never have the full meaning of the Gospel, till we throw away our written sermons.

3. A minister's course of study and training for his work should be *exclusively theological*.

I mean just as I say. I am not now going to discuss the question whether all education ought not to be theological. But I say education for the ministry should be exclusively so. But you will ask: Should not a minister understand science? I would answer: Yes; the more the better. I would that ministers might understand all science. But it should all be in connection with theology. Studying science is studying the works of God. And studying theology is studying God.

Let a scholar be asked, for instance, this question: "Is there a God?" To answer it, let him ransack the universe, let him go out into every department of science to find the proofs of *design*, and in this way to learn the existence of God. Let him ransack creation to see whether there is such a *unity* of design as evinces that there is *one God*. In like manner, let him inquire concerning the attributes of God, and His character. He will learn science here, but will learn it as a part of theology. Let him search every field of knowledge to bring forward his proofs. What was the design of this plan? What was the end of that arrangement? See whether everything you find in the universe is not calculated to produce happiness, unless perverted.

Would the student's heart get hard and cold in study, as cold and hard as college walls, if science were pursued in this way? Every lesson brings him right up before God, and is, in fact, communion with God, which warms his heart, and makes him more pious, more solemn, more holy. The very distinction between classical and theological study is a curse to the Church, and a curse to the world. The student spends four years in college at *classical* studies, with no God in them; and then three years in the seminary, at *theological* studies; and what then? Poor young man! Set him to work, and you will find that he is not educated *for the ministry* at all. The Church groans under his preaching, because he does not preach with unction, or with power. He has been spoiled in training.

4. We learn what *revival preaching* is. All ministers should be revival ministers, and all preaching should be revival

preaching; that is, it should be calculated to promote holiness. People say: "It is very well to have some men in the Church, who are revival preachers, and who can go about and promote revivals; but then you must have others to *indoctrinate* the Church." Strange! Do they know that a revival indoctrinates the Church faster than anything else? And a minister will never produce a revival if he does not indoctrinate his hearers. The preaching I have described is full of doctrine, but it is doctrine *to be practised*. And that is revival preaching.

5. There are *two objections* sometimes brought against the kind of preaching which I have recommended.

(*a*) That it is *letting down the dignity* of the pulpit to preach in this colloquial, lawyer-like style. They are shocked at it. But it is only on account of its novelty, and not for any impropriety there is in the thing itself. I heard a remark made by a leading layman in regard to the preaching of a certain minister. He said it was the first preaching he had ever heard, that he understood, and the minister was the first he had heard who spoke as if he believed his own doctrine, or meant what he said. The layman further said that when first he heard the minister preach—as if he really meant what he said—he came to the conclusion that such a preacher must be crazy! But, eventually, he was made to see that it was all true, and then he submitted to the truth, as the power of God for the salvation of his soul.

What is the dignity of the pulpit? What an idea, to see a minister go into the pulpit to sustain its dignity! Alas, alas! During my foreign tour, I heard an English missionary preach exactly in that way. I believe he was a good man, and out of the pulpit he would talk like a man who meant what he said. But no sooner was he in the pulpit than he appeared like a perfect automaton—swelling, mouthing, and singing, enough to put all the people to sleep. And the difficulty seemed to be that he wanted to maintain the *dignity of the pulpit*.

(*b*) It is objected that this preaching is *theatrical*. The Bishop of London once asked Garrick, the celebrated actor, why it was that actors, in representing a mere fiction, should move an assembly, even to tears, while ministers, in representing the most solemn realities, could scarcely obtain a hearing. The philosophical Garrick well replied: "It is because we represent fiction as reality, and you represent reality as a fiction."[1] This is telling the whole story. Now, what is the design of the actor in a threatical representation? It is so to throw himself into the spirit and meaning of the writer, as to adopt his sentiments, and make them his own: to feel them, embody them, throw them out upon the audience as a living reality.

Now, what is the objection to all this in preaching? The actor suits the action to the word, and the word to the action. His looks, his hands, his attitudes, and everything, are designed to express the *full meaning* of the writer. Now, this should be the aim of the preacher. And if by "theatrical" be meant the strongest possible representation of the sentiments expressed, then the more theatrical the sermon is, the better. And if ministers are too stiff, and the people too fastidious, to learn even from an actor, or from the stage, the best method of swaying mind, of enforcing sentiment, and diffusing the warmth of burning thought over a congregation, then they must go on with their prosing, and reading, and sanctimonious starch. But let them remember, that while they are thus turning away and decrying the art of the actor, and attempting to support the "dignity of the pulpit," the theatres can be thronged every night. The common sense of the people *will* be entertained with that manner of speaking, and sinners will go down to hell.

6. A congregation may learn *how to choose a minister*. When a vacant Church is looking out for a minister, there are two leading points on which attention is commonly fixed. (1) That he should be *popular*. (2) That he should be *learned*. These are very well. But the point that should be the first in their inquiries is: "Is he wise to win souls?" No matter how eloquent a minister is, or how learned, no matter how pleasing and how popular are his manners, if it is a matter of fact that sinners are not converted under his preaching, it shows that he has not *this* wisdom, and your children and neighbours will go down to hell under his preaching.

---

[1]On the other hand, Garrick said of Romaine: "He has the *hears*, as well as the art, of preaching."

I am happy to know that many Churches *will* ask this question about ministers, and if they find that a minister is destitute of this vital quality, they will not have him. And if ministers can be found who *are* wise to win souls, the Churches *will have* such ministers. It is in vain to contend against it, or to pretend that they are not well educated, or not learned, or the like. It is in vain for the schools to try to force down the throats of the Churches a race of ministers who are learned in everything but what they most need to know.

It is very difficult to say what needs to be said on this subject, without being in danger of begetting a wrong spirit in the Church towards ministers. Many professors of religion are ready to find fault with ministers when they have no reason; insomuch, that it becomes very difficult to say of ministers what is true, and what needs to be said, without one's remarks being perverted and abused by this class of professors. I would not, for the world, say anything to injure the influence of a minister of Christ, who is really endeavouring to do good. But, to tell the truth will not injure the influence of those ministers who, by their lives and preaching, give evidence to the Church that their object is to do good, and win souls for Christ. *This* class of ministers will recognise the truth of all that I have said, or wish to say. They see it all and deplore it. But if there be ministers who are doing no good, who are feeding themselves and not the flock, such ministers *deserve* no influence. If they are doing no good, it is time for them to betake themselves to some other profession. They are but leeches on the very vitals of the Church, sucking out its heart's blood. They are useless and worse than useless. And the sooner they are laid aside and their places filled with those who will *exert* themselves for Christ, the better.

Finally. It is the duty of the Church to pray for us, ministers. Not one of us is such as he ought to be. Like Paul, we can say: "Who is sufficient for these things?" (2 Cor. 2. 16.) But who among us is like Paul? Where will you find such ministers as Paul? They are not here. We have been wrongly educated, all of us. Pray for the schools, and colleges, and seminiaries. And pray for young men who are preparing for the ministry. Pray for ministers, that God would give them this wisdom to win souls. And pray that God would bestow upon the Church the wisdom and the means to educate a generation of ministers who will go forward and convert the world. The church must *travail* in prayer, and groan and agonise for this. This is now the pearl of price to the Church—to have a supply of the *right sort* of ministers. The coming of the millennium depends on having a different sort of ministers, who are more thoroughly educated *for their work*. And this we shall have so sure as the promise of the Lord holds good. Such a ministry as is now in the Church will never convert the world, but the world *is to be* converted, and therefore God intends to have ministers who will do it. "Pray ye therefore the Lord of the harvest, that He would send forth labourers into His harvest" (Luke 10. 2).

LECTURE XIII

HOW CHURCHES CAN HELP MINISTERS

> And it came to pass, when Moses held up his hand, that Israel
> prevailed: and when he let down his hand, Amalek prevailed. But
> Moses' hands were heavy; and they took a stone, and put it under him,
> and he sat thereon; and Aaron and Hur stayed up his hands, the one
> on the one side, and the other on the other side; and his hands were
> steady until the going down of the sun. And Joshua discomfited
> Amalek and his people with the edge of the sword.—Exod. 17. 11-13.

You who read your Bibles will recollect the connection in
which these verses stand. The people of God, in subduing their
enemies, came to battle against the Amalekites, and these
incidents took place. It is difficult to conceive why importance
should be attached to the circumstance of Moses holding up his
hands, unless the expression is understood to denote the
attitude of prayer. But then his holding up his hands, and the
success attending it, will teach us the importance of prayer to
God, for His aid in all our conflicts with His enemies. The co-
operation and support of Aaron and Hur have been generally
understood to represent the duty of Churches to sustain and
assist ministers in their work, and the importance of this co-
operation to the success of the preached Gospel. I shall make
this use of it on the present occasion. As I have spoken of the
duty of ministers to labour for revivals, I shall now consider
the importance of the co-operation of the Church in producing

and carrying on a revival.

There are various things, the importance of which in promoting a revival have not been duly considered by Churches or ministers—things which, if not attended to, will make it impossible that revivals should extend, or even continue for any considerable time. In my last two Lectures, I have been dwelling on the duties of ministers, for it was impossible for me to deliver a course of lectures on revivals, without entering more or less extensively into that department of means. I have not done with that part of the subject, but have thought it important here to step aside and discuss some points, in which the members of the Church must stand by and aid the minister, if they expect to enjoy a revival. In discussing the subject, I propose to mention: 1. Several things which Christians must *avoid*, if they would support ministers. II. Some things to which they must *attend*.

I. *THINGS THAT MUST BE AVOIDED.*

1. By all means keep clear of the idea, both in theory and practice, that *a minister alone is to promote revivals*. Many professing Christians are inclined to take a passive attitude on this subject, and feel as if they had nothing to do. They have employed a minister, and paid him to feed them with instruction and comfort, and now they have nothing to do but to sit and swallow the food he gives. They are to pay his salary and attend on his preaching—and they think that is doing a great deal. And he, on his part, is expected to preach good, sound, *comfortable* doctrine, to bolster them up, and make them feel comfortable. So, they expect to go to heaven. I tell you THEY WILL GO TO HELL if this is their religion! That is not the way to heaven!

Rest assured that where this spirit prevails in the Church, however good the minister may be, the Church has taken the course to prevent a revival. Be the minister ever so faithful, ever so devoted, ever so talented and eloquent, though he may wear himself out, and perhaps destroy his life, he will have little or no revival.

Where there are very few members, or none, a revival may be promoted without any organised effort of the Church, because there is no Church to organise; and in such a case, God accommodates His grace to the circumstances, as He did when the apostles went out, single-handed, to plant the Gospel in the world. I have seen instances of powerful revivals where such was the case. But where there are means, God will have them used. I had rather have no Church in a place, than attempt to promote a revival in a place where there is a Church which will not work. God will be inquired of by His people, to bestow His blessings. The counteracting influence of a Church that will not work, is worse than infidelity. There is no possibility of occupying neutral ground, in regard to a revival, though some professors imagine they are neutral. If a professor will not give himself to the work, he opposes it. Let such a one attempt to take middle ground, and say he is "going to wait and see how affairs shape"—why, that is the very ground the devil wants him to take. Professors can in this way do his work a great deal more effectually than by open opposition. If they should take open ground in opposition, everybody will say they have no religion. But, by taking this middle course they retain their influence, and thus do the devil's work more effectually.

In employing ministers Churches must remember that they have only employed *leaders* to lead them on to action in the cause of Christ. People would think it strange if any country should propose to support a general, and then let him go and fight alone! This is no more absurd, or destructive, than for a minister to attempt to go forward alone. The Church misconceives the design of the ministry, if the minister is left to work alone. It is not enough that they should hear his sermons. That is only the word of command, which the Church is bound to follow.

2. Do not *complain of your minister* because there is no revival, if you are *not doing your duty*, for if you are not doing your duty, *that alone* is a sufficient reason why there should be no revival. It is a most cruel and abominable thing for Church members to complain of their minister, when they themselves are fast asleep. It is very common for professors of religion to take great credit to themselves, and quiet their own consciences, by complaining of their ministers. And when the importance of ministers being awake is spoken of, such people are always ready to say: "We never shall have a revival with

such a minister"; when the fact is that their minister is much more awake than they are themselves.

Another thing is true in regard to this point, and worthy of notice. When the Church is sunk down in a low state, professors of religion are very apt to complain of the *Church*, and of the low state of religion. That intangible and irresponsible being, the "Church," is greatly complained of by them, for being asleep. Their complaints of the low state of religion, and of the coldness of the Church or of the minister, are poured out dolefully, without any seeming realisation that the Church is composed of individuals, and that until each one will take *his own* case in hand, complain of *himself*, and humble himself before God, and repent, and wake up, the Church can never have any efficiency, and there never can be a revival. If, instead of complaining of your minister, or of the Church, you would wake up as individuals, and not complain of him or them until you can say you are pure from the blood of all men, and are doing your duty to save sinners, the minister would be apt to feel the justice of your complaints, and if he would not, God would either wake him up or remove him.

3. Do not let your minister *kill himself* by attempting to *carry on the work alone*, while you refuse to help him. It sometimes happens that a minister finds the ark of the Lord will not move unless he lays out his utmost strength, and he has been so desirous of a revival that he has done this, and has died. And he was willing to die for it. I could mention cases in which ministers have died in consequence of their labours to promote a revival where the Church hung back from the work.

A minister, some years since, was labouring where there was a revival; and was visited by an elder of a Church at some distance, who wanted him to go and preach there. There was no revival there, and never had been. The elder complained about their state, and said they had had two excellent ministers, one of whom had worn himself completely out, and died; and the other had exhausted himself, grown discouraged, and left them. They were a poor and feeble Church, and their prospects very dark, unless they could have a revival, and so he begged this minister to go and help them.

The minister at last replied by asking: "Why did you never have a revival?" "I do not know," said the elder; "our minister laboured very hard, but the Church did not seem to wake up, and somehow there seemed to be no revival." "Well, now," said the minister, "I see what you want; you have killed one of God's ministers, and broke down another so that he had to leave you; and now you want to get another there and kill *him*; and the devil has sent you here to get me to go and rock your cradle for you. You had one good minister to preach for you, but you slept on, and he exerted himself till he absolutely died in the work. Then the Lord let you have another, and still you lay and slept, and would not wake up to your duty. And now you have come here in despair, and want another minister, do you? God forbid that you should ever have another while you do as you have done. God forbid that you should ever have a minister till the Church will wake up to duty."

The elder was affected, for he was a good man. The tears came into his eyes, and he said it was no more than they deserved. "And now," said the minister, "will you be faithful, and go home and tell the Church what I say? If you will, and they will be faithful, and wake up to duty, they shall have a minister, I will warrant them that." The elder said he would, and he was true to his word; he went home and told the members how cruel it was for them to ask for another minister to come among them, unless they would wake up. They felt it, and confessed their sins, and wakened up to duty, and a minister was sent to them, and a precious and powerful revival followed.

Churches do not realise how often their coldness and backwardness may be absolutely the cause of the death of ministers. The state of the people, and of sinners, rests upon their mind; they travail in soul night and day; and they labour in season and out of season, beyond the power of the human constitution to bear, till they wear out and die. The Church knows not the agony of a minister's heart, when he travails for souls, and labours to wake up the members to help, but still sees them in the slumber of death. Perhaps they will sometimes rouse up to spasmodic effort for a few days, and then all is cold again. And so many a faithful minister wears himself out and dies, and then these heartless professors are the first to blame him for doing *so much*.

I recollect a case of a good minister, who went to a place

where there was a revival, and while there heard a pointed sermon to ministers. He received it like a man of God; he did not rebel against God's truth, but he promised God that he never would rest until he saw a revival among his people. He returned home and went to work; the Church would not wake up, except a few members, and the Lord blessed *them*, and poured out His Spirit; but the minister laid himself down on his bed and died, in the midst of the revival.

4. Be careful not to complain of plain, pointed preaching, *even when its reproofs fasten on yourselves*. Churches are apt to forget that a minister is responsible only to God. They want to make rules for a minister to preach by, so as to have his discourses *fit them*. If he bears down upon the Church, and exposes the sins that prevail among the people, they call it "personal," and rebel against the truth. Or they say: "He should not preach so plainly to the Church *before the world*, for it exposes religion; he ought to take members by themselves and preach to the Church alone, and not tell sinners how bad Christians are." But there are cases where a minister can do no less than show the house of Jacob their sins. If you ask: "Why not do it when we are by ourselves?" I answer: "Just as if sinners do not know you do wrong! I will preach to you by yourselves, about your sins, when you will get together by yourselves to sin. But as the Lord liveth, if you sin before the world, you shall be rebuked before the world. It is not a fact that sinners do know how you live, and that they stumble over you into hell? Then do not blame ministers, when they see it to be their duty to rebuke the Church openly, before the world. If you are so proud that you cannot bear this, you need not expect a revival. Do not call the preaching 'too plain,' simply because it exposes the faults of the Church. There is no such thing as preaching too plainly."

5. Sometimes professors take alarm lest the minister should *offend the ungodly* by plain preaching. And they will begin to caution him against it, and ask him if he had not better alter a little so as to avoid giving offence, and the like. This fear is specially excited if some of the more wealthy and influential members of the congregation are offended, lest they should withdraw their support, no longer give their money to help to pay the minister's salary, and so cause the burden to come the

heavier on the Church. They can never have a revival in such a Church. Why, the Church ought to pray, above all things, that the truth may come on the ungodly like fire. What if they *are* offended? Christ can get along very well without their money. Do not blame your minister, or ask him to change his mode of preaching so as to please and conciliate the ungodly. It is of no use for a minister to preach to the impenitent, unless he can preach the truth to them. And it will do no good for *them* to pay for the support of the Gospel, unless it is preached in such a way that they may be searched and saved.

Sometimes Church members will talk among themselves about the minister's imprudence, and create a party, and get into a very wrong spirit, because the wicked are displeased. There was a place where there was a powerful revival, and great opposition. The Church became alarmed, for fear that if the minister was not less plain and pointed, some of the impenitent would go and join some other congregation. And so one of the leading men in the Church was appointed to go to the minister, and ask him not to preach quite so hard, for, if he continued to do so, such-and-such persons would leave the congregation. The minister asked: "Is not the preaching true?" "Yes." "Does not God bless it?" "Yes." "Did you ever see the like of this work before in this place?" "No, I never did." "Then, 'get thee behind me, Satan.' You have come upon the devil's errand! You see God is blessing the preaching, the work is going on, and sinners are converted every day; and now you come to get me to let down the tone of preaching, so as to ease the minds of the ungodly." The man felt the rebuke, and took it like a Christian; he saw his error and submitted, and never again was heard to find fault with plainness in preaching.

In another town where there was a revival, a woman who had some influence (not pious) complained very much about "plain, pointed, personal preaching,' as she called it. But, by and by, she herself became a subject of the work. After this some of her impenitent friends reminded her of what she used to say against the preacher for "preaching so hot." She said her views were altered now, and she did not care how hot the truth was preached; not even if it was *red hot!*

6. *Do not take part with the wicked in any way*. If you do it at all, you will strengthen their hands. If the wicked should

accuse the minister of being imprudent or personal; and if the Church members, without admitting that the minister is so, should merely agree that "personal preaching is wrong," and talk about "the impropriety of personal preaching," the wicked would feel themselves strengthened by such remarks. Do not unite with them at all, for they will feel that they have you on their side against the minister; you adopt their principles, use their language, and are understood as sympathising with them. What *is* personal preaching? No individual is ever benefited by preaching until he is made to feel that it means *him*. Such preaching is always personal. It often appears so personal to wicked men that they feel as if they were just going to be called out by name before the congregation. A minister was once preaching to a congregation, and, when describing certain characters, he said: "If I were omniscient, I could call out by name the very persons that answer to this picture." A man cried out: "Name me!" And he looked as if he were going to sink into the earth. He afterwards said that he had no idea of speaking out; but the minister described him so perfectly that he really thought he was going to call him by name. The minister did not actually know that there was such a man. It is common for men to think their own conduct is described, and they complain: "Who has been telling him about me? Somebody has been talking to him about me, and getting him to preach to me!" I suppose I have heard of five hundred or a thousand just such cases. Now, if the Church members will admit that it is *wrong* for a minister to *mean* anybody in his preaching, how can he do any good? If you be not willing your minister should mean anybody, or preach to anybody, you had better dismiss him. To whom must he preach, if not to the persons, the individuals before him? And how can he preach to them, when he does not mean them?

7. If you wish to stand by your minister in promoting a revival, do not, *by your lives contradict* his preaching. If he preaches that sinners are going to hell, do not give the lie to it, and smile it all away, by your levity and unconcern. I have heard sinners speak of the effect produced on the minds by levity in Christians after a solemn and searching discourse. *They* feel solemn and tender, and begin to feel alarmed at their

condition; and they see these professors, instead of weeping over them, all light and easy: as much as to say: "Do not be afraid, sinners, it is not so bad, after all; keep cool and you will do well; do you think we would laugh and joke if you were going to hell of fast? We would not laugh if only your house were on fire; still less if we saw you burning in it!" Of what use is it for a minister to preach to sinners in such a state of things?

8. Do not *needlessly take up the time* of your minister. Ministers often lose a great deal of time by individuals calling on them, to talk, when they have nothing of importance to talk about, and have come on no particular errand. The minister, of course, is glad to see his friends, and often too willing to spend time in conversation with his people, as he loves and esteems them. Professors of religion should remember, however, that a minister's time is worth more than gold, for it can be employed in that which gold can never buy. If the minister be kept from his knees, or from his Bible, or from his study, that they may indulge themselves in his conversation, they do a great injury. When you have a *good reason* for it, you should never be backward to call upon him, and even take up all the time that is necessary. But if you have nothing in particular to say that is important, keep away.

9. Be sure not to sanction anything that is calculated to *divert public attention* from the subject of religion. Often, when it comes the time of year to work, when the evenings are long, and business is light, and the very time to make an extra effort; at this moment somebody in the Church will "give a party," and invite some Christian friends, so as to have it a *religious* party. And then some other family must do the same, to return the compliment. Then another, and another, till it grows into an organised system of parties that consumes the whole winter. Abominable! This is the grand device of the devil, because it appears so innocent, and so proper, to promote good feeling, and increase the acquaintance of Christians with each other. And so, instead of prayer-meetings, they will have these parties.

The evils of these parties are very great. They are often got up at great expense; and the most abominable gluttony is practised in them.[1] I have been told that in some instances

---

[1]John Angell James wrote similarly, a few years later, in

professed Christians have made great entertainments, and excused the ungodly prodigality in the use of Jesus Christ's money, by giving what was left, after the feast was ended, *to the poor!* Thus making it a virtue to feast and riot, even to surfeiting, on the bounties of God's providence, under pretence of benefiting the poor. This is the same in principle with a splendid ball which was given some years ago, in a neighbouring city. The ball was got up for the benefit of the poor, and each gentleman was to pay a certain sum, and after the ball was ended, whatever remained of the funds thus raised, was to be given to the poor. Truly this is strange charity: to eat, and drink, and dance, and when they have rioted and feasted until they can enjoy it no longer, they deal out to the poor the crumbs that have fallen from the table. I do not see, however, why such a ball is not quite as pious as such Christian parties. The evil of balls does not consist simply in the exercise of dancing, but in the dissipation, and surfeiting, and temptations connected with them.

But it is said they are *Christian* parties, and that they are all, or nearly all, professors of religion, who attend them. And furthermore, that they are concluded, often, with prayer. Now

---

referring more especially to dinner-parties in England: "It may be seriously questioned whether, among professing Christians, the propensity for entertainments has not ripened into something like a passion for worldly pleasures. Dinner-parties, among the wealthier classes of professors, have become frequent and expensive; viands the most costly, and wines the most various, are set forth with a profusion which proves at what an outlay the entertainment has been served up to gratify the vanity of the host and the palate of his guests" (see "The Church in Earnest"). James also quotes an experience of Thomas Scott, the commentator, who, attending "a large party at the house of an opulent tradesman, suggested that, as regards Christians, such expensive dinners should be exchanged for more frugal entertainments and for the better feeding of the poor, the maimed, and the blind." Scott's remarks were warmly disapproved, but he went home "as one who had thrown a great burden from his back." He found himself under a sort of tacit excommunication from that worldly circle. The opulent tradesman, however, accepted the rebuke to this extent: he invited Scott once again and treated him to the simplicity of one dish only, a piece of boiled beef.

I regard this as one of the worst features about them; that after the waste of time and money, the excess in eating and drinking, the vain conversation, and nameless *fooleries*, with which such a season is filled up, an attempt should be made to sanctify it, and palm it off upon God, by concluding it with prayer. Say what you will, it would not be more absurd or incongruous, or impious, to close a ball, or a theatrical performance, or a card party with prayer.

Has it come to this; that professors of religion (who profess to desire the salvation of the world), when calls are made upon them from the four winds of heaven, to send the Gospel, to furnish Bibles, and tracts, and missionaries, to save the world from death, should waste large sums of money in an evening, and then go to the Missionary Meeting and pray for the heathen?

In some instances, I have been told, they find a salve for their consciences in the fact that their *minister* attends their parties. This, of course, would give weight to such an example; for if one professor of religion made a party and invited the minister, others would do the same. The next step they take may be for each to give a ball, and appoint their minister a manager! Why not? And perhaps, by and by, he will do them the favour to play the fiddle. In my estimation he might quite as well do it, as go and conclude such a party with prayer. I should advise any congregation that is calculating to have a circle of parties, in the meantime to dismiss their minister, and let *him* go and preach where the people would be ready to receive the Word and profit by it, rather than have him stay and be grieved, and killed, by attempting to promote religion among them, while they are engaged, heart and hand, in the service of the devil.

Professors of religion should never arrange anything that *may* divert public attention from religion, without having first consulted their minister, and made it a subject of special prayer. And if they find it will have an adverse effect, they ought never to do it. Subjects will often come up before the public which have this tendency; some course of Lectures, some show, or the like. Professors ought to be wise, and understand what they are about, and not give countenance to any such thing until they see what influence it will have, and whether it will hinder a revival. If it will do that, let them have nothing to do with it. Every such thing should be estimated by its bearing upon Christ's Kingdom.

II. *SEVERAL THINGS WHICH CHURCHES MUST DO.*

That is to say, things which they must do if they would promote a revival and aid their minister.

1. They must attend to his *temporal wants*. A minister who gives himself wholly to his work cannot be engaged in worldly employments, and *of course* is entirely dependent on his people for the supply of his temporal wants, including the support of his family. I need not argue this point here, for you all understand this perfectly. It is the command of God, that "they which preach the Gospel should live of the Gospel" (1 Cor. 9. 14). But now look around and see how many Churches do in this matter. For instance, when they want a minister, they will cast about and see *how cheaply* they can get one. They will calculate to a farthing how much his salt will cost, and how much his flour, and then set his salary so low as to subject him to extreme inconvenience to pay his way and keep his family. A minister must have his mind at ease, to study and labour with effect, and he cannot screw down prices, and barter, and look out for the best chances to buy to advantage what he needs. If he be obliged to do this, his mind is embarrassed. Unless his temporal wants are so supplied, that his thoughts may be abstracted from them, how can he do his duty?

2. *Be honest with your minister.* Do not measure out and calculate with how much salt and how many bushels of grain he can possibly get along. Remember, you are dealing with Christ, and He calls you to place His ministers in such a situation, that, with ordinary prudence, temporal embarrassment may be out of the question.

3. *Be punctual with him.* Sometimes Churches, when they are about to welcome a minister, have a great deal of pride about giving a salary, and they will get up a subscription list, and make out, in the total, an amount which they never do pay, and very likely never expected to pay. And so, after one, two, three, or four years, the society gets three or four hundred dollars in debt to the minister, and then they expect him to forego it. And all the while they wonder why there is no

revival! This may be the very reason—because the Church has LIED. They have faithfully promised to pay so much, and have not done it. God cannot consistently pour out His Spirit on such a Church.

4. *Pay him his salary without being asked*. Nothing is so embarrassing to a minister as to be obliged to *dun* his people for his salary. Often he creates enemies and gives offence by being obliged to call, and call, for his money—even then not getting it as he was promised. They would have paid it if their *credit* had been at stake; but when it is nothing but *conscience* and the blessing of God, they "let it lie along." If any one of them had a note due at the bank, you would see him careful and prompt to be on the ground before three o'clock, lest he should lose his character. But they know the minister will not *sue* them for his salary, so they are careless, and then let it run into arrears, and he must suffer the inconvenience. This is not so common in the city as it is in the country. But in the country I have known some heartrending cases of distress and misery, by the negligence and cruelty of congregations in *withholding* that which was due. Churches live in habitual lying and cheating, and then wonder why they have no revival. How can they wonder?

5. *Pray for your minister*. Even the apostles used to urge the Churches to pray for them. This is more important than you imagine. Ministers do not ask people to pray for them simply as men, nor that they may be filled with an abundance of the Spirit's influences, merely to promote their own personal enjoyment. But they know that unless the Church greatly desires a blessing upon the labours of a minister, it is tempting God for him to expect it. How often does a minister go into his pulpit, feeling that his heart is ready to break for the blessing of God, while he also feels that there is no room to expect it, for there is no reason to believe that the Church desires it! Perhaps he has been for hours on his knees in supplication, and yet, because the Church does not desire a blessing, he feels as if his words would bound back in his face.

I have seen Christians who would be in an agony, when the minister was going into the pulpit, for fear his mind should be in a cloud, or his heart cold, or he should have no unction, and so a blessing should not come. I have laboured with a man of this sort. He would pray until he got an assurance in his mind that God would be with me in preaching, and sometimes he would pray himself ill. I have known the time when he has been in darkness for a season, while the people were gathering, and his mind was full of anxiety, and he would go again and again to pray, till finally he would come into the room with a placid face, and say: "The Lord has come, and He will be with us." And I do not know that I ever found him mistaken.[1]

I have known a Church bear up their minister in prayer from day to day, and watch with anxiety unutterable, to see that he had the Holy Ghost with him in his labours! When Christians feel and pray thus, oh, what feelings and what looks are manifest in the congregation! They have felt anxiety unutterable to have the Word come with power and take effect; and when they see their prayer answered, and when they hear a word or a sentence come WARM from the heart, taking effect among the people, you can see their whole souls look out of their eyes! How different is the case where the Christians feel that the *minister* is praying, and so there is no need for *them* to do so. They are mistaken. The Church must desire and pray for the blessing. God says He will be inquired of *by the house of Israel*. I wish you to feel that there can be no substitute for this.

I have seen cases in revivals, where the Church was kept in the background in regard to prayer, and persons from abroad were called on to pray in all the meetings. This is always unhappy, even if there should be a revival, for the revival must

---

[1]Undoubtedly this is another reference to "Father" Nash (see footnote, p. 91), who delighted to accompany Finney upon revival campaigns. In the revival at Gouverneur (in which the great majority of the inhabitants, Finney believed, were converted), Nash rose very early and went into a wood to pray. "It was one of those clear mornings," said Finney, "on which it is possible to hear sounds at a great distance." Three-quarters of a mile away lived an unconverted man who was at this time out of doors and who was suddenly arrested by hearing the voice of prayer. He could distinguish that it was Nash's voice, and this brought to him such a sense of the reality of religion as he had never before experienced; he experienced no relief until he found it in Christ.

be less powerful and less salutary in its influences upon the Church. I do not know but that I have sometimes offended Christians and ministers from other places, by continuing to call on members of the Church to pray, and not on visitors. It was not from any disrespect, but because the object was to get *that Church* which was chiefly concerned, to desire, and pray, and agonise for a blessing.

In a certain place, a "protracted meeting" was held, with no good results; but, on the contrary, great evils were produced. I was led to make inquiry for the reason, and it came out that throughout their meetings not one member of their own Church was called on to pray, but all the prayers were made by persons from elsewhere. No wonder there was no good done. The leader of the meeting meant well, but he undertook to promote a revival without getting the Church into the work. He let a lazy Church lie still and do nothing, and so there could be no good result.

Churches should pray for ministers as the agents for breaking down sinners with the word of truth. Prayer for a minister is often made in a set and formal way, and confined to the prayer-meetings. They will *say* their prayers in the old way, as they have always done: "Lord, bless Thy ministering servant whom Thou hast stationed on this part of Zion's walls!" and so on; and it amounts to nothing, because there is no heart in it. The fact often is that they never thought of praying for him in secret; they never have agonised in private for a blessing on his labours. They may not omit it wholly in their meetings, for if they do *that*, it becomes evident that they care very little indeed about the labours of their minister. But that is not the most important place. The way to present *effectual* prayer for your minister is, when you are in secret, to wrestle with God for success to attend his labours.

I knew a case of a minister in ill-health, who became depressed and cast down in his mind, and was very much in darkness, so that he did not feel as if he could preach any longer. An individual of the Church was awakened to feel for the minister in such a situation, and to pray that he might have the Holy Ghost to attend his preaching. One Sabbath morning, this person's mind was very much exercised, so that he began to pray as soon as it was light, and prayed again and again for a blessing *that day*. And the Lord in some way directed the minister within hearing of his prayer. The person was telling the Lord just what he thought of the minister's situation and state of mind, and pleading, as if he would not be denied, for a blessing. The minister went into the pulpit and preached, and the light broke in upon him, and the Word was with power, and a revival commenced that very day.

6. A minister should be provided for *by the Church*, and his support guaranteed, *irrespective of the ungodly*. Otherwise he may be obliged either to starve his family, or to keep back a part of the truth so as not to offend sinners. I once expostulated with a minister whom I found was afraid to come out fully with the truth. I told him I was surprised he did not bear upon certain points. He told me he was so situated that he *must* please certain men, who would be touched thereby. It was the ungodly that chiefly supported him, and this made him dependent and temporising. And yet perhaps that very Church which left the minister dependent on the ungodly for his bread, would turn round and abuse him for his want of faith, and his fear of men. The Church ought always to say to the minister: "We will support you; go to work; let the truth pour down on the people, and we will stand by you."

7. See that everything is so arranged that people can sit *comfortably* in the meeting. If people do not sit in ease, it is difficult to get or to keep their attention. And if they are not attentive, they cannot be converted. They have come to hear for their lives, and they ought to be so situated that they can hear with all their souls, and have nothing in their bodily position to call for attention. Churches do not realise how important it is that the place of meeting should be made comfortable. I do not mean *showy*. All your glare and glory of rich chandeliers, and rich carpets, and splendid pulpits, make for the opposite extreme, taking off the attention just as effectually, and defeating every object for which a sinner should come to a meeting. You need not expect a revival *there*.

8. See that the house of God is kept *clean*. The house of God should be kept as clean as you want your own house to be kept. Churches are often kept excessively slovenly. I have seen them where people used so much tobacco, and took so little care about neatness, that it was impossible to preach with comfort.

Once, in a protracted meeting, the thing was charged upon the Church (and they had to acknowledge it), that they paid more money for tobacco than they did for the cause of Missions. There is an importance in these things, which is not realised. See that man! What is he doing? I am preaching to him about eternal life, and he is thinking about the dirty pew.

9. It is important that the house should be *just warm enough*, but not too warm. Suppose a minister comes into a house and finds it cold; he sees, as soon as he gets in, that he might as well have stayed at home; the people are shivering, their feet are chilled, and they feel as if they should take cold; and the minister wishes he were at home, for he knows he cannot do anything; but he must preach, or the congregation will be disappointed.

Or, he may find the house too warm, and the people, instead of listening to the truth, are fanning themselves and panting for breath. By and by a woman faints, and makes a stir, and the train of thought and feeling is all lost, and so a whole sermon is wasted. These little things take off the attention of people from the words of eternal life. And very often it is so, that if you drop a single link in the chain of argument, you lose the whole, and the people are damned, just because the careless Church does not see to the proper regulation of these little matters.

10. The house should be *well ventilated*. Of all houses, a church shoud be the most perfectly ventilated. If there be no change of the air, it passes through so many lungs that it becomes bad; its vitality is exhausted, and the people pant, they know not why, and feel an almost irresistible desire to sleep; the minister preaches in vain; the sermon is lost, and worse than lost. I have often wondered that this matter should be so little the subject of thought. The elders and officials will sit and hear a whole sermon, while the people are all but ready to die for the want of air, and the minister is wasting his strength in preaching where the room is just like an exhausted receiver; there they sit and never think to do anything in the matter. They should take it upon themselves to see that this is regulated rightly; that the house is just warm enough, and the air kept pure. How important it is that they should be awake on this subject; that the minister may labour to the best

advantage, and the people give their undivided attention to the truth which is to save their souls.

It is very common, when things are wrong, to have it all laid to the sexton, or caretaker. Often, however, the sexton is not to blame. If the building is cold and uncomfortable, very often it is because the fuel is not good, or the stoves not suitable, or the place is so open it cannot be warmed. If it is warm, perhaps somebody has intermeddled, and heaped on fuel without discretion. Or, if the sexton is in fault, perhaps it is because the Church does not pay him enough for his services, and he cannot afford to give the attention necessary to keep the place in order. Churches sometimes screw down the sexton's salary to the lowest point, so that he is obliged to slight his work. Or they will select one who is incompetent, for the sake of getting him cheap. Let an adequate payment be made for the work, and it can be done, and done faithfully. If one sexton will not do it rightly, another will, and the Church must see that it is done aright. What economy! To pay a minister's salary, and then, for the want of a small sum added to the sexton's wages, everything is so out of order that the minister's labours are all lost, souls are lost, and your children and neighbours go down to hell!

Sometimes this uncleanliness, and negligence, and confusion, are chargeable to the minister. Perhaps he uses tobacco, and sets the example of defiling the house of God. Perhaps the pulpit will be the filthiest place in the house. I have sometimes been in pulpits that were too loathsome to be occupied by human beings. If a minister has no more piety and decency than this, no wonder things are "at loose ends" in the congregation. And generally it is even so.

11. People should leave their *very young* children *at home*. I have often known children to cry just at that stage of the services that would most effectually destroy the effect of the meeting. If children weep, they should *instantly* be removed. I have sometimes known a mother, or a nurse, sit and toss her child, while its cries were diverting the attention of the whole congregation.

12. The members of the Church should aid the minister by *visiting from house to house*, and trying to save souls. Do not leave all this to the minister. It is impossible he should do it,

even if he were to give all his time, and neglect his study and private prayer. Church members should take pains and qualify themselves for this duty, so that they can be useful in it.

13. They should hold *Bible classes*. Suitable individuals should be selected to hold Bible classes, for the instruction of the young people, and where those who are awakened or affected by the preaching, can be received and be converted. As soon as persons are seen to be touched, let them be invited to join the Bible class, where they will be properly treated, and probably they will be converted. The Church should select the best men for this service, and should all be on the look out to fill up the Bible classes. It has been done in this congregation. It is a very common thing when persons are impressed, that they are observed by somebody, and invited to join the Bible class. They accept the invitation, and there they are converted. We want more teachers, able and willing to take charge of such classes.

14. Churches should sustain *Sabbath Schools*, and in this way aid their minister in saving souls. How can a minister attend to this and preach? Unless the Church will take off these responsibilities, and cares, and labours, he must either neglect them, or be crushed. Let the members be WIDE AWAKE, let them watch and bring in children to the school, teach them faithfully, and lay themselves out to promote a revival in the school.

15. They should *watch over the members of the Church*. They should visit each other, in order to stir each other up, know each other's spiritual state, and "consider one another to provoke unto love and to good works" (Heb. 10. 24). The minister cannot do it, he has not time; it is impossible he should study and prepare sermons, and at the same time visit all the members of the Church as often as is necessary to keep them advancing. The members are bound to watch over each other's spiritual welfare. But how is this done? Many do not know one another. They meet and pass as strangers, and never ask about one another's spiritual condition. But if they hear anything bad of one, they go and tell it to others. Instead of watching over them for their good, they watch for their halting. How can they watch for good when they are not even acquainted with each other?

16. The Church should *watch for the effect of preaching*. If the members are *praying* for the success of the preached Word, they will watch for it, of course. They should keep a look-out, and when any in the congregation give evidence that the Word of God has taken hold of them, they should follow it up. Wherever there are any exhibitions of feeling, those persons should be attended to, instantly, and not left till their impressions wear off. They should be spoken to, or visited, or got into the anxious meeting, or into the Bible class, or brought to the minister. If the members do not attend to this, they neglect their duty. If they attend to it, they may do incalculable good.

There was a pious young woman, who lived in a very cold and wicked place. She alone had the spirit of prayer, and she had been praying for a blessing upon the Word. At length she saw an individual in the congregation who seemed to be affected by the preaching, and as soon as the minister came from the pulpit, she came forward, agitated and trembling, and begged him to go and converse with the person immediately. He did so, the individual was soon converted, and a revival followed. Now, one of your stupid professors would not have seen that that individual was awakened, but would have stumbled over half a dozen such without noticing. Professors should watch every sermon, and see how it affects the congregation. I do not mean that they should be stretching their necks and staring about the house; but they should observe, as they may, and if they find any person affected by preaching, they should put themselves in his way, and guide him to the Saviour.

17. Beware, and do *not give away all the preaching* to others. If you do not take your portion, you will starve, and become like spiritual skeletons. Christians should take their portion to themselves. Though the sermon should be quite searching to them, they should still make the honest application, lay it alongside their heart, and practise it, and live by it. Otherwise, the preaching will do *them* no good.

18. Be ready to aid your minister in carrying out *his plans for doing good*. When the minister is wise to devise plans for usefulness, and the Church ready to execute them, they may carry all before them. But when the members hang back from

every enterprise until they are actually dragged into it—when they are opposing every proposal, because it will *cost something*, they are a dead weight upon a minister.

I was once attending a "protracted meeting," where we were embarrassed because there were no lamps to the building. I urged the people to get them, but they thought the expense would be too much! I then proposed to get them myself, and was about to do it, but found it would give offence, and we went without. But the blessing did not come, to any great extent. How could it? The Church began by calculating to a nicety how much it would cost, and they would not go beyond that exact figure to save souls from hell.

So, where a minister appoints such a meeting, such people object, because it will cost something. If they can offer unto the Lord that which costs nothing, they will do it. Miserable helpers they are! Such a people can have no revival. A minister might as well have a millstone about his neck, as such a Church. He had better leave them, if he cannot teach them better, and go where he will not be so hampered.

19. Church members should make it a point *to attend prayer-meetings*, and *attend in time*. Some will always attend the preaching, because they have nothing to do but to sit and hear and be entertained, but they will not attend prayer-meetings for fear they should be called on to do something. Such members tie up the hands of the minister, and discourage his heart. Why do they employ a minister? Is it to amuse them by preaching? Or is it that he may teach them the will of God, that they may do it?

20. Church members ought *to study and inquire what they can do, and then do it*. Christians should be trained like a band of soldiers. It is the duty and office of a minister to train them for usefulness, to teach and direct them, and lead them on in such a way as to produce the greatest amount of moral influence. And then the Christians should stand their ground and do their duty, otherwise they will be right in the way. But I could write a book as large as this Bible before me, in detailing the various particulars which ought to be attended to.

REMARKS.

1. You see that a minister's want of success may not be

wholly on account of a want of wisdom in the exercise of his office. I am not excusing negligent ministers; I never will spare ministers from the naked truth, nor apply flattering titles to men. If they are blameworthy, let them be blamed. And, no doubt, they are always more or less to blame when the Word produces no effect. But it is far from being true that they are always the *principal* persons to blame. Sometimes the Church is much more to blame than the minister; if an apostle or an angel from heaven, were to preach, he could not produce a revival of religion in that Church. Perhaps they are dishonest to their minister, or covetous, or careless about the conveniences of public worship. Alas! what a state many country churches are in, where, for the want of a small expenditure, everything is inconvenient and uncomfortable, and the labours of the preacher are lost. They "dwell in ceiled houses" themselves, and let "the house of God lie waste" (Hag. 1. 4). Or the professors of religion counteract all the influence of the preaching by their ungodly lives. Or perhaps their worldly show (as in most of the Churches in this city) annihilates the influence of the Gospel.

2. Churches should remember that they are exceedingly guilty, to employ a minister and then not aid him in his work. The Lord Jesus Christ has sent an ambassador to sinners, to turn them from their evil ways, and he fails to his errand, because Churches refuse to do their duty. Instead of recommending his message, and seconding his entreaties, and holding up his hands in all the ways that are proper, they stand right in the way, and contradict his message, and counteract his influence, and souls perish. No doubt, in most of the congregations in the United States, the minister is often hindered so much that for a great part of the time he might as well be on a foreign mission as be there, for any effect of his preaching in the conversion of sinners, for he has to preach over the heads of an inactive and stupid Church.

Yet these very Churches are not willing to have their minister absent a few days to attend a "protracted meeting." "We cannot spare him; he is *our* minister, and we like to have our minister here"; while at the same time, they hinder all he can do at home. If he could, he would tear himself right away, and go where there is no minister, and where the people would be willing to receive the Gospel. But there he must stay, though he cannot get the Church into a state to have a revival once in three years, to last three months at a time. It might be well for him to say to the Church: "Whenever you are determined to take one of these long naps, I wish you would let me know it, so that I can go and labour somewhere else in the meantime, till you are ready to wake again."

3. Many Churches cannot be blessed with a revival, because they are "sponging" out of other Churches, and out of the treasury of the Lord, for the support of their minister, when they are abundantly able to support him themselves. Perhaps they are depending on the Home Missionary Society, or on other Churches, while they are not exercising any *self-denial* for the sake of the Gospel. I have been amazed to see how some Churches live. One Church, as I have said, actually confessed that the members spent more money for tobacco than they gave for Missions. And yet they had no minister, because "they were not able to support one"! There is actually *one man* in that Church who is himself able to support a minister, but still they have no minister and no preaching!

The Churches have not been instructed in their duty on this subject. I stopped in a place where there was no preaching. I inquired of an elder in the Church why it was so, and he said it was "because they were so poor." I asked him how much he was worth; he did not give me a direct answer, but said that another elder's income was about five thousand dollars a year; and I finally found out that this man's was about the same. "Here," said I, "are two elders, each of you able to support a minister, and because you cannot get outside help, you have no preaching. Why, if you *had* preaching, it would not be blessed." Finally, he confessed that he was able to support a minister, and the two together agreed that they would do it.

It is common for Churches to ask for help, when in fact they do not need any help, and when it would be a great deal better for them to support their own minister. If they get funds from the Home Missionary Society, when they ought to raise sufficient themselves, they may expect the curse of the Lord upon them, and this will be a sufficient reason for the Gospel proving to them a curse, rather than a blessing. Of how many might it be said: "Ye have robbed God, even this whole

Church" (Mal. 3. 9).

I know a Church which employed a minister for half the time, and felt unable to pay his salary for that. A Women's Working Society in a neighbouring town appropriated their funds to this object, and assisted this Church in paying the minister's salary. The result was, as might be expected; he did them little or no good. They had no revival under his preaching, nor could they ever expect any, while acting on such a principle. There was one man in that congregation who could support a minister all the time. I was informed by a member, that the Church members were supposed to be worth *two hundred thousand dollars*. Now if this be true, here is a Church with an income, at seven per cent., of fourteen thousand dollars a year, who felt themselves too poor to pay two hundred dollars for the support of a minister to preach half the time, but would suffer the women of a neighbouring town to work with their own hands to aid them in paying the sum. Among the elders of this Church, I found, too, that several used tobacco; two of them, however, subsequently signed a covenant, written on the blank leaf of their Bible, in which they pledged themselves to abandon that sin for ever.

It was in a great measure simply for want of right instruction that this Church was pursuing such a course, for, when the subject was taken up, and their duty laid before them, the wealthy man of whom I am speaking said that he would pay the whole salary himself, if he thought it would not be resented by the congregation, and do more hurt than good; and that if the Church would procure a minister, and go ahead and raise a part of his salary, he would make up the remainder. They can now not only support a minister half the time, but all the time, and pay his salary themselves. And they will find it good and profitable to do so.

As I have gone from place to place labouring in revivals, I have always found that Churches were blessed in proportion to their liberality. Where they have manifested a disposition to support the Gospel, and to pour out their substance liberally into the treasury of the Lord, they have been blessed both in spiritual and in temporal things. But where they have been parsimonious, and let the minister preach for them for little or nothing, these Churches have been cursed instead of blessed.

And, as a general thing, in revivals of religion, I have found it to be true that young converts are most inclined to join those Churches which are most liberal in making efforts to support the Gospel.

The Churches are very much in the dark on this subject. They have not been taught their duty. I have, in many instances, found an exceeding readiness to respond, when the subject was laid before them. I knew an elder who was talking about getting a minister for half the time, because the Church was poor, although his own income was considerable. I asked him whether *his* income would not enable him alone to support a minister all the time? He said it would. And on being asked what other use he could make of the Lord's money which he possessed, that would prove so beneficial to the interest of Christ's Kingdom, as to employ a minister not only half, but all the time, in his own town, he concluded to set himself about it. A minister has been obtained accordingly, and I believe they find no difficulty in paying him his full salary.

The fact is, that a minister can do but little by preaching only half the time. If on one Sabbath an impression be made, it is lost before a fortnight comes round. As a matter of economy, a Church should lay itself out to support the Gospel all the time. If they get the right sort of a minister, and keep him steadily at work, they may have a revival, and thus the ungodly will be converted, and come in and help them; so that in one year they may have a great accession to their strength. But if they employ a minister only half the time, year after year may roll away, while sinners are going to hell, and no accession be made to the strength of the Church from the ranks of the ungodly.

The fact is, that professors of religion have not been made to feel that all their possessions are the Lord's. Hence they have talked about *giving their property* for the support of the Gospel! As if the Lord Jesus Christ were a begger, and they were called upon to support His Gospel as an act of almsgiving!

A certain merchant was paying a large part of his minister's salary: one of the members of the Church was relating the fact to a minister from another place, and spoke of the *sacrifice* which this merchant was making. At this moment the merchant came in. "Brother," said the minister, "you are a merchant. Suppose you employ a clerk to sell goods, and a schoolmaster to teach your children; and you order your clerk to pay your schoolmaster, out of the store, such an amount, for his services in teaching. Now, suppose your clerk gave out that *he* had to pay this schoolmaster his salary, and should speak of the sacrifices that *he* was making to do it: what would you say to this?" "Why," said the merchant, "I shoud say it was ridiculous." "Well," said the minister, "God employs you to teach His children, and He requires you to pay the salary out of the income of the store. Now, do you call this *your* sacrifice, and say that you are making a great sacrifice to pay this minister's salary? No: you are just as much bound to sell goods for God as he is to preach for God. You have no more right to sell goods for the purpose of laying up money than he has to preach the Gospel for the same purpose. You are bound to be as pious, and aim *as singly* at the glory of God, in selling goods, as he is in preaching the Gospel. And thus you are as fully to give up your whole time for the service of God as he does. You and your family may lawfully live out of the profits of this store, and so may the minister and his family, just as lawfully. If you sell goods from these motives, selling goods is just as much serving God as preaching; and a man who sells goods on these principles; and acts in conformity to them, is just as pious—just as much in the service of God—as he is who preaches the Gospel. Every man is bound to serve God *in his calling*; the minister by teaching; the merchant by selling goods; the farmer by tilling his fields; and the lawyer and the physician by plying the duties of their professions. It is *equally* unlawful for any one of these to labour for the meat that perisheth. All they do is to be for God, and all they earn, after comfortably supporting their families, is to be dedicated to the spread of the Gospel and the salvation of the world."

It has lone enough been supposed that ministers must be more pious than other men, that *they* must not love the world, that *they* must labour for God: that *they* must live as frugally as possible, and lay out their whole time, and health, and strength, and life, to build up the Kingdom of Jesus Christ. This is true. But although other men are not called to labour in the same field, and to give up their time to public instruction, yet they are just as *absolutely* bound to consider their whole

257

time as God's; and have no more right to love the world, or accumulate wealth, or lay it up for their children, or spend it upon their lusts, than ministers have.

It is high time for the Church to be acquainted with these principles. The Home Missionary Society may labour till the Day of Judgment to convert people, but will never succeed, till the Churches are led to understand and feel their duty in this respect. Why, the very fact that they are asking and receiving aid in supporting their minister from the Society while they are able to support him themselves, is probably the very reason why his labours among them are not more blessed.

I would that the American Home Missionary Society possessed a hundred times the means that it now does, of aiding feeble Churches that are unable to help themselves. But it is neither good economy nor piety to give funds to those who are able, but unwilling, to support the Gospel. For it is in vain to attempt to help them, while they are able, but unwilling, to help themselves.

If the Missionary Society had a ton of gold, it would be no charity to give it to such a Church. But let the Church bring in all the tithes to God's storehouse, and He will open the windows of heaven and pour down a blessing (Mal. 3. 10). But let the Churches know assuredly that, if they are unwilling to help themselves to the extent of their ability, they show the reason why such small success attends the labours of their ministers. Here they are, "sponging" their support from the Lord's treasury! How many Churches lay out their money for tea, and coffee, and tobacco, and then come and ask aid from the Home Missionary Society! I will protest against aiding a people who use tea and tobacco, and live without the least self-denial, wanting to offer God only that which costs them nothing (2 Sam. 24. 24).

Finally: if they mean to be blessed, let them do their duty—*all* their duty, put their shoulder to the wheel, gird on the Gospel armour, and come up to the work. *Then*, if the Church is *in the field*, the car of salvation will move on, though all hell oppose, and sinners will be converted and saved. But if a Church will leave all the labour to the minister, and sit still and look on while he is working, and themselves doing nothing but complain of him, they will not only fail of a revival of religion, but, if they continue slothful and censorious, will, by and by, find themselves in hell for their disobedience and unprofitableness in the service of Christ.

LECTURE XIV

MEASURES TO PROMOTE REVIVALS

These men, being Jews, do exceedingly trouble our city, and teach
customs, which are not lawful for us to receive, neither to observe,
being Romans.—Acts 16. 20, 21

"These men," here spoken of, were Paul and Silas, who
went to Philippi to preach the Gospel, and very much
disturbed the people of that city, who supposed that the
preaching would interfere with their worldly gains. And so
they arraigned the preachers of the Gospel before the
magistrates of the city, as culprits, and charged them with
teaching doctrines, and especially employing measures, that
were not lawful.

In discoursing from these words I design to show: I. That,
under the Gospel dispensation, God has established no
particular system of measures to be employed, and invariably
adhered to, in promoting religion. II. That our present forms
of public worship, and everything, so far as *measures* are
concerned, have been arrived at by degrees, and by *a succession
of New Measures.*

I. *GOD HAS ESTABLISHED NO PARTICULAR MEASURES.*

Under the *Jewish* dispensation, there were particular forms
enjoined and prescribed by God Himself, from which it was
not lawful to depart. But these forms were all *typical*, and were

designed to shadow forth Christ, or something connected with the new dispensation that Christ was to introduce. And therefore they were fixed, and all their details particularly prescribed by Divine authority. But it *was never so* under the Gospel. When Christ came, the ceremonial or typical dispensation was abrogated, because the design of those forms was fulfilled, and they were therefore of no further use. He being the Antitype, the types were of course done away at His coming. THE GOSPEL was then preached as the appointed means of promoting religion; and it was left to the discretion of the Church to determine, from time to time, what *measures* should be adopted, and what *forms* pursued, in giving the Gospel its power.

We are left in the dark as to the measures pursued by the apostles and primitive preachers, except so far as we can gather from occasional hints in the Book of Acts. We do not know how many times they sang, how many times they prayed, in public worship, nor even whether they sang or prayed at all in their ordinary meetings for preaching. When Jesus Christ was on earth, labouring among His disciples, He had nothing to do with forms or measures. He did from time to time in this respect just as it would be natural for any man to do in such cases, without anything like a set form or mode. The Jews accused Him of disregarding their forms. His object was to preach and teach mankind the true religion. And when the apostles preached afterwards, with the Holy Ghost sent down from heaven, we hear nothing about their having a particular system of measures for carrying on their work; nor do we hear of one apostle doing a thing in a particular way because others did it in that way. Their commission was: "Go and preach the Gospel, and disciple all nations." It did not prescribe any forms. It did not admit any. No person can pretend to get any set of forms or particular directions as to measures, out of this commission. Do it—the best way you can; ask wisdom from God; use the faculties He has given you; seek the direction of the Holy Ghost; go forward and do it. This was their commission. And their object was to make known the Gospel in the *most effectual way*, to make the truth stand out strikingly, so as to obtain the attention and secure the obedience of the greatest number possible. No person can find any form of doing this laid down in the Bible. It is *preaching the Gospel* which there stands out prominently as the great thing. The form is left out of the question.

It is manifest that in preaching the Gospel there must be *some* kind of measures adopted. The Gospel must be presented before the minds of the people, and measures must be taken so that they *can* hear it, and be induced to attend to it. This is done by building churches, holding stated or other meetings, and so on. Without some measures, the Gospel can never be made to take effect among men.

II. *PRESENT FORMS ARRIVED AT BY DEGREES.*

Our present forms of public worship, and everything so far as *measures* are concerned, have been arrived at *by degrees*, and by a *succession of New Measures.*

1. I will mention some things in regard to the *ministry*.

Many years ago, ministers were accustomed to wear a *peculiar habit*. It is so now in Roman Catholic countries. It used to be so here. Ministers had a peculiar dress as much as soldiers. They used to wear a cocked hat, bands (instead of a cravat or stock), small clothes, and a wig. No matter how much hair a man had on his head, he must cut it off and wear a wig. And he must wear a gown. All these things were customary, and every clergyman was held bound to wear them, and it was not considered proper for him to officiate without them.[1] All these had doubtless been introduced by a succession of innovations, for we have no good reason for believing that the apostles and primitive ministers dressed differently from other men.

---

[1] The regular preaching costume of the eighteenth century now gains its familiarity (apart from the political squibs and social burlesques of Rowlandson, Gillray, and others) chiefly through popular pictures illustrating the careers of Wesley and Whitefield, *e.g.*, Wesley preaching from his father's tombstone, in Epworth churchyard, and Whitefield at Moorfields. The more modern items which Finney goes on to specify have themselves passed into history. The picturesque attire of the latter part of the eighteenth century, the costume of Chesterfield and Charles James Fox and Goldsmith—with his "Tyrian bloom satin grain coat and garter-blue silk breeches" (for which William Filby hopefully charged him

But now all these things have been given up, one by one, in America, by a succession of innovations or new measures, until now, in many places, a minister can go into the pulpit and preach without attracting special notice, although dressed like any other man. And in regard to each of these alterations the Church complained as much as if it had been a Divine institution given up. It was denounced as an *innovation*. When ministers began to lay aside their cocked hats, and wear headgear like other men's, it grieved the elderly people very much; it looked so "undignified," they said, for a minister to wear a round hat. When, in 1827, I wore a fur cap, a minister said: "That is too bad, for a minister."

When ministers first began, a few years since, to wear white hats, it was thought by many to be a sad and very undignified innovation. And even now they are so bigoted in some places that a clergyman lately told me how, in travelling through New England last summer, with a white hat, he could perceive that it injured his influence. This spirit should not be looked upon as harmless; I have good reason to know that it is not harmless. There is at this day scarcely a minister in the land who does not feel himself obliged to wear a black coat, as much as if it were a Divine institution. The Church is yet filled with a kind of superstitious reverence for such things. Thinking men see this to be mere bigotry, and are exceedingly in danger of viewing everything about religion in the same light on this account.

So, in like manner, when ministers laid aside their *bands*, and wore cravats or stocks, it was said they were becoming secular, and many found fault. Even now, in some places, a minister would not dare to be seen in the pulpit in a cravat or stock. The people would feel as if they had no clergyman, if he had no bands. A minister in this city asked another, but a few days since, "if it would do to wear a black stock in the pulpit?" He wore one in his ordinary intercourse with his people, but

---

£8 2s. 7d.), gave place to that of the Regency and Beau Brummell and the styles so quaintly perpetuated in Cruikshank's drawings. Then, as the nineteenth century grew older, the fashion changed again, and elaborate neckwrappings were a thing of the past. Archbishop Sumner (1780-1862) was probably the last of Anglican dignitaries to wear (quite in the early part of his episcopal career) a wig.

doubted whether it would do to wear it in the pulpit.

So in regard to small clothes: they used to be thought essential to the ministerial character. Even now, in Roman Catholic countries, every priest wears small clothes. Even the little boys there, who are training for the priest's office, wear their cocked hats, and black stockings, and small clothes. This would look ridiculous amongst us. But it used to be practised in America. The time was when good people would have been shocked if a minister had gone into the pulpit wearing pantaloons instead of small clothes.[1] They would have thought he was certainly going to ruin the Church by his innovations. I have been told that, some years ago, in New England, a certain elderly clergyman was so opposed to the "new measure" of a minister's wearing pantaloons that he would, on no account, allow them in his pulpit. A young man who was going to preach for him had no small clothes, and the old minister would not let him officiate in pantaloons, but said: "My people would think I had brought a fop into the pulpit, if they saw a man there with pantaloons on; and it would produce an excitement among them." And so, finally, the young man was obliged to borrow a pair of the old gentleman's clothes, and they were too short for him, and he made a ridiculous figure enough. But anything was better than such a terrible innovation as preaching in pantaloons! Reason, however, has triumphed.

Just so it was in regard to *wigs*. I remember one minister, who, though quite a young man, used to wear an enormous white wig. And the people talked as if there were a Divine right about it, and it was as hard to give it up, almost, as to give up the Bible itself. *Gowns* also were considered essential to the ministerial character. And even now, in many congregations in this country, the people will not tolerate a minister in the pulpit, unless he has a flowing silk gown, with enormous sleeves as big as his body. Even in some of the Congregational churches in New England, they cannot bear to give it up.

Now, how came people to suppose a minister must have a gown or a wig, in order to preach with effect? Why was it that every clergyman was held obliged to use these things? How is

[1] *i.e.*, long trousers in place of the old-fashioned knee-breeches.

it that not one of these things has been given up in the Churches, without producing a shock among them? They have all been given up, one by one, and many congregations have been distracted for a time by the innovation. But will any one pretend that the cause of religion has been injured by it? People felt as if they could hardly worship God without them, but plainly their attachment to them was no part of their religion, that is, no part of the Christian religion. It was mere superstition. And when these things were taken away, they complained, as Micah did: "Ye have taken away my gods" (Judg. 18. 24). No doubt, however, religious character was improved by removing these objects of superstitious reverence. So that the Church, on the whole, has been greatly the gainer by the innovations. Thus you see that the present mode of a minister's dress has been gained by a series of new measures.

2. In regard to the *order of public worship*.

The same difficulties have been met in the effecting of every change, because the professing Christians have felt as if God had established just the *mode which they were used to*.

(a) *Psalm Books*. Formerly it was customary to sing the Psalms. By and by there was introduced a version of the Psalms in rhyme. This was "very bad," to be sure. When ministers tried to introduce them, the Churches were distracted, the people displayed violent opposition, and great trouble was created by the innovation. But the new measure triumphed.

Yet when another version was brought forward, in a better style of poetry, its introduction was opposed, with much contention, as yet a further new measure. Finally came Watts's version, which is still opposed in many Churches. No longer ago than 1828, when I was in Philadelphia, I was told that a minister there was preaching a *course of Lectures* on Psalmody, to his congregation, for the purpose of bringing them to use a better version of psalms and hymns than the one they were accustomed to. And even now, in a great many congregations, there are people who will rise and leave, if a psalm or hymn is given out from a new book. If Watts's version of the Psalms should be adopted, they would secede and form a new congregation, rather than tolerate such an innovation!

The same sort of feeling has been excited by introducing the "Village Hymns" in prayer-meetings. In one Presbyterian congregation in New York, within a few years, the minister's wife wished to introduce the Village Hymns into the women's prayer-meetings, not daring to go any further. She thought she was going to succeed. But some of the careful souls found out that it was "made in New England," and refused to admit it.

(b) *"Lining" the Hymns.* Formerly, when there were but few books, it was the custom to "line" hymns, as it was called. The deacon used to stand up before the pulpit, and read the psalm or hymn, a line at a time, or two lines at a time, when then the rest would join in. By and by, they began to introduce books, and let every one sing from his own book. And what an innovation! Alas, what confusion and disorder it made! How could the good people worship God in singing without having the deacon to "line" the hymn in a "holy" tone; for the holiness of it seemed to consist very much in the tone, which was such that you could hardly tell whether he was reading or singing.

(c) *Choirs.* Afterwards, another innovation was brought in. It was thought best to have a select choir of singers sit by themselves, so as to give an opportunity to improve the music. But this was bitterly opposed. How many congregations were torn and rent in sunder by the desire of ministers and some leading individuals, to bring about an improvement in the cultivation of music, by forming choirs! People talked about "innovations," and "new measures," and thought great evils were coming to the Churches, because the singers were seated by themselves, and cultivated music, and learned new tunes that the old people could not sing. It used not to be so when they were young, and they would not tolerate such novelties in the Church.

(d) *Pitchpipes.* When music was cultivated, and choirs seated together, then the singers wanted a pitchpipe. Formerly, when the lines were given out by the deacon or clerk, he would strike off into the tune, and the rest would follow as well as they could. But when the leaders of choirs began to use pitchpipes for the purpose of pitching all their voices on precisely the same key, what vast confusion it made! I heard a clergyman say that an elder in the town where he used to live, would get up and leave the service whenever he heard the chorister blow his pipe. "Away with your whistle," said he; "what, whistle in the house of God!" He thought it a profanation.

(e) *Instrumental music.* By and by, in some congregations, various instruments were introduced for the purpose of aiding the singers, and improving the music. When the bass viol was first introduced, it made a great commotion. People insisted they might just as well have a *fiddle* in the house of God. "Why, *it is* a fiddle, it is made just like a fiddle, only a little larger; and who can worship where there is a fiddle? By and by you will want to dance in the meeting-house." Who has not heard these things talked of as though they were matters of the most vital importance to the cause of religion and the purity of the Church? Ministers, in grave ecclesiastical assemblies, have spent days in discussing them. In a synod in the Presbyterian Church, it was seriously talked of by some, as a matter worthy of discipline in a certain Church, that "they had an organ in the house of God." This was only a few years ago. And there are many Churches now that would not tolerate an organ. They would not be half so much excited on being reminded that sinners are going to hell, as on hearing that "there is going to be an organ in the meeting-house."[1] In how many places is it easier to get the Church to do anything else than work in a

---

[1] The feeling against the organ (and, primarily, against all "human" hymns as well as against solo-singing), although greatly lessened through the campaigns of Messrs. Moody and Sankey— with Mr. Sankey's "Kist o'whustles," has little American organ— still prevails among many sincere Christians. When the American evangelists began their work at Edinburgh, in November, 1873, the first meeting (in the Music Hall) was packed, but Mr. Moody was absent through illness, and Mr. Sankey was left to face the ordeal of criticism alone. He chose "Jesus of Nazareth passeth by," and the intense silence that prevailed was an index of earnest appreciation. At the third meeting, Mr. Sankey selected "Yet there is room" (with the chorus, "Room, room, still room!"), the music being his own composition—to the words which Dr. Horatius Bonar had written to them, as a spiritual reply to Tennyson's song in "Guinevere" ("Idylls of the King") "Late, late, so late!" Mr. Sankey, as he took his seat at the instrument found that he was close to Dr. Bonar himself—who ministered in a Church where the Psalms only were

natural way to do what is needed, and wisest, and best, for promoting religion and saving souls? They act as if they had a "Thus saith the Lord" for every custom and practice that has been handed down to them, or that they have long followed themselves, even though it is absurd and injurious.

(f) Extemporary prayers. How many people are there who talk just as if the Prayer Book was of Divine institution! And I suppose multitudes believe it is. And in some parts of the Church a man would not be tolerated to pray without his book being before him.

(g) Preaching without notes. A few years since a lady in Philadelphia was invited to hear a certain minister preach, and she refused, because he did not *read* his sermons. She seemed to think it would be profane for a man to go into the pulpit and *talk*, just as if he were talking to the people about some interesting and important subject.[1] Just as if God had enjoined the use of notes and written sermons. They do not know that notes themselves are an innovation, and a modern one too. They were introduced in a time of political difficulty in England. The ministers were afraid they should be accused of preaching something against the Government, unless they could show what they had preached, by having all written beforehand. And, with a time-serving spirit, they yielded to political considerations, and imposed a yoke of bondage upon the Church. And now, in many places, extempore preaching is not tolerated.

(h) Kneeling in prayer. This has made a great disturbance in many parts of the country. The time has been in the

---

used, his own beautiful hymns suffering exclusion with the rest. At the close, Dr. Bonar remarked, with a smile: "Well, Mr. Sankey, you 'sang the Gospel' to-night." "Singing the Gospel" was then a phrase of almost startling novelty (Ira D. Sankey's "My Life and Sacred Songs").

[1]Probably another autobiographical reference. It was said *of* him: "Finney don't preach, he only explains what other people preach"; and *to* him: "Why, anybody could preach as you do; you just talk as though you were at home in your own parlour." But there was more than a felicitous homeliness; Thomas W. Seward said: "His intellectual force attracted many who would not have listened to a less gifted expounder of the Divine Law."

Congregational Churches in New England, when a man or woman would be ashamed to be seen kneeling at a prayer-meeting, for fear of being taken for a Methodist. I have prayed in families where I was the only person that would kneel. The others all stood. Others, again, talk as if there were no other posture but kneeling, that could be acceptable in prayer.

3. In regard to the *labours of laymen.*

(a) *Lay prayers.* Much objection was formerly made against allowing any man to pray or to take a part in managing a prayer-meeting, unless he was a clergyman. It used to be said that for a layman to pray in public, was interfering with the dignity of ministers, and was not to be tolerated. A minister in Pennsylvania told me that a few years ago he appointed a prayer-meeting in the Church, and the elders opposed it and "turned it out of house." They said they would not have such work; they had hired a minister to do the praying, and he should do it; and they were not going to have common men praying.

Ministers and many others have very extensively objected against a layman's praying in public, *especially* in the presence of a minister; that would let down the authority of the clergy, and was not to be tolerated. At a synod held in this State, there was a synodical prayer-meeting appointed. The committee of arrangements, as it was to be a formal thing, designated beforehand the persons who were to take part, and named two clergymen and one layman. The layman was a man of talent and information equal to most ministers. But a Doctor of Divinity got up and seriously objected to a layman being asked to pray before that synod. It was not usual, he said; it infringed upon the rights of the clergy, and he wished no innovations! What a state of things!

(b) *Lay exhortation.* This has been made a question of vast importance, one which has agitated all New England and many other parts of the country, whether laymen ought to be allowed to exhort in public meetings. Many ministers have laboured to shut up the mouths of laymen entirely.[1] Such

---

[1] Two of the objections taken to the preaching of James Davenport, at Boston, as early as 1742, were, that he "acted to the disservice of religion, by going with his friends singing through the

persons overlooked the practice of the primitive Churches. So much opposition was made to this practice, nearly a hundred years ago, that President Edwards had actually to take up the subject, and write a laboured defence of the rights and duties of laymen. But the opposition has not entirely ceased to this day. "What, a man that is not a minister, to talk in public! It will create confusion; it will let down the ministry: what will people think of ministers, if we allow common men to do the same things that *we* do?" Astonishing!

But now all these things are gone by in most places, and laymen can preach and exhort without the least objection. The evils that were feared, from the labours of laymen, have not been realised, and many ministers are glad to induce laymen to exercise their gifts in doing good.

4. *Women's prayer-meetings.* Within the last few years women's prayer-meetings have been extensively opposed. What dreadful things! A minister said that when he first attempted to establish these meetings, he had all the clergy around opposed to him. "Set women to pray? Why, the next thing, I suppose, will be to set them to preach!" Serious apprehensions were entertained for the safety of Zion if women should be allowed to get together to pray, and even now it is not tolerated in some Churches.

So it has been in regard to all the active movements of the Church. Missions and Sunday Schools have been opposed, and have gained their present hold only by a succession of struggles and a series of innovations. A Baptist Association in Pennsylvania, some years since, disclaimed all fellowship with any minister that had been liberally educated, or that supported Missions, Bible Societies, Sabbath Schools, Temperance Societies, etc. All these were denounced as New Measures, not found in the Bible, and that would necessarily lead to distraction and confusion in the Churches. The same thing has been done by some among the German Churches.

---

streets and highways, to and from the houses of worship, on Lord's days and other days"; and against his "encouraging private brethren to pray and exhort in assemblies gathered for that purpose" (Declaration with regard to James Davenport, by "We, the Associated Pastors of Boston and Charlestown").

And in many Presbyterian Churches there are found those who will take the same ground, and denounce all these things, with the exception, perhaps, of an educated ministry, as innovations, new measures, "going in your own strength," and the like, and as calculated to do great evil.

5. I will mention several men who, in Divine providence, have been set forward as prominent in *introducing innovations*.

(a) *The apostles*—who were great innovators, as you all know. After the Resurrection, and after the Holy Spirit was poured out upon them, they set out to re-model the Church. They broke down the Jewish system of measures, and rooted it out, so as to leave scarcely a vestige.

(b) *Luther and the Reformers*. You all know what difficulties they had to contend with, and the reason was, that they were trying to introduce new measures—new modes of performing the public duties of religion, and new expedients to bring the Gospel with power to the hearts of men. All the strange and ridiculous things of the Roman Catholics were held to by Rome with pertinacious obstinacy, as if they were of Divine authority; and such an excitement was raised by the attempt to change them, as wellnigh involved all Europe in bloodshed.

(c) *Wesley and his coadjutors*. Wesley did not, at first, break from the Established Church in England, but formed little classes everywhere, which grew into a Church within a Church. He remained in the Episcopal Church; but he introduced so much of new measures as to fill all England with excitement, and uproar, and opposition; and he was everywhere denounced as an innovator and a stirrer up of sedition—a teacher of new things which it was not lawful to receive.

Whitefield was a man of the same school, and, like Wesley, was an innovator. I believe he and several individuals of his associates were expelled from College for getting up such a new measure as a social prayer-meeting.[1] They would pray

---

[1]Whitefield joined the "Holy Club" at Oxford about the end of 1734 or the beginning of 1735, when the Methodist fraternity numbered only fifteen menbers. He was not expelled, although

together and expound the Scriptures, and this was such a daring novelty that it could not be borne. When Whitefield came to America what an astonishing opposition was raised! Often he well nigh lost his life, and barely escaped by the skin of his teeth.[1] Now, everybody looks upon him as the glory of the age in which he lived. And many of our own denomination have so far divested themselves of prejudice as to think Wesley not only a good, but a wise and pre-eminently useful man. Then, almost the entire Church viewed them with animosity, fearing that the innovations they introduced would destroy the Church.

(d) President Edwards. This great man was famous in his day for new measures. Among other innovations, he refused to baptize the children of impenitent parents. The practice of baptizing the children of the ungodly had been introduced into the New England Churches in the preceding century, and had become nearly universal. President Edwards saw that the practice was wrong, and he refused to do it, and the refusal shook all the Churches of New England. A hundred ministers joined and determined to put him down. He wrote a book on

---

persecutions were frequent and the Master of Pembroke threatened him with ejection for the specific fault of visiting in the homes of the poor). Continuing his earnest stand, his room became the daily resort of bands of devout disciples. Later, in 1768, six Methodist students were expelled from the University for taking upon themselves to pray, reading and expounding the Scriptures, and singing hymns in private houses—and because they had been tradesmen before entering as students.

[1] He was not disturbed, however. "I am sorry to see you at Boston," said a distinguished but critical preacher. "So is the devil," remarked Whitefield. And, despite the intensity of the opposition of which he was the target, he wrote, for example, of one meeting (attended by fifteen thousand people, but merely one out of many similar gatherings): "Oh, how did the Word run! It rejoiced me to see such numbers greatly affected so that some, I believe, could scarcely abstain from crying out, that the place was no other than a Bethel, and the gate of heaven. The power and presence of the Lord accompanied me. Many now wept exceedingly and cried out under the Word, like persons that were hungering and thirsting after righteousness."

the subject, and defeated them all. It produced one of the greatest excitements there ever was in New England. Nothing, unless it was the Revolutionary War, ever produced an equal excitement.

The General Association of Connecticut refused to countenance Whitefield, he was such an innovator. "Why, he will preach out of doors, and anywhere!" Awful! What a terrible thing that a man should preach in the fields or in the streets! Cast him out![1]

All these were devoted men, seeking out ways to do good and save souls. And precisely the same kind of opposition was experienced by all, obstructing their path and trying to destroy their character and influence. A *book*, still extant, was written in President Edwards' time, by a doctor of divinity, and signed by a multitude of ministers, against Whitefield and Edwards, their associates and their measures. A letter was published in this city by a minister against Whitefield, which brought up the same objections against innovations that we hear now. In the time of the late opposition to revivals in the State of New York, a copy of this letter was taken to the editor of a religious

---

[1]Various Associations of ministers denounced Whitefield. The Faculty of Harvard College, too, protested (1744) that they looked upon his "going about in an itinerant way (especially as he hath so much of an enthusiastical turn of mind), as utterly inconsistent with the peace and order, if not the very being of these Churches of Christ." The same protest urged that the left the care of the Orphan House "to a person whom we have reason to believe is little better than a Quaker." An Association which met at Weymouth in the following year solemnly condemned, *inter alia*, his "practice of singing hymns in the public roads, when riding from town to town." An Association convened at Marlborough (1745) complained that "when Mr. Whitefield first came among us, he used his utmost cunning to engage the affections of the people, and when he had wrought them up to a loud opinion of his excellences, and they began to look upon him as one endowed with an uncommon measure of the Spirit, he continued to insinuate that unconverted ministers could do little or no good to souls." Some of the ministers who signed the associated "Testimonies" were, however, opposers of the revival from the beginning." (See Tracy's "The Great Awakening.")

periodical with a request that he would publish it. He refused, and gave for a reason, that if published, many would apply it to the controversy that is going on now. I mention it merely to show how identical is the opposition that is raised in different ages against all new measures designed to advance the cause of religion.[1]

6. *In the present generation,* many things have been introduced which have proved useful, but have been opposed on the ground *that they were innovations.* And as many are still unsettled in regard to them, I have thought it best to make some remarks concerning them. There are three things, in particular, which have chiefly attracted remark, and therefore I shall speak of them. They are: *anxious meetings, protracted meetings,* and the *anxious seat.* These are all opposed, and are called "new measures."

(a) Anxious meetings. The first that I ever heard of under that name were in New England, where they were appointed for the purpose of holding personal conversation with anxious sinners, and to adapt instruction to the cases of individuals, so as to lead them immediately to Christ. The design of them is evidently philosophical, but they have been opposed because they were new. There are two modes of conducting an anxious meeting, either of which may effect the object in view.

(1) By spending a few moments in personal conversation, in order to learn the state of mind of each individual, and then,

[1]The present Lecture may be described as Finney's *Apologia.* He justifies his whole conduct and procedure in the promotion of revival as against the party which persistently and sometimes virulently attacked him on account of his "new measures" (see footnote, p. 226). A copy of the letter of fulmination against Whitefield had been found, pasted in a book, by Judge Jonas Platt (who with his son and daughter had been converted in the revival which broke out at Utica, under Finney's preaching). Judge Platt took the letter to Mr. Morse, of the *New York Observer,* but that gentleman declined to publish it, since its reprinting would assuredly be regarded as a suggestion that Finney's opponents were manifested of old towards Whitefield. This refusal had weight in leading Finney's friends to establish these Lectures were originally published. The opposition died down, for "the results of the revivals were such as to shut the mouths of gainsayers."

in an address to the whole meeting, to take up their errors and remove their difficulties.

(2) By going round to each, and taking up each individual case, and going over the whole ground with each one separately, and getting them to promise to give their hearts to God. Either way the meetings are important, and have been found most successful in practice. But multitudes have objected against them because they were new.

(b) Protracted meetings.[1] These are not new, but have always been practised, in some form or another, ever since there was a Church on earth. The Jewish festivals were nothing else but protracted meetings. In regard to the *manner*, they were conducted differently from what they are now. But the *design* was the same: to devote a series of days to religious services, in order to make a more powerful impression of Divine things on the minds of the people. All denominations of Christians, when religion prospers among them, hold protracted meetings. In Scotland they used to begin on Thursday, at all their Communion seasons, and continue until after the Sabbath. The Episcopalians, Baptists, and Methodists, all hold protracted meetings. Yet now, in our day, they have been opposed, particularly among Presbyterians,[1] and called "new measures," and regarded as fraught with all manner of evil, notwithstanding that they have been so manifestly and so extensively blessed. I will suggest a few things that ought to be considered in regard to them.

[1]Or, as we should say nowadays, a special evangelistic mission or Gospel campaign. Finney's "protracted meetings" sometimes lasted for months. The teaching was" (to use his own words) "that the only obstacle in the way of their conversion was their own stubborn will; that God was trying to gain their unqualified consent to give up their sins and accept the Lord Jesus Christ as their righteousness and salvation." "Protracted meetings are, in fact," wrote Dr. Ashbel Green (formerly of Princeton), "only a modification of the protracted sacramental solemnities, well known in Scotland and in some parts of our own country." (Appendix to Sprague's "Lectures on Revivals of Religion.")

[1]It is well to bear in mind, with regard to Finney's frequent references to the Presbyterian Church, its administration, methods, theology, and more especially its general spiritual condition, that it

(1) In appointing them, regard should be had *to the circumstances of the people*; whether the Church is able to give attention and devote time to carrying on the meeting. In some instances this rule has been neglected. Some have thought it right to break in upon the necessary business of the community. In the country they would appoint the meeting in the harvest-time, and in the city in the height of the business season, when all the men are *necessarily* occupied, and pressed with their temporal labours. In defence of this course it is said, that *our* business should always be made to yield to *God's* business; that eternal things are of so much more importance than temporal things, that worldly business of any kind, and *at any time*, should be made to yield and give place to a protracted meeting. But the worldly business in which we are engaged is not *our* business. It is as much *God's* business, and as much our duty, as our prayers and protracted meetings are. If we do not consider our business in this light, we have not yet taken the first lesson in religion; we have not learned to do all things to the glory of God. With this view of the subject—separating our business from religion, we are living six days for ourselves, and the seventh for God. REAL DUTIES NEVER INTERFERE WITH EACH OTHER. Weekdays have *their* appropriate duties, and the Sabbath *its* appropriate duties, and we are to be equally pious on every day of the week, and in the

---

was in connection with the Presbyterian Church which he was attending at the time of his conversion, that he first spoke in public. Then, in 1822, he placed himself under the care of his Presbytery as a candidate for the ministry, and although he declined to proceed to college (on the ground that the system of education and training was radically wrong, since it did not produce ministers who were soul-winners) he duly became a Presbyterian minister. After he had accepted a call to New York, in 1832, and had laboured there for some time, a number of Finney's friends and supporters erected the Tabernacle, in Broadway, with the understanding that he would become pastor. They formed a Congregational Church, and, said Finney: "I took my dismission from the Presbytery and became pastor of that Congregational Church." Family circumstances had rendered it desirable that he should settle in a Church; nevertheless he continued to evangelise, as indeed, he delighted to do, after he had become President of Oberlin College.

performance of the duties of every day. We are to plough, and sow, and sell our goods, and attend to our various callings, with the same singleness of view to the glory of God, with which we go to Church on the Sabbath, and pray in our families, and read our Bibles. This is a first principle in religion. He that does not know and act on this principle, has not learned the "A B C" of piety, as yet. Now, there are particular seasons of the year, in which God, in His providence, calls upon men to attend to business, because worldly business at the time is particularly urgent, and must be done at that season, if done at all; seed-time and harvest for the farmer, and the business seasons for the merchant. And we have no right to say, in those particular seasons, that we will quit *our business* and have a protracted meeting. The fact is, the business *is not* ours. And unless God, by some special indication of His providence, shows it to be His pleasure that we should turn aside and have a protracted meeting at *such times*, I look upon it as tempting God to appoint one. It is saying: "O God, this worldly business is *our* business, and we are willing to lay it aside for *Thy* business." Unless God has indicated it to be His pleasure to pour out His Spirit, and revive His work at such a season, and has thus *called upon* His people to quit, for the time being, their ordinary employments, and attend especially to a protracted meeting, it appears to me that God might say to us in such circumstances: "Who hath required this at your hand?"

God has a right to dispose of our time as He pleases, to require us to give up any portion of our time, or all our time, to duties of instruction and devotion. And when circumstances plainly call for it, it is our duty to lay aside every other business, and make direct and continuous efforts for the salvation of souls. If we transact our business upon right principles, and from right motives, and wholly for the glory of God, we shall never object to go aside to attend a protracted meeting, whenever there appears to be a call for it in the providence of God.

A man who considers himself a steward or a clerk, does not consider it a hardship to rest from his labours on the Sabbath, but a privilege. The selfish *owner* may feel unwilling to suspend his business on the Sabbath. But the *clerk* who transacts business, not for himself, but for his employer, considers it a privilege to rest on the Sabbath. So we, if we do our business for God, will not think it hard if He makes it our duty to suspend our worldly business and attend a protracted meeting. We should rather consider it in the light of a holiday. Whenever, therefore, you hear a man pleading that he cannot leave his business to attend a protracted meeting—that it is his duty to attend to business, there is reason to fear that he considers the business as his own, and the meeting as God's business. If he felt that the business of the store or the farm was as much God's business as attending a protracted meeting, he would, doubtless, be very willing to rest from his worldly toils, and go up to the house of God and be refreshed, whenever there was an indication on the part of God, that the community was called to that work. It is highly worthy of remark, that the Jewish festivals were appointed at those seasons of the year when there was the least pressure of indispensable worldly business.

In some instances, such meetings have been appointed in the very pressure of business seasons, and have been followed with no good results, evidently for the want of attention to the rule here laid down. In other cases, meetings have been appointed in seasons when there was a great pressure of worldly business, and have been signally blessed. But in those cases the blessing followed because the meeting was appointed in obedience to the indications of the will of God, and by those who had spiritual discernment, and understood the signs of the times. In many instances, doubtless, individuals have attended who *really supposed* themselves to be giving up their *own* business to attend to God's business, and in some cases they made what they supposed to be a real sacrifice, and God in mercy granted them the blessing.

(2) Ordinarily, a protracted meeting should be conducted throughout, and the labour chiefly performed, by *the same minister*, if possible. Sometimes protracted meetings have been held, and dependence placed on ministers coming in from day to day, and there has been no blessing. The reason has been obvious. They did not come in a state of mind which was right for entering into such work; and they did not know the state of people's minds, so as to know what to preach. Suppose a person who is sick should call a different physician

every day. Neither would know what the symptoms had been, what was the course of the disease or of the treatment, what remedies had been tried, or what the patient could bear. The method would certainly kill the patient. Just so in a protracted meeting, carried on by a succession of ministers. None of them get into the spirit of it, and generally they do more harm than good.

A protracted meeting should not, ordinarily, be appointed, unless they can secure the right kind of help, and get a minister or two who will agree to stay on the ground till the meeting is finished. Then they will probably secure a rich blessing.

(3) There should not be *so many public meetings* as to interfere with the *duties of private prayer and of the family*. Otherwise Christians will lose their spirituality and let go their hold of God; and the protracted meeting will prove a failure.

(4) *Families* should not put themselves out so much, in entertaining strangers, as to *neglect prayer and other duties*. It is often the case that when a protracted meeting is held, some of the principal families in the Church, I mean those who are principally relied on to sustain the meetings, do not get into the work at all. And the reason is, that they are "cumbered with much serving." They often take needless trouble to provide for guests who come from a distance to the meeting, and lay themselves out very foolishly to make an entertainment, not only comfortable but sumptuous. It should always be understood that it is the duty of families to have as little working and parade as possible, and to get along with their hospitality in the easiest way, so that they may all have time to pray, and go to the meeting, and to attend to the things of the Kingdom.

(5) By all means guard against *unnecessarily keeping late hours*. If people keep late hours, night after night, they will inevitably wear out the body; their health will fail, and there will be a reaction. They sometimes allow themselves to get so excited as to lose their sleep, and become irregular in their meals, till they break down. Unless the greatest pains are taken to keep regular, the excitement will get so great, that nature will give way, and the work will stop.

(6) *All sectarianism* should be carefully avoided. If a

sectarian spirit breaks out, either in the preaching, or praying, or in conversation, it will counteract all the good of the meeting.

(7) Be watchful against *placing dependence* on a protracted meeting, *as if that of itself would produce a revival*. This is a point of great danger, and has always been so. This is the great reason why the Church in successive generations has always had to give up her measures—because Christians had come to rely on them for success. So it has been in some places, in regard to *protracted meetings*. They have been so blessed, that in some places the people have thought that if they could only have a protracted meeting, they would have a blessing, and sinners would be converted *of course*. And so they have appointed their meeting, without any preparation in the Church, and have just sent for some minister of note and set him to preaching, as if that would convert sinners. It is obvious that the blessing would be withheld from a meeting got up in this way.

(8) Avoid adopting the idea that a revival cannot be enjoyed *without a protracted meeting*. Some Churches have got into a morbid state of feeling on this subject. Their zeal has become all spasmodic and feverish, so that they never think of doing anything to promote a revival, *only in that way*. When a protracted meeting is held, they seem to be wonderfully zealous, but then sink down to a torpid state till another protracted meeting produces another spasm. And now multitudes in the Church think it is necessary to give up protracted meetings because they are abused in this way. This ought to be guarded against, in every Church, so that they may not be driven to give them up, and lose all the benefits that protracted meetings are calculated to produce.

(c) The anxious seat.[1]

---

[1]The "anxious seat" was a sore subject of contention among the alleged "new measures." A striking instance of this opposition was seen at Rochester, N.Y. A judge, of much influence in the place, especially among its many lawyers, warmly opposed the method of invitation, yet he attended the meetings regularly, and Finney cherished the hope that he would be converted. One night the judge vacated his seat, and Finney, who was preaching a sermon specially applicable to him, concluded that he had gone home. Presently;

By this I mean the appointment of some particular seat in the place of meeting, where the anxious may come and be addressed particularly, and be made subjects of prayer, and sometimes be conversed with individually. Of late, this measure has met with more opposition than any of the others. What is the great objection? I cannot see it. The *design* of the anxious seat is undoubtedly philosophical, and according to the laws of mind. It has two bearings:

(*a*) When a person is seriously troubled in mind, everybody knows there is a powerful tendency to conceal it. When a person is borne down with a sense of his condition, if you can get him willing to have it known, if you can get him to break away from the chains of pride, you have gained an important point towards his conversion. This is agreeable to the philosophy of the human mind. How many thousands are there who will bless God to eternity, that, when pressed by the truth, they were ever brought to take this step, by which they threw off the idea that it was a dreadful thing to have anybody know that they were serious about their souls.

(*b*) Another bearing of the anxious seat is to detect deception and delusion, and thus prevent false hopes. It has been opposed on the ground that it was calculated to create delusion and false hopes. But this objection is unreasonable. The truth is the other way.

Suppose I were preaching on the subject of Temperance, and that I should first show the evils of intemperance, and bring up the drunkard and his family, and show the various evils produced, till every heart were beating with emotion. Then I portray the great danger of *moderate* drinking, and show how it leads to intoxication and ruin, and that there is no

---

however, Finney felt his coat pulled, and he found, just behind him, the judge, who said: "Mr. Finney, please pray for me by name; also, I will go to the anxious seat." The effect was electrical as the judge made his way to the front of the pulpit and knelt down. Prayer and weeping prevailed through the meeting, and the judge was immediately joined by many—lawyers and others—who crowded to the front, filling every place where there was room to kneel. Finney was naturally interested in the conversion of lawyers, and expressed the opinion that "in proportion to their numbers more of them have been converted than of any other class."

safety but in TOTAL ABSTINENCE, till a hundred hearts are ready to say: "I will never drink another drop of ardent spirit in the world; if I do, I may expect to find a drunkard's grave." Now I stop short, and let the pledge be circulated, and every one that is fully resolved is ready to sign it. But how many will begin to draw back and hesitate, when you call on them to *sign a pledge* of total abstinence! One says to himself: "Shall I sign it or not? I thought my mind was made up, but this signing a pledge *never* to drink again—I do not know about that." Thus you see that when a person is called upon to give a pledge, if he is found not to be decided, he makes it manifest that he was not sincere. That is, that he never came to that resolution on the subject, which could be relied on to control his future life.

Just so with the awakened sinner. Preach to him, and, at the moment, he thinks he is willing to do anything; he thinks he is determined to serve the Lord; but bring him to the test; call on him to do one thing, to take one step, that shall identify him with the people of God or cross his pride, and his pride comes up, and he refuses; his delusion is brought out, and he finds himself a lost sinner still; whereas, if you had not done it, he might have gone away flattering himself that he was a Christian. If you say to him: "There is the anxious seat, come out and avow your determination to be on the Lord's side," and if he is not willing to do so small a thing as that, then he is not willing to do *anything*, and there he is, brought out before his own conscience. It uncovers the delusion of the human heart, and prevents a great many spurious conversions, by showing those who might otherwise imagine themselves willing to do anything for Christ that in fact they are willing to do *nothing*.

The Church has always felt it necessary to have something of the kind to answer this very purpose. In the days of the apostles *baptism* answered this purpose. The Gospel was preached to the people, and then all those who were willing to be on the side of Christ were called on to be *baptized*. It held the precise place that the anxious seat does now, as a public manifestation of a determination to be a Christian.

In modern times, even those who have been violently opposed to the anxious seat, have been obliged to adopt some substitute, or they could not get along in promoting a revival. Some have adopted the expedient of inviting the people who are anxious for their souls, to stay, for conversation, after the rest of the congregation have retired. But what is the difference? This is as much setting up a test as the other. Others, who would be much ashamed to employ the anxious seat, have asked those who have any feeling on the subject, to retain their seats when the rest retire. Others have called the anxious to withdraw into a Lecture-room. The object of all these is the same, and the principle is the same—to bring people out from the refuge of false shame. One man I heard of, who was very far gone in his opposition to new measures. In one of his meetings he requested all those who were willing to submit to God, or desired to be made subjects of prayer, to signify it by leaning forward and putting their heads down upon the pew before them. Who does not see that this was a mere evasion of the anxious seat, that it was designed to answer the same purpose, and that the plan was adopted because it was felt that something of the kind was important?

Now, what objection is there against taking a particular seat, or rising up, or going into the Lecture-room? They all mean the same thing; and they are not novelties in principle at all. The thing has always been done in substance. In Joshua's day he called on the people to decide what they would do, and they spoke right out in the meeting: "The Lord our God will we serve, and His voice will we obey" (Josh. 24. 24).

REMARKS

1. If we examine the history of the Church we shall find that there never has been an extensive reformation, except by new measures. Whenever the Churches get settled down into a *form* of doing things, they soon get to rely upon the outward doing of it, and so retain the form of religion while they lose the substance. And then it has always been found impossible to arouse them so as to bring about a reformation of the evils, and produce a revival of religion, by simply pursuing that established form. Perhaps it is not too much to say, that it is impossible for God Himself to bring about reformations but by new measures. At least, it is a fact that God has *always chosen* this way, as the wisest and best that He could devise or adopt. And although it has always been the case, that the very

measures which God has chosen to employ, and which He has blessed in reviving His work, have been opposed as new measures, and have been denounced, yet He has continued to act upon the same principle. When He has found that a certain mode has lost its influence by having become a form, He has brought up some new measure, which would BREAK IN upon lazy habits, and WAKE UP a slumbering Church. And great good has resulted.

2. The same distinctions, in substance, that now exist, have always existed, in all seasons of reformation and revival of religion. There have always been those who particularly adhered to their forms and notions, and precise way of doing things, as if they had a "Thus saith the Lord" for every one of them. They have called those that differed from them, who were trying to roll the ark of salvation forward, "Methodists," "New Lights," "Radicals," "New School," "New Divinity," and various other opproprious names. And the declensions that have followed have been uniformly owing to two causes, which should be by no means overlooked by the Church.

(*a*) The Old School, or Old Measure party, have perservered in their opposition, eagerly seizing hold of any real or apparent indiscretions in the friends of the work. In such cases the Churches have gradually lost their confidence in the opposition to new measures, and the cry of "innovation" has ceased to alarm them. Thus the scale has turned.

(*b*) But now mark me: right here, in this state of things, the devil has, again and again, taken the advantage. When the battle has been fought and the victory gained, the rash zeal of some well-meaning, but head-strong individuals, has brought about a reaction, that has spread a pall over the Churches for years. This was the case, as is well known, in the days of President Edwards.[1] Here is a rock, upon which a lighthouse is

---

[1]Finney's criticisms are of course beyond dispute, but are not to be taken as implying any reflection upon the revival in general or upon Jonathan Edwards' part therein, in particular, or as suggesting that the Northampton (Mass.) revivals of 1734-6 and 1740 failed to effect a lasting improvement in Church and public life. Writing Dec. 21, 1743, Edwards himself said: "Ever since the great work of God that was wrought here about nine years ago there has been a great,

now built, and upon which if the Church now run aground, both parties are entirely without excuse. It is now well known, or ought to be known, that the declension which followed the revival in those days, together with the declensions which have repeatedly occurred, were owing to the combined influence of the continued and pertinacious opposition of the Old School, and the ultimate bad spirit and recklessness of some individuals of the New School.

The note of alarm should be distinctly sounded to both parties, lest the devil should prevail against us at the very point, and under the very circumstances, where he has so often prevailed. Will the Church never learn wisdom from experience? When will it come to pass that the Church will be revived, and religion prevail, without exciting such opposition *in the Church* as eventually brings about a reaction?

3. It is truly astonishing that grave ministers should really feel alarmed at the new measures of the present day, as if new measures were something new under the sun, and as if the present form and manner of doing things had descended from the aspostles, and were established by a "Thus saith the Lord"; when the truth is, that every step of the Church's advance from the gross darkness of Popery, has been through the introduction of one new measure after another. We now look with astonishment, and are inclined to look almost with

---

abiding alteration in this town in many respects. There has been vastly more religion kept up in the town, among all sorts of persons, in religious exercises and in common conversation." And of the 1740 revival he wrote (Nov. 12, 1743): "One circumstance wherein this work differed from that which had been in the town five or six years before, was that conversions were wrought more sensibly and visibly: the progress of the Spirit of God in conviction more apparent. The preceding season had been very remarkable on this account, beyond what had been before, but this more remarkable than that." ("The Christian History"—a journal which was of itself of strong revival interest, being "so far as is known the first periodical for the diffusion of contemporary religious intelligence, ever established." It was suggested by Jonathan Edwards' "Thoughts on the Revival,' and was conducted by Thomas Prince, jun. The first number was issued March 5, 1743, and it was continued, in weekly numbers of eight pages, for two years.)

contempt, upon the cry of "innovation" that has preceded our day; and as we review the fears that multitudes in the Church have entertained in bygone days, with respect to innovation, we find it difficult to account for what appear to us the groundless and absurd, at least, if not ridiculous, objections and difficulties which they made. But, is it not wonderful, at this late day, after the Church has had so much experience in these matters, that grave and pious men should seriously feel alarmed at the introduction of the simple, the philosophical, and greatly-prospered measures of the last ten years? As if new measures were something not to be tolerated, of highly disastrous tendency, that should wake the notes and echoes of alarm in every nook and corner of the Church.

4. We see why it is that those who have been making the ado about new measures *have not been successful in promoting revivals*.

They have been taken up with the *evils*, real or imaginary, which have attended this great and blessed work of God. That there have been evils, no one will pretend to deny. But I believe that no revival ever existed since the world began, of as great power and extent as the one that has prevailed for the last ten years, which has not been attended with as great or greater evils. Still, a large portion of the Church have been frightening themselves and others, by giving constant attention to the *evils* of revivals. One of the professors in a Presbyterian Theological Seminary felt it his duty to write a series of letters to Presbyterians, which were extensively circulated, the object of which seemed to be to sound the note of alarm through all the borders of the Church, in regard to the evils attending revivals. While men are taken up with the evils instead of the excellences following a blessed work of God, how can it be expected that they will be useful in promoting it? I would say all this in great kindness, but it is a point upon which I must not be silent.

5. Without new measures it is impossible that the Church should succeed in gaining the attention of the world to religion. There are so many exciting subjects constantly brought before the public mind, such a running to and fro, so many that cry "Lo here!" and "Lo there!" that the Church cannot maintain her ground without sufficient novelty in

measures, to get the public ear. The measures of politicians, of infidels, and heretics, the scrambling after wealth, the increase of luxury, and the ten thousand exciting and counteracting influences that bear upon the Church and upon the world, will gain men's attention, and turn them away from the sanctuary and from the altars of the Lord, unless we increase in wisdom and piety, and wisely adopt such new measures as are calculated to get the attention of men to the Gospel of Christ. I have already said that novelties should be introduced no faster than they are really called for; they should be introduced with the greatest wisdom, and caution, and prayerfulness, and in a manner calculated to excite as little opposition as possible. But new measures we must have. And may God prevent the Church from settling down in any set of forms, or getting the present or any other edition of her measures *stereotyped*.

6. It is evident that we must have more arousing preaching, to meet the character and wants of the age. Ministers are generally beginning to find this out. And some of them complain of it, and suppose it to be "owing to new measures," as they call them. They say that such ministers as our fathers would have been glad to hear, cannot now be heard, cannot get a pastorate, nor secure an audience. And they think that new measures have perverted the taste of the people. But this is not the difficulty. The character of the age is changed, but these men retain the same stiff, dry, prosing style of preaching, that answered half a century ago.

Look at the Methodists. Many of their ministers are unlearned, in the common sense of the term—many of them taken right from the shop or farm, and yet they have gathered congregations, and pushed their way, and won souls everywhere. Whenever the Methodists have gone, their plain, pointed and simple, but warm and animated, mode of preaching has always gathered congregations. Few Presbyterian ministers have gathered such large assemblies, or won so many souls. Now, are we to be told that we must pursue the same old, formal mode of doing things, amidst all these changes? As well might the North River be rolled back, as the world converted under such preaching. Those who adopt a different style of preaching, as the Methodists have done, will run away from us. We must have powerful preaching, or the devil will have the people, except what the Methodists can save! Many ministers are finding out already, that a Methodist preacher, without the advantages of a liberal education, will draw a congregation around him which a Presbyterian minister, with perhaps ten times as much learning, cannot equal, because he has not the earnest manner of the other, and does not pour out fire upon his hearers when he preaches.

7. We see the importance of having *young ministers obtain right views of revivals*. In a multitude of cases I have seen that great pains are taken to frighten our young men, who are preparing for the ministry, about "the evils of revivals," and the like. Young men in some theological seminaries are taught to look upon new measures as if they were the very inventions of the devil. How can such men have revivals? So when they come out, they look about and watch, and start, as if the devil were there. Some young men in Princeton a few years ago came out with an essay upon the "Evils of Revivals." I should like to know, now, how many of those young men have *enjoyed* revivals among their people, since they have been in the ministry; and if any have, I should like to know whether they have not repented of that piece about "the evils of revivals"?

If I had a voice so loud as to be heard at Princeton, I would speak to those young men on this subject. It is high time to talk plainly. The Church is groaning in all her borders for the want of suitable ministers. Good men are labouring, and are willing to labour night and day, to assist in educating young men for the ministry, to promote revivals of religion; and yet when young men come out of the seminary some of them are as shy of all the measures that God blesses as they are of Popery itself.

Shall it be so always? Must we educate young men for the ministry, and have them come out frightened to death about new measures? They ought to know that new measures are no new thing in the Church. Let them go to work, and keep at work, and not be frightened. I have been pained to see that some men, in giving accounts of revivals, have evidently felt it necessary to be particular in detailing the measures used, to avoid the inference that *new* measures were introduced; evidently feeling that even the Church would undervalue the revival unless it appeared to have been promoted without new measures. Besides, this caution in detailing the measures in order to demonstrate that there is nothing new, looks like admitting that new measures are wrong because they are new, and that a revival is more valuable when it is not promoted by new measures. In this way, I apprehend that much evil has been done; and if the practice is to continue, it must come to this, that a revival must be judged of by the fact that it occurred in connection with new, or with old, measures. I never will countenance such a spirit, or condescend to guard an account of a revival against the imputation of old or new measures. I believe new measures are *right*; that is, that it is no objection to a measure, that it is new, or old.

Let a minister enter fully into his work, and pour out his heart to God for a blessing, and whenever he sees the want of any measure to bring the truth more powerfully before the minds of the people, let him adopt it and not be afraid, and God will not withhold His blessing. If ministers will not go forward, if they will preach the Gospel with power and earnestness, if they will not turn out of their tracks to do anything *new* for the purpose of saving souls, they will grieve the Holy Spirit away, and God will visit them with His curse, and raise up other ministers to do His work in the world.

8. *It is the right and duty of ministers to adopt new measures* for promoting revivals. In some places the Church members have opposed their minister when he has attempted to employ those measures which God has blessed for a revival, and have gone so far as to give up their prayer-meetings, and give up labouring to save souls, and stand aloof from everything, because their minister has adopted what they call "new measures"—no matter how reasonable the measures are in themselves, nor how seasonable, nor how much God may bless them. It is enough that they are called "new"; they will not have anything to do with new measures, nor will they tolerate them among the people. And thus they fall out by the way, and grieve away the Spirit of God, and put a stop to the revival, when the world around them is going to hell.

Finally, this zealous adherence to particular forms and modes of doing things which has led the Church to resist innovations *in measures, savours strongly of fanaticism.* And what is not a little singular, is, that fanatics of this stamp are always the first to cry out "fanaticism." What is that but fanaticism in the Roman Catholic Church, which causes them to adhere with such pertinacity to their particular modes, and forms, and ceremonies, and fooleries? They act as if all these things were established by Divine authority; as if there were a "Thus saith the Lord" for every one of them. Now, we justly style this a spirit of fanaticism, and esteem it worthy of rebuke. But it is just as absolutely fanatical for the Presbyterian Church, or any other, to be sticklish for her particular forms, and to act as if *they* were established by Divine authority. The fact is that God has established, in no Church, any particular *form*, or manner of worship, for promoting the interests of religion. The Scriptures are entirely silent on these subjects, under the Scriptures are entirely silent on these subjects, under the Gospel dispensation, and the Church is left to exercise her own discretion in relation to all such matters. And I hope it will not be thought unkind, when I say again, that to me it appears that the unkind, angry zeal, for a certain mode and manner of doing things, and the overbearing, exterminating cry against new measures, SAVOUR STRONGLY OF FANATICISM.

The only thing insisted upon under the Gospel dispensation, in regard to measures, it that there should be *decency and order*. "Let all things be done decently and in order" (I Cor. 14. 40). We are required to guard against all confusion and disorderly conduct. But what is meant by decency and order? Will it be said that an anxious meeting, or a protracted meeting, or an anxious seat, is inconsistent with decency and order? I should most sincerely deprecate, and most firmly resist, whatever was indecent and disorderly in the worship of God's house. But I do not suppose that by "order," we are to understand any particular set mode, in which any Church may have been accustomed to perform its service.

Lecture XV

HINDRANCES TO REVIVALS

I am doing a great work, so that I cannot come down: why should the work cease, whilst I leave it, and come down to you?—Neh. 6. 3.

This servant of God had come down from Babylon to rebuild the temple and re-establish the worship of God at Jerusalem, the city of his fathers' sepulchres. When it was discovered by Sanballat and certain individuals who were his allies, who had long enjoyed the desolations of Zion, that the temple and the holy city were about to be rebuilt, they raised a great opposition. Sanballat and the other leaders tried, in several ways, to divert Nehemiah and his friends, and prevent them from going forward in their work; at one time they threatened them, and then complained that they were going to rebel against the king. They found, however, that they could not frighten Nehemiah, and then they sought to delude him by artifice and fraud, and draw him off from the vigorous prosecution of his work. But the words sum up his position: "I am doing a great work, so that I cannot come down: why should the work cease, whilst I leave it, and come down to you?"

It has always been the case, whenever any of the servants of God do anything in His cause, and there appears to be *a probability* that they will succeed, that Satan by his agents regularly attempts to divert their minds and nullify their labours. So it has been during the last ten years, in which there have been such remarkable revivals through the length and breadth of the land. These revivals have been very great and powerful, and extensive. It has been estimated that not less than TWO HUNDRED THOUSAND persons have been converted by God in that time. And the devil has been busy in his devices to divert and distract the people of God, and turn off their energies from pushing forward the great work of salvation.

In remarking upon the subject, I propose: I. To show that a revival of religion is a great work. II. To mention several things which may put a stop to it. III. To show what must be done for the continuance of this great revival.

I. *A REVIVAL OF RELIGION IS A GREAT WORK.*

It is a great work, because in it are *great interests involved.* In a revival of religion, there are involved both the glory of God, so far as it respects the government of this world, and the salvation of men; two things, therefore, that are of infinite importance are involved in it. The greatness of a work is to be estimated by the greatness of the consequences depending on it; this is the measure of its importance.

II. *THINGS WHICH MAY STOP A REVIVAL.*

Some have talked very foolishly on this subject, as if nothing could hinder a genuine revival. They say: "If your revival is a work of God, it cannot be stopped: can any created being stop God?" Now I ask if this is common sense? Formerly, it used to be the established belief that a revival could not be stopped, because it was the work of God. And so they supposed it would go on, whatever might be done to hinder it, in the Church or out of it. But the farmer might just as well reason so, and think he could go and cut down his wheat and not hurt the crop, because it is God that makes grain grow. A revival is the work of God, and so is a crop of wheat; and God is as much dependent on the use of means in one case as the other. And therefore a revival is as liable to be injured as a wheat field.

1. A revival will stop whenever the *Church believes it is going to cease.* The Church is the instrument with which God

carries on this work, and Christians are to work in it voluntarily and with their hearts. Nothing is more fatal to a revival than for its friends to predict that it is going to stop. No matter what the *enemies* of the work may say about it, predicting that it will come to nothing, they cannot stop it in this way; but the friends must labour and pray in faith to carry it on. It is a contradiction to say they are labouring and praying in faith to carry on the work, and yet believe that it is going to stop. If they lose their faith, it will stop, of course. Whenever the friends of revivals begin to prophesy that the revival is going to stop, they should be instantly rebuked, in the name of the Lord. If the idea should once begin to prevail, and if you cannot counteract it and root it out, the revival will infallibly cease; for it is indispensable to the work that Christians should labour and pray in faith to promote it, and it is a contradiction to say that they can labour in faith for its continuance while they believe that it is about to cease.

2. A revival will cease *when Christians consent that it should cease.* Sometimes Christians see that the revival is in danger of ceasing, and that if something effectual is not done, it will come to a standstill. If this should distress them, and drive them to prayer, and to fresh efforts, the work will not cease. When Christians love the work of God and the salvation of souls so well that they are distressed at a mere apprehension of a decline, it will drive them to agony and effort to prevent its ceasing; but if they see the danger, and do not try to avert it, or to renew the work, *they consent that it should stop.* There are many people who see revivals declining, and that they are in great danger of ceasing altogether, and yet they manifest but little distress, and seem to care but little about it. Whole Churches see the position that must ensue unless there can be an awakening; and yet they are at ease, and do not groan and agonise in prayer that God would revive His work. Some are even predicting that there is now going to be a great reaction, and a great dearth come over the Church, as there did after the day of Whitefield and Edwards. And yet they are not startled at their own forebodings. THEY CONSENT TO IT. It seems as if they were the devil's trumpeters, sent out to scatter dismay throughout the ranks of God's elect.

3. A revival will cease whenever *Christians become*

mechanical in their attempts to promote it. When their faith is strong, and their hearts are warm and mellow, and their prayers full of holy emotion, and their words with power, then the work goes on. But when their prayers begin to be cold and without emotion, and they begin to labour mechanically, and to use words without feeling, then the revival will cease.

4. The revival will cease, whenever Christians get the idea that *the work will go on without their aid.* They are co-workers with God in promoting a revival, and the work can be carried on just as far as the Church will carry it on, and no farther. God has been for one thousand eight hundred years trying to get the Church into the work. He has been calling and urging, commanding, entreating, pressing and encouraging, to get Christians to take hold. He has stood all this while ready to *make bare His arm* to carry on the work with them. But the Church has been unwilling to do her part, seeming determined to leave it to God alone to convert the world, and saying: "If He wants the world converted, let Him do it." The Church ought to know that this is impossible. Sinners cannot be converted without their own agency, for conversion consists in their voluntary turning to God. Nor can sinners be converted without the appropriate moral influences to turn them; that is, without truth and the reality of things being brought full before their minds either by direct revelation or by *men.* God cannot convert the world by physical omnipotence, but He is dependent on the moral influence of the Church.

5. The work will cease when the Church *prefers to attend to selfish concerns* rather than God's business. I do not admit that men *have* any business which is properly *their own*, but they think so, and in fact prefer to attend to what they consider as their own, rather than work for God. They begin to think they *cannot afford* sufficient time from their worldly employments, to carry on a revival. They pretend they are obliged to give up attending to religion, and they let their hearts go out again after the world. And the work must cease, of course.

6. When Christians *get proud* of their "great revival," it will cease. I mean those Christians who have been instrumental in promoting it. It is almost always the case in a revival, that a part of the Church proves too proud or too worldly to take any part in the work. They are determined to

stand aloof, and wait, and see what it will come to. The pride of this part of the Church cannot stop the revival, for the revival never rested on them. It began without them, and it can go on without them. They may fold their arms and do nothing but look out and find fault; and still the work may go on. But when the part of the Church that does the work begins to think what a great revival they have had, how they have laboured and prayed, how bold and how zealous they have been, and how much good they have done, then the work will be likely to decline. Perhaps it has been published in the papers what a revival there has been in that Church, and how absorbed the members have been, so they think how high they will stand in the estimation of other Churches, all over the land, because they have had such a great revival. And so they get puffed up, and vain, and they can no longer enjoy the presence of God. The Spirit withdraws from them, and the revival ceases.

7. The revival will stop when the Church *gets exhausted by labour*. Multitudes of Christians commit a great mistake here in time of revival. They are so thoughtless, and have so little judgment, that they will break up all their habits of living, neglect to eat and sleep at the proper hours, and let the excitement run away with them, so that they overdo their bodies, and are so imprudent that they soon become exhausted, and it is impossible for them to continue in the work. Revivals often cease from negligence and imprudence, in this respect, on the part of those engaged in carrying them on, and declensions follow.

8. A revival will cease when the Church begins *to speculate about abstract doctrines*, which have nothing to do with practice. If the Christians turn their attention away from the things of salvation, and go to studying or disputing about abstract points, the revival will cease, of course.

9. *When Christians begin to proselytise*. When the Baptists are so opposed to the Presbyterians, or the Presbyterians to the Baptists, or both against the Methodists, or Episcopalians against the rest, that they begin to make efforts to get the converts to join their Church, you soon see the last of the revival. Perhaps a revival will go on for a time, and all sectarian difficulties are banished, till somebody circulates a book, privately, to gain proselytes. Perhaps some over-zealous

deacon, or some mischief-making woman, or some proselytising minister, cannot keep still any longer, but begins to work the work of the devil, by attempting to gain proselytes, and so stirs up bitterness; and, raising a selfish strife, grieves away the Spirit, and drives Christians into parties. No more revival there!

10. When Christians *refuse to render to the Lord according to the benefits recieved*. This is a fruitful source of religious declensions. God has opened the windows of heaven to a Church, and poured them out a blessing, and then He reasonably expects them to bring in the tithes into His storehouse, and devise and execute liberal things for Zion; but they have refused; they have not laid themselves out accordingly to promote the cause of Christ, and so the Spirit has been grieved, and the blessing withdrawn, and in some instances a great reaction has taken place, because the Church would not be liberal, when God had been so bountiful. I have known Churches which were evidently cursed with barrenness for such a course. They had a glorious revival, and afterwards perhaps their buildings needed repairing, or something else was needed which would cost a little money, and they refused to do it, and so for their niggardly spirit God gave them up.

11. When the Church, in any way, *grieves the Holy Spirit*.

(a) When Christians *do not feel their dependence on the Spirit*. Whenever they get strong in their own strength, God curses their blessings. In many instances, they sin against their own mercies, because they get lifted up with their success, and take the credit to themselves, and do not give all the glory to God. As He says: "If ye will not hear, and if ye will not lay it to heart, to give glory unto My name, saith the Lord of hosts, I will even send a curse upon you, and I will curse your blessings: yea, I have cursed them already, because ye do not lay it to heart" (Mal. 2. 2). There has been a great deal of this, undoubtedly. I have seen many things in the newspapers that suggested a disposition in men to take credit for success in promoting revivals. There is doubtless a great temptation to this, and it requires the utmost watchfulness, on the part of ministers and Churches, to guard against it, and not to grieve the Spirit away by vainglorying in men.

(*b*)   The Spirit may be grieved *by a spirit of boasting of the revival*. Sometimes, as soon as a revival commences, you will see it blazed out in the newspapers. And most commonly this will kill the revival. There was a case in a neighbouring State, where a revival commenced, and instantly there came out a letter from the pastor, telling that he had a revival. I saw the letter, and said to myself, "That is the last we shall hear of this revival." And so it was. In a few days the work totally ceased. I could mention cases and places, where persons have published such things as to puff up the Church, and make the people so proud that little more could be done for the revival.

Some, under pretence of publishing things to the praise and glory of God, have published things that savoured so strongly of a disposition to exalt themselves—making their own agency stand out conspicuously—as were evidently calculated to make an unhappy impression. At a protracted meeting held in this Church, a year ago last fall, there were five hundred hopefully converted, whose names and places of residence we knew. A considerable number of them joined this Church. Many of them united with other Churches. Nothing was said of this in the papers. I have several times been asked why we were so silent on the subject. I could only reply, that there was such a tendency to self-exaltation in the Churches, that I was afraid to publish anything on the subject. Perhaps I erred. But I have so often seen mischief done by premature publications, that I thought it best to say nothing about it. In the revival in this city, four years ago, so much was said in the papers that appeared so much like self-exaltation, that I was afraid to publish. I am not speaking against the practice itself, of publishing accounts of revivals. But the manner of doing it is of vast importance. If it be done so as to excite vanity, it is always fatal to the revival.

(*c*)   So, too, the Spirit is grieved by *saying or publishing things* that are calculated to *undervalue the work of God.* When a blessed work of God is spoken lightly of, not rendering to God the glory due to His Name, the Spirit is grieved. If anything be said about a revival, give only the plain and naked *facts*, just as they are, and let them pass for what they are worth.

12. A revival may be expected to cease, *when Christians*

lose the spirit of brotherly love. Jesus Christ will not continue with people in a revival any longer than they continue in the exercise of brotherly love. When Christians are in the spirit of a revival, they feel this love, and then you will hear them call each other "Brother" and "Sister," very affectionately. But when they begin to get cold, they lose this warmth and glow of affection for one another, and then this calling "Brother" and "Sister" will seem silly, and they will leave it off. In some Churches they never call each other so; but where there is a revival Christians naturally do it. I never saw a revival, and probably there never was one, in which they did not do it. But as soon as this begins to cease, the Spirit of God is grieved, and departs from among them.

13. A revival will decline and cease, unless *Christians are frequently re-converted.* By this I mean, that Christians, in order to keep in the spirit of revival, commonly need to be frequently *convicted*, and humbled and broken down before God, and "re-converted." This is something which many do not understand, when we talk about a Christian being re-converted. But the fact is, that in a revival, the Christian's heart is liable to get crusted over, and lose its exquisite relish for Divine things; his unction and prevalence in prayer abate, and then he must be converted over again. It is impossible to keep him in such a state as not to do injury to the work, unless he passes through such a process every few days. I have never laboured in revivals in company with any one who would keep in the work and be fit to manage a revival continually, who did not pass through this process of breaking down as often as once in two or three weeks.

Revivals decline, commonly, because it is found impossible to make Christians realise their guilt and dependence, so as to break down before God. It is important that ministers should understand this, and learn how to break down the Church, and break down themselves when they need it, or else Christians will soon become mechanical in their work, and lose their fervour and their power of prevailing with God. This was the process through which Peter passed, when he had denied the Saviour, and by which breaking down, the Lord prepared him for the great work on the day of Pentecost. I was surprised, a few years since, to find that the phrase *"breaking down"* was a stumbling-block to certain ministers and professors of religion. They laid themselves open to the rebuke administered to Nicodemus: "Art thou a master of Israel, and knowest not these things?" (John 3. 10.) I am confident that until some of them know what it is to be "broken down," they will never do much more for the cause of revival.

14. A revival cannot continue *when Christians will not practise self-denial*. When the Church has enjoyed a revival, and begins to grow fat upn it, and to run into self-indulgence, the revival will soon cease. Unless they sympathise with the Son of God, who gave up all to save sinners; unless they are willing to give up their luxuries, and their ease, and devote themselves to the work, the Christians need not expect that the Spirit of God will be poured out upon them. This is undoubtedly one of the principal causes of personal declension. Let Christians in a revival BEWARE, when they first find an inclination creeping upon them to shrink from self-denial, and to give in to one self-indulgence after another. It is the device of Satan, to "bait" them off from the work of God, and make them dull and gross, lazy and fearful, useless and sensual; and so drive away the Spirit and destroy the revival.

15. A revival will be stopped *by controversies about new measures*. Nothing is more certain to overthrow a revival than this.

16. Revivals can be put down *by the continued opposition of the Old School, combined with a bad spirit in the New School*. If those who do nothing to promote revivals continue their opposition, and if those who are labouring to promote them allow themselves to get impatient, and get into a bad spirit, the revival will cease. When the Old School write letters in the newspapers, against revivals or revival men, and the New School write letters back again, in an angry, contentious spirit, revivals will cease. LET THEM KEEP ABOUT THEIR WORK, and neither talk about the opposition, nor preach upon it, nor rush into print about it. If others choose to publish "slang," let the Lord's people keep to their work. None of the slander will stop the revival, while those who are engaged in it mind their business, and keep to the work.

In one place where there was a revival, certain ministers

formed a combination against the pastor of the Church, and a plan was set on foot to ruin him, and they actually got him prosecuted before his Presbytery, and had a trial that lasted six weeks, right in the midst of the revival; but the work still went on. The praying members of the Church laid themselves out so in the work, that it continued triumphantly throughout the whole scene. The pastor was called off, to attend his trial, but there was another minister that laboured among the people, and the members did not even go to the trial, but kept praying and labouring for souls, and the revival rode out the storm. In many places, opposition has risen up in the Church, but a few humble souls have kept at their work, and our gracious God has stretched out His naked arm and made the revival go forward in spite of all opposition.

But whenever those who are actively engaged in promoting a revival get excited at the unreasonableness and pentinacity of the opposition, and feel as if they must answer the cavils, and refute the slanders, then they get down to the plain of Ono (Neh. 6. 2) and the work must cease.

17. *Any diversion of the public mind* will hinder a revival. In the case I have specified, where the minister was put on trial before his Presbytery, the reason why it did not ruin the revival was, that the praying members of the Church *would not suffer* themselves to be diverted. They kept on praying and labouring for souls, and so public attention was kept to the revival, in spite of all the efforts of the devil.

But whenever Satan succeeds in *absorbing* public attention in any other subject, he will put an end to the revival. No matter what the subject is. If an angel from heaven were to come down, and preach, or pass about the streets, it might be the worst thing in the world for a revival, for it would turn sinners off from their own sins, and turn the Church off from praying for souls, to follow this glorious being, and gaze upon him, and the revival would cease.

18. *Resistance to the Temperance reformation* will put a stop to revivals in a Church. The time has come that it can no longer be innocent in a Church to stand aloof from this glorious reformation. The time was when this could be done ignorantly. The time has been when ministers and Christians could enjoy revivals, notwithstanding that ardent spirit was

used among them. But since light has been thrown upon the subject, and it has been found that the use is injurious, no member or minister can be innocent and stand neutral in the cause. They must speak out and take sides. And if they do not take ground on our side, their influence is on the other. Show me a minister that has taken ground against the Temperance reformation who has had a revival. Show me one who now stands aloof from it who has a revival. Show me one who now temporises upon this point, who does not come out and take a stand in favour of Temperance who has a revival. It used not to be so. But now the subject has come up, and has been discussed, and is understood, no man can shut his eyes upon the truth. The man's hands are RED WITH BLOOD who stands aloof from the Temperance cause. And can *he* have a revival?

19. Revivals are hindered when ministers and *Churches take wrong ground in regard to any question involving human rights*. Take the subject of SLAVERY,[1] for instance. The time was when this subject was not before the public mind. John Newton continued in the slave trade after his conversion.[2]

---

[1]The Slavery question was now becoming crucial. Finney's uncompromising position in the matter was speedily made clear. Party animosity was so fierce that, following the dissemination of a report that in his Broadway Tabernacle (then in course of erection) whites and blacks would have to sit together, the building was set on fire, and as the firemen refused to extinguish the conflagration, the interior and roof were consumed. However, the friends who had undertaken the erection duly completed it. Despite the intense feeling, a quarter of a century was yet to elapse ere, at the Confederate attack on Fort Sumter, the first shot was fired in the Civil War. Two days after that event Lincoln called for seventy-five thousand men to put down the rebellion: when the war concluded (with the surrender of Lee, at Appomattox Court House, April 9, 1865) the North had more than a million men under arms; and perhaps a million lives had been lost in the terrible struggle which was waged to maintain (in the words of Lincoln, in the famous Gettysburg address) "the proposition that all men are created equal" and that "this nation, under God, shall have a new birth of freedom."

[2]Newton's words were: "During the time I was engaged in the slave trade I never had the least scruple as to its lawfulness... It is, indeed, accounted a genteel employment... However, I considered

And so had his mind been perverted, and so completely was his conscience seared, in regard to this most nefarious traffic, that the sinfulness of it never occurred to his thoughts until some time after he became a child of God. Had light been poured upon his mind previously to his conversion, he *never could* have been converted without previously abandoning this sin. And after his conversion, when convinced of its iniquity, he could no longer enjoy the presence of God without abandoning the sin forever.

So, doubtless, many slave dealers and slave holders in our country have been converted, notwithstanding their participation in this abomination, because the sinfulness of it was not apparent to their minds. So ministers and Churches, to a great extent throughout the land, have held their peace, and borne no testimony against this abomination, existing in the Church and in the nation. But recently, the subject has come up for discussion, and the providence of God has brought it distinctly before the eyes of all men. Light is now shed upon this subject, as it has been upon the cause of Temperance. Facts are exhibited, and principles established, and light thrown in upon the minds of men, and this monster is dragged from his horrid den, and exhibited before the Church, and it is demanded of Christians: "IS THIS SIN?" Their testimony *must* be given on this subject. They are God's witnesses. They are sworn to tell "the truth, the whole truth, and nothing but the truth." It is impossible that their testimony should not be given, on one side or the other. Their silence can no longer be accounted for upon the principle of ignorance, that they have never had their attention turned to the subject. Consequently,

---

myself as a sort of gaoler or turnkey; and I was sometimes shocked with an employment that was perpetually conversant with chains, bolts, and shackles. In this view I had often petitioned that the Lord would be pleased to fix me in a more humane calling, and place me where I might have more frequent converse with His people. My prayers were answered." They were answered through an illness which, just as he was to sail in command of a ship, detained him in England. Then followed his appointment to the curacy of Olney, his friendship with Cowper, and the production of the Olney Hymns. He continued at Olney for sixteen years, when he became rector of St. Mary Woolnoth, close to the Mansion House, London.

the silence of Christians upon the subject is virtually saying *that they do not* consider slavery as a sin.

The truth is, this is a subject on which they cannot be silent without guilt. The time has come, in the providence of God, when every southern breeze is loaded down with the cries of lamentation, mourning, and woe. Two millions of degraded heathen in our own land stretch their hands, all shackled and bleeding, and send forth to the Church of God the agonising cry for help. And shall the Church, in her efforts to reclaim and save the world, deafen her ears to this voice of agony and despair? God forbid! The Church cannot turn away from this question. It is a question for the Church and for the nation to decide, and God will push it to a decision. It is in vain for us to resist it for fear of distraction, contention, and strife. It is in vain to account it an act of *piety* to turn away the ear from hearing this cry of distress.

The Church must testify, and testify "the truth, the whole truth, and nothing but the truth," on this subject, or she is perjured, and the Spirit of God departs from her. She is under oath to testify, and ministers and Churches who do not pronounce it sin, bear false testimony for God. It is doubtless true, that one of the reasons for the low state of religion at the present time is that many Churches have taken the wrong side on the subject of slavery, have suffered prejudice to prevail over principle, and have feared to call this abomination by its true name.

20. Another thing that hinders revivals is, *neglecting the claims of Missions*. If Christians confine their attention to their own Church, do not read even their *Missionary Magazine*, or use any other means to inform themselves on the subject of the claims of the world, but reject the light, and will not do what God calls them to do in this cause, the Spirit of God will depart from them.

21. *When a Church rejects the calls of God upon it for educating young men for the ministry*, it will hinder and destroy a revival. Look at the Presbyterian Church. Look at the two hundred thousand souls converted within ten years: consider that there are resources sufficient to fill the world with ministers, and yet observe that the ministry is not increasing so fast as the population of our own country; so that

unless something more can be done to provide ministers, we shall become heathen ourselves. The Churches do not press upon young men the duty of going into the ministry. God pours His Spirit on the Churches, and converts hundreds of thousands of souls, and if then the labourers do not come forth into the harvest, what can be expected but that the curse of God will come upon the Churches, and His Spirit will be withdrawn, and revivals will cease? Upon this subject no minister, no Church, should be silent or inactive.

22. *Slandering revivals* will often put them down. The great revival in the days of President Edwards suffered greatly by the conduct of the Church in this respect. It is to be expected that the enemies of God will revile, misrepresent, and slander revivals. But when *the Church* herself engages in this work, and many of her most influential members are aiding and abetting in calumniating and misrepresenting a glorious work of God, it is reasonable that the Spirit should be grieved away. It cannot be denied that this has been done to a grievous and God-dishonouring extent. It has been estimated that in one year, since the revival commenced, ONE HUNDRED THOUSAND SOULS were converted to God in the United States. This is undoubtedly the greatest number that were ever converted in one year, since the world began.[1] It could not be expected that, in an excitement of this extent, among *human beings*, there should be nothing to deplore. To expect perfection in such a work as this, of such extent, and carried on by human instrumentality, is utterly unreasonable and absurd. Evils doubtless did exist and have existed. They were to be expected of course, and guarded against as far as possible. But I do not believe the world's history can furnish one instance in which a revival, approaching to this in extent and influence, has been attended with so few evils, and with so little that is honestly to be deplored.

But how has this blessed work of God been treated! Admitting all the evils complained of to be real, which is far

---

[1]"This," added Finney, in 1868, "was in 1831. There have been more extensive revivals since. In 1857-8 it was estimated that fifty thousand conversions per week occurred for six or eight weeks in succession, in the northern parts of the United States."

from being true, they would only be like spots upon the disc of the glorious sun; things hardly to be thought of in comparison with the infinite greatness and excellence of the work. And yet how has a great portion of the Presbyterian Church received and treated this blessed work of God? At the General Assembly, that grave body of men that represent the Presbyterian Church, in the midst of this great work, instead of appointing a day of thanksgiving, instead of praising and glorifying God for the greatness of His work, we hear from them the voice of rebuke. From the reports that were given of the speeches, it appears that the house was filled with complainings. Instead of devising measures to forward the work, their attention seemed to be taken up with the comparatively trifling evils that were incidental to it. And after much complaining, they absolutely appointed a committee, and sent forth a "Pastoral Letter," calculated to excite suspicion, to quench the zeal of God's people, and to turn them from giving glory to God for the greatness of the blessing into finding fault and carping about "the evils." When I heard what was done at that General Assembly, when I read their speeches, when I saw their Pastoral Letter, my soul was sick, an unutterable feeling of distress came over my mind, and I felt that God would "visit" the Presbyterian Church for conduct like this. And ever since, the glory has been departing, and revivals have been becoming less and less frequent—less and less powerful.

And now I wish it could be known whether those ministers who poured out those complainings on the floor of the General Assembly, and who were instrumental in getting up that Pastoral Letter, have since been blessed in promoting revivals of religion; whether the Spirit of God has been upon them; and whether their Churches can witness that they have an unction from the Holy One.

23. *Ecclesiastical difficulties* are calculated to grieve away the Spirit, and destroy revivals. It has always been the policy of the devil to turn off the attention of ministers from the work of the Lord to disputes and ecclesiastical litigations. President Edwards was obliged to be taken up for a long time in disputes before ecclesiastical councils; and in our days, and in the midst of these great revivals of religion, these difficulties have been

alarmingly and shamefully multiplied. Some of the most efficient ministers in the Church have been called off from their direct efforts to win souls to Christ, to reply to charges preferred against them, or against their fellow-labourers in the ministry, which could never be sustained. Oh, tell it not in Gath! When will those ministers and professors of religion, who do little or nothing themselves, let others alone, and let them work for God?

24. Another thing by which revivals may be hindered is *censoriousness, on either side*, and *especially in those who have been engaged in carrying forward a revival*. It is to be expected that the opposers of the work will watch for the halting of its friends, and be sure to censure them for all that is wrong, and not infrequently for that which is right, in their conduct. Especially is it to be expected that many censorious and unchristian remarks will be made about those who are the most prominent instruments in promoting the work. This censoriousness on the part of the *opposers* of the work, whether in or out of the Church, will not, however, of itself put a stop to the revival. While its promoters keep humble, and in a prayerful spirit, while they do not retaliate, but possess their souls in patience, while they do not suffer themselves to be diverted, to recriminate, and grieve away the spirit of prayer, the work will go forward.

Censoriousness in those who are opposed to the work is but little to be dreaded, for they have not the Spirit, and nothing depends on them, for they can hinder the work only just so far as they themselves have influence personally. But the others have the power of the Holy Spirit, and the work depends on their keeping in a right temper. If they get wrong, and grieve away the Spirit, there is no help: the work must cease. Whatever provocation, therefore, the promoters of the blessed work may have had, if it ceases, the responsibility will be theirs. And one of the most alarming facts in regard to this matter is that, in many instances, those who have been engaged in carrying forward the work appear to have lost the Spirit. They are becoming diverted; are beginning to think that the opposition is no longer to be tolerated, and that they must come out and reply in the newspapers. It should be known, and universally understood, that whenever the friends and promoters of this greatest of revivals suffer themselves to be called off to newspaper janglings, to attempt to defend themselves, and reply to those who write against them, the work will cease. Nothing is more detrimental to revivals of religion (and so it has always been found) than for the promoters of it to listen to the opposition, and begin to reply. This was found to be true in the days of President Edwards, as those who are acquainted with his book on Revivals[1] are well aware.

III. *THINGS WHICH OUGHT TO BE DONE.*

I proceed to mention some things *which ought to be done* to continue this great and glorious revival of religion, which has been in progress for the last ten years.

1. *There should be great and deep repentings on the part of ministers.* WE, my brethren, must humble *ourselves* before God. It will not do for us to suppose that it is enough to call on the *people* to repent. We must take the lead in repentance, and then call on the Churches to follow.

Especially must those repent who have taken the lead in producing feelings of opposition and distrust in regard to revivals. Some ministers have confined their opposition against revivals and revival measures to their own congregations, and have created such suspicions among their own people as to prevent the work from spreading and prevailing among them. Such ministers will do well to consider the remarks of President Edwards on this subject:

'If ministers preach never so good doctrine, and are never so painful and laborious in their work, yet, if at such a day as this, they show to their people that they are not well-affected to this work, but are very doubtful and suspicious of it, they will be very likely to do their people a great deal more hurt than good; for the very fame of such a great and extraordinary work of God, if their people were suffered to believe it to be His work, and the example of other towns, together with what preaching they might hear occasionally, would be likely to have a much greater influence upon the minds of their people, to awaken and animate them in religion, than all their labours with them.

---

[1]"Thoughts on the Revival," etc.

And besides, their minister's opinion would not only beget in them a suspicion of the work they hear of abroad, whereby the mighty hand of God that appears in its loses its influence upon their minds, but it will also tend to create a suspicion of everything of the like nature, that shall appear among themselves, as being something of the same distemper that has become so epidemical in the land; and that is, in effect, to create a suspicion of all vital religion, and to put the people upon talking against it, and discouraging it, wherever it appears, and knocking it on the head as fast as it rises. And we that are ministers, by looking on this work, from year to year, with a displeased countenance, shall effectually keep the sheep from their pasture, instead of doing the part of shepherds to them by feeding them; and our people had a great deal better be without any settled minister at all at such a day as this."[1]

Others have been more public, having aimed at exerting a wider influence. Some have written pieces for the public papers. Some men, in high standing in the Church, have circulated letters which were never printed; others have had their letters printed and circulated. There seems to have been a system of letter-writing about the country calculated to create distrust. In the days of President Edwards, substantially the same course was pursued, in view of which he says, in his work on Revivals:

"Great care should be taken that the press should be improved to no purpose contrary to the interest of this work. We read that when God fought against Sisera, for the deliverance of His oppressed Church, *they that handled the pen of the writer* came to the help of the Lord (Judg. 5. 14). Whatever class of men in Israel they were that are intended, yet as the words were indited by a Spirit that had a perfect view of all events to the end of the world, it is not unlikely that they have respect to authors, those that should fight against the kingdom of Satan with their pens. Those, therefore, that publish pamphlets ot the disadvantage of this work, and tending either directly or indirectly to bring it under suspicion, and to discourage or hinder it, would do well thoroughly to

---

[1]"Thoughts on the Revival," etc. Part 2: "Obligations to promote this work."

consider whether this be not indeed the work of God; and whether, if it be, it is not likely that God will go forth as fire, to consume all that stand in His way, and so burn up those pamphlets; and whether there be not danger that the fire that is kindled in them will scorch the authors."[1]

All these must repent. God never will forgive them, nor will they ever enjoy His blessing on their preaching, or be honoured to labour in revivals, till they repent. This duty President Edwards pressed upon ministers in his day, in the most forcible terms. There doubtless have been now, as there were then, faults on both sides. And there must be deep repentance, and mutual confessions of faults on both sides.

"There must be a great deal done at confessing of faults on both sides: for undoubtedly many and great are the faults that have been committed, in the jangling and confusions, and mixtures of light and darkness, that have been of late. There is hardly any duty more contrary to our corrupt dispositions and mortifying to the pride of man; but it must be done. Repentance of faults is, in a peculiar manner, a proper duty, when the kingdom of heaven is at hand, or when we especially expect or desire that it should come as appears by John the Baptist's preaching. And if God does now loudly call upon us to repent, then He also calls upon us to make proper manifestations of our repentance.

"I am persuaded that those who have *openly opposed* this work, or have from time to time spoken lightly of it, cannot be excused in the sight of God, without openly confessing their fault therein: especially if they be ministers. If they have in any way, either directly or indirectly, opposed the work, or have so behaved in their public performances or private conversation as to prejudice the minds of their people against the work; if, hereafter, they shall be convinced of the goodness and divinity of what they have opposed, they ought by no means to palliate the matter, and excuse themselves, and pretend that they always thought so, and that it was only such and such imprudences that they objected against; but they ought openly to declare their conviction, and condemn themselves for what

---

[1]"Thoughts on the Revival," etc. Part 2: "Obligations to promote this work."

they have done; for it is Christ that they have spoken against, in speaking lightly of, and prejudicing others against, this work. And though they have done it ignorantly and in unbelief, yet when they find out Who it is that they have opposed, undoubtedly God will hold them bound publicly to confess it.

"And on the other hand, if those who have been *zealous to promote* the work have, in any of the forementioned instances, openly gone much out of the way, and done that which was contrary to Christian rules, whereby they have openly injured others or greatly violated good order, and so done that which has wounded religion, they must publicly confess it, and humble themselves, as they would gather out the stones, and prepare the way of God's people. They who have laid great stumbling-blocks in others' way by their *open transgression*, are bound to remove them by their *open repentance*."[1]

There are ministers in our day, I say it not in unkindness, but in faithfulness, and I would that I had them all here before me while I say it, who seem to have been engaged much of their time, for years, in doing little else than acting and talking and writing in such a way as to create suspicion in regard to revivals. And I cannot doubt that their Churches would, as President Edwards says, be better with no minister at all, unless they will repent and regain God's blessing.

2. *Those Churches which have opposed revivals* must humble themselves and repent. Churches which have stood aloof, or hindered the work, must repent of their sin, or God will not go with them. Look at those Churches which have been throwing suspicion upon revivals. Do they enjoy revivals? Does the Holy Ghost descend upon them, to enlarge them and build them up? There is one of the Churches in this city, where the Session has been publishing in the newspapers what it calls its "Act and Testimony," calculated to excite an unreasonable and groundless suspicion against many ministers who are labouring successfully to promote revivals. And what is the state of that Church? Have they had a revival?

---

[1] "Thoughts on the Revival," etc., Part 5:—"What ought to be done to promote this work."

Why, it appears from the official report, that it has dwindled in one year twenty-seven per cent. And all such Churches will continue to dwindle, in spite of everything else that can be done, unless they repent and have a revival. They may pretend to be mighty pious, and jealous for the honour of God, but God will not believe they are sincere. And He will manifest His displeasure by not pouring out His Spirit. If I had a voice loud enough, I should like to make all those Churches and ministers that have slandered revivals, hear me, when I say that I believe they have helped to bring the pall of death over the Church, and that the curse of God is on them already, and will remain unless they repent. God has already sent leanness into their souls, and many of them know it.

3. *Those who have been engaged in promoting the work* must also repent. Whenever a wrong spirit has been manifested, or they have got irritated and provoked at the opposition, and lost their temper, or mistaken Christian faithfulness for hard words and a wrong spirit, they must repent. Those who are opposed can never stop a revival alone, unless those who promote it get wrong. So we must repent if we have said things that were censorious, or proud, or arrogant, or severe. Such a time as this is no time to stand justifying ourselves. Our first call is to repent. Let each one repent of his own sins, and not fall out about who is most to blame.

4. *The Church must take right ground in regard to politics.* Do not suppose that I am going to preach a political sermon, or that I wish to have you join in getting up a *Christian party* in politics. No, you must not believe that. But the time has come that Christians must vote for honest men, and take consistent ground in politics. They must let the world see that the Church will uphold no man in office who is known to be a knave, or an adulterer, or a Sabbath-breaker, or a gambler, or a drunkard. Such is the spread of intelligence and the facility of communication in our country, that every man can know for whom he gives his vote. And if he will give his vote only for honest men, the country will be obliged to have upright rulers. All parties will be compelled to put up honest men as candidates. But the time has come when they must act differently. As on the subjects of Slavery and Temperance, so

on this subject the Church must act rightly or the country will be ruined. God cannot sustain this free and blessed country, which we love and pray for, unless the Church will take right ground. Politics are a part of a religion in such a country as this, and Christians must do their duty to the country as a part of their duty to God. It seems sometimes as if the foundations of the nation are becoming rotten, and Christians seem to act as if they think God does not see what they do in politics. But I tell you He does see it, and He will bless or curse this nation, according to the course they take.

5. *The Churches must take right ground on the subject of Slavery.* Here the question arises, What is right ground? *(a)* I will state some of the *things that should be avoided.*

1. First of all, a *bad spirit* should be avoided. Nothing is more calculated to injure religion, and to injure the slaves themselves, than for Christians to get into an angry controversy on the subject. It is a subject upon which there needs to be no angry controversy among Christians. Slave-holding professors, like rum-selling professors, may endeavour to justify themselves, and may be angry with those who press their consciences, and call upon them to give up their sins. Those proud professors of religion, who think a man to blame, or think it is a shame to him, to have a black skin, may allow their prejudices so far to prevail, as to shut their ears and be disposed to quarrel with those who urge the subject upon them. But I repeat it, the subject of Slavery is a subject upon which Christians, praying men, *need not* and *must not* differ.

2. Another thing to be avoided is *an attempt to take neutral ground* on this subject. Christians can no more take neutral ground on this subject, since it has come up for discussion, than they can take neutral ground on the subject of the sanctification of the Sabbath. It is a great national sin. It is a sin of the Church. The Churches, by their silence, and by permitting slave-holders to belong to their communion, have been consenting to it. All denominations have been more or less guilty, although the Quakers have of late years washed their hands of it. It is in vain for the Churches to pretend it is merely a political sin. I repeat, it is the sin of the Church, to which all denominations have consented. They have virtually

declared that it is lawful. The very fact of suffering slave-holders quietly to remain in good standing in their Churches, is the strongest and most public expression of their view that it is not sin. For the Church, therefore, to pretend to take neutral ground on the subject, is perfectly absurd. The fact is that she is not on neutral ground at all. While she tolerates slave-holders in her communion SHE JUSTIFIES THE PRACTICE. And as well might an enemy of God pretend that he was neither a saint nor a sinner, that he was going to take neutral ground, and pray, "good Lord and good devil," because he did not know which side would be the most popular!

3. Great care should be taken to *avoid a censorious spirit on either side*. It is a subject on which there has been, and probably will be for some time to come, a difference of *opinion* among Christians, as to the best method of disposing of the question: and it ought to be treated with great forbearance.

(*b*) I will mention several things that, in my judgment, the Church is imperatively *called upon to do*, on this subject:

1. Christians, of all denominations, should lay aside prejudice, and *inform themselves* on this subject, without any delay. Vast multitudes of professors of religion have indulged prejudice to such a degree, as to be unwilling to read and hear, and come to a right understanding of the subject. But Christians cannot pray in this state of mind. I defy any one to possess the spirit of prayer while he is too prejudiced to examine this or any other question of duty. If the light did not shine, Christians might remain in the dark upon this point, and still possess the spirit of prayer. But if they *refuse to come to the light*, they cannot pray. Where ministers, individual Christians, or whole Churches, *resist* truth upon this point, when it is so extensively diffused and before the public mind, I do not believe they will or can enjoy a revival of religion.

2. Writings, containing temperate and judicious discussions on this subject, and such developments of facts as are before the public, should be quietly and extensively circulated, and should be carefully and prayerfully examined by the whole Church. I do not mean by this, that the attention of the Church should be so absorbed by this as to neglect the main question of saving souls in the midst of them; I do not mean that such premature movements on this subject should be made, as to

astound the Christian community, and involve them in a broil; but that praying men should act judiciously, and that, as soon as sufficient information can be diffused through the community, the Churches should meekly, but *firmly* take decided ground on the subject, and express, before the whole nation and the world, their abhorrence of this sin.

The anti-masonic excitement which prevailed a few years since made such desolations in the Churches, and produced so much alienation of feeling and ill-will among ministers and people, and the introduction of *this* subject has been attended with such commotions, that many good ministers, who are themselves entirely opposed to slavery, dread to introduce the subject, through fear that their people have not religion enough to consider it calmly, and decide upon it in the spirit of the Gospel. I know there is danger of this. But still, the subject must be presented to the Churches. Let there be no mistake here. William Morgan's *exposé* of freemasonry was published in 1826; the subsequent discussion continued until 1830. In the meantime the Churches had very generally borne testimony against freemasonry, and resolved that they could not have adhering masons in fellowship. As a consequence, the masonic lodges generally disbanded. There was a general stampede of Christians from the lodges. This prepared the way, and in 1830 the greatest revival the world had then seen commenced in the centre of the anti-masonic region, and spread over the whole field where the Church action had been taken.

Perhaps no Church in this country has had a more severe trial upon this subject, than this, which was a Church of young, and for the most part, inexperienced Christians. And many circumstances conspired, in my absence,[1] to produce confusion and wrong-feeling among them. But so far as I am now acquainted with the state of feeling in this Church, I know of no ill-will among the members on this subject. There are doubtless those who feel upon this subject, in very different degrees: and yet I can honestly say that I am not aware of the least difference in *sentiment* among them. We have from the beginning taken the same ground on the subject of Slavery

---

[1]   On his trip to the Mediterranean, following a breakdown in health. (See Lecturer's Preface.)

that we have on Temperance. We have excluded slave-holders, and all concerned in the traffic, from our Communion. By some, out of this Church, this course has been censured as unwarrantable and uncharitable, and I would by no means make my own judgment, or the example of this Church, a rule for the government of other ministers and Churches. Still, I conscientiously believe that the time is not far distant, when the Churches will be united in this expression of abhorrence against this sin. If I do not baptize slavery by some soft and Christian name, if I call it SIN, both consistency and conscience conduct to the inevitable conclusion, that while this sin is persevered in, its perpetrators cannot be fit subjects for Christian communion and fellowship.

To this it is objected that there are *many ministers* in the Presbyterian Church who are slaveholders. And it is said to be very inconsistent that we should refuse to suffer slave-holders to come to our Communion, and yet belong to the same Church with them, sit with them in ecclesiastical bodies, and acknowledge them as ministers. To this I answer, that I have not the power to deal with those ministers, and certainly I am not to withdraw from the Church because some of its ministers or members are slave-holders. My duty is to belong to the Church, even if the devil should belong to it. When I *have authority*, I exclude slave-holders from the Communion, and I always will as long as I live. But where I have no authority, if the table of Christ be spread, I will sit down to it in obedience to His commandment, whoever else may sit down or stay away.

I do not mean, by any means, to denounce all those slave-holding ministers and professors as hypocrites, and to say that they are not Christians. But this I say, that while they continue in this attitude, the cause of Christ and of humanity demands that they should not be recognised as such, unless we mean to be partakers of other men's sins. It is no more inconsistent to exclude slave-holders because they belong to the Presbyterian Church, than it is it exclude persons who drink or sell ardent spirit. For there are many rum-sellers belonging to the Presbyterian Church.

I believe the time has come—although I am no prophet, I believe it will be found to have come, that the revival in the

United States will prevail no further and no faster than the Church takes right ground upon this subject. The Church is God's witness. The fact is, that Slavery is, pre-eminently, the *sin of the Church*. It is the very fact that ministers and professors of religion of different denominations hold slaves, which sanctifies the whole abomination, in the eyes of ungodly men. Who does not know that on the subject of Temperance, every drunkard in the land will skulk behind some rum-selling deacon, or wine-drinking minister? It is the most common objection and refuge of the intemperate, and of moderate drinkers, that it is practised by professors of religion. It is *this* that creates the imperious necessity for excluding traffickers in ardent spirit, and rum-drinkers, from the Communion. Let the Churches of all denominations speak out on the subject of Temperance; let them close their doors against all who have anything to do with the death-dealing abomination, and the cause of Temperance is triumphant. A few years would annihilate the traffic. Just so with Slavery.

It is the Church that mainly supports this sin. Her united testimony upon the subject would settle the question. Let Christians of all denominations meekly, but firmly, come forth, and pronounce their verdict; let them wash their hands of this thing; let them give forth and write on the head and front of this great abomination, "SIN," and in three years, a public sentiment would be formed that would carry all before it, and there would not be a shackled slave, nor a bristling, cruel slave-driver, in this land.

Still it may be said, that in many Churches, this subject *cannot* be introduced without creating confusion and ill-will. This may be. It has been so on the subject of Temperance, and upon the subject of revivals too. In some Churches, neither Temperance nor revivals can be introduced without producing dissension. Sabbath Schools, and missionary operations, and everything of the kind, have been opposed, and have produced dissensions in many Churches. But is this a sufficient reason for excluding these subjects? And where Churches have excluded these subjects for fear of contention, have they been blessed with revivals? Everybody knows that they have not. But where Churches have taken firm ground on these subjects, although individuals, and sometimes numbers, have opposed, still they have been blessed with revivals. Where any of these subjects are carefully and prayerfully introduced; where they are brought forward with a right spirit, and the true relative importance is attached to each of them; if in such cases, there are those who will make disturbance and resist, *let the blame fall where it ought.* There are some individuals, who are *themselves* disposed to quarrel with this subject, who are always ready to exclaim: "Do not introduce these things into the Church, they will create opposition." And if the minister and praying people feel it their duty to bring the matter forward, they will themselves create a disturbance and then say: "There, I told you so; now see what your introducing this subject has done; it will tear the Church all to pieces." And while they are themselves doing all they can to create a division, they are charging the division upon the subject, and not upon themselves. There are some such people in many of our Churches. And neither Sabbath Schools, nor Missions, nor Anti-slavery, nor anything else that honours God or benefits the souls of men, will be carried on in the Churches, without these careful souls being offended by it.

There might infinitely better be no Church in the world, than that she should attempt to remain neutral, or give a false testimony on a subject of such importance as Slavery, especially since the subject has come up, and it is impossible, from the nature of the case, that her testimony should not be in the scale, on the one side or the other.

Do you ask: "What shall be done? Shall we make it the all-absorbing topic of conversation, and divert attention from the all-important subject of the salvation of souls in the midst of us?" I answer: "No." Let a Church express its opinion upon the subject, and be at peace. So far as I know, *we* are entirely at peace upon this subject. We have expressed our opinion; we have closed our Communion against slave-holders, and are attending to other things. I am not aware of the least unhealthy excitement among us on this subject. And where it has become an absorbing topic of conversation in places, in most instances, I believe, it has been owing to the pertinacious and unreasonable opposition of a few individuals against even granting the subject a hearing.

6. If the Church wishes to promote revivals, *she must*

sanctify the Sabbath. There is a vast deal of Sabbath-breaking in the land. Merchants break it, travellers break it, the Government breaks it. A few years ago an attempt was made in the western part of this State, to establish and sustain a Sabbath-keeping line of boats and coaches. But it was found that the *Church* would not sustain the enterprise. Many professors of religion would not travel in these coaches, and would not have their goods forwarded in canal-boats that would be detained from travelling on the Sabbath. At one time, Christians were much engaged in petitioning Congress to suspend the Sabbath mails, and now they seem to be ashamed of it. But one thing is most certain, that unless something is done, and done speedily, and done effectually, to promote the sanctification of the Sabbath by the Church, the Sabbath will go by the board, and we shall not only have our mails running on the Sabbath, and post-offices open, but, by and by, our courts of justice, and the halls of legislation, will be kept open on the Sabbath. And what can the Church do, what will this nation do, *without any Sabbath?*

7. The Church must *take right ground* on all the subjects of practical morality which come up for discussion from time to time.

There are those in the Churches who are standing aloof from the subject of moral reform, and who are afraid to have anything said in the pulpit against lewdness. On this subject, the Church need not expect to be permitted to take neutral ground. In the providence of God, it is up for discussion. The evils have been exhibited; the call has been made for reform. And what is to reform mankind but the truth? And who shall present the truth if not the Church and the ministry? Away with the idea, that Christians can remain neutral, and yet enjoy the approbation and blessing of God!

In all such cases, the minister who holds his peace is counted among those on the other side. Everybody knows that it is so in a revival. It is not necessary for a person to rail out against the work. If he will only keep still and take neutral ground, the enemies of the revival will all consider him as on their side. So on the subject of Temperance. It is not needful that a person should rail at the Cold-water Society, in order to be on the best terms with drunkards and moderate drinkers. Only let him plead for the moderate use of wine, only let him continue to drink it as a luxury, and all the drunkards account him on their side. On all these subjects, when they come up, the Churches and ministers must take the right ground, and take it openly, and stand to the cause, and carry it through, if they expect to enjoy the blessing of God in revivals. They must cast out from their communions such members as, in contempt of the light that is shed upon them, continue to drink or traffic in ardent spirit.

8. *There must be more done for all the great objects of Christian benevolence.* There must be much greater effort for the cause of Missions, and Education, and the Bible, and all other branches of religious enterprise, or the Church will displease God. Look at it. Think of the mercies we have received, of the wealth, numbers and prosperity of the Church. Have we rendered unto God according to the benefits we have received, so as to show that the Church is bountiful, and willing to give money, and to work for God? No. Far from it. Have we multiplied our means and enlarged our plans, in proportion as the Church has increased? Is God satisfied with what has been done, or has He reason to be? After such a revival as has been enjoyed by the Churches of America for the last ten years, we ought to have done ten times as much as we have for Missions, Bibles, Education, Tracts, Churches, and for all causes that are designed to promote religion and save souls. If the Churches do not wake up this subject, and lay themselves out on a larger scale, they may expect that the revival in the United States will cease.

9. If Christians expect revivals to spread and prevail, till the world is converted, they must give up writing letters and publishing pieces *calculated to excite suspicion and jealousy in regard to revivals,* and must take hold of the work themselves. If the whole Church, as a body, had gone to work ten years ago, and continued it as a few individuals, whom I could name, have done, there might not now have been an impenitent sinner in the land. The millennium would have fully come into the United States before this day. Instead of standing still, or writing letters, let ministers who think we are going wrong, just buckle on the harness and *go forward, and show* us a more excellent way. Let them teach us by their example how to do

better. I do not deny that some may have made mistakes and committed errors. I do not deny that many things which are wrong have been done in revivals. But is that the way to correct them, brethren? So did not Paul. He corrected his brethren by telling them kindly that he would show them a more excellent way. Let our brethren take hold and go forward. Let us hear the cry from all their pulpits: "To the work!" Let them lead on where the Lord will go with them and make bare His arm, and I, for one, will follow. Only let them GO ON, and let us have the people converted to God, and let all minor questions cease.

If not, and if revivals do cease in this land, the ministers and Churches will be guilty of all the blood of all the souls that shall go to hell in consequence of it. There is no need that the work should cease. If the Church will do all her duty, the millennium may come in this country in three years. But if it is to be always so, that in the time of revival, two-thirds of the Church will hang back and do nothing but find fault, the curse of God will be on this nation, and that before long.

REMARKS.

1. It is high time there should be *great searchings of heart* among Christians and ministers. Brethren, this is no time to resist the truth, or to cavil and find fault because the truth is spoken out plainly. It is no time to recriminate or to strive, but we must search *our own* hearts, and humble ourselves before God.

2. We must repent and forsake our sins, and amend our ways and our doings, or the revival will cease. Our ecclesiastical difficulties MUST CEASE, and all minor differences must be laid aside and given up, to unite in promoting the great interests of religion. If not, revivals will cease from among us, and the blood of lost millions will be found on our skirts.

3. If the Church would *do all her duty*, she would soon complete the triumph of religion in the world. But if a system of insinuation and denunciation is to be kept up, not only will revivals cease, but the blood of millions who will go to hell before the Church will get over the shock, will be found on the skirts of the men who have got up and carried on this dreadful contention.

4. Those who have *circulated slanderous reports* in regard to revivals, must repent. A great deal has been said about heresy, and about some men's denying the Spirit's influence, which is wholly groundless, and has been made up out of nothing. And those who have made up the reports, and those who have circulated them against their brethren, must repent and pray to God for His forgiveness.

5. We see the *constant tendency there is* in Christians to declension and backsliding. This is true in all converts of all revivals. Look at the revival in President Edwards' day. The work went on till thirty thousand souls had been converted, and by this time so many ministers and Christians got into such a state, by writing books and pamphlets, on one side and the other, that they carried all by the board, and the revival ceased. Those who had opposed the work grew obstinate and violent, and those who promoted it lost their meekness, and got ill-tempered, and were then driven into the very evils that had been falsely charged upon them.

And now, what shall we do? This great and glorious work of God seems to be indicating a decline. The revival is not dead— blessed be God for that—it is not dead! Now, we hear from all parts of the land that Christians are reading on the subject, and inquiring about the revival. In some places there are now powerful revivals. And what shall we do, to lift up the standard, to move this entire nation and turn all this great people to the Lord? We must DO RIGHT. We must all have a better spirit, we must get down in the dust, we must act unitedly, we must take hold of this great work with all our hearts, and then God will bless us, and the work will go on.

What is the condition of this nation? No doubt God is holding the rod of WAR over the heads of this nation. He is waiting, before He lets loose His judgments, to see whether the Church will do right. The nation IS under His displeasure, because the Church has acted in such a manner with respect to revivals. And now suppose war should come, where would be our revivals? How quickly would war swallow up the revival spirit. The spirit of war is anything but the spirit of revival. Who will attend to the claims of religion when the public mind is engrossed by the all-absorbing topic of war. See now how this nation is, *all at once*, brought upon the brink of war. God brandishes His blazing sword over our heads. Will the Church repent? It is THE CHURCH that God chiefly has in view. How shall we avoid the curse of war? Only by a reformation in the Church. It is in vain to look to politicians to avert war. Perhaps they would generally be in favour of war. Very likely the things they would do to avert it would run us right into it. If the Church will not feel, will not awaken, will not act, where shall we look for help? If the Church absolutely *will not* move, will not tremble in view of the just judgments of God hanging over our heads, we are certainly nigh unto cursing, as a nation.

6. Whatever is done *must be done quickly*. The scales are on a poise. If we do not go forward, we must go back. Things cannot remain as they are. If we do not have a more powerful revival than we have had, very soon we shall have none at all. We have had such a great revival that now small revivals do not interest the public mind. You must act as individuals. *Do your own duty.*

7. It is common, when things get all wrong in the Church, for each individual to find fault both with the Church, and with his brethren, and to overlook his own share of the blame. But, as individual members of the Church of Christ, let each one act rightly, and get down in the dust, and never speak proudly, or censoriously. GO FORWARD. Who would leave such a work, and go down into the plain of Ono? Let us mind our work, and leave the issue with God.[1]

---

[1]Many years later Finney said, commenting upon the revivals and their critics: "Time has settled the question of the purity and inestimable value of those revivals, against which so much mistaken opposition existed. The disastrous reaction predicted by opposers has not been witnessed. It must be admitted that the converts of those revivals have composed the strength of the Churches, and that their Christian influence has been felt throughout the land. No revivals have ever existed, the power and purity of which have been more thoroughly established by time and experience, than that great and blessed work of God, against which such a storm of opposition was raised. Upon the question of Slavery, the Church was too late in her testimony to avoid the war. But the slaveholders were much alarmed by the constantly growing opposition throughout that region of the North where revival influences had been felt. They took up arms to defend and perpetuate the abomination, and by doing so abolished it."

LECTURE XVI

THE NECESSITY AND EFFECT OF UNION

Again I say unto you, That if two of you shall agree on earth as touching anything that they shall ask, it shall be done for them of My Father which is in heaven.—Matt. 18. 19

I have already used this text in preaching upon the subject of prayer-meetings. At present I design to enter more into the spirit and meaning of the words. The evident design of our Lord, in this text, was to teach the importance and influence of union in prayer and effort to promote religion. He states the strongest possible case, by taking the number "two," as the least number between whom there can be an agreement, and says that "where two of you shall agree on earth as touching anything that they shall ask, it shall be done for them of My Father which is in heaven." It is the fact of their *agreement* upon which He lays the stress; and mentioning the number "two" appears to have been designed merely to afford encouragement to the smallest number between whom there can be an agreement. But what are we to understand by being "agreed as touching" the things we shall ask? I will answer this question under the two following heads: I. We are to be agreed in prayer. II. We are to be agreed in everything that is essential to obtaining the blessing that we seek.

I. *AGREEING IN PRAYER.*

In order to come within the promise, we are to be agreed in

prayer. I. We should *agree in our desires* for the object. It is necessary to *have desires* for the object, and to be agreed in those desires. Very often individuals pray *in words* for the same thing, when they are by no means agreed in desiring that thing. Nay, perhaps some of them, in their hearts, desire the very opposite. People are called on to pray for an object, and they all pray for it in words, but God knows they often do not desire it; and perhaps He sees that the hearts of some are, all the while, resisting the prayer.

2. We must *agree in the motive* from which we desire the object. It is not enough that our desires for an object should be the same, but the *reason why* must be the same. An individual may desire a revival, for the glory of God and the salvation of sinners. Another member of the Church may also desire a revival, but from very different motives. Some, perhaps, desire a revival in order to have the congregation built up and strengthened, so as to make it more easy for them to pay their expenses in supporting the Gospel. Another desires a revival for the sake of having the Church increased so as to be more numerous and more respectable. Others desire a revival because they have been opposed or evil spoken of, and they wish to have it known that whatever may be thought or said, *God* blesses them. Sometimes people desire a revival from mere natural affection, so as to have their friends converted and saved. If they mean to be so united in prayer as to obtain a blessing, they must not only desire the blessing, and be agreed in desiring it, but they must also agree in desiring it for the same reasons.

3. We must be agreed in desiring it *for good reasons.* These desires must not only be united, and from the same motives, but they must be from *good* motives. The supreme motive must be *to honour and glorify God.* People may even desire a revival, and agree in desiring it, and agree in the motives, and yet if these motives are not good, God will not grant their desires. Thus, parents may be agreed in prayer for the conversion of their children, and may have the same feelings and the same motives, and yet if they have no higher motives than because they are *their children,* their prayers will not be granted. They are agreed in the reason, but it is not the *right* reason.

In like manner, any number of persons might be agreed in their desires and motives, but if their motives are selfish, their being *agreed* in them will only make them more offensive to God. "How is it that ye have *agreed together* to tempt the Spirit of the Lord?" (Acts 5. 9). I have seen a great deal of this, where Churches have been engaged in prayer for an object, and their motives were evidently selfish. Sometimes they are engaged in prayer for a revival, and you would think by their earnestness and union that they would certainly move God to grant the blessing, till you find out their reason. And what is it? Why, they see *their* congregation is about to be broken up, unless something can be done. Or they see some other denomination gaining ground, and there is no way to counteract this but by having a revival in *their* Church. All their praying is therefore only an attempt to get the Almighty to help them out of their difficulty; it is purely selfish and therefore offensive to God. A woman, in Philadelphia, was invited to attend a women's prayer-meeting at a certain place. She inquired what they met *there* for, and for what they were going to pray? She was answered that they were going to pray for the outpouring of the Spirit upon the city. "Well," she said, "I shall not go; if they were going to pray for *our congregation*, I would go, but I am not going there to pray for other Churches!" Oh, what a spirit!

I have had a multitude of letters and requests that I would visit such-and-such places, and endeavour to promote a revival, and many reasons have been urged why I should go; but when I came to weigh their reasons, I have sometimes found every one of them to be selfish. And God would look upon every one with abhorrence.

In prayer-meetings, too, how often do we hear people offer such reasons why they desire certain blessings, as are not right in the sight of God; reasons which, if they are the true ones, would render their prayers not acceptable to God, because their motive was not right.

There are many things said in favour of the cause of Foreign Missions, which are of this character, appealing to wrong motives. How often are we told of six hundred millions of heathens, who are *in danger* of going to hell, and how little is said of the *guilt* of six hundred millions engaged as rebels against God, or of the *dishonour* and contempt poured upon God our Maker by such a world of outlaws. Now, I know that God refers to those motives which appeal to our mere natural sympathies, and compassion, and uses them, but always in subordination to His glory. If these lower motives be placed foremost, it must always produce a defective piety, and a great deal that is false. Until the Church will look at the dishonour done to God, little will be done. It is this which must be made to stand out before the world, it is this which must be deeply felt by the Church, it is this which must be fully exhibited to sinners, before the world can ever be converted.

Parents never agree in praying for the conversion of their children in such a way as to have their prayers answered, until they feel that their children are rebels. Parents often pray very earnestly for their children, because they wish God to save them, and they almost think hardly of God if He does not save *their* children. But if they would have their prayers prevail, they must come to take God's part against their children, even though for their perverseness and incorrigible wickedness He should be obliged to send them to hell. I knew a woman who was very anxious for the salvation of her son, and she used to pray for him with agony, but still he remained impenitent, until at length she became convinced that her prayers and agonies had been nothing but the fond yearnings of parental feeling, and were not dictated at all by a just view of her son's character as a wilful and wicked rebel against God. And there was never any impression made on his mind until she was made to take strong ground against him as a rebel, and to look on him as deserving to be sent to hell. And then he was converted. The reason was, she never before was influenced by the right motive in prayer—desiring his salvation with a supreme regard to the glory of God.

4. If we would be so united as to prevail in prayer, *we must agree in faith.* That is, we must concur in expecting the blessing prayed for. We must understand the reason why it is to be expected, we must see the evidence on which faith ought to rest, and must *absolutely believe* that the blessing will come, or we do not bring ourselves within the promise. Faith is always understood as an indispensable condition of prevailing prayer. If it is not expressed in any particular case, it is always

implied, for no prayer can be effectual but that which is offered in faith. And in order that *united* prayer may prevail, there must be united faith.

5. So, again, we must be agreed as to the *time* when we desire the blessing to come. If two or more agree in desiring a particular blessing, and one of them desires to have it come *now,* while others are not quite ready to have it yet, it is plain they are not agreed. They are not united in regard to one essential point. If the blessing is to come in answer to their united prayer, it must come as they prayed for it. And if it comes, it must come *at some time.* But if they disagree as to the time when they shall have it, plainly it can never come in answer to their prayer.

Suppose a Church should undertake to pray for a revival, and should all be agreed in desiring a revival, but not as to the time when it shall be. Suppose some wish to have the revival come now, and are all prepared, with their hearts waiting for the Spirit of God to come down, and are willing to give time and attention and labour to it NOW. But others are not quite ready, they have something else to attend to just at present, some worldly object which they want to accomplish, some piece of business in hand, wanting just to finish this thing, and *then* they would have the revival come. They cannot possibly find time to attend to it *now;* they are not prepared to humble themselves, to search their hearts, and break up their fallow ground, and put themselves in a posture to receive the blessing. Is it not plain that there is no real union, for they are not agreed in that which is essential? While some are praying that the revival may come *now,* others are praying, with equal earnestness, that it may *not.*

Suppose the question were now put to *this* Church, whether you are agreed in praying for a revival of religion here? Do you all desire a revival, and would you all like to have it now? Would you be heartily agreed now to break down in the dust, and open your hearts to the Holy Ghost, if He should come to-night? I do not ask what you would *say,* if I should propose the question. Perhaps if I should put it now, you would all rise up and *vote* that you were agreed in desiring a revival, and agreed to have it now. You know how you ought to feel, and what you ought to say, and you know you ought to be ready for a revival *now*. But, I ask: "Would GOD see to it to be so in your hearts, that you are agreed on this point, and prayed accordingly? If not, when will you be agreed on this point? Have *any two* of you agreed on this point, and prayed accordingly? If not, when will you be agreed to pray for a revival? And if this Church cannot be agreed among themselves, how can you expect a revival? It is of no use for you to stand up here and say you are agreed, when God reads the heart, and sees that you are not agreed. Here is the promise: "Again I say unto you, that if two of you shall agree on earth as touching anything that they shall ask, it shall be done for them of My Father which is in heaven." Now this is either true or false. Which ground will you take? If it is true, then it is true that you are not agreed, and never have been, except in those cases where you have had a revival.

But we must agree, not only on *a* time, but it must be the *present* time, or we are not agreed in everything essential to the work. Unless we agree to have a revival *now*, we shall not *now* use the means, and until the means are used it cannot come. It is plain, then, that we must be agreed on the present time; that is, we are not agreed, in the sense of the text, until we are agreed that *now* we will have the blessing, and act accordingly. to agree upon a future time is of no use, for when that future time comes we must *then* be agreed upon that *present time*, and use means accordingly; so that you see you are never properly agreed, until you agree that *now* is the time.

II. *AGREEMENT IN ESSENTIAL THINGS.*

You see the language of the text: "If two of you shall agree *as touching* anything that they shall ask." Many people seem to read it as if it referred merely to an agreement *in asking*, and they understand it to promise, that whenever two are agreed *in asking* for any blessing, it shall be given. But Christ says there must be an agreement "as touching" the thing prayed for. That is, the agreement or union must comprise everything that is essential to the bestowment and reception of the blessing.

1. If Christians would enjoy the benefits of this promise in praying for a revival, they must be agreed *in believing revivals of religion to be realities*. There are many individuals, even in the Church, who do not in their hearts believe that the revivals

which take place are the work of God. Some of them may pray in words for an outpouring of the Spirit and a revival of religion, while in their hearts they doubt whether there are any such things known in modern times. In united prayer there must be no hypocrisy.

2. They must agree *in feeling the necessity of revivals*. There are some who believe in the reality of revivals, as a work of God, while at the same time, they are unsettled as to the necessity of having them in order to the success of the Gospel. They think there is a real work of God in revivals, but, after all, perhaps it is quite as well to have sinners converted and brought into the Church in a more quiet and gradual way, and without so much excitement. Whenever revivals are abroad in the land, and prevail, and are popular, they may appear in favour of them, and may put up their cold prayers for a revival, while at the same time they would be sorry, on the whole, to have a revival come among them. They think it is so much safer and better to indoctrinate the people, and spread the matter before them in a calm way, and so bring them in gradually, and not run into the danger of having "animal feeling" or "wild fire" in their congregations!

3. They must be agreed *in regard to the importance of revivals*. Men are not blessed with revivals, in answer to prayers that are not half in earnest. They must feel the infinite importance of a revival, before they will pray so as to prevail. Blessings of this kind are not granted but in answer to such prayers as arise from a sense of their importance. As I have shown before, on the subject of prevailing prayer, it is when men desire the blessing with UNUTTERABLE AGONY, that they offer such prayer as will infallibly prevail with God. Those who feel less as to the importance of a revival may pray for it in words, but they will never have the blessing. But when a Church has been united in prayer, and really felt the importance of a revival, it has never failed of having one. I do not believe a case can be found, of such a Church being turned empty away. Such an agreement, when sincere, will secure an agreement also on all other subjects that are indispensable.

4. They must be agreed also, in having correct *Scriptural views about several things connected with revivals*.

(a) The necessity of Divine agency to produce a revival. It is

not enough that they all hold this in *theory,* and pray for it *in words.* They must fully understand and deeply feel this necessity; they must realise their entire dependence on the Spirit of God, or the whole will fail.

(*b*) *Why* Divine agency is necessary. There must be an agreement on correct principles in regard to the reason that Divine agency is so indispensable. If they get wrong ideas on this point they will be hindered. If Christians get the idea that this necessity of Divine influence lies in the *inability* of sinners, or if they feel as if God were under obligation to give the Holy Spirit, in order to make sinners *able* to obey the Gospel, they insult God, and their prayers will not avail. For in that case they must feel that it is a mere matter of common justice for God to pour out His Spirit, before He can justly require Christians to work, or sinners to repent.

Suppose a Church gets the idea that sinners are poor unfortunate creatures, who come into the world with such a nature that they cannot help sinning, and that sinners are just as unable to repent and believe the Gospel as they are to fly to the moon, how can it be felt that the sinner is a rebel against God, and that he deserves to be sent to hell? How can they feel that the sinner is *to blame*? And how can they take God's part when they pray? If they do not take God's part against the sinner, they cannot expect God will regard their prayers, for they do not pray with right motives. No doubt one great reason why so many prayers are not answered, is, that those who pray do in fact take the sinner's part against God. They pray as if the sinner were a poor unfortunate being, to be pitied, rather than as if he were a guilty wretch, to be blamed. And the reason is, that they do not believe sinners are able to obey God. If a person does not believe that sinners are *able* to obey their Maker, and really believes that the Spirit's influences are necessary to make them *able*, it is impossible, with these views, to offer acceptable and prevailing prayer for the sinner; and it is not wonderful that persons with these views should not prevail with God, and should doubt about the efficacy of the prayer of faith.

How often do you hear people pray for sinners in this style: "O Lord, *help* this poor soul to do what he is required to do; O Lord, *enable* him to do so-and-so." Now this language implies that they take the sinner's part, and not God's. If it were understood by those who use it, as it is sometimes explained, and if people meant by it what they ought to mean when they plead for sinners, I would not find so much fault with it. The truth is, that when people use this language, they often mean just what the language itself would be naturally, at first sight, understood to mean, which is just as if they should pray: "Lord, Thou commandest these poor sinners to repent, when, O Lord, Thou knowest they cannot repent, unless Thou givest them Thy Spirit to *enable* them to do so, though Thou hast declared that Thou wilt send them to hell if they do not, whether they ever receive Thy Spirit or not; and now, Lord, this seems very hard, and we pray Thee to have pity upon these poor creatures, and do not deal so hardly with them, for Christ's sake."

Who does not see that such a prayer, or a prayer which *means* this, in whatever language it may be couched, is an insult to God, charging Him with infinite injustice, if He should continue to exact from sinners a duty which they are unable to perform without that aid which He will not grant! People may pray in this way till the Day of Judgment, and never obtain a blessing, because they take the sinner's part against God. They cannot pray successfully, until they understand that the sinner is a rebel, and obstinate in his rebellion—so obstinate, that he never will, without the Holy Spirit, do what he might, as well as not, instantly do, and that this obstinacy is the reason, and the only reason, why he needs the influence of the Holy Spirit for his conversion. The only ground on which the sinner needs Divine agency is, to overcome his obstinacy, and make him *willing* to do what he *can* do, and what God justly requires him to do. And Christians are never in an attitude in which God can hear their united prayers, unless they are agreed in so understanding their dependence on God, as to feel it in perfect consistency with the sinner's blame. If it is the other way, they are agreed in understanding it wrongly, and their prayers for Divine help to the unfortunate, instead of Divine favour to make a rebel submit, are wide of the mark, are an insult to God, and they never will obtain favour in heaven.

(c) They must be agreed in understanding that *revivals are not miracles, but that they are brought about by the use of means*, like other events. No wonder revivals formerly came so seldom and continued so short a time, when people generally regarded them as miracles, or like a mere shower of rain, that will come on a place, continue a little while, and then blow over; that is, as something over which we have no control. For what can people do to get a shower of rain? Or how can they make it rain any longer than it does rain? It is necessary that those who pray should be agreed in understanding a revival as something to be brought about by means, or they never will be agreed in using them.

(*d*) They must be agreed in understanding that *human agency is just as indispensable to a revival as Divine agency*. Such a thing as a revival of religion, I venture to say, never did occur without Divine agency, and never did occur without human agency. How often do people say: "God *can*, if He pleases, carry on the work *without* means." But I have no faith in it, for there is no evidence for it. What is religion? Obedience to God's law. But the law cannot be obeyed unless it is known. And how can God make sinners obey but by making known His commandments? And how can He make them known but by revealing them Himself, or sending them to others—that is, by bringing THE TRUTH to bear on a person's mind till he obeys it? God never did, and never can, convert a sinner, except with the truth. What is conversion? Obeying the truth. He may Himself directly communicate it to the sinner; but then, the sinner's own agency is indispensable, for conversion consists in the right employment of the sinner's own agency. And ordinarily, He employs the agency of others also, in printing, writing, conversation, and preaching. God has put the Gospel treasure in earthen vessels. He has seen fit to employ *men* in preaching the Word; that is, He has seen that human agency is that which He can best employ in saving sinners. And if there ever was a case (of which we have no evidence), there is not one in a thousand, if one in a million, converted in any other way than through the truth, made known and urged by human instrumentality. And as Christians must be united in using those means, it is plainly necessary that they should be united in understanding the true reason why means are to be used, and the true principles on which they are to be governed and applied.

5. It is important that there should be union in regard to the *measures essential to the promotion of a revival*. Let individuals agree to do anything whatever, yet if they are not agreed in their measures, they will run into confusion, and counteract one another. Set them to sail a ship, and they never can get along without agreement. If they attempt to do business, as merchants, when they are not agreed in their measures, what will they do? Why, they will only undo each other's work, and thwart the whole business of the concern. All this is preeminently true in regard to the work of promoting a revival. Otherwise, the members of the Church will counteract each other's influence, and they need not expect a revival.

(a) The Church must be agreed in regard to *the meetings which are held*, as to what meetings, and how many, and where and when they shall be held. Some people always desire to multiply meetings in a revival, as if the more meetings they had, the more religion there would be. Others are always opposed to *any* new meetings in a revival. Some are always for having a protracted meeting; and others are never ready to hold a protracted meeting at all. Whatever difference there may be, it is essential that the Church should come to a good understanding on the subject, so that they can go on together in harmony, and labour with zeal and effect.

(b) They must be agreed as to the *manner of conducting meetings*. It is necessary that the Church should be united and cordial on this subject, if it is expected to offer united prayer with effect. Sometimes there are individuals who want to adopt every new thing they can hear of or imagine, while others are totally unwilling to have anything altered in regard to the management of the meetings, but would have everything done precisely in the way to which they are accustomed. The ought to be *agreed* in some way, either to have the meetings altered, or to keep them on in the old way. The best possible way is, for the Church to agree in this, that they will let the meetings go on and take their course, just as the Spirit of God shapes them, and not even attempt to make the two meetings just alike. The Church never will give the fullest effect to the truth, until there is agreement in this

principle: That, in promoting a revival, they will accommodate their measures to circumstances, and not attempt to interrupt the natural course which pious feeling and sound judgment indicate, but cast themselves entirely upon the guidance and direction of the Holy Spirit, introducing any measure, at any time, that shall seem called for in the Providence of God, without laying any stress upon its being new or old.

6. They must be agreed in the *manner of dealing with impenitent sinners*. It is a point immensely important that the Church should be agreed as to the treatment of sinners. Suppose that there is no agreement, so that one will tell a sinner one thing and another another. What confusion! How can they agree in prayer, when it is plain that they are not agreed as to the things for which they shall pray? Go among such a people, and hear them pray for sinners; attend a prayer-meeting and listen. Here is one man who prays that the sinners present may repent. Another prays that they may be convicted; and perhaps, if he be very much concerned, will go so far as to pray that they may be *deeply* convicted. Another prays that sinners may go home solemn and pensive, and silent, meditating on the truths they have heard. Another prays in such a manner that you can see he is afraid to have them converted now. Another prays very solemnly that they may not attempt to do anything in their own strength. And so on. How easy it is to see that the Church is not agreed *as touching* the things they ask for; hence they have no interest in the promise.

If you set such people to talk with sinners, they will be just as discordant, for it is plain that they are not agreed, and have no clear views in regard to what a sinner must do to be saved, or of what ought to be said to sinners in order to bring them to repent. The consequence is, that sinners who are awakened and anxious presently get confounded, and do not know what to do; and perhaps they give up in despair, or conclude that in reality there is nothing rational or consistent in religion. One will tell the sinner he must *repent* immediately. Another will give him a book (Doddridge's "Rise and Progress of Religion in the Soul," perhaps), and tell him to read it. Another will tell him to pray and persevere, and then, in God's time, he will obtain the blessing. A revival can never go on for any length of time, amidst such difficulties. Even if it should begin, it must soon run out; unless, perhaps, the body of the Church will keep still and say nothing, letting others carry on the work. And even then the work will suffer materially for want of co-operation and support. A Church ought to be agreed. Christians ought to have a clear understanding of this subject, and all speak the same thing and give the same directions; then, the sinner will find no one to take his part, but will get no relief or comfort till he repents.

7. They must be agreed *in removing the impediments to a revival*. If a Church expects a revival, it must clear the stumbling-blocks out of the way.

(a) In the exercise of discipline. If there are rotten members in the Church, they should be removed, and the Church should agree to cut them off. If they remain, they are such a reproach to religion as to hinder a revival. Sometimes when an attempt is made to cast them out, this creates a division, and thus the work is stopped. Sometimes the offenders are persons of influence, or they have family friends who will take their part, and make a party, and thus create a bad spirit, and prevent a revival.

(b) In mutual confessions. Whenever wrong has been done to any, there should be a full confession. I do not mean a cold and forced acknowledgment, such as saying: "*If* I have done wrong, I am sorry for it;" but a hearty confession, going the full length of the wrong, and showing that it comes out of a broken heart.

(c) Forgiveness of enemies. A great obstruction to revivals is often found in the fact that active and leading individuals harbour a revengeful and unforgiving spirit towards those who have injured them, which destroys their spirituality, makes them harsh and disagreeable in their manner, and prevents them from enjoying either communion with God in prayer, or the blessing of God to give them success in labour. But let the members of the Church be truly agreed, in confessing their faults, and in cherishing a tender, merciful, forgiving, Christ-like spirit toward any who, they think, have done them wrong, and then the Spirit will come down upon them not by measure.

8. They must be agreed *in making all the necessary preparations for a revival*. They should be agreed in having all necessary preparation made, and in bearing their part of the labour or expense involved. There should be an equality, a few should not be burdened while the rest do little or nothing, but every one should bear his proportion, according to his ability. Then there will be neither envying nor jealousy, nor any of those mutual recriminations and altercations and disrespectful remarks about one another, which are so inconsistent with brotherly love, and put such a stumbling-block in the way of sinners.

9. They must be agreed in *doing heartily whatever is necessary to be done for the promotion of the revival*. Sometimes a slight disagreement about a very little thing will be allowed to break in and destroy a revival. A minister told me that he once went to labour in a place as an evangelist, and the Spirit of God was evidently present, and sinners began to inquire, and things looked quite favourable, until some of the members of the Church began to agitate the inquiry: how they should pay the evangelist. They said: "If he stays among us any longer, he will expect us to give him something"; and they did not see how they could afford to do so. And they talked about it, until the minds of the brethren got distracted and divided, and the preacher went away. Look at it. There God stood in the door of that Church, with His hands full of mercies, but these parsimonious and wicked professors thought it would cost something to have a revival, and their expenses were about as much as they felt willing or able to bear; and so they let the preacher depart, and the work ceased. He would not have left, at the time, whether they gave him anything or not; for what he should receive, or whether he should receive anything from them, was a question about which he felt not concern. But the Church, by its parsimonious spirit, got into such a state as to grieve the Spirit, and he saw that to stay longer with them would do no good. Oh, how will those professors feel when they meet sinners from that town in judgment, when it will all come out, that God was ready and waiting to grant them a blessing, but they allowed themselves to get agitated and divided by inquiring how much they should have to pay!

10. They must be agreed *in labouring to carry on the work*. It

is not enough that they should agree to pray for a revival, but they should agree also in labouring to promote it. They should set themselves to it systematically, to visit and converse and pray with their neighbours; to look out for opportunities of doing good; to watch the effect of the preaching, and watch the signs of the times, that they may know when anything needs to be done, and do it. They should be agreed *to labour*: they should be agreed *how* to labour: they should be agreed to live *accordingly*.

11. They must agree in a *determination to persevere*. It will not answer for some members to begin to move and bluster about, and then as soon as the least thing happens that seems unfavourable, to get discouraged, and faint, and one-half of them give over. They should be all united, and agreed to persevere, and labour, and pray, and hold on, until the blessing comes.

In a word, if Christians expect to unite in prayer and effort, so as to prevail with God, they must be agreed in speaking and doing the same things, in walking by the same rule, and maintaining the same principles, and in persevering till they obtain the blessing, so as not to hinder or thwart each other's efforts. All this is evidently implied in being agreed *as touching* the things for which they are praying.

REMARKS

1. We see why it is that so many of the children of professing parents are not converted.

It is because the parents have not been agreed *as touching* the things they should pray for in behalf of their children. Perhaps they never had any kind of agreement respecting them. Perhaps they were never agreed even as to what was the very *best thing* they could ask for them. Sometimes parents are not agreed in anything, but their opinions clash, and they are perpetually disagreeing, and their children see it. Then it is no wonder that the children remain unconverted.

Or perhaps they may not be agreed as touching *the salvation* of their children. Are they sincere in desiring it? Do they agree to seek it, and agree from right motives? Do they agree in regard to the importance of it? Are they agreed how the children ought to be dealt with, so as to effect their conversion;

what shall be said to them; how it shall be said; when; and by whom? Probably few cases will be found where children remain unconverted, but where inquiry would prove that the parents were never truly agreed as touching these things. In many cases, indeed, it is quite evident that they are not agreed.

Often there is such disagreement that we could not expect any good to result, or, indeed, anything but ruin to the children. The husband and wife often disagree entirely and fundamentally in regard to the manner of bringing up their children. Perhaps the wife is fond of dress, and display, and visiting; while the husband is plain and humble, and is grieved and distressed, and mourns and prays to see how his children are puffed up with vanity. or it may be that the father is ambitious, and wants to have his daughters fashionably educated and make a display, and his sons become great men; so he will send his daughters to a fashionable school, where they may learn anything but their duty to God, and will be all the while pushing his sons forward, and goading their ambitions; while the mother grieves and weeps in secret to see her dear children hurried on to destruction, her influence counteracted, and her sons and daughters trained up to serve the god of this world, and to go to hell.

2. We see the hypocrisy of those who profess to be praying for a revival while they are doing nothing to promote it. There are many who appear to be very zealous in praying for a revival, while they are not *doing* anything at all to bring it about. What do they mean? Are they agreed *as touching* the things they ask for? Certainly not. They cannot be agreed in offering acceptable prayer for a revival until they are prepared to do what God requires them to do to promote it. What would you think of the farmer who should pray for a crop and neither plough nor sow? Would you think such prayers pious, or an insult to God?

3. We see why so many prayers that are offered in the Church are never answered. It is because those who offered them never were agreed *as touching* the things they asked for. Perhaps the minister never laid the subject before them, never explained what it is to be agreed, nor showed them its importance, nor set before them the great encouragement which the promise before us affords to Churches that will

agree. Perhaps the members have never conferred together, to compare views, to see whether they understood the subject alike—whether they were agreed in regard to the motives, grounds, and importance of being united in prayer and labour for a revival. Suppose you were to go through the Churches and learn the precise views and feelings of the members on this subject. How many would you find who are agreed even in regard to the essential and indispensable things, concerning which it is necessary Christians should be agreed in order to unite in prevailing prayer? Perhaps no two could be found who are agreed, and if two were found whose views and desires are alike, it would probably be ascertained that they are unacquainted with each other, and, of course, neither act nor pray together.

4. We see why it is that the text has been generally understood to mean something different from what it says. People have first read it wrongly. They have read as if it were: "If any two of you shall agree *to ask* anything, it shall be done." And as they have often agreed to ask for things, and the things were not done, they have said: "The literal meaning of the text cannot be true, for we have tried it and know it is not true. How many prayer-meetings have we held, and how many petitions have we put up, in which we have perfectly agreed in asking for blessings, and yet they have not been granted." Now the fact is, that they have never yet understood what it is to be agreed *as touching* the things they are to ask for. I am sure this is no strained construction of the text, but is its true and obvious meaning, as a plain, pious reader would understand it, if he inquired seriously and earnestly the true import. They must be agreed not only *in asking*, but in everything else that is indispensable to the existence of the thing prayed for. Suppose two of you agree in desiring to go to London together. If you are not agreed in regard to the means, what route you shall take, and what ship you will go in, you will never get there together. Just so in praying for a revival: you must be agreed in regard to the means and circumstances, and everything essential to the existence and progress of a revival.

5. We may ordinarily expect a revival of religion to prevail and extend among those *without* the Church, just in proportion to the union of prayer and effort *within*. If there is

a general union within the Church, the revival will be general. If the union continues so will the revival. If anything outside breaks in upon this perfect union in prayer and effort, it will limit the revival. How great and powerful would be the revival in a city, if all the Churches in the city were thus united in promoting it.

There is another fact, which I have witnessed, worthy of notice. I have observed that a revival will prevail *outside* the Church, among persons in that *class of society*, amongst whom it prevails *within* the Church. If the women in the Church are most awake and prayerful, the work may ordinarily be expected to prevail mostly amongst women out of the Church, and more women will be converted than men. If the young people in the Church are most awake, then assuredly the work is most likely to prevail among the youth. If the heads of families and the principal men in the Church are awake, the revival is, I have observed, more likely to prevail among that class out of the Church. I have known a revival mostly confined to women, with few men converted, apparently because the men within the Church did not take active part. Again, I have repeatedly known the greatest number of converts to be among men, owing apparently to the fact that the men within the Church were the most active. When the revival does not reach a particular class of the impenitent, pains should be taken to arouse that portion of the Church who are of their own age and standing, to make more direct efforts for their conversion.

There seems to be a philosophy in this fact, which has often been illustrated. Different classes of professors naturally feel a sympathy for the impenitent of *their own sex* and *age* and *rank*, and more naturally pray for them, and for more influence over them; and this seems to be at least one of the reasons why revivals are apt to be the most powerful and general in that class without the Church who are most awake within the Church. Christians should understand this, and feel their responsibility. One great reason why, in revivals, so few of the principal men are converted, doubtless is that that class in the Church are often so worldly that they cannot be aroused. The revival will generally prevail mostly in those families where the professors belonging to them are awake; and the impenitent belonging to those families where the professors are not awake are apt to be left unconverted. One principal reason obviously is that when the professors in a family or neighbourhood are awake, there is not only prayer offered for sinners in the midst of them, but there are corresponding influences acting on the impenitent among them. If they are awake, their looks and lives and warnings all tend to promote the conversion of their impenitent friends. But if they are asleep, all their influence tends to prevent such conversions. Their coldness grieves the Spirit, their worldliness contradicts the Gospel, and all their intercourse with their impenitent friends is in favour of impenitence, and calculated to perpetuate it.

6. We see why different denominations have been suffered to spring up in the Church, and under the government of God.

Christians often see and deplore the evils that have arisen to the Church of God, from the division of His people into jarring sects; and they have wondered and been perplexed to think that God should suffer it to be so. But in the light of this subject we can see that, considering what diversities of opinions and feelings and views actually exist in the Church, much good results from this division. Considering this diversity of opinion, many would never agree to pray and labour together, so as to do it with success, and so it is better they should separate, and let those unite who are agreed. In all cases where there cannot be a cordial agreement in labour, it is better that each denomination should labour by itself, so long as the difference exists. I have sometimes seen revivals broken up by attempting to unite Christians of different denominations in prayer and labour together, *while they were not agreed* as to the principles or measures by which the work was to be promoted. They would undo each other's work, destroy each other's influence, perplex the anxious, and give occasion to the enemies of God to blaspheme; and soon their feelings would get soured, and, the Spirit being grieved away, the work would stop, and perhaps painful confusion and controversy follow.

7. We see why God sometimes suffers Churches to be divided. It is because He finds that the members are so much at variance that they *will not* pray and labour together with

effect. Sometimes Church communities that are in such a state will still keep together from worldly considerations and worldly policy, because it is so much easier for the whole to support public worship; and so they continue, jealous and jangling, for years, accomplishing little or nothing for the salvation of sinners. In such cases God has often let something occur among them, that would *tear them asunder*, and then each party would go to work in its own way, and perhaps both would prosper. As soon as they were separated, everything settled down in peace. I have known some cases where this has been done with the happiest results, and both Churches have been speedily blessed with revivals.

8. It is evident that many more Churches *need* to be divided. How many there are that hold together, and yet do no good, for the simple reason that they are not sufficiently agreed. They do not think alike, nor feel alike, on the subjects connected with revivals, and while this is so, they never can work together. Unless they can be brought to such a change of views and feelings on the subject as will unite them, they are only a hindrance to each other and to the work of God. In many cases they see and feel that this is so, and yet they keep together, conscientiously, for fear a division should dishonour religion, when in fact the division that now exists may be making religion a by-word and a reproach. Far better would it be if they would agree to divide amicably, like Abraham and Lot. "If thout wilt take the left hand, then I will go to the right; or if thou depart to the right hand, then I will go to the left" (Gen. 13. 9). Let them separate, and each party work in its own way; and they may both enjoy the blessing.

9. We see why a few individuals, who are perfectly united, may be successful in gathering and building up a new Church, and may prosper much more than a much larger number who are not agreed among themselves. If I were going to gather a new Church, I would rather have five persons, or three, or even two, who were perfectly agreed *as touching* the things they were to pray for, and the manner in which they should labour for all that is essential to the prosperity of a Church, and who would stand by me, and stand by each other, than begin with a Church of five hundred members, who were not agreed.

10. We see what glorious things may be expected for Zion,

whenever the Churches generally shall be agreed on these subjects. When ministers shall lay aside their prejudices, and their misconstructions, and their jealousies, and shall see eye to eye; and when the Churches shall understand the Bible alike, and see their duty alike, and pray alike, and shall be "agreed *as touching* the things that they shall ask," a nation shall be born in a day. Only let them feel as the heart of one man, and be agreed as to what ought to be done for the salvation of the world, and the millennium will come at once.

11. There is vast ignorance in the Churches on the subject of revivals. After all the revivals that have been enjoyed, and all that has been said and written and printed concerning revivals, there are very few who have any real, consistent knowledge on the subject. And when there is a revival, how few are there who can take hold to labour and promote it as if they understood what they were about. How few persons are to be found who have ever taken up revivals of religion as a subject to be studied and understood. Everybody knows that in a revival Christians must pray, and do some things which they have not been in the habit of doing. But multitudes know nothing of the REASON WHY they should do this, or why one thing is better than another, and, having no principles to guide them, when anything occurs which they did not expect, they are all at fault, and know not what to do.

If men should go to work to build a house of worship, and know as little how to proceed as many ministers and professors know how to build the spiritual temple of God, they never would get a house up; and yet people make themselves believe that they are building the Church of God, when they know not what they are about, but are utterly unable to give a reason why they are doing as they do, or why one thing should be done rather than another. There are multitudes in the Church who never seem to suppose that the work of promoting revivals of religion is one that requires study, and thought, and knowledge of principles, and skill in applying the Word of God so as to give every one his portion in season. And so they go on, generally doing little or nothing, because they are attempting nothing; and if they ever do awaken, they go headlong to work, without any system or plan, as if God had left this part of our duty out of the reach of sound judgment and good sense.

12. There is vast ignorance among ministers upon this subject, and one great reason of this ignorance is that many get the idea that they already understand all about revivals, when in reality they know next to nothing about them. I once knew a minister come in where there was a powerful revival, and bluster about and find fault with many things, speaking of his "knowledge of revivals," that he had "been in seventeen of them," and so on, when it was evident that he knew nothing as he ought of revivals.

13. How important it is that the Church should be trained and instructed, so as to know what to do in a revival. Members should be trained and disciplined like an army; each one having a place to fill, and something to do, knowing where he belongs, and what he has to do, and how to do it. Instead of this, how often do you see a Church in a time of revival take hold of the work to promote it, just like a troop of children thinking to build a house. How few there are who really know how to do—what? Why, the very thing for which God suffers Christians to live in this world, the very thing for which ALONE He would ever let them remain away from heaven a day; and this is the very thing, of all others, that they do not study, and do not try to understand.

14. We see why revivals are often so short, and why they so often produce a reaction. It is because the Church does not understand the subject. Revivals are short, because professors have been stirred up to a kind of spasmodical action. They have gone to work by impulse, rather than from deliberate conviction of duty, and have been guided by their feelings rather than by a sound understanding of what they ought to do; they did not know either what to do, what they could do, what they could not, or how to husband their strength, or what the state of things would bear. Perhaps their zeal led them into some indiscretions, and they lost their hold on God, and so the enemy prevailed. The Church ought to be so trained as to know what to do, so as never to fail, and never to suffer defeat or reaction, when an attempt is made to promote a revival. Christians should understand all the tactics of the devil, and know where to guard against his devices, so that they may know him when they see him—and not mistake him for an

angel of light come to give them lessons of wisdom in promoting the revival—and so that they can co-operate wisely with the minister, and with one another, and with the Holy Ghost, in carrying on the work. No person who has been conversant with revivals can overlook the fact that the ignorance of professors of religion concerning revivals, and their blunders in the matter, are among the common things that put revivals down, and bring back a fearful reaction upon the Church. How long shall this be so? It ought not to be so; it need not be so; shall it always be so?

15. We see that every church is justly responsible for the souls that are in its charge. If God has given such a promise, and if it is true that where so many as two are agreed, *as touching* the things they ask for, it shall be done, then certainly Christians are responsible, and if sinners are lost, their blood will be found upon the Church.

16. We see the guilt of ministers, in not informing themselves, and rightly and speedily instructing the Churches, upon this momentous subject. Why, what is the end of the Christian ministry? What have they to do, but to instruct and marshal the sacramental host, and lead them on to conquest? What, will they let the Church remain in ignorance on the very subject, and the only point of duty, for the performance of which they are in the world—the salvation of sinners? Some ministers have acted as *mysteriously* about revivals as if they thought Christians were either incapable of understanding how to promote them, or that it was of no importance that they should know. But this is all wrong. No minister has yet begun even to understand his duty, if he has neglected to teach his people to work for God in the promotion of revivals. What is he about? What does he mean? Why is he a minister? To what end has he taken the sacred office? Is it that he "may eat a piece of bread"? (I Sam. 2. 36).

17. We see that pious parents can render the salvation of their children certain. Only let them pray in faith, and be agreed *as touching* the things they shall ask for, and God has promised them the desire of their hearts. Who can be agreed so well as parents? Let them be agreed in prayer, and agreed what to do, and agreed in doing all their duty; let them thus train up their children in the way they should go, and when

they are old they *will not* depart from it.

And now, do you believe you are agreed, according to the meaning of this promise? I know that where a few individuals may be agreed in some things, they may produce some effect. But while the body of the Church is not agreed, there will always be so many things to counteract, that they will accomplish but little. THE CHURCH MUST BE AGREED. Oh, if we could find but one Church perfectly and heartily agreed in al these points, so that they could pray and labour together, all as one, what good would be done! Oh, what do Christians think, how can they keep still, when God has brought down His blessings so that if any two were agreed as touching the things they ask for, it would be done? Alas! alas! how bitter will be the remembrance of the janglings in the Church, when Christians come to see the crowds of lost souls that have gone down to hell, because *we* were not agreed to labour and pray for their salvation.

Finally, in the light of this promise we see the awful guilt of the Church. God has given it to be the precious inheritance of His people at all times, and in all places, that, if His people *agree*, their prayers will be answered. We see the awful guilt of the members of this Church, who listen to Lectures about revivals, and then go away and *have no revival*; and also the guilt of members of other Churches who hear and go home and *refuse to do their duty*. How can you meet the thousands of impenitent sinners around you, at the bar of God, and see them sink away into everlasting burnings? Have you been united in heart to pray for them? If you have not, why have you disagreed? Why have you not prayed with this promise until you have prevailed.

You will now either be agreed, and pray for the Holy Ghost, and receive Him before you leave the place, or the anger of the Lord will be upon you. Should you now agree to pray in the sense of this promise, for the Spirit of God to come down on this city, the Heavenly Dove would fly through this city in the midst of the night and would rouse the consciences and break up the guilty slumbers of the wicked. What, then, is the crimson guilt of those professors of religion who are *sleeping in sight of such a promise*? They seem to have skipped over it,or entirely to have forgotten it. Multitudes of sinners are going to hell in all directions, and yet this blessed promise is neglected; yea, more, is practically despised by the Church. There it stands in the solemn record, and the Church might take hold of it in such a manner that vast numbers might be saved[1]—but they are not agreed, therefore souls will perish. And where is the responsibility? Who can take this promise and look the perishing in the face at the Day of Judgment?

---

[1] In all Finney's writings we find him urgent and expectant on the subject of immediate conversion. In his addresses the effect appears to have been still more intense. For instance, Dr. Joseph T. Thompson (one of Finney's successors at Broadway Tabernacle) said of him: "He was unconsciously dramatic, never theatrical. One of the most impressive sermons I ever heard him deliver was on the text: "Judgment also will I lay to the line, and righteousness to the plummet: and the hail shall sweep away the refuge of lies" (Isa. 28. 17). Right before our eyes, he conjured up such a storm of wind, rain, and hail that I grew chilled through and through. I shivered and buttoned up my coat...I was never more astonished than when I went outside and saw the world bathed in sunlight, the birds twittering, and all as calm and serene as a June day could ever be. How he did it I cannot tell." Dr. Cuyler said: "Finney's sermons were chain lightning, flashing conviction into the hearts of the stoutest sceptics, and the links of his logic were so compact that they defied resistance."

Lecture XVII

FALSE COMFORTS FOR SINNERS

How then comfort ye me in vain, seeing in your answers there remaineth falsehood?—Job 21. 34.

Job's three friends insisted that the afflictions which he suffered were sent as a punishment for his sins, and were evidence conclusive that he was a hypocrite, and not a good man, as he professed to be. A lengthy argument ensued, in which Job referred to all past experience, to prove that men are not dealt with in this way according to their character; that the distinction is not observed in the allotments of Providence. His friends maintained the opposite, and intimated that this world is also a place of rewards and punishments, in which men receive good or evil, according to their deeds. In this chapter, Job urges, by appealing to common sense and common observation and experience, that this cannot be true, because it is a matter of fact that the wicked are often prosperous in this world and throughout life, and hence he infers that their judgment and punishment must be reserved for a future state. "The wicked is *reserved* to the day of destruction," and "they shall be brought forth to the day of wrath" (*v*. 30). And inasmuch as the friends who came to comfort him, being in the dark on this fundamental point, had not been able to understand his case, and so could not afford him any comfort, but rather aggravated his grief, Job insisted upon it that he would still look to a future state for consolation. he rebuked them by exclaiming, in the bitterness of his soul: "How then comfort ye me in vain, seeing in your answers there remaineth falsehood?"

My present purpose is to make some remarks upon the various methods employed in comforting anxious sinners; and I design: I. To notice briefly the necessity and design of instructing anxious sinners. II. To show that anxious sinners are always seeking comfort. Their supreme object, indeed, is to get comfort in their distress. III. To notice some of the false comforts often administered.

I. *INSTRUCTING ANXIOUS SINNERS.*

The very idea of anxiety implies some instruction. A sinner will not be anxious at all about his future state, unless he has light enough to know that he is a sinner, and that he is in danger of punishment and needs forgiveness. But men are to be converted, not by physical force, nor by a change wrought in their nature or constitution by creative power, but by the truth, made effectual by the Holy Spirit. Conversion is yielding to the truth. Therefore, the more the truth can be brought to bear on the mind, *other things being equal*, so much the more probable is it that the individual will be converted. Unless the truth is brought to bear upon him, it is certain he *will not* be converted. If it be brought to bear, it is not absolutely certain that it will be effectual, but the probability is in proportion to the extent to which the truth *is* brought to bear.

The great design of dealing with an anxious sinner is to clear up all his difficulties and darkness, do away with all his errors, sap the foundation of his self-righteous hopes, and sweep away every vestige of comfort that he can find in himself. There is often much difficulty in all this, and much instruction is required. Sinners often cling with a death-grasp to their false dependences. The last place to which a sinner ever betakes himself for relief is to Jesus Christ. Sinners had rather be saved in any other way in the world. They had rather make any sacrifice, go to any expense, or endure any suffering, than just throw themselves as guilty and lost rebels upon Christ alone for salvation. This is the very last way in which they are ever willing to be saved. It cuts up all their self-righteousness, and annihilates their pride and self-satisfaction so completely that they are exceedingly unwilling to adopt it. But it is as true in philosophy as it is in fact, that this is, after all, the only way in which a sinner could find relief. If God should attempt to relieve sinners and save them without humbling their pride and turning them from their sins, He could not do it.

Now, the object of instructing an anxious sinner should be to bring his mind, by the shortest route, to the practical conclusion that there is, in fact, no other way in which he can be relieved and saved, but to renounce himself, and rest in Christ alone. To do this with effect requires great skill. It requires a thorough knowledge of the human heart, a clear understanding of the plan of salvation, and a precise and definite idea of the very thing that a sinner MUST DO in order to be saved. The ability to impart such instruction effectually is one of the rarest qualifications in the ministry. It is distressing to see how few ministers and how few professors of religion there are who have in their own mind so distinct an idea of *the thing to be done*, that they can go to an anxious sinner and tell him exactly what he has to do, and how to do it, and can show him clearly that there is no possible way for him to be saved, but by doing that very thing which they tell him, and can make him feel the certainty that he *must* do it, and that unless he does that very thing he will be lost.

II. *ANXIOUS SINNERS ARE ALWAYS SEEKING COMFORT.*

Sinners often imagine they are seeking *Jesus Christ*, and seeking *religion*, but this is a mistake. No person ever sought religion, and yet remained irreligious. What is religion? It is obeying God. Seeking religion is seeking to obey God. The soul that hungers and thirsts after righteousness is the soul of a Christian. To say that a person can seek to obey God, and yet not obey Him, is absurd; for, if he is seeking *religion*, he is not an impenitent sinner. To seek *religion* implies a willingness to obey God, and a willingness to obey God is religion. It is a contradiction to say that an impenitent sinner is seeking religion. It is the same as to say that he seeks and actualy longs to obey God, and God will not let him; or that he longs to embrace Jesus Christ, and Jesus Christ will not let him come. The fact is, the anxious sinner is seeking a hope, he is seeking pardon, and comfort, and deliverance from hell. He is anxiously looking for some one to comfort him and make him feel better, without being obliged to conform to such humiliating conditions as those of the Gospel. And his anxiety and distress continue, only because he will not yield to these terms. Unfortunately, anxious sinners find comforters enough to their liking. Miserable comforters they are, too, "seeing in their answers there remaineth falsehood." No doubt, millions and millions are now in hell, because there were those around them who gave them false comfort, who had so much false pity, or were themselves so much in the dark, that they would not let sinners remain in anxiety till they had submitted their hearts to God, but administered falsehood.

III. *WAYS IN WHICH FALSE COMFORT IS GIVEN.*

There is an endless variety of ways in which false comfort is given to anxious sinners. The more I observe the ways in which even good people deal with anxious sinners, the more I feel grieved at the endless falsehoods with which they attempt to comfort their anxious friends, and thus, in fact, deceive them and beguile them out of their salvation. It often reminds me of the manner in which people act when any one is ill. Let any one of you be ill, with almost any disease in the world, and you will find that every person you meet with has a remedy for *that* disorder, a certain cure, a specific, a panacea; and you will find such a world of quackery all around you that if you do not take care and SHUT IT ALL OUT, you will certainly lose your life. A man must exercise his own judgment, for he will find as many remedies as he has friends, and each one is tenacious of his own medicine, and perhaps will think it hard if it is not taken. And no doubt this miserable system of quackery kills a great many people.

This is true to no greater extent respecting the diseases of the body than respecting the diseases of the mind. People have their specifics and their panaceas, to comfort distressed souls; and whenever they begin to talk with an anxious sinner, they will bring in their false comforts—so much that if he does not TAKE CARE, and mind the Word of God, he will infallibly be deceived to his own destruction. I propose to mention a few of the falsehoods that are often brought forward in attempting to comfort anxious sinners. Time would fail me even to *name* them *all*.

The direct object of many persons is to *comfort* sinners; and they are often so intent upon this that when they see their friends distressed, they pity them, they feel very compassionate: "Oh, oh, I cannot bear to see them so distressed, I must comfort them somehow"; and so they try one way, and another, and all to *comfort* them! Now, God desires they should be comforted. He is benevolent, and has kind feelings, and His heart yearns over them, when He sees them so distressed. But He sees that there is *only one way* to give a sinner real comfort. He has more benevolence and compassion than all men, and wishes to comfort them. But he has fixed the terms, as unyielding as His Throne, on which He will give a sinner relief. He will not alter. He knows that nothing else will do the sinner effectual good, for nothing can make him happy, until he repents of his sins and forsakes them, and turns to God. And therefore God will not yield. Our object should be the same as that of God. We should feel compassion to give comfort, but we should also be sure that it is of the right kind.

Our prime object should be to induce the sinner to *obey God*. His comfort ought to be, both with us and with himself, only a secondary object; and while we are more anxious to *relieve his distress* than to have him cease to abuse and dishonour God, we are not likely, by our instructions, to do him any real good. This is a fundamental distinction in dealing with anxious sinners, but it is evidently overlooked by many, who seem to have no higher motives than sympathy or compassion for the sinner. If in preaching the Gospel or instructing the anxious, we are not actuated by a high regard to the honour of God, and rise no higher than to desire to relieve the distressed; this is going no farther than a constitutional sympathy, or compassion, would carry us. The overlooking of this principle has often misled professors of religion, and when they have heard others dealing faithfully with anxious sinners, they have accused them of cruelty. I have often had professors bring anxious sinners to me, and beg me to *comfort* them; and then, when I have probed the conscience of the sinner to the quick, they have shuddered, and sometimes taken his part. It is sometimes impossible to deal effectually with young people who are anxious, in the presence of their parents, because the parents have so much more compassion for their children than regard to the honour of God. This is a position which is all wrong; and with such views and feelings you had better hold your tongue than say anything to the anxious.

1. One of the ways in which people give false comfort to distressed sinners is by asking them: "What have you done? *You are not so bad!*" They see them distressed and cry out: "Why, what have you done?" as if they had never done anything wicked, and had in reality no occasion to feel distressed at all. A fashionable lady was spiritually awakened, and she was going to see a minister, to converse with him, when she was met by a friend, who turned her back, and drove off her anxiety by the cry: "What have you done to make you feel so? I am sure you have never committed any sin that need make you feel so!"

I have often met with cases of this kind. A mother will tell her son, who is anxious, what an obedient child he has always been, how good and how kind, and she begs him "not to take on so." So a husband will tell his wife, or a wife her husband: "How good you are!" and say: "Why, you are not so bad. You have been to hear that frightful minister, who frightens people, and you have got excited. Be comforted, for I am sure you have not been bad enough to justify such distress." When the truth is, they have been a great deal worse than they think they have. No sinner ever has an idea of his sins greater than they really are. No sinner ever has an adequate idea of how great a sinner he is. It is not probable that any man could live under a full sight of his sins. God has, in mercy, spared all His creatures on earth that worst of sights, a naked human heart. The sinner's guilt is much more deep and damning than he thinks, and his danger is much greater than he thinks it is; and if he should see his sins as they are, probably he would not live one moment. True, a sinner may have false notions on the subject, which may create distress, but which have no foundation. He may think he has committed the unpardonable sin, or that he has grieved away the Spirit, or sinned away his day of grace. But to tell the most moral and naturally amiable person in the world that he is good enough, or that he is not so bad as he thinks he is, is not giving him rational comfort, but is deceiving him and ruining his soul. Let those who do it, beware.

2. Others tell awakened sinners that "conversion is *a progressive work*," and in this way ease their anxiety. When a man is distressed, because he sees himself to be such a sinner, and that unless he turns to God he will be lost, it is a great relief to have some friend hold out the idea that he can get better by degrees, and that he is *now* "coming on," little by little. They tell him: "You cannot expect to get along all at once; I do not believe in these *sudden* conversions, you must wait and let it work; you have begun well, and, by and by, you will get comfort." All this is false as the bottomless pit. The truth is, regeneration, or conversion, *is not* a progressive work. What is regeneration? What is it but the beginning of obedience to God? And is the beginning of a thing progressive? It is the first act of genuine obedience to God—the first voluntary action of the mind, that is what God approves, or that can be regarded as obedience to God. That is conversion. When persons talk about conversion as a progressive work, it is absurd. They show that *they know* just as much about regeneration or conversion as Nicodemus did. They know nothing about it as they ought to know, and are no more fit to conduct an anxious meeting, or to advise or instruct anxious sinners, than Nicodemus was.

3. Another way in which anxious sinners are deceived with false comfort is by being advised to "*dismiss the subject for the present*." Men who are supposed to be wise and good have assumed to be so much wiser than God, that when God is dealing with a sinner, by His Spirit, and is endeavouring to bring him to an *immediate* decision, they think God is crowding too hard, and that it is necessary for them to interfere. They will advise the person to take a ride, or to go into company, or engage in business or do something that will

relieve his mind a little, at least for the present. They might just as well say to God in plain words: "O God, Thou art too hard, Thou goest too fast, Thou wilt make him crazy, or kill him; he cannot stand it, poor creature; if he be so pressed he will die." Just so they take sides against God, and practically tell the sinner himself: "God will make you crazy if you do not dismiss the subject, and resist the Spirit, and drive Him away from your mind."

Such advice, if it be truly conviction of sin that distresses the sinner, is, in no case, either safe or lawful. The strivings of the Spirit, to bring the sinner to Christ, will never hurt him, nor drive him crazy. He may make himself deranged by resisting; but it is blasphemous to think that the blessed, wise, and benevolent Spirit of God would ever act with so little care, as to derange and destroy the soul which He came to sanctify and save. The proper course to take with a sinner, when the striving of the Spirit throws him into distress, is, to instruct him, clear up his views, correct his mistakes, and make the way of salvation so plain, that he may see it right before him. Not to dismiss the subject, but to fall in with the Spirit, and thus hush all those dreadful agonies which are produced by resisting the Holy Ghost. REMEMBER, if an awakened sinner should voluntarily dismiss the subject once, probably he will never take it up again.

4. Sometimes an awakened sinner is comforted by being told that *"religion does not consist in feeling bad."* I once heard of a Doctor of Divinity giving an anxious sinner such counsel, when he was actually writhing under the arrows of the Almighty. Said he: "Religion is cheerful, religion is not gloomy; do not be distressed, but dismiss your fears; be comforted, you should not feel so bad," and such like miserable comforts, when, in fact, the man had infinite reason to be distressed, for he was resisting the Holy Ghost, and was in danger of grieving Him away for ever.

It is true, religion does not consist in "feeling bad"; but the sinner has reason to be distressed, because *he has no religion.* If he had religion, he would not feel so. Were he a Christian, he would rejoice. But to tell an impenitent sinner to be cheerful! Why, you might as well preach this doctrine in hell, and tell them there: "Cheer up here, cheer up: do not feel so bad!"

The sinner is on the very verge of hell, he is in rebellion against God, and his danger is infinitely greater than he imagines. Oh, what a doctrine of devils it is to tell a rebel against Heaven not to be distressed! What is all his distress but rebellion itself? He is not comforted, because he refuses to be comforted. God is ready to comfort him. You need not think to be more compassionate than God. He will fill the sinner with comfort, in an instant, on submission. There stands the sinner, struggling against God, and against the Holy Ghost, and against conscience, until he is distressed almost to death, but still he will not yield; and now some one comes in, saying: "Oh, I hate to see you feel so bad, do not be so distressed; cheer up, cheer up; religion does not consist in being gloomy; be comforted." Horrid!

5. Whatever *involves the subject of religion in mystery* is calculated to give a sinner false comfort. When a sinner is anxious on the subject of religion, very likely, if you becloud it in mystery, he will feel relieved. The sinner's distress arises from the pressure of present obligation. Enlighten him on this point, and clear it up, and if he will not yield, it will only increase his distress. But tell him that regeneration is all a mystery, something he cannot understand, and, by leaving him all in a fog, you relieve his anxiety. It is his clear view of the nature and duty of repentance, that produces his distress. It is the light that brings agony to his mind, while he refuses to obey. It is that which makes up the pains of hell. And it will almost make hell in the sinner's breast here, if only made clear enough. Only cover up this light, and his anxiety will immediately become far less acute and thrilling, but if you take up a clear light, and flash it broadly upon his soul, then, if he will not yield, you kindle up the tortures of hell in his bosom.

6. Whatever *relieves the sinner from a sense of blame* is calculated to give him false comfort. The more a man feels himself to blame, the deeper is his distress; so, anything that lessens his sense of blame, of course lessens his distress—but it is a comfort full of death. If anything will help him to divide the blame, and throw a part of it upon God, it will afford him comfort, but it is a relief that will destroy his soul.

7. To *tell him of his inability* is false comfort. Suppose you say to an anxious sinner: "What can you do? You are a poor

feeble creature, you can do nothing." You will thereby make him feel a kind of despondency, but it is not that keen agony of remorse with which God wrings the soul when He is labouring to bring the sinner to repentance.

If you tell him he is unable to comply with the Gospel, he naturally falls in with that relief. He says to himself: "Yes, I *am* unable, I am a poor, feeble creature, I cannot do this, and certainly God cannot send me to hell for not doing what I cannot do." Why, if I believed that a sinner was *unable*, I would tell him plainly: "Do not be afraid, you are not to blame for not complying with the call of the Gospel: for you are unable, and God will not send you to hell for not doing what you have no strength to do—'Shall not the Judge of all the earth do right?'" I know it is not common for those who talk about the sinner being "unable," to be so consistent, and carry out their theory. But the sinner *infers* all this, and so he feels relieved. It is all false, and all the comfort derived from it is only treasuring up wrath against the Day of Wrath.

8. Whatever makes the impression on a sinner's mind that he is to be *passive in religion* is calculated to give him false comfort. Give him the idea that he has nothing to do but to wait God's time; tell him conversion is the work of God, and he ought to leave it to Him; and that he must be careful not to try to take the work out of God's hand; and he will *infer* as before, that he is not to blame, and will feel relieved. If he has only to stand still, and let God do the work, just as a man holds still to have his arm amputated, he feels relieved. But such instruction as this, is all wrong. If the sinner is thus to stand still, and let God do it, he instantly infers that *he* is not to blame for not doing it himself; and the inference is not only natural but legitimate.

It is true that there is a sense in which conversion is the work of God. But it is false, as it is often represented. It is also true that there is a sense in which conversion is the sinner's own act. It is ridiculous, therefore, to say that a sinner is passive in regeneration, or passive in being converted, for conversion is his own act. The thing to be done is that which cannot be done for him. It is something which *he must do*, or it will never be done.

9. Telling a sinner to *wait God's time*. Some years ago, in

Philadelphia, I met a woman who was anxious about her soul, and had been a long time in that state. I conversed with her, and endeavoured to learn her state. She told me a good many things, and finally said she knew she ought to be willing to wait on God as long as He had waited upon her. She said that God had waited on her a great many years before she would give any attention to His call, and now she believed it was her duty to wait God's time to show mercy to her and convert her soul. And she said this was the instruction she had received. She must be patient, she thought, and wait God's time, and, by and by, He would give her relief. Oh, amazing folly!

Here is the sinner in rebellion. God comes with pardon in one hand and a sword in the other, and tells the sinner to repent and receive pardon, or refuse and perish. And now here comes a minister of the Gospel and tells the sinner to "wait God's time." Virtually he says that God is not ready to have him repent *now*, and is not ready to pardon him *now*, and thus, in fact, throws off the blame of his impenitence upon God. Instead of pointing out the *sinner's* guilt, in not submitting at once to God, he points out *God's* "insincerity"—in making an offer, when, in fact, He was not ready to grant the blessing!

I have often thought such teachers needed the rebuke of Elijah, when he met the priests of Baal. "Cry aloud: for he is a god; either he is talking, or he is pursuing, or he is in a journey, or peradventure he sleepeth, and must be awakened" (I Kings 18. 27). The minister who ventures to intimate that God is not ready, and tells the sinner to wait God's time, might almost as well tell him that God is asleep, or gone on a journey, and cannot attend to him at present. Miserable comforters, indeed! It is little less than outrageous blasphemy of God. How many have gone to the judgment, red all over with the blood of souls that they have deceived and destroyed—by telling them God was not ready to save them, and that they must wait God's time. No doubt such a doctrine is exceedingly calculated to afford present relief to an anxious sinner. It warrants him to say: "God is not ready, I must wait God's time, and so I can live in sin a while longer, till He gets ready to attend to me, and then I will get religion."

10. It is false comfort to tell an anxious sinner to do anything for relief, *which he can do, and not submit* his heart to God. An

anxious sinner is often willing to do anything else, but the very thing which God requires him to do. He is willing to go to the ends of the earth, or to pay his money, or to endure suffering, or do anything but make full and instantaneous submission to God. Now, if you will compromise the matter with him, and tell him of something else that he may do, and yet evade *that point*, he will be very much comforted. He likes that instruction. He says: "Oh, yes, I will do that; I like that minister, he is not so severe as others, he seems to understand my particular case, and knows how to make allowances."

It often reminds me of the conduct of a patient who is very sick, but has a great dislike for a certain physician and a particular medicine, but that is the very physician who alone understands treating his disease, and that the only remedy for it. Now, the patient is willing to do anything else, and call in any other physician. He is anxious and in distress, is asking all his friends if they cannot tell him what he shall do. He will take all the nostrums and quack medicines in the country—before he will submit to the *only course* that can bring him relief. By and by, after he has tried everything without receiving any benefit, if he survives the experiment he gives up this unreasonable opposition, calls in the physician, takes the proper medicine, and is cured. Just so it is with sinners. They will eagerly do anything, if you will only let them off from this intolerable pressure of present obligation to submit to God.

I will mention a few of the things the telling of which to sinners distracts their attention from the point of immediate submission. *(a)* Telling a sinner he must *use the means*—attend meetings and pray. Tell an anxious sinner this: "You must use the means"; and he is relieved. "Oh, yes, I will do that, if that be all. I thought that God required me to repent and submit to Him now. But if "using the means" will answer, I will do that with all my heart." He was distressed before, because he was cornered, and did not know which way to turn. Conscience had beset him, like a wall of fire, and urged him to repent NOW. But this relieves him at once; he feels better, and is very thankful that he has found such a good adviser in his distress! But he may "use the means," as he says, till the Day of Judgment, and not be a particle the better for it, but only hasten his way to death. What is the sinner's use of means, but rebellion against God? God uses means—the Church uses means, to convert and save sinners, to impress them, and bring them to submission. But what has the sinner to do with such means? It is just telling him: "You need not submit to God now, but just use the means awhile, and see if you cannot melt God's heart down to you, so that He will yield this point of unconditional submission." It is a mere cavil to evade the duty of immediate submission to God. It is true that sinners, actuated by a regard to their own happiness, often give attention to the subject of religion, attend meetings, and pray, and read, and many such things. But in all this they have no regard to the honour of God, nor do they so much as intend to obey Him. Their design is not obedience, for if it were, they would not be impenitent sinners. They are not, therefore, using means to be *Christians*, but to obtain pardon, and a hope. It is absurd to say that an impenitent sinner is using means to repent, for this is the same as to say he is willing to repent; or, in other words, that he does repent, and so is not an impenitent sinner. So, to say that an unconverted sinner uses means with the design to become a Christian, is a contradiction; for it is saying that he is willing to be a Christian, which is the same as to say he is a Christian already.

(*b*) Telling a sinner to *pray for a new heart*. I once heard a celebrated Sunday-school teacher do this. He was almost the father of Sunday Schools in America. He called a little girl up to him, and began to talk to her. "My littl girl, are you a Christian?" "No, sir." "Well, you cannot be a Christian yourself, can you?" "No, sir." "No, you cannot be a Christian yourself, you cannot change your heart yourself, but you must pray for a new heart, that is all you can do; pray to God, God will give you a new heart." He was an aged and venerable man, but I almost felt disposed to rebuke him in the name of the Lord; I could not bear to hear him deceive that child, telling her, practically, she could not be a Christian. Does God say: "Pray for a new heart"? Never. He says: "Make you a new heart" (Ezek. 18. 31). The sinner is not to be told to pray to God to do his duty for him, but to go and do it himself. I know the Psalmist prayed: "Create in me a clean heart, and renew a right spirit within me" (Psa. 51. 10). He had *faith*, and prayed in faith. But that is a very different thing from setting an obstinate rebel to pray for a new heart. An anxious sinner will be delighted with such instruction, saying: "I knew I needed a new heart, and that I ought to repent, but I thought I must do it myself. I am very willing to ask God to do it; I hated to do it myself, but have no objection that God should do it, if He will, and I will pray for it, if that is all that is required."

(c) Telling the sinner to *persevere*. And suppose he does persevere? He is as certain to be lost as if he had been in hell ever since the foundation of the world. His anxiety arises only from his resistance; and if he would submit, it would cease; and will you tell him to persevere in the very thing that causes his distress? Suppose my child should, in a fit of passion, throw a book or something on the floor. I tell him: "Take it up," but instead of minding what I say he runs off and plays. "Take it up!" He sees I am in earnest, and begins to look serious. "Take it up, or I shall get a rod." And I put up my arm to get the rod. He stands still. "Take it up, or you must be whipped." He comes slowly along to the place, and begins to weep. "Take it up, my child, or you will certainly be punished." Now he is in distress, and sobs and sighs as if his bosom would burst; but he still remains as stubborn as if he knew I could not punish him. Now I begin to press him with motives to submit and obey, but there he stands, in agony, and at length bursts out: "Oh, father, I do feel so bad, I think I am growing better." And now, suppose a neighbour to come in and see the child standing there, in all his agony and stubbornness. The neighbour asks him what he is standing there for, and what is he doing. "Oh, I am using means to pick up that book." If this neighbour should tell the child: "Persevere, persevere, my boy, you will get it by and by," what should I do? Why, I would ask him to leave the house; what does he mean by encouraging my child in rebellion?

Now, God calls the sinner to repent, He threatens him, He draws the glittering sword, He persuades him, He uses motives, and the sinner is distressed to agony, for he sees himself driven to the dreadful alternative of giving up his sins or going to hell. he ought instantly to lay down his weapons, and break his heart at once. But he resists, and struggles against conviction, and that creates his distress. Now, will you tell him to persevere? Persevere in what? In struggling against God! That is just the direction the devil would give. All the devil wants is, to see him persevere just in the way he is going on, and his destruction is sure.

(d) Telling a sinner to *press forward*. That is, to say to him: "You are in a good way, only press forward, and you will get to heaven." This is on the supposition that his face is toward heaven, when in fact his face is toward hell, and he is pressing forward, and never more rapidly than now, while he is resisting the Holy Ghost. Often have I heard this direction given, when the sinner was in as bad a way as he could be. What you ought to tell him is: "STOP, sinner, stop, do not take another step that way, it leads to hell." God tells him to stop, and because he does not wish to stop, he is distressed. Now, why should you attempt to comfort him in this way?

(e) Telling a sinner that he must *"try" to repent and give his heart to God*. "Oh, yes," says the sinner, "I am willing to try, I have often tried to do it, and I will try again." Does God tell you to "try" to repent? All the world would be willing to "try" to repent, in their way. Giving this direction implies that it is very difficult to repent, and perhaps impossible, and that the best thing a sinner can do is, to *try* and see whether he can do it or not. What is this, but substituting your own commandment in the place of God's. God requires nothing short of repentance and a holy heart; anything short of that is comforting the sinner in vain, "seeing in your answers there remaineth falsehood."

(f) Telling him to *pray for repentance*. "Oh, yes, I will pray for repentance, if that is all. I was distressed because I thought God required *me* to repent; but I can wait." And so he feels relieved, and is quite comfortable.

(g) Telling a sinner to *pray for conviction*, or *pray for the Holy Ghost* to show him his sins, or to *labour to get more light* on the subject of his guilt, in order to increase his conviction.

All this is just what the sinner wants, because it lets him off from the pressure of *present* obligation. He wants just a little more *time*. Anything that will defer that *present pressure* of obligation to repent immediately, is a relief. What does he want more conviction for? Does God give any such direction to an impenitent sinner? God takes it for granted that he has conviction enough already. And so he has. Do you say he cannot realise all his sins? If he can realise *only one* of them, let him repent of that one, and he is a Christian. Suppose he could see them all, what reason is there to think he would repent of them all, any more than he would repent of that one that he does see? All this is comforting the sinner by setting him to do that which he can do, and yet not submit his heart to God.

11. Another way in which false comfort is given to anxious sinners is, to tell them God is *trying their faith by keeping them in the furnace*, and they must wait patiently upon the Lord. Just as if God were in fault, or stood in the way of a sinner becoming a Christian. Or as if an impenitent sinner had faith! What an abomination! Suppose somebody should tell my child, while he was standing by the book as I have described: "Wait patiently, my boy, your father is trying your faith." No. The sinner is trying the patience and forbearance of God. God is not setting Himself to torture a sinner, and teach him a lesson of patience. But He is waiting upon him, and labouring to bring him *at once* into such a state of mind as will render it consistent to fill his soul with the peace of heaven. And shall the sinner be encouraged to resist, by the idea that God is bantering? TAKE CARE! God has said His Spirit shall not always strive.

12. Another false comfort is, saying to the sinner: "*Do your duty, and leave your conversion with God.*" I once heard an elder of a Church say to an anxious sinner: "Do your duty, and leave your conversion to God; He will do it in His own time and way." That was just the same as telling him, that it was not his duty to be converted NOW. He did not say: "Do your duty, and leave your *salvation* with God." That would have been proper enough, for it would have been simply telling him to submit to God, and would have included conversion as the first duty of all. But he told him to leave his *conversion* to God. And this elder, that gave such advice, was a man of liberal education too. How absurd! As if the sinner could do his duty and not be converted! God has required him: "Make you a new heart" (Ezek. 18. 31); and do you beware how you comfort him with an answer of falsehood.

13. Sometimes professors of religion will try to comfort a sinner, by telling him: "*Do not be discouraged; I was a long*

time in this way before I found comfort." They will tell him: "I was under conviction so many weeks—or perhaps so many months, or sometimes years—and have gone through all this, and know just how you feel; your experience is the same as mine precisely. After so long a time I found relief; and I doubt not you will find it by and by. Do not despair, God will comfort you soon." Tell a sinner to take courage in his rebellion! Oh, horrible! Such professors ought to be ashamed. Suppose you were under conviction so many weeks, and afterwards found relief, it is the very last thing you ought to tell an anxious sinner. What is it but encouraging him to hold out, when his business is to submit? Did you hold out so many weeks while the Spirit was striving with you? You only deserved so much the more to be lost, for your obstinacy and stupidity.

Sinner! it is no sign that God will spare *you* so long, or that His Spirit will remain with you to be resisted. And remember, if the Spirit is taken away, you will be sent to hell.

14. Another false comfort is to say: "I *have faith to believe* you will be converted." You have faith to believe? On what does your faith rest? On the promise of God? On the influences of the Holy Ghost? Then you are counteracting your own faith. The very design and object of the Spirit of God is to tear away from the sinner his last vestige of a hope while remaining in sin; to annihilate every crag and twig he may cling to. And the object of your instruction should be the same. You should fall in with the plan of God. It is only in this way that you can ever do any good—by urging him to submit at once, and leave his soul in the hands of God. But when one that he thinks is a Christian, tells him: "I have faith to believe you will be converted," it upholds him in a false expectation. Instead of tearing him away from his false hopes, and throwing him upon Christ, you just turn him aside to depend upon your faith, and to find comfort because you have faith for him. This is all false comfort, that worketh death.

15. Sometimes professors of religion try to comfort an anxious sinner by telling him: "I *will pray for you*." This is false comfort, for it leads the sinner to trust in those prayers, instead of trusting in Christ. The sinner says: "He is a good man, and God hears the prayers of good men; no doubt his prayers will prevail, some time, and I shall be converted: I do

not think I shall be lost." And his anxiety, his agony, is all gone. A woman said to a minister: "I have no hope now, but I have faith in your prayers." Just such faith is this as the devil wants them to have—faith in prayers instead of faith in Christ.

16. It is equally false comfort to say: "I rejoice to see you in this way, and I hope you will be faithful, *and hold out.*" What is this but rejoicing to see him in rebellion against God? For that is precisely the ground on which he stands. He is resisting conviction, and resisting conscience, and resisting the Holy Ghost, and yet you rejoice to see him in this way, and hope he will be faithful, and hold out! There is a sense, indeed, in which it may be said that his situation is more hopeful than when he was in stupidity. For God has convinced him, and may suceed in turning and subduing him. But that is not the sense in which the sinner himself will understand it. He will suppose that you think him in a hopeful way, because he is doing better than formerly; when, in fact, his guilt and danger are greater than they ever were before. Instead of rejoicing, you ought to be distressed and in agony, to see him thus resisting the Holy Ghost, for every moment he does this, he is in danger of being left of God, and given up to hardness of heart and to despair.

17. Again, it is said: "You will have your pay for this, by-and-by: God *will reward* you." I once heard a sinner say: "I feel very bad, I have strong hopes that I shall get my reward." But that individual afterwards said: "Nowhere can there be found so black a sinner as I am, and no sin of my life seems so black as that expression." He was overwhelmed with contrition, that he should ever have had such an idea, as to think that God should reward him for suffering so much distress, when he had brought it all upon himself, needlessly, by his wicked resistance to the truth. The truth is, what such "instructors" are seeking is, to *comfort* the sinner; being all in the dark themselves on the subject of religion, they, of course, give him false comfort.

18. Another false comfort is, to tell the sinner *he has not repented enough*. The truth is, he has not really repented at all. As soon as the sinner repents, God always comforts him. This direction implies that his feelings are right as far as they go. To tell him that he has any repentance, is to tell him a lie, and cheat him out of his soul.

19. People sometimes comfort a sinner by telling him: "*If you are elected*, you will be brought in." I once heard of a case where a person under great distress of mind was sent to converse with a neighbouring minister. They talked for a long time. As the person went away, the minister said to him: "I should like to send a line by you to your father." His father was a pious man. The minister wrote the letter, and forgot to seal it. As the sinner was going home, he saw that the letter was not sealed, and he thought to himself, that probably the minister had written about him, and his curiosity at length led him to open and read it. And there he found it written to this purport: "Dear Sir,—I found your son under conviction, and in great distress, and it seems not easy to say anything to give him relief. But, if he is one of the elect, he is sure to be brought in." He had wanted to say something to comfort the father; but now, mark: that letter had wellnigh ruined the son's soul; for he settled down on the doctrine of Election, saying: "If I am elected, I shall be brought in;" and his conviction was gone. Years afterwards he was awakened and converted, but only after a great struggle, and never until that false impression had been obliterated from his mind, and he had been made to see that he had nothing at all to do with the doctrine of Election, but that if he did not repent he would be lost.

20. It is very common for some people to tell an awakened sinner: "You are in a very prosperous way. I am glad to see you so, and *feel encouraged* about you." It sometimes seems as if the Church were in league with the devil to help sinners to resist the Holy Ghost. The thing that the Holy Ghost wants to make the sinner feel is, that all his ways are wrong, and that they lead to hell. And everybody is conspiring to make the opposite impression! The Spirit is trying to discourage him, and they are trying to encourage him; the Spirit to distress him by showing him that he is all wrong, and they to comfort him by saying he is doing well. Has it come to this, that the worst counteraction to the truth and the greatest obstacle to the Spirit, shall spring from the Church. Sinner, do not believe them! You are not in a hopeful way. You are not doing well, but ill—as ill as you can, while resisting the Holy Ghost.

21. Another fatal way in which false comfort is given to sinners, is by applying to them *certain Scripture promises*

which were designed only for saints. This is a grand device of the devil. It is much practised by the Universalists. But Christians often do it. For example:

(*a*) "Blessed are they that mourn: for they shall be comforted" (Matt. 5. 4). How often has this passage been applied to anxious sinners, who were in distress because they would not submit to God. "Blessed are they that mourn." That is true, where they mourn with godly sorrow. but what is this sinner mourning about? He is mourning because God's law is holy, and the terms of salvation so fixed that he cannot bring them down to his mind. Will you tell such a rebel: "Blessed are they that mourn"? You might just as well apply it to those that are in hell! There is mourning there, too. The sinner is mourning because there is no other way of salvation, because God is so holy that He requires him to give up all his sins, and he feels that the time has come, that he must either give them up, or be lost. Shall we tell him, he shall be comforted? Shall we tell the devil: "You mourn now; but the Bible says, you are blessed if you mourn; and you shall be comforted by and by!"

(*b*) "Seek, and ye shall find" (Matt. 7. 7). This is said to sinners in such a way as to imply that the anxious sinner is seeking religion. This promise was made in reference to Christians, who ask in faith, and seek to do the will of God, and it is not applicable to those who are seeking hope or comfort; but to holy seeking. To apply it to an impenitent sinner is only to deceive him, for his seeking is not of this character. To tell him: "You are seeking, are you? Well, seek, and you shall find," is to cherish a fatal delusion. While he remains impenitent, he has not a desire which the devil might not have, and yet remain a devil still.

If the sinner had a desire to do his duty, if he were seeking to do the will of God, and give up his sins, he would be a Christian. But to comfort an impenitent sinner with such a promise—you might just as well comfort Satan!

(*c*) "Let us not be weary in well doing: for in due season we shall reap, if we faint not" (Gal. 6. 9). To apply this for a sinner's comfort, is absurd. As if he were doing something to please God! He has never done well, and never has done more ill than now. Suppose my neighbor, who came in while I was trying to subdue my child, should say to the child, "In due season you shall reap, if you faint not," what should I say? "Reap? Yes, you shall reap; if you do not give up your obstinacy, you shall reap indeed, for I will apply the rod." So the struggling sinner shall reap the damnation of hell, if he does not give up his sins.

22. Some professors of religion, when they attempt to converse with awakened sinners, are very fond of saying: "I will *tell you my experience*." This is a dangerous snare, and often gives the devil a handle to lead the sinner to hell, by getting him to copy your experience. If you tell it to the sinner, and he thinks it is a Christian experience, he will almost infallibly be trying to imitate it, so that, instead of following the Gospel, or the leadings of the Spirit in his own soul, he is following your example. This is absurd as well as dangerous. No two were ever exercised just alike. Men's experiences are as much unlike as are their countenances. Such a course is likely to mislead him. The design is, often, to encourage him at the very point where he ought not to be encouraged, *before* he has submitted to God. And it is calculated to impede the work of God in his soul.

23. How many times will people tell an awakened sinner that *God has begun* a good work in him, and will carry it on. I have known parents talk so with their children, and, as soon as they have seen their children awakened, give up all anxiety about them, and settle down at ease, thinking that now God had begun a work in their children He would carry it on. It would be just as rational for a farmer to say about his grain, as soon as it comes up out of the ground: "Well, God has begun a good work in my field, and He will carry it on." What would be thought of a farmer who should neglect to put up his fence, because God has begun the work of giving him a crop of grain? If you tell a sinner so, and he believes you, it will certainly be his destruction, for it will prevent his doing that which is absolutely indispensable to his being saved. If, as soon as the sinner is awakened, he is taught that, God having begun a good work, that only needs to be carried on, He will surely carry it on, he sees that thee is no further occasion to be anxious, for, in fact, he has nothing more to do. And so he will be relieved from that intolerable pressure of present obligation to repent

and submit to God. And if he is relieved from his sense of obligation to do it, he will never do it.

24. Some will tell the sinner: "Well, you have *broken off your sins*, have you?" "Oh, yes," says the sinner; when it is all false; he has never forsaken his sins for a moment, he has only exchanged one form of sin for another; only placed himself in a new attitude of resistance. And to tell him that he has broken them off is to give him false comfort.

25. Sometimes this direction is given for the purpose of relieving the agony of an anxious sinner: "Do *what you can*, and God will do the rest"; or: "Do what you can, and God will help you." This is the same as telling a sinner: "You cannot do what *God requires* you to do, but if you do what you can, God will help you as to the rest." Now, sinners often get the idea that they *have done* all they can, when, in fact, they have done nothing at all, except that they have resisted God with all their might. I have often heard them say: "I have done all I can, and I get no relief, what can I do more?" Now, you can see how comforting it must be to such a one to have a professor of religion come in and say: "If you will do what you can, God will help you." It relieves all his keen distress at once. He may be uneasy, and unhappy, but his agony is gone.

26. Again, they say: "You should *be thankful for what you have*, and hope for more." If the sinner is convicted, they tell him he should be thankful for conviction, and hope for conversion. If he has any feeling, he should be thankful for what feeling he has, just as if his feeling were religious feeling, when he has no more religion than Satan. He *has* reason to be thankful indeed: thankful that he is out of hell, and thankful that God is yet waiting on him. But it is ridiculous to tell him that he should be thankful in regard to the state of his mind, when he is all the while resisting his Maker with all his might.

IV. *ERRORS MADE IN PRAYING FOR SINNERS.*

I will here mention a few errors that are made in praying for sinners, by which an unhappy impression is made on their minds, in consequence of which they often obtain false comfort in their distress.

1. People sometimes pray for sinners as if they deserved TO

BE PITIED more than BLAMED. They pray for them as "MOURNERS": "Lord, help these pensive mourners"! As if they were just mourners, like one that had lost a friend, or met with some other calamity, which he could not help, and so were greatly to be pitied, sitting there, sad, pensive, and sighing. The Bible never talks so. It pities sinners, but it pities them as mad and guilty rebels, deserving to go to hell; not as poor pensive mourners, who want to be relieved, but can do nothing but sit and mourn.

2. Praying for them as "*poor sinners.*" Does the Bible ever use such language as this? The Bible never speaks of them as "poor sinners," as if they deserved to be pitied more than blamed. Christ pities sinners in His heart. And so does God pity them. He feels in His heart all the gushings of compassion for them, when He sees them going on, obstinate and wilful in gratifying their own lusts, at the peril of His eternal wrath. But He never lets an impression escape from Him, as if the sinner were just a "poor creature"—to be pitied, as if he could not help his position. The idea that he is poor, rather than wicked; unfortunate, rather than guilty, relieves the sinner greatly. I have seen the sinner writhe with agony under the truth, in a meeting, until somebody began to pray for him as a "*poor*" creature. And then he would gush out into tears, and weep profusely, and think he was greatly benefited by such a prayer, saying: "Oh, what a good prayer that was!" If you go now and converse with that sinner, you will probably find that he is still pitying himself as a poor unfortunate creature—perhaps even weeping over his unhappy condition: but his *conviction of sin*, his deep impressions of *awful guilt*, are all gone.

3. Praying that God would "*help the sinner to repent.*" "O Lord, *enable* this poor sinner to repent *now.*" This conveys the idea to the sinner's mind, that he is now trying with all his might to repent, and that he cannot do it, and therefore Christians are calling on God to help him, and enable him to do it. Most professors of religion pray for sinners, not that God would make them *willing* to repent, but that He would *enable* them, or make them able. No wonder their prayers are not heard. They relieve the sinner of his sense of responsibility, and that relieves his distress. But it is an insult to God, as if God had commanded a sinner to do what He could not do.

4. People sometimes pray: "Lord, these sinners are *seeking Thee, sorrowing*." This language is an allusion to what took place at the time when Jesus was a little boy, and went into the Temple to talk with the rabbis and doctors. His parents, you recollect, went a day's journey towards home before they missed him; then they turned back, and, after looking all around, they found the little Jesus standing in the Temple disputing with the learned men. Then "His mother said unto Him, Son, why hast Thou thus dealt with us? behold, Thy father and I have sought Thee sorrowing" (Luke 2. 48). And so this prayer represents sinners as seeking Jesus, but He hides Himself from them, and they look all around, and hunt, and try to find Him, and wonder where He is, and say: "Lord, we have sought Jesus these three days sorrowing." It is a LIE! No sinner ever sought Jesus with all his heart three days, or three minutes, and could not find Him. Jesus "stands at the door, and knocks" (Rev. 3. 20). he is right before the sinner, pleadng with him, and facing him with all his false pretences. Seeking Jesus! The sinner may cry: "Oh, how I am sorrowing, and seeking Jesus," but it is no such thing; Jesus is seeking him. And yet how many oppressed consciences are relieved and comforted by hearing one of these prayers.

5. "Lord, have mercy on these sinners, who are *seeking Thy love to know*." This is a favourite expression with many; as if sinners were seeking to get to heaven without Jesus Christ. As if they were seeking it, and He was so hard-hearted that He would not let them have it!

6. "Lord, have mercy on these *penitent souls*"; calling anxious sinners "penitent souls"! If they are truly penitent, they are Christians. To make the impression on an unconverted sinner that he is penitent, is to make him believe a lie. But it is very comforting to the sinner, and he likes to take it up, and pray it over again: "O Lord, I am a poor penitent soul, I am very penitent, I am so distressed, Lord, have mercy on a poor penitent." Dreadful delusion, to lead an impenitent sinner to pray as a penitent!

7. Sometimes people pray for anxious sinners as "*humble souls*." "O Lord, these sinners have humbled themselves." But that is not true, they have not humbled themselves; if they had, the Lord would have raised them up and comforted them, as

He has promised. There is a hymn of this character that has done much mischief. It begins:

> Come, HUMBLE sinner, in whose breast
> A thousand thoughts revolve.

This hymn was once given by a minister to an awakened sinner, as one applicable to his case. He began to read: "Come, humble sinner." He stopped: "Humble sinner: that is not applicable to me, I am not a *humble* sinner." Ah, how well was it for him that the Holy Ghost had taught him better than the hymn! If the hymn had said: "Come, *anxious sinner,*" or "*guilty sinner,*" or "*trembling sinner,*" it would have been well enough, but to call him a "*humble*" sinner would not do. There are vast numbers of hymns of the same character. It is very common to find sinners quoting the false sentiments of some hymn, to excuse themselves in rebellion against God.

A minister told me he heard a prayer, quite lately, in these words: "O Lord, these sinners have humbled themselves, and come to Thee as well as they know how; if they knew any better, they would do better; but, O Lord, as they have come to Thee in the best manner they can, we pray Thee to accept them and show mercy." Horrible!

8. Many pray: "Father, forgive them; for they know not what they do" (Luke 23. 34). This is the prayer which Christ made for His murderers; and, in their case, it was true; they did not know what they were doing, for they did not believe that Jesus Christ was the Messiah. But it cannot be said of sinners under the Gospel that they do no know what they are doing. They *do know* what they are doing. They do not see the full extent of it; but they do know that they are sinning against God, and rejecting Christ; and the difficulty is that they are unwilling to submit to God. But such a prayer is calculated to make the sinner feel relieved, and make him say: "Lord, how canst Thou blame me so? I am a poor ignorant creature, I *do not know* how to do what is required of me; if I knew how, I would do it."

9. Another expression is: "Lord, direct these sinners, who are *inquiring the way to Zion with their faces thitherward.*" But this language is only applicable to Christians. Sinners have not their faces towards Zion; their faces are set towards hell!

And how can a sinner be said to be "inquiring the way" to Zion, when he has no disposition to go there? The real difficulty is that he is unwilling to WALK in the way in which he knows he ought to go.

10. People pray that sinners "may have *more conviction.*" Or, they pray that sinners may "*go home solemn* and tender, and take the subject into consideration," instead of praying that they may *repent now.* Or, they pray as if they supposed the *sinner to be willing* to do what is required. All such prayers are just such prayers as the devil wants; he wishes to have such prayers, and I dare say he does not care how many such are offered.

Sometimes, in an anxious meeting, or when sinners have been called to the anxious seats, after the minister has made plain the way of salvation, and taken away all stumbling-blocks out of the path, just when the sinners are ready to YIELD some one will be called on to pray, and instead of praying that they may *repent now*, he begins: "O Lord, we pray that these sinners may be solemn, that they may have a deep sense of their sinfulness, that they may go home impressed with their lost condition, that they may attempt nothing in their own strength, that they may not lose their convictions, and that, in Thine own time and way, they may be brought into the glorious light and liberty of the sons of God."

Instead of bringing them right up to the point of *immediate* submission, on the spot, it gives them time to breathe, it lessens the pressure of conviction, so that a sinner breathes freely again, and feels relieved, and sits down at his ease. Thus, when the sinner is brought up, as it were, and stands at the gate of the Kingdom, such a prayer, instead of pushing him in, sets him back again: "There, poor thing, sit there till God helps you."

11. Christians sometimes pray in such a manner as to make the impression that CHRIST IS THE SINNER'S FRIEND in a different sense from that in which God the Father is his Friend. They pray to Christ: "O Thou Friend of sinners," as if God were full of vengeance, just going to crush the poor wretch, till Jesus Christ comes in and takes his part, and delivers him. Now, this is all wrong. The Father and the Son are perfectly agreed, their feelings are all the same, and both

are equally disposed to have sinners saved. And to make such an impression deceives the sinner, and leads to wrong feelings towards God. To represent God the Father as standing over him, with the sword of justice in His hand, eager to strike the blow, till Christ interposes, is not right. The Father is as much the sinner's Friend as the Son. His compassion is equal. But if the sinner get this unfavourable idea of God the Father, how is he ever to love Him with all his heart, so as to say: "Abba, Father"?

12. The impression is often made, by the manner of praying, that you do not expect sinners to repent *now*, or that you expect God to fulfil what is *their* duty, or that you wish to encourage them to trust in your prayers. And so, sinners are ruined. Never pray so as to make the impression on sinners, that you secretly hope they are Christians already, or that you feel strong confidence they will be, by and by, or that you half believe they are converted now. This is always unhappy. In this way, multitudes are deceived with false comfort, and prevented, just at the critical point, from making the final surrender of themselves to God.

REMARKS.

1. Many persons who deal in this way with anxious sinners, do so from false pity. They feel so much sympanthy and compassion, that they cannot bear to tell sinners the truth which is necessary to save them. As well might a surgeon, when he sees that a man's arm must be amputated, or death must result, indulge this feeling of false pity, and just put on a plaster, and give him an opiate. There is no benevolence in that. True benevolence would lead the surgeon to be cool and calm, and with a keen knife, cut the limb off, and save the life. It is false tenderness to do anything short of that. I once saw a woman under distress of mind, who for months had been driven well nigh to despair. Her friends had tried all the false comforts without effect, and they brought her to see a minister. She was emaciated, and worn out with agony. The minister set his eye upon her, and poured in the truth upon her mind, and rebuked her in a most pointed manner. The woman who was with her interfered: she thought it cruel, and said: "Oh, do comfort her, she is so distressed, do not trouble her

any more, she cannot bear it." Whereupon the minister turned, and rebuked *her*, and sent her away, and then poured in the truth upon the anxious sinner like fire, so that in five minutes she was converted, and went home full of joy. The plain truth swept all her false notions away, and in a few moments she was joyful in God.

2. The treatment of anxious sinners, which ministers such false comforts is, in fact, *cruelty*. It is cruel as the grave, as cruel as hell, for it is calculated to send the sinner down to the burning abyss. Christians feel compassion for the anxious, and so they ought. But the last thing they ought to do is to flinch just at the point where it comes to a crisis. They should feel compassion, but they should show it just as the surgeon does, when he deliberately goes to work, in the right and best way, and cuts off the man's arm, and thus cures him and saves his life. Just so Christians should let the sinner see their compassion and tenderness, but they should take God's part, fully and decidedly. They should lay open to the sinner the worst of his case, expose his guilt and danger, and then lead him right up to the cross, and insist on instant submission. They must have firmness enough to do this work thoroughly; and, if they see the sinner distressed and in agony, still they must press him right on, and not give way in the least till he yields.

To do this often requires nerve. I have often been placed in circumstances where I have realised this. I have found myself surrounded with anxious sinners, in such distress as to make every nerve tremble; some overcome with emotion and lying on the floor; some applying camphor to prevent their fainting; others shrieking out as if they were just going to hell. Now, suppose any one should give false comfort in such a case as this? Suppose he had not nerve enough to bring them right up to the point of instant and absolute submission? How unfit would such a man be, to be trusted in such a case!

3. Sometimes sinners become deranged through despair and anguish of mind. Whenever this is the case, it is almost always because those who deal with them try to encourage them with false comfort, and thus lead them to such a conflict with the Holy Ghost. They try to hold them up, while God is trying to break them down. And, by and by, the sinner's mind gets

confused with this contrariety of influences, and he either goes deranged, or is driven to despair.

4. If you are going to deal with sinners, remember that you are soon to meet them in Judgment, therefore be sure to treat them in such a way that if they are lost, it will be their own fault. Do not try to comfort them with false notions *now*, and have them reproach you with it *then*. Better to suppress your false sympathy, and let the naked truth "pierce even to the dividing asunder of soul and spirit, and of the joints and marrow" (Heb. 4. 12), than to soothe them with false comfort, and beguile them away from God!

5. Sinner, if you converse with any Christians, and they tell you to do anything, first ask: "If I do *that*, shall I be saved?" You may be anxious, and not be saved. You may pray, and not be saved. You may use means,in your own way, and not be saved. Whatever they tell you to do, if you can do it and not be saved, do not attend to such instructions. They are calculated to give you false comfort, and divert your attention from the main thing to be done, and beguile you down to hell. Do not follow any such directions, lest you should die while doing so, for then there is no retrievement.

Finally; let a Christian never tell a sinner anything, or give him any direction, that will lead him to stop short of, or that does not include, submission to God. To let him stop at any point short of this, is infinitely dangerous. Suppose you are at an anxious meeting, or a prayer-meeting, and you tell a sinner to pray, or to read, or to do anything that comes short of saving repentance, and he should fall and break his neck that night, of whom would his blood be required? A youth in New England once met a minister in the street,and asked him "what he should do to be saved?" The minister told him to go home, and go into his room, and kneel down and give his heart to God. "Sir," said the boy, "I feel so bad, I am afraid I shall not live to get home." The minister saw his error, felt the rebuke thus unconsciously given by a youth, and then told him: "Well, then, give your heart to God here, and then go home to your room and tell Him of it."

It is enough to make one's heart bleed to see so many miserable comforters for anxious sinners "in whose answers there remaineth falsehood." What a vast amount of spiritual quackery there is in the world, and how many "forgers of lies" there are, "physicians of no value" (Job 13. 4) who know no better than to comfort sinners with false hopes, and delude them with their "old wives' fables" (I Tim. 4. 7) and nonsense, or who give way to false tenderness and sympathy, till they have not firmness enough to see the sword of the Spirit applied, cutting men to the soul, and laying open the sinner's naked heart. Alas, that so many are ever put into the ministry, who have not skill enough to stand by and see the Spirit of God to do His work, in breaking up the old foundations, and crushing all the rotten hopes of a sinner, and breaking him down at the feet of Jesus.

LECTURE XVIII

DIRECTIONS TO SINNERS

What must I do to be saved?—Acts 16. 30.

These are the words of the jailer at Philippi—the question which he put to Paul and Silas, who were then under his care as prisoners. Satan had, in many ways, opposed these servants of God in their work of preaching the Gospel, and had been as often defeated and disgraced. But here he devised a new and peculiar project for frustrating their labours. There was a certain woman at Philippi, who was possessed with a spirit of divination, or, in other words, the spirit of the devil, and brought her masters much gain by her soothsaying. The devil set this woman to follow Paul and Silas about the streets, and as soon as they had begun to gain the attention of the people, she would come in and cry: "These men are the servants of the most high God, which shew unto us the way of salvation" (*v*. 17). That is, she undertook to second the exhortations of the preachers, and added her testimony, as if to give additional weight to their instructions.

The effect of it was just what Satan desired. The people all knew that this was a wicked, base woman; and when they heard her attempting to recommend this new preaching, they were disgusted, and concluded that it was all of a piece. The devil knew that it would not do him any good to set such a person to oppose the preaching of the apostles, or to speak against it. The time had gone by for that to succeed. And, therefore, he takes the opposite ground, and by setting her to praise them as the servants of God, and to bear her polluted testimony in favour of their instructions, he led people to suppose the apostles were of the same character with her, and had the same spirit that she had. Paul saw that if things went on so, he would be totally baffled, and could never succeed in establishing a Church at Philippi. So he turns round upon her, and commands the foul spirit, in the name of Jesus Christ, to come out of her. "When her masters saw that the hope of the gains was gone" they raised a great persecution, and "caught Paul and Silas," and made a great ado, and brought them before the magistrates, and raised such a clamour that the magistrates shut up the messengers of the Gospel in prison, and the jailer "made their feet fast in the stocks."

Thus, the enemy thought they had put down the excitement. But "at midnight Paul and Silas prayed, and sang praises unto God: and the prisoners heard them" (*v*. 25). This old prison, that had so long echoed to the voice of blasphemy and oaths, now resounded with the praises of God; and these walls, that had stood so firm, now trembled under the power of prayer. The stocks were unloosed, the gates thrown open, and every one's bands broken. The jailer was aroused from his sleep, and when he saw the prison doors open, he drew his sword, knowing that if the prisoners had escaped he must pay for it with his life, and was about to kill himself. But Paul, who had no notion of escaping clandestinely, cried out to him instantly: "Do thyself no harm: for we are all here." And the jailer "called for a light, and sprang in, and came trembling, and fell down before his prisoners, Paul and Silas, and brought them out, and said, Sirs, what must I do to be saved?"

In my last Lecture, I dwelt at some length on the false instructions given to sinners under conviction, and the false comforts too often administered, and the erroneous instructions which such persons receive. It is my design now, to show what are *the instructions* that should be given to anxious sinners in order to their speedy and effectual conversion; or, in other words, to explain to you, what answer should be given to those who make the inquiry: "What must I do to be saved?" I propose: I. To show what is *not a proper direction* to be given to sinners,when they make the inquiry in the text. II. To show what *is a proper answer* to the inquiry. III. To *specify several errors* into which anxious sinners are apt to fall.

I. WHAT ARE NOT PROPER DIRECTIONS.

No more important inquiry was ever made than this: "What must I do to be saved?" Mankind are apt enough to inquire: "What shall I eat, and what shall I drink?" and the question may be answered in various ways, with little danger. But when a sinner asks in earnest: "What must I do to be saved?" it is of infinite importance that he should receive the right answer.

1. No direction should be given to a sinner that will *leave him still* "in the gall of bitterness, and in the bond of iniquity" (Acts 8. 23). No answer is proper to be given, by complying with which he would not go to heaven, if he should die the next moment.

2. No direction should be given that does not include a change of heart, or a right heart, or hearty obedience to Christ. In other words, nothing is proper which does not imply actually becoming a Christian. Any other direction that falls short of this, is of no use. It will not bring him any nearer to the Kingdom, it will do no good, but will lead him to defer the very thing which he must do in order to be saved. The sinner should be told plainly, at once, what he must do if he would not be lost; and he should be told nothing that does not include a right state of heart. Whatever you may do, sinner, that does not include a right heart, is sin. Whether you read the Bible or not, you are in sin, so long as you remain in rebellion. Whether you go to religious services or stay away; whether you pray or not, it is nothing but rebellion, every moment. It is surprising that a sinner should suppose himself to be doing service to God when he prays, and reads his Bible. Should a rebel against the Government read the statute-book while he continues in rebellion, and has no design to obey; should he ask for pardon while he holds on to his weapons of resistance and warfare; would you think him doing his country a service, and lay it

under obligation to show him favour? No; you would say that all his reading and praying were only an insult to the majesty both of the lawgiver and the law. So you, sinner, while you remain in impenitence, are insulting God, and setting him at defiance, whether you read His Word, and pray, or let it alone. No matter what place or what attitude your body is in, on your knees or in the house of God; so long as your heart is not right, so long as you resist the Holy Ghost, and reject Christ, you are a rebel against your Maker.

II. *WHAT IS A PROPER ANSWER.*

Generally, you may give the sinner any direction, or tell him to do anything, that includes a right heart; and if you make him understand, and he follows the directions, he will be saved. The Spirit of God, in striving with sinners, suits His strivings to the state of mind in which He finds them. His great object in striving with them is, to dislodge them from their hiding-places, and bring them to submit to God at once. These objections, difficulties, and states of mind, are as various as the circumstances of mankind—as many as there are individuals. The characters of individuals afford and endless diversity. What is to be done with each one, and how he is to be converted, depends on his particular errors. It is necessary to ascertain his errors; to find out what he understands, and what he needs to be taught more perfectly; to see what points the Spirit of God is pressing upon his conscience, and to press the same things, and thus bring him to Christ.

The most common directions are the following:

1. It is generally in point, and a safe and suitable direction, to tell a sinner to *repent*. I say, *generally*. For sometimes the Spirit of God seems not so much to direct the sinner's attention to his *own sins* as to some other thing. In the days of the apostles, the minds of the people seem to have been agitated mainly on the question, whether Jesus was the true Messiah. And so the apostles directed much of their instruction to this point, to prove that he was the Christ. And whenever anxious sinners asked them what they must do, they most commonly exhorted them to "believe on the Lord Jesus Christ." They bore down on this point, because here was where the Spirit of God was striving, and this was the subject

that especially agitated the minds of the people, and, consequently, this would probably be the first thing a person would do on submitting to God. It was the grand point at issue between God and the Jew and Gentile of those days, whether Jesus Christ was the Son of God. It was the point in dispute. To bring the sinner to yield this controverted question was the way the most effectually to humble him.

At other times, it will be found that the Spirit of God is dealing with sinners chiefly in reference to their own sins. Sometimes He deals with them in regard to a particular duty, as prayer—perhaps family prayer. The sinner will be found to be contesting that point with God, whether it is right for him to pray, or whether he ought to pray in his family. I have known striking cases of this kind, where the individual was struggling on this point, and as soon as he fell on his knees to pray, he yielded his heart, showing that this was the very point which the Spirit of God was contesting, and the hinge on which his controversy with God all turned. That was conversion.

The direction to repent is always *proper*, but will not always be effectual, for there may be some other thing that the sinner needs to be told also. And where it is the pertinent direction, sinners need not only to be told to repent, but to have it explained to them what repentance is. Since there has been so much mysticism, and false philosophy, and false theology, thrown round the subject, it has become necessary to tell sinners not only what you mean by repentance, but also to tell them what you *do not* mean. Words that used to be plain, and easily understood, have now become so perverted that they need to be explained to sinners, or they will often convey a wrong impression to their minds. This is the case with the word "repentance." Many suppose that *remorse*, or a sense of guilt, is repentance. Then, hell is full of repentance, for it is full of remorse, unutterable and eternal. Others feel *regret* that they have done such a thing, and they call that repenting. But they only regret that they have sinned, because of the consequences, and not because they abhor sin. This is not repentance. Others suppose that convictions of sin and strong fears of hell are repentance. Others consider the remonstrances of conscience as repentance; they say: "I never do anything wrong without repenting and feeling sorry I did it." Sinners must be shown that all these things are not repentance. They are not only consistent with the utmost wickedness, but the devil might have them all and yet remain a devil. Repentance is a change of mind, as regards God and towards sin. It is not only a change of views, but a change of the ultimate preference or choice of the soul. It is a voluntary change, and by consequence involves a change of *feeling* and of *action toward God and toward sin*. It is what is naturally understood by a change of mind on any subject of interest and importance. We hear that a man has changed his mind in politics; everybody understands that he has undergone a change in his views, his feelings, and his *conduct*. This is repentance, on that subject: it is a change of mind, but not toward God. Evangelical repentance is a change of willing, of feeling, *and of life, in respect to God.*

Repentance always implies abhorrence of sin. It of course involves the love of God and the forsaking of sin. The sinner who truly repents does not feel as impenitent sinners think they should feel at giving up their sins, if they should become religious. Impenitent sinners look upon religion in this way: that if they become pious, they should be *obliged* to stay away from balls and parties, and *obliged* to give up theatres, or gambling, or other things that they now take delight in. And they see not how ever they could enjoy themselves, if they should break off from all those things. But this is very far from being a correct view of the matter, Religion does not make them unhappy, by shutting them out from things in which they delight, because the first step in it, is, to repent, to change their mind in regard to all these things. They do not seem to realise, that the person who has repented has no disposition for these things; he has given them up, and turned his mind away from them. Sinners feel as if they should *want* to go to such places, and want to mingle in such scenes, just as much as they do now, and that it will be such a continual sacrifice as to make them unhappy. This is a great mistake.

I know there are some professors, who would be very glad to betake themselves to their former practices, were it not that they feel constrained, by fear of losing their character, or the like. But, mark me: if they feel so, it is because they have no religion; they do not hate sin. If they desire their former ways, they have no religion, they have never repented; for repentance always consists in a change of views and feelings. If they were really converted, instead of choosing such things, they would turn away from them with loathing. Instead of lusting after the flesh-pots of Egypt, and desiring to go into their former circles, parties, balls, and the like, they would find their highest pleasure in obeying God.

2. Sinners should be told to *believe* the Gospel. Here, also, they need to have it explained to them, and to be told *what is not* faith, and what is. Nothing is more common, than for a sinner, when told to believe the Gospel, to say: "I do believe it." The fact is, he has been brought up to admit the fact that the Gospel is true, but he does not *believe* it: he knows nothing about the evidence of it, and all his faith is a mere admission without evidence. He holds it to be true, in a kind of loose, indefinite sense, so that he is always ready to say: "I do believe the Bible." It is strange that they do not see that they are deceived in thinking that they believe, for they must see that they have never acted upon these truths, as they do upon those things which they do believe. Yet it is often quite difficult to convince them that they do not believe.

But the fact is, that the careless sinner does not believe the Gospel at all. The idea that the careless sinner is an *intellectual* believer, is absurd. The devil is an intellectual believer, and that is what makes him tremble. What makes a sinner anxious is, that he begins to be an intellectual believer, and that makes him feel. No being in heaven, earth, or hell, can intellectually believe the truths of the Gospel, and not feel on the subject. The anxious sinner has faith of the same kind with devils, but he has not so much of it, and, therefore, he does not feels so much. The man who does not feel or act at all, on the subject of religion, is an infidel, let his professions be what they may. He who feels nothing, and does nothing, believes nothing. This is a philosophical fact.

Faith does not consist in an intellectual conviction that Christ died for you in particular, or in a belief that you are a Christian, or that you ever shall be, or that your sins are forgiven. But faith is that trust or confidence in God, and in Christ, which commits the whole soul to Him in all His relations to us. It is a voluntary trust in His person, His veracity, His word. This was the faith of Abraham: he had that confidence in what God said, which led him to act as accepting its truth. This is the way the apostle illustrates it in the eleventh chapter of Hebrews. "Faith is the substance of things hoped for, the evidence of things not seen" (*v.* 1). And he goes on to illustrate it by various examples. "Through faith we understand that the worlds were framed" (*v.* 3); that is, we believe this, and act accordingly.

Take the case of Noah. Noah was warned of God of things not seen as yet, that is, he was assured that God was going to drown the world, and he believed it, and acted accordingly; he prepared an ark to save his family, and by so doing, he condemned the world that would not believe; his actions gave evidence that he was sincere. Abraham, too, was called of God to leave his country, with the promise that he should be the gainer by it; and he obeyed and went out, without knowing whither he went. Read the whole chapter, and you will find many instances of the same kind. The whole design of the chapter is to illustrate the nature of faith, and to show that it invariably results in action. The sinner should have it explained to him, and be *made to see* that the faith which the Gospel requires, is just that confidence in Christ which leads him to act on what He say as being a certain fact. This is believing in Christ.

3. Another direction, proper to be given to the sinner, is, that he should *give his heart to God.* God says: "My son, give Me thine heart" (Prov. 23. 26). But here also there needs to be explanation, to make him understand what it is. It is amazing that there should be any darkness here. It is the language of common life, in everybody's mouth, and everybody understands just what it means, when we use it in regard to anything else. But when it comes to religion, they seem to be all in the dark. Ask a sinner, no matter what may be his age, or education, what it means to give the heart to God, and, strange as it may appear, he is at a loss for an answer. Ask a woman, what it is to give her heart to her husband; or a man, what it is to give his heart to his wife; and they understand it. But then they are totally blind as to giving their hearts to God. I suppose I have asked more than a thousand anxious sinners this

question. When I have told them, they must give their hearts to God, they have always said that they were willing to do it, and sometimes, that they were anxious to do it, and they have even seemed to be in an agony of desire about it. Then I have asked them, what they understood to be *meant* by giving their hearts to God, since they were so willing to do it. And very seldom have I received a correct or rational answer from a sinner of any age. I have sometimes had the strangest answers that could be imagined.

Now, to give your heart to God is the same thing as to give your heart to anybody else; the same as for a woman to give her heart to her husband. Ask that woman if she understands this. "Oh, yes, that is plain enough; it is to place my affections with him, and strive to please him in everything." Very well, place your affections on God, and strive to please Him in everything. But when they come to the subject of religion, people suppose there is some wonderful mystery about it. Some talk as if they suppose it means taking out this bundle of muscles, or fleshy organ, in their bosom, and giving it to God. Sinner, what God asks of you, is, that you should love Him supremely.

4. "*Submit to God*," is also a proper direction to anxious sinners. And oh, how dark sinners are here, too! Scarcely a sinner can be found who will not tell you that he is willing to submit to God. But they do not understand. They need to be told what true submission is. Sometimes they think it means that they should be willing to be sent to perdition. Sometimes they place themselves in this attitude, and call it submission; they say that, if they are elected they will be saved; and if not, they will be lost. This is not submission. True submission is yielding obedience to God. Suppose a rebel, in arms against the Government, is called on to submit, what would he understand by it? Why, that he should yield the point, and lay down his arms, and obey the laws. That is just what it means for a sinner to submit to God. He must cease his strife and conflict against his Maker, and take the attitude of a willing and obedient child, willing to be and do whatever God requires. "Here am I" (I Sam. 3. 8); "Lord, what wilt Thou have me to do?" (Acts 9. 6.)

Suppose a company of soldiers had rebelled, and the Government had raised an army to put them down, and had driven them into a stronghold, where they were out of provisions, and had no way to escape. Suppose the rebels to have met, in this extremity, to consider what should be done; and one rises up, saying: "Well, comrades, I am convinced we are all wrong from the beginning, and now the reward of our deeds is likely to overtake us, and we cannot escape; and as for remaining here to die, I am resolved not to do it; I am going to throw myself on the mercy of the commander-in-chief." That man submits. He ceases from that moment to be a rebel in his heart, just as soon as he comes to this conclusion. So it is with the sinner when he yields the point, and consents in his heart to do, and be, whatever God shall require. The sinner may be in doubt what to do, and may feel afraid to put himself in God's hands, thinking that if he does, perhaps God will send him down to hell, as he deserves. But it is his business to leave all that question with God, to resist his Maker no longer, to make no conditions, but to trust wholly to God's benevolence and wisdom to appoint his future condition. Until he has done this, he has done nothing to the purpose.

5. Another proper direction to be given to sinners, is to *confess and forsake their sins*. They must confess to God their sins against God, and confess to men their sins against men; and forsake them all. A man does not forsake his sins till he has made all the reparation in his power. If he has stolen money, or defrauded his neighbour out of poverty, he does not forsake his sins by merely resolving not to steal any more, not to cheat again; he must make reparation to the extent of his power.[1] So, if he has slandered any one, he does not forsake his sin by merely saying he will not do so again; he must make

---

[1] Restitution was a prominent feature in Finney's campaigns. For example, a young woman in New York, who became converted at one of his meetings, had been a wholesale pilferer practically all her life; but after her conversion she commenced the work of restoring, so far as she could, all the articles she had stolen—and these varied from a handkerchief belonging to a schoolmate to a shawl which was the property of a Bishop's daughter. At Bolton, Lancs., after Finney had preached upon Restitution, some hundreds—indeed, it was believed thousands—of pounds sterling were restored to persons from whom money had been dishonestly obtained or withheld; the sums varied from small amounts up to a single payment of £300. (*The Revival*, March 17, 1860.)

reparation. So, in like manner, if he has robbed God, as all sinners have, he must make reparation, as far as he has power. Suppose a man has made money in rebellion against God, and has withheld from Him his time, talents, and service, has lived and rioted upon the bounties of His providence, and refused to lay himself out for the salvation of the world; he has robbed God. Now, if he should die, feeling this money *to be his own*, and should he leave it to his heirs without consulting the will of God—why, he is just as certain to go to hell as a highway robber. He has never made any satisfaction to God. With all his whining and pious talk, he has never confessed HIS SIN to God, nor forsaken his sin, for he has neither felt nor acknowledged himself to be the steward of God. If he refuses to hold the property in his possession as the steward of God; if he accounts it his own, and as such gives it to his children, he says in effect, to God: "That property is not Thine, it is mine, and I will give it to my children." He has continued to persevere in his sin, for he does not relinquish the ownership of that of which he has robbed God.

What would a merchant think if his clerk should take all the capital and set up a store of his own, and die with it in his hands? Will such a man go to heaven? "No," you say. God would prove Himself unjust, to let such a character go unpunished. What, then, shall we say of the man who has robbed God all his life? God sent him to be His clerk, to manage some of His affairs, but he has stolen all the money, and says it is his; he keeps it, and, dying, leaves it to his children, as if it were all his own lawful property. Has that man forsaken sin? I tell you, No. If he has not surrendered himself and all he has to God, he has not taken the first step in the way to heaven.

6. Another proper direction to be given to sinners is: "*Choose you this day whom ye will serve*" (Josh. 24. 15). Under the Old Testament dispensation, this, or something equivalent to it, was the most common direction given. It was not common to call on men to *believe in Christ* until the days of John the Baptist. He baptized those who came to him, with the baptism of repentance, and directed them to believe on Him who should come after him. Under Joshua, the text was something which the people all understood more easily than

they would a call to believe on the distant Messiah; it was: "Choose you this day whom ye will serve." On another occasion, Moses said to them: "I call heaven and earth to record this day against you, that I have set before you life and death, blessing and cursing: therefore choose life, that both thou and thy seed may live" (Deut. 30. 19). The direction was accommodated to the people's knowledge. And it is as good now as it was then. Sinners are called upon to choose—what? Whether they will serve God or the world; whether they will follow holiness or sin. Let them be made to understand what is meant by choosing, and what is to be chosen, and then if the thing be done from the heart, they will be saved.

Any of these directions, if complied with, will constitute true conversion. The particular exercises may vary in different cases. Sometimes the first exercise in conversion is submission to God, sometimes repentance, sometimes faith, sometimes the choice of God and His service; in short, whatever their thoughts are taken up with at the time. If their thoughts are directed to Christ at the moment, the first exercise will be faith. If to sin, the first exercise will be repentance. If to their future course of life, it is choosing the service of God. If to the Divine government, it is submission. It is important to find out just where the Holy Spirit is pressing the sinner at the time, and then take care to push that point. If it is in regard to Christ, press that; if it is in regard to his future course of life, push him right up to an immediate choice of obedience to God.

It is a great error to suppose that any one particular exercise is always foremost in conversion, or that every sinner must have faith first, or submission first. It is not true, either in philosophy or in fact. There is a great variety in people's exercises. Whatever point is taken hold of between God and the sinner, when the sinner YIELDS that, he is converted. Whatever the particular exercise may be, if it includes *obedience of heart to God on any point*, it is true conversion. When he yields one point to *God's authority*, he is ready to yield all. When he changes his mind, and obeys in one thing, because it is God's will, he will obey in other things, so far as he sees it to be God's will. Where there is right choice, then, whenever the mind is directed to any one point of duty, he is ready to follow. It matters very little which of these directions be given, if it is only made plain, and if it is to the point, so as to serve as a test of *obedience to God*. If it is to the point that the Spirit of God is debating with the sinner's mind, so as to fall in with the Spirit's work, and not to divert the sinner's attention from the very point in controversy, let it be made perfectly clear, and then pressed till the sinner yields, and he will be saved.

III. *ERRORS INTO WHICH ANXIOUS SINNERS ARE APT TO FALL.*

1. The first error is, in supposing that they must make themselves better, or prepare themselves, so as in some way to recommend themselves to the mercy of God. It is marvellous that sinners will not understand that all they have to do is to *accept* salvation, all prepared to their hands, from God. But they all, learned or unlearned, at first betake themselves to a legal course to get relief. This is one principal reason why they will not become Christians at once. They imagine that they must be, in some way or other, *prepared* to come. They must change their dress, and make themselves look a little better; they are not willing to come just as they are, in their rags and poverty. They must have something more on, before they can approach God. They should be shown, at once, that it is impossible they should be any better until they do what God requires. Every pulse that beats, every breath they draw, they are growing worse, because they are standing out in rebellion against God, so long as they do not do the *very thing* which God requires of them as the first thing to be done.

2. Another error is, in supposing that they must *suffer a considerable time under conviction*, as a kind of punishment, before they are properly ready to come to Christ. So they will pray for conviction; and they think that if they are ground down to the earth with distress, for a sufficient time, then God will pity them, and be more ready to help them when He sees them so very miserable! They should be made to understand clearly that they are thus unhappy and miserable, *merely because* they refuse to accept the relief which God offers.

3. Sometimes sinners imagine they must wait for *different feelings* before they submit to God. They say: "I do not think I feel right yet, to accept Christ; I do not think I am prepared to

be converted yet." They ought to be made to see that what God requires of them is to *will* right. If they obey and submit with the *will*, the *feelings* will adjust themselves in due time. It is not a question of *feeling*, but of *willing* and *acting*.

The *feelings* are involuntary, and have no moral character except what they derive from the action of the will, with which action they sympathise. Before the will is right, the feelings will not be, of course. The sinner should come to Christ by accepting Him at once; and this he must do, not in obedience to his *feelings*, but in obedience to his *conscience*. Obey, submit, trust. Give up all instantly, and your feelings will come right. Do not wait for better feelings, but commit your whole being to God at once, and this will soon result in the feelings for which you are waiting. What God requires of you is the present act of your mind, in turning from sin to holiness, and from the service of Satan to the service of the living God.

4. Another error of sinners is to suppose that they *must wait* till their *hearts are changed*. "What?" say they, "am I to believe in Christ before my heart is changed? Do you mean that I am to repent before my heart is changed?" Now, the simple answer to all this is that the change of heart is the very thing in question. God requires sinners to love Him: *that is* to change their hearts. God requires the sinner to believe the Gospel. *That is* to change his heart. God requires him to repent. *That is* to change his heart. God does not tell him to wait till his heart is changed, and then repent and believe, and love God. The very word itself, *repent*, signifies a change of mind or heart. To do either of these things is to change your heart, and to "make you a new heart" (Ezek. 18. 31), just as God requires.

5. Sinners often get the idea that they are perfectly willing to do what God requires. Tell them to do this thing, or that, to repent, or believe, or give God their hearts, and they say: "Oh, yes, I am *perfectly willing* to do that; I wish I could do it, I would give anything if I could do it." They ought to understand that being truly *willing* is doing it, but there is a difference between willing and desiring. People often *desire* to be Christians, when they are wholly *unwilling* to be so. When we see anything which appears to be a good, we are so constituted that we desire it. We necessarily desire it when it is before our minds. We cannot help desiring in in proportion as its

goodness is presented to our minds. But yet we may not be *willing* to have it, under all the circumstances. A man may desire on many accounts to go to Philadelphia, while, for still more weighty reasons, he *chooses* not to go there. So the sinner may desire to be a Christian. He may see that if he were a Christian he would be a deal more happy, and that he should go to heaven when he dies; but yet he is not willing to be a Christian. WILLING to obey Christ is to be a Christian. When an individual actually *chooses* to obey God, he is a Christian. But all such desires do not terminate in actual choice, are nothing.

6. The sinner will sometimes say that he *offers* to give God his heart, but he intimates that God is unwilling. But this is absurd. What does God ask? Why, that you should love Him. Now for you to say that you are willing to give God your heart, but that God is unwilling, is the same as saying that you are willing to love God, but God is not willing to be loved by you, and will not suffer you to love Him. It is important to clear up all these points in the sinner's mind, that he may have no dark and mysteious corner to rest in, where the truth will not reach him.

7. Sinners sometimes get the idea that they repent, when they are only convicted. Whenever the sinner is found resting in any LIE let the truth sweep it away, however much it may pain and distress him. If he has any error of this kind, you must tear it away from him.

8. Sinners are often wholly taken up with *looking at themselves*, to see if they cannot find something there, some kind of feeling or other, that will recommend them to God. Evidently for want of proper instruction, David Brainerd was a long time taken up with his *state of mind*, looking for some *feelings* that would recommend him to God. Sometimes he imagined that he had such feelings, and would tell God, in prayer, that now he felt as he should, in order to receive His mercy; and then he would see that he had been all wrong.[1]

---

[1] Dr. Andrew A. Bonar, in his Diary (July 20, 1890) expressed a similar thought regarding Brainerd—whose Diary and Journal have of course taken their place, as a spiritual classic, with Augustine's "Confessions," Bunyan's "Grace Abounding," the Letters of Rutherford and of Cowper, and the Journal and letters in which

Thus the poor man, for want of correct instruction, was driven almost to despair, and it is easy to see that his Christian exercises through life were greatly modified, and his comfort and usefulness much impaired, by the false philosophy he had adopted on this point.[2] You must turn the sinner away from himself.

Henry Martyn records, or tells to Lydia Grenfell, the moving account of his wrestlings with self, his aspirations after righteousness, and, as he "burnt out for God," his agonisings for India. "Sometimes," writes Brainerd, "after enlargement in duty and considerable affection, I hoped I had made a good step towards heaven. Sometimes I thought I should soon be reconverted to God, while the whole was founded on mere presumption. The Spirit of God was powerfully at work with me, and I was inwardly pressed to relinquish all hopes of helping myself...I at once saw that all my contrivances to effect or procure deliverance and salvation for myself wee utterly in vain." But (July 12, 1739) "as I was walking in a dark, thick grove, *unspeakable glory* seemed to open to the view and apprehension of my soul...The way of salvation opened to me with such infinite wisdom, suitableness, and excellency, that I was amazed I had not dropped my own contrivances and complied with this lovely, blessed,and excellent way before...I wondered that all the world did not see and comply with this way of salvation, entirely by *the righteousness of Christ*." Brainerd had continually to battle against physical inability. "My soul was filled with light and love; my body was so weak that I could scarcely stand."

² It is not surprising that Finney was warmly interested in Brainerd, for the Journal of that saintly man, describing his experiences among the North American Indians, abounds in incidents of a revival character. Thus, the entry for August 8, 1745, runs: "Preached to them [the Indians] from Luke 14. 16-23. There was much visible concern while I was preaching. Afterwards the power of God seemed to descend upon the assembly like a rushing mighty wind, and with an astonishing energy bore down all before it. Old men and women who had been drunken wretches for many years appeared in distress for their souls; and little children, as well as middle-aged persons. Another man, who had been a murderer and notorious drunkard, was brought to cry for mercy with many tears. They were almost universally praying and crying in every part of the house, and many out of doors, and some could neither go nor stand. It was, indeed, a surprising day of God's power and seemed enough to convince an atheist of the truth, importance, and power of God's Word."

REMARKS.

1. The labour of ministers is greatly increased, and the difficulties in the way of salvation are greatly multiplied, by the false instructions that have been given to sinners. The consequence has been that directions which used to be plain are now obscure. People have been taught so long that there is something awfully mysterious and unintelligible about conversion, that they do not try to understand it.

It was once sufficient, as we learn from the Bible, to tell sinners to repent, or to believe on the Lord Jesus Christ; but now, faith has been talked about as a *principle*, instead of an act; and repentance as something put into the mind, instead of an exercise of the mind; and sinners are perplexed. Ministers are charged with preaching heresy, because they presume to teach that faith is an exercise, and not a principle; and that sin is an act, and not a part of the constitution of man. And sinners have become so sophisticated, that you have to be at great pains in explaining, not only what you do mean, but what you do not mean, otherwise they will be almost sure to misunderstand you, and either gain a false relief from their anxiety, by throwing their duty off upon God, or else run into despair from the supposed in practicability of doing what is requisite for their salvation. It is often a matter of the greatest dificulty to lead sinners out of the theological labyrinths and mazes into which they have been deluded, and to lead them along the straight and simple way of the Gospel. It seems as if the greatest ingenuity had been employed to mystify the minds of the people, and to weave a most sublte web of false philosophy, calculated to involve a sinner in endless darkness. It is necessary to be as plain as A B C, and the best educated have to be talked to like children. Tell a sinner to *believe*, and he stares, saying: "Why, how you talk! Is not faith a principle? And how am I to believe till I get this principle?" So, if a minister tells a sinner, in the very words that the apostle used in the great revival on the Day of Pentecost: "Repent, every one of you" (Acts 2. 38), he is answered: "Oh, I guess you are an Arminian; I do not want any of your Arminian teaching; do you not deny the Spirit's influences?" It is enought to make humanity weep, to see the fog and darkness that have been thrown around the plain directions of the Gospel.

2. These false instructions to sinners are infinitely worse than none. The Lord Jesus Christ found it more difficult to get the people to yield up their false notions of theology than anything else. This has been the great difficulty with the Jews to this day, that they have received false notions in theology, have perverted the truth on certain points, and you cannot make them understand the plainest points in the Gospel. So it is with sinners: the most difficult thing to be done is to get them away from these "refuges of lies," which they have found in false theology. They are so fond of holding on to these refuges (because they excuse the sinner, and condemn God), that it is found to be the most perplexing, and difficult, and discouraging part of a minister's labour, to drive them out.

3. No wonder the Gospel has taken so little effect, encumbered as it has been with these strange dogmas. The truth is, that very little of the Gospel has come out upon the world, for these hundreds of years, without being clogged and obscured by false theology. People have been told that they must repent, and, in the same breath, told they could not repent, until the truth itself has been all mixed up with error, so as to produce the same practical effect with error. The Gospel that was preached has been another gospel, or no gospel at all.

4. You can understand what is meant by "healing slightly the hurt of the daughter of God's people" (Jer. 6. 14; 8. 11), and the danger of doing it. It is very easy, when sinners are under conviction, to say something that shall smooth over the case, and relieve their anxiety, so that they will either get a false hope, or will be converted with their views so obscure, that they will always be poor, feeble, wavering, doubting inefficient Christians.

5. Much depends on the manner in which a person is dealt with, when under conviction. Much of his future comfort and usefulness depends on the clearness, strength, and firmness with which the directions of the Gospel are given, when he is under conviction. If those who deal with him are afraid to use the probe thoroughly, he will always be a poor, sickly, doubting Christian. The true mode is to deal thoroughly and plainly with the sinner, to tear away every excuse he can offer, and to show him plainly what he is and what he ought to be; then he

will bless God to all eternity that he fell in with those who would be so faithful with his soul. For the want of this thorough and searching management, many are converted who seem to be stillborn; and the reason is, they never were faithfully dealt with. We may charitably hope they are Christians, but still it is uncertain and doubtful: their conversion seems rather a change of opinion than a change of heart. But if, when sinners are under conviction, you pour in the truth, put in the probe, break up the old foundations, sweep away their "refuges of lies," and use the Word of God like fire and like a hammer, you will find that they will come out with clear views, and strong faith, and firm principles— not doubting, halting, irresolute Christians, but such as follow the Lord wholly. That is the way to make strong Christians. This has been eminently the case in many revivals of modern days. I have heard old Christians say of the converts: "These converts have, at the very outset, all the clearness of view, and strength of faith, of old Christians. They seem to understand the doctrines of religion, and to know what to do, and how to promote revivals, better than one in a hundred of the old members in the Church."

I once knew a young man who was converted away from home. The place where he lived had no minister, and no preaching, and no religion. He went home three days after he was converted, and immediately set himself to work to labour for a revival. He set up meetings in his neighbourhood, and prayed and laboured, and a revival broke out—of which he had the principal management throughout a powerful work, in which most of the principal men of the place were converted. The truth was, he had been so dealt with that he knew what he was about. He understood the subject and knew where he stood himself. He was not all the while troubled with doubts, whether he was himself a Christian. He knew that he was serving God, and that God was with him, and so he went boldly and resolutely forward to his object. But if you undertake to make converts, without clearing up all their errors and tearing away their false hopes, you may make a host of hypocrites, or of puny, dwarfish Christians, always doubting and easily turned back from a revival spirit, and worth nothing. The way is, to bring them right out to the light. When a man is converted in this way, you can depend on him, and will know where to find him.

6. Protracted seasons of conviction are generally owing to defective instruction. Wherever clear and faithful instructions are given to sinners, there you will generally find that convictions are *deep and pungent*, but *short*.

7. Where clear and discriminating instructions are given to convicted sinners, if they do not soon submit, their convictions will generally leave them. Convictions in such cases are generally short. Where the truth is brought to bear upon the sinner's mind, and he directly resists the very truth that must convert him, there is nothing mroe to be done. The Spirit will soon leave him, for the very weapons He uses are resisted. Where instructions are not clear, but are mixed up with errors, the Spirit may strive, even for years, in great mercy, to get sinners through the fog of false instruction; but not so where their duty is clearly explained to them, and they are brought right up to the single point of immediate submission, all their false pretences being exposed, and the path of duty made perfectly plain. Then, if they do not submit, the Spirit of God forsakes them, and their state is wellnigh hopeless.

If there be sinners in this house, and you see your duty clearly, TAKE CARE how you delay. If you do not submit, you may expect the Spirit of God will forsake you, and you are LOST.

8. A vast deal of the direction given to anxious sinners amounts to little less than the popish doctrine of indulgences. The Pope used to sell indulgences to sin, and this led to the Reformation under luther. Sometimes people would purchase and indulgence to sin for a certain time, or to commit some particular sin, or a number of sins. Now, there is a vast deal in Protestant Churches which is little less than the same thing. What does it differ from this, to tell a sinner to wait? It amounts to telling him to continue in sin for a while longer, while he is waiting for God to convert him. And what is that but an indulgence to commit sin? Any direction given to sinners that does not require them *immediately* to obey God is an indulgence to sin. It is in effect giving them liberty to continue in sin against God. Such directions are not only wicked, but ruinous and cruel. If they do not destroy the soul, as

no doubt they often do, they *defer*, at all events, the sinner's enjoyment of God and of Christ, and he stands a great chance of being lost for ever, while listening to such instructions. Oh, how dangerous it is to give a sinner reasons to think he may wait a moment, before giving his heart to God!

9. So far as I have had opportunity to observe, those persons with whom conversion was most sudden have commonly turned out to be the best Christians. I know the reverse of this has often been held and maintained. But I am satisfied there is no reason for it, although multitudes, even now, regard it as a suspicious circumstance, if a man has been converted very suddenly. But the Bible gives no warrant for this supposition. There is not a case of protracted conviction recorded in the whole Bible. All the conversions recorded there are sudden conversions. And I am persuaded there never would be such multitudes of tedious convictions (which often end in nothing, after all), if it were not for those theological perversions which have filled the world with *Cannot-ism.* In Bible days, sinners were told to repent, and they did it *then.* Cannot-ism had not been broached in that day. It is this speculation about the inability of sinners to obey God, that lays the foundation for all the protracted anguish and distress, and perhaps ruin, into which so many are led. Where a sinner is brought to see what he has to do, and he takes his stand at once, AND DOES IT, you generally find that such a person proves a decided character. You will not find him one of those that you always have to *warp up* to duty, like a ship, against wind and tide. Look at those professors who always have to be dragged forward in duty, and you will generally find that they had not clear and consistent directions when they were converted. Most likely, too, they will be very much "afraid of these sudden conversions."

Afraid of sudden conversions! Some of the best Christians of my acquaintance were convicted and converted in the space of a few minutes. In one-quarter of the time that I have been speaking, many of them were awakened, and came right out on the Lord's side, and have been shining lights in the Church ever since, and have generally manifested the same decision of character in religion that they did when they first came out and took a stand on His side.

Lecture XIX

INSTRUCTIONS TO CONVERTS

Feed My lambs.—John 21. 15.

Those who read their Bibles will recollect the connection in which these words occur, and by whom they were spoken. They were addressed by the Lord Jesus Christ to Peter, after he had denied his Lord, and had subsequently professed repentance. Our Lord asked him this question, to remind him, in an affecting manner, at once of his sin and of the love of Christ: "Simon, son of Jonas, lovest thou Me more than these?"—strongly implying a doubt whether he *did* love Him. Peter answers: "Yea, Lord; Thou knowest that I love Thee." Then Christ said unto Him: "Feed My lambs"; and repeated the question, as if He would read his inmost soul: "Simon, son of Jonas, lovest thou Me?" Peter was still firm, and promptly answered again: "Yea, Lord; Thou knowest that I love Thee." Jesus still asked him the question again, the third time, emphatically. He seemed to urge the point, as if He would search his inmost thoughts, to see whether Peter would ever deny Him again. Peter was touched; he was "grieved," it is said; he did not fly into a passion, nor did he boast, as formerly: "Though I should die with Thee, yet will I not deny Thee" (Matt. 26. 35); but he was grieved; he was subdued; he spoke tenderly; he *appealed* to the Saviour Himself, as if he would implore Him not to doubt his sincerity any longer: "Lord, Thou knowest all things; Thou knowest that I love Thee." Christ then gave him his final charge: "Feed My sheep" (*v*. 17).

By the terms "sheep" and "lambs" the Saviour undoubtedly designated Christians, members of His Church; the lambs probably represent young converts, those that have but little experience and but little knowledge of religion, and therefore need to have special attention and pains taken with them, to guard them from harm, and to train them for future usefulness. And when our Saviour told Peter to feed His sheep, He doubtless referred to the important part which Peter was to perform in watching over the newly-formed Churches in different parts of the world, and in training the young converts, and leading them along to usefulness and happiness.

My last Lecture was on the subject of giving right instruction to anxious sinners; this naturally brings me to consider the manner in which young converts should be treated, and the instructions that should be given to them.

In speaking on this subject it is my design to state: I. Several things that ought to be considered, in regard to the hopes of young converts. II. Several things respecting their making a profession of religion, and joining the Church. III. The importance of having correct instruction given to young converts. IV. What should not be taught to young converts. V. What particular things are specially necessary to be taught to young converts. VI. How young converts should be treated by Church members.

I. THE HOPES OF YOUNG CONVERTS.

1. Nothing should be said *to create a hope*. That is to say, nothing should ordinarily be intimated to persons under conviction calculated to make them think they have experienced religion, till they find it out themselves. I do not like this term, "experienced religion," and I use it only because it is a phrase in common use. It is an absurdity in itself. What is religion? Obedience to God. Suppose you should hear a good citizen say he had experienced obedience to the Government of the country! You see that it is nonsense. Or suppose a child

should talk about experiencing obedience to his father. If he knew what he was saying, he would say he had *obeyed his father*; just as the apostle Paul says to the Roman believers: "Ye have *obeyed from the heart* that form of doctrine which was delivered you" (Rom. 6. 17).

What I mean to say is that ordinarily it is best to let their hope or belief that they are converted spring up spontaneously in their own minds. Sometimes it will happen that persons may be really converted, but, owing to some notions which they have been taught about religion, they do not realise it. Their views of what religion is, and its effect upon the mind, are so entirely wide of the truth that they do not think they have it. I will give you an illustration on this point.

Some years since, I laboured in a place where a revival was in progress, and there was in the place a young lady from Boston. She had been brought up a Unitarian. She was a person of considerable education, and was intelligent on many subjects; but on the subject of religion she was very ignorant. At length she was convicted of sin. She became awfully convinced of her horrible enmity against God. She had been so educated as to have a sense of propriety; but her enmity against God became so great, and broke out so frightfully, that it was horrible to hear her talk. She used to come to the anxious meetings, where we conversed with each person separately; and her feelings of opposition to God were such that she used to create disturbance. By the time I came within two or three seats of her, where she could hear what I said in a low voice to the others, she would begin to make remarks in reply, so that they could be heard. And she would say the most bitter things against God, against His providence, and His method of dealing with mankind, as if God were an infinite tyrant. I would try to hush her, and make her keep still, because she distracted the attention of others. Sometimes she would stop and command her temper for a time, and sometimes she would rise and go out. I have seldom seen a case where the enmity of the heart rose so high against God. One night, at the anxious meeting, after she had been very restless, as I went towards her, she began as usual to reply, but I hushed her, and told her I could not converse with her there. I invited her to see me the next morning, when I told her I would talk with her.

She promised to come; but, said she: "God is unjust—He is infinitely unjust. Is He not almighty? Why, then, has He never shown me my enmity before? Why has He let me run on so long? Why does He let my friends at Boston remain in this ignorance? They are the enemies of God as much as I am, and they are going to hell. Why does He not show them the truth in regard to their condition?" And in this temper she left the room.

The next morinig she came to see me, as she had promised. I saw, as soon as she came in, that her countenance was changed, but I said nothing about it. "Oh," said she, "I have changed my mind, as to what I said last night about God; I do not think He has done me any wrong, and I think I shall 'get religion' some time, for now I love to think about God. I have been all wrong; the reason why I had never known my enmity before was that I would not. I used to read the Bible, but I always passed over the passages that would make me feel as if I were a lost sinner; and those passages that spoke of Jesus Christ as God I passed over without consideration; but now I see that it was my fault, not God's fault, that I did not know any more about myself; I have changed my mind now." She had no idea that this was religion, but she was encouraged now to expect religion at some future time, because she loved God so much. I said nothing to make her imagine that I thought her a Christian, but left her to find it out. And, for a time, her mind was so entirely occupied with thinking about God that she never seemed to ask whether she "had religion" or not.

It is a great evil, ordinarily, to encourage persons to hope they are Christians. Very likely you may judge prematurely. Or if not, it is better, in any case, that they should find it out for themselves—that is, supposing they do not see it at once.

2. When persons express a hope, and yet express doubts, too, it is generally because the work is not thorough. If they are converted, they need breaking up. They are still lingering around the world, or they have not broken off effectually from their sins, and they need to be pushed back, rather than urged forward. If you see reason to doubt, or if you find that they have doubts, most probably there is some good reason to doubt. Sometimes persons express a hope in Christ, and afterwards remember some sin that needs to be confessed to men; or

some case where they have slandered, or defrauded, where it is necessary to make satisfaction, and where either their character, or their purse, is so deeply implicated that they hesitate, and refuse to perform their duty. This grieves the Spirit, brings darkness over their minds, and justly leads them to doubt whether they are truly converted. If a sould is truly converted, it will generally be found that, where there are doubts, there is on some point a neglect of duty. They should be searched as with a lighted candle, and brought up to the performance of duty, and not suffered to hope until they do it. *Ordinarily*, it is proper just to throw in some plain and searching truth, that will go through them, something that will wither their false hopes. Do it while the Spirit of God is dealing with them, and do it in a right way, and there is no danger of its doing harm.

To illustrate this: I knew a person who was a member of the Church, but an abominable hypocrite—proved to be so by her conduct, and afterwards fully confessed to be so. In a revival of religion she was awakened and deeply convicted, and after a while she got a hope. She went to a minister to talk with him about her hope, and he poured the truth into her mind in such a manner as to annihilate all her hopes. She then remained under conviction many days, and at last she broke out in hope again. The minister knew her temperament, and knew what she needed, and he tore away her hope again. Then she broke down. So deeply did the Spirit of God PROBE her heart that, for a time, it took away all her bodily strength. Then she came out subdued. Before, she had been one of the proudest of rebels against God's government, but now she became humbled, and was one of the most modest, tender, and lovely of Christians. No doubt that was just the way to deal with her. It was just the treatment that her case required.

It is often useful to deal with individuals in this way. Some persons are *naturally* unamiable in their temper, and unlovely in their deportment. And it is particularly important that such persons should be dealt with most thoroughly whenever they first begin to express hope in Christ. Unless the work with them is, in the first place, uncommonly deep and thorough, they will be vastly less useful, and interesting, and happy, than they would have been had the probe been thoroughly dealt with; if they are left to go on as though all were well; if they are not sufficiently probed and broken down, these unlovely traits of character will remain unsubdued, and will be always breaking out, to the great injury both of their personal peace and their general influence and usefulness as Christians.

It is important to take advantage of such characters while they are just in these peculiar circumstances, so that they can be moulded into proper form. Do not spare, though it should be a child, or a brother, or a husband, or a wife. Let it be a thorough work. If they express a hope, and you find they bear the image of Christ, they are Christians. But if it should appear doubtful—if they do not appear to be fully changed, just tear away their hope, by searching them with discriminating truth, and leave the Spirit to do the work more deeply. If still the image is not perfect, do it again—break them down into a childlike spirit, and then let them hope. They will then be clear and thorough Christians. By such a mode of treatment I have often known people of the crookedest and most hateful natural character so transformed, in the course of a few days, that they appeared like different beings. You would think the work of a whole life of Christian cultivation had been done at once. Doubtless this was the intent of our Saviour's dealing with Peter. He had been converted, but became puffed up with spiritual pride and self-confidence, and then he fell. After that, Christ broke him down again by three times searching him with the inquiry: "Simon, son of Jonas, lovest thou Me?" After which he seems to have been a stable and devoted saint the rest of his days.

3. There is no need of young converts *having or expressing doubts as to their conversion.* There is no more need of a person doubting whether he is now in favour of God's government than there is for a man to doubt whether he is in favour of our Government or another. It is, in fact, on the face of it, absurd for a person to talk of doubting on such a point, if he is intelligent and understands what he is talking about. It has long been supposed to be a virtue, and a mark of humility, for a person to doubt whether he is a Christian, but this notion that there is virtue in doubting is a device of the devil. "I say, neighbour, are you in favour of our Government, or do you prefer that of Russia?" "Why, I have some hopes that I love

our own Government, but I have many doubts." Wonderful! "Woman, do you love your children?" "Why, sir, I sometimes have a trembling hope that I love them, but you know the best have doubts." "Wife, do you love your husband?" "I do not know—I sometimes think I do, but you know the heart is deceitful, and we ought to be careful and not be too confident." Who would have such a wife? "Man, do you love your wife, do you love your family?" "Ah, you know we are poor creatures, we do not know our own hearts. I think I do love them, but perhaps I am deceived." Ridiculous!

Ordinarily, the very idea of a person expressing doubts renders his piety truly doubtful. A real Christian has no need to doubt; and when one is full of doubts, ordinarily you ought to doubt for him and help him doubt. Affection to God is as much a matter of consciousnes as any other affection. A woman *knows* she loves her child. How? By consciousness. She is conscious of the exercise of this affection. And she sees it carried into action every day. In the same way a Christian may know that he loves God; by his consciousness of this affection, and by seeing that it influences his daily conduct.

In the case of young converts, truly such, these doubts generally arise from their having been wrongly dealt with, and not sufficiently taught,or not thoroughly humbled. In any case they should never be left in such a state, but should be brought to such a thorough change that they will doubt no longer.

It is inconsistent with usefulness for a Christian to be always entertaining doubts; it not only makes him gloomy, but it makes his religion a stumbling-block to sinners. What do sinners think of such a religion? They say: "These converts are afraid to think they have got anything real; they are always doubting whether it is a reality, and they ought to know whether there is anything in it or not. If it is anything, these people seem to have it, but I am inclined to think it rather doubtful. At any rate, I will let it pass for the present; I do not believe God will condemn me for not attending to that which appears so uncertain." No, a settled hope in Christ is indispensable to usefulness; and therefore you should deal so with young converts, as to lead them to a consistent, well-grounded, stable hope. Ordinarily, this may be done,if pursued wisely, at the proper time, and that is at the commencement of their religious life. They should not be left till it is done.

I know there are exceptions; there are cases where the best instructions will be ineffectual; but these depend on the state of the health, and the condition of the nervous system. Sometimes you find a person incapable of reasoning on a certain topic, and so his errors will not yield to instruction. But most commonly they mistake the state of their own hearts, because they judge under the influence of a physical disease. Sometimes persons under a nervous depression will go almost into despair. Persons who are acquainted with physiology would easily explain the matter. The only way to deal with such cases is first to recruit their health, and get their nervous system into a proper tone, and thus remove the physical cause of their gloom and depression; then they will be able to receive and apply your instructions. But if you cannot remove their gloom and doubts and fears in this way, you can at least avoid doing the positive harm that is wrought by giving wrong instructions.

I have known even experienced Christians to have fastened upon them the error of thinking it was necessary, or was virtuous, or a mark of humility, to be always in doubt; and Satan would take advantage of it, and of the state of their health, and drive them almost to despair. You ought to guard against this, by avoiding the error when teaching young converts. Teach them that instead of there being any virtue in doubting, it is a sin to have any reason to doubt, and a sin if they doubt without any reason, and a sin to be gloomy and to disgust sinners with their despondency. And if you teach them thoroughly what religion is, and make them SEE CLEARLY what God wishes to have them do, and lead them to do it promptly and decidedly, ordinarily they will not be harrassed with doubts and fears, but will be clear, open-hearted, cheerful, and growing Christians—an honour to the religion they profess, and a blessing to the Church and the world.

II. *MAKING A PROFESSION OF RELIGION.*

I proceed to mention some things worthy of consideration in regard to young converts making a profession of religion, or joining the Church.

1. Young converts should, ordinarily, *offer themselves for admission to some Church of Christ immediately*. By

"immediately," I mean that they should do it the *first* opportunity they have. They should not *wait*. If they set out in religion by waiting, most likely they will always be waiting, and never do anything to much purpose. If they are taught to wait under conviction, before they give themselves to Christ; or if they are taught to wait after conversion, before, by joining the Church, they give themselves publicly to God, they will probably go halting and stumbling through life. The first thing they should be taught, always is: NEVER WAIT, WHERE GOD HAS POINTED OUT YOUR DUTY. We profess to have given up the waiting system; let us carry it through and be consistent.

2. While I say it is the duty of young converts to offer themselves to the Church immediately, I do not say that, in all cases, they should *be received* immediately. The Church has an undoubted right to assume the responsibility of receiving them immediately or not. If the Church is not satisfied in the case, it has the power to bid candidates wait till inquiries can be made as to their character and their sincerity. This is more necessary in large cities than it is in the country, because so many applications are received from persons who are entire strangers. But if the Church thinks it necessary to postpone an applicant, the responsibility is not his. *He* has not postponed obedience to the dying command of Christ, and so he has not grieved the Spirit, and so he may not be essentially injured if he is faithful in other respects. Whereas, if *he* had neglected the duty voluntarily, he would soon have got into the dark, and would very likely have backslidden.

If there is no particular reason for delay, ordinarily the Church ought to receive them when they apply. If they are sufficiently instructed on the subject of religion to know what they are doing, and if their general character is such that they can be trusted as to their sincerity and honesty in making a profession, I see no reason why they should be delayed. But if there are sufficient reasons, in the view of the Church, for making them wait a reasonable time, let the Church so decide, on its responsibility to Jesus Christ. It should be remembered, however, what is the responsibility which the Church thereby assumes, and that if those are kept out of the Church who ought to be in it, the Holy Spirit is grieved.

It is impossible to lay down particular rules on this subject, applicable to all cases. There is so great a variety of reasons which may warrant keeping persons back, that no general rules can reach them all. Our practice, in this Church, is to propound persons for a month after they make application, before they are received into full communion. The reason of this is, that the Session may have opportunity to inquire respecting individuals who offer themselves, as so many of them are strangers. But in the country, where there are regular congregations, and all the people have been instructed for their youth in the doctrines of religion, and where everybody is perfectly known, the case is different, and ordinarily I see no reason why persons of good character should not be admitted immediately. If a person has not been a drunkard, or otherwise of bad character, let him be admitted at once, as soon as he can give a rational and satisfactory account of the hope that is in him.

That is evidently the way the apostles did. There is not the least evidence in the New Testament that they ever put off a person who wanted to be baptized and to join the Church. I know this does not satisfy some people, because they think the case is different. But I do not see it so. They say the apostles were inspired. That is true; but it does not follow that they were so inspired to read the characters of men, as to be prevented from making mistakes in this matter. On the other hand, they did make mistakes, just as ministers may do now; and, therefore, it is not true that their being inspired men alters the case on this point. Simon Magus was supposed to be a Christian, and was baptized and admitted into communion, remaining in good standing until he undertook to purchase the Holy Ghost with money.

The apostles used to admit converts from heathenism immediately, and without delay. If they could receive persons who, perhaps, never heard more than one Gospel sermon, and who never had a Bible, nor ever attended a Sabbath School or Bible Class in their lives, surely it is not necessary to create an outcry and alarm, if a Church should think proper to receive persons of good character, who have had the Bible all their lives, and have been trained in the Sabbath School, and have sat under the preaching of the Gospel, and who, therefore, may be supposed to understand what they are about, and not to profess what they do not feel.

I know it may be said that persons who make a profession of religion now, are not obliged to make such sacrifices for their religion as the early believers were, and, consequently, people may be more ready to play the hypocrite. And, to some extent, that is true. But then, on the other hand, it should be remembered that, with the instructions which they have on the subject of religion, they are not so easily led to deceive themselves, as those who were converted without the precious advantages of a religious education. They may be strongly tempted to deceive others, but I insist that, with the instructions which they have received, the converts of these great revivals are not half so liable to deceive themselves, and take up with a false hope, as were those in the days of the apostles. And on this ground I believe that those Churches that are faithful in dealing with young converts, and that exhibit habitually the power of religion, are not likely to receive so many unconverted persons as the apostles did.

It is important that the Churches should act wisely on this point. Great evil has been done by this practice of keeping persons out of the Church a long time in order to see if they were Christians. This is almost as absurd as it would be to throw a young child out into the street, to see whether it will live; to say: "If it lives, and promises to be a healthy child, we will take care of it," when that is the very time it wants nursing and taking care of, the moment when the scale is turning whether it should live or die. Is that the way to deal with young converts? Should the Church throw her new-born children out to the winds, and say: "If they live there, let them be taken care of; but if they die there, then they ought to die"? I have not a doubt that thousands of converts, in consequence of this treatment, have gone through life without joining any Church, but have lingered along, full of doubts and fears, and darkness, and in this way have spent their days, and gone to the grave without the comforts and usefulness which they might have enjoyed, simply because the Church, in her folly, has suffered them to wait outside the pale, to see whether they would grow and thrive, without those ordinances which Jesus Christ established particularly for their benefit.

Jesus Christ says to His Church: "Here, take these lambs, and feed them, and shelter them, and watch over them, and protect them": and what does the Church do? Why, turn them out alone upon the cold mountains, among the wild beasts, to starve or perish, to see whether they are alive or not! The whole system is as unphilosophical as it is unscriptural. Did Jesus Christ tell His Churches to do so? Did the God of Abraham teach any such doctrine as this, in regard to the children of Abraham? Never. He never taught us to treat young converts in such a barbarous manner. The very way to lead them into doubts and darkness, is to keep them away from the Church, from its fellowship, and its ordinances.

I have understood there is a church which has passed a resolution that no yong converts shall be admitted till they have "had a hope" for at least six months. Where did they get any such rule? Not from the Bible, nor from the example of the early Churches.

3. In examining young converts for admission their consciences should not be ensnared by examining them too extensively or minutely *on doctrinal points*. From the manner in which examinations are conducted in some Churches, it would seem as if they expected that young converts would be all at once acquainted with the whole system of divinity, and able to answer every puzzling question in theology. The effect of it is that young concerts are perplexed and confused, and give their assent to things they do not understand, and thus their conscience is ensnared, and consequently weakened. Why, one great design of receiving young converts into the Church is to teach them doctrines; but if they are to be kept out of the Church until they understand the whole system of doctrines, this end is defeated. Will you keep them out till one main design of receiving them is accomplished by other means? It is absurd. There are certain cardinal doctrines of Christianity, which are embraced in the experience of every true convert; and these young converts will testify to them, on examination, if questioned in such a way as to draw out knowledge, and not in such a way as to puzzle and confound. The questions should be such as are calculated to draw out from them what they have learned by experience, and not what they may have got in theory before or since their

conversion. The object is, not to find out how much they know, or how good scholars they are in divinity, as you would examine a school; it is to find out whether they have a *change of heart*, to learn whether they have experienced the great truths of religion by their power in their own souls.[1] You see therefore how absurd, and injurious too, it must be, to examine, as is sometimes done, like a lawyer at the bar cross-examining a suspicious witness. It should rather be like a faithful physician anxious to find out his patient's true condition, and therefore leading him, by inquiries and hints, to disclose the real symptoms of the case.

You will always find, if you put your questions rightly, that real converts will see clearly those great fundamental points—the Divine authority of the Scriptures, the necessity of the influences of the Holy Spirit, the Deity of Christ, the doctrines of total depravity and regeneration, the necessity of the atonement, justification by faith, and the justice of the eternal punishment of the wicked. By a proper course of inquiries you will find all these points come out, if you put your questions in such a way that they are understood.

A Church Session in this city has, as we are informed, passed a vote, that no person shall join that Church till he will give his assent to the whole Presbyterian Confession of Faith, and adopt it as his "rule of faith and practice and Christian obedience." That is, they must read the book through, which is about three times as large as this hymn-book which I hold, and

---

[1] After D. L. Moody had presented himself as an applicant for membership in Mount Vernon Church, Boston (in May, 1855), the following minute was entered regarding him: "Dwight L. Moody. Has been baptized. First awakened on the 16th of May. Became anxious about himself. Saw himself a sinner, and sin now seems hateful and holiness desirable. Thinks he has repented; has purposed to give up sin; feels dependent on Christ for forgiveness. Loves the Scripture. Prays. Desires to be useful. Religiously educated. Been in the city a year. Is not ashamed to be known as a Christian. Eighteen years old." Nevertheless, the committee "deferred recommending him for admission." When Moody first spoke in a prayer-meeting a deacon assured him that he "would serve God best by keeping still." ("The Life of Dwight L. Moody." By his son, W. R. Moody.)

must understand it, and agree to it all, before they can be admitted to the Church, before they can make a profession of religion, or obey the command of Christ. By what authority does a Church say that no one shall join their communion till he understands all the points and technicalities of this long Confession of Faith? Is that their charity, to cram this whole Confession of Faith down the throat of a young convert, before they let him so much as come to the Communion? He says: "I love the Lord Jesus Christ, and wish to obey His command. "Very well, but do you understand and adopt the Confession of Faith?" He says: "I do not know, for I never read that, but I have read the Bible, and I love that, and wish to follow the directions in it, and to come to the table of the Lord." "Do you love the Confession of Faith? If not, YOU SHALL NOT COME," is the reply of this charitable Session; "you shall not sit down at the Lord's table till you have adopted all this Confession of Faith." Did Jesus Christ ever authorise a Church Session to say this—to tell that child of God, who stands there with tears, and asks permission to obey his Lord, and who understands the grounds of hope—to tell him he cannot join the Church till he understands the Confession of Faith? Shut the door against young converts till they swallow the Confession of Faith! Will such a Church prosper? Never!

No Church on earth has a right to impose its extended Confession of Faith on a young convert who admits the fundamentals of religion. They may let the young convert know their own faith on ever so many points, and they may examine him, if they think it necessary, as to his belief; but suppose he has doubts on some points not essential to Christian experience,—the doctrine of Infant Baptism, or of Election, or the Perseverance of the Saints; and suppose he honestly and frankly tells you he has not made up his mind concerning these points? Has any minister or Church a right to say, he shall not come to the Lord's table till he has finished all his researches into these subjects, that he shall not obey Christ till he has fully made up his mind on such points, on which Christians, and devoted ones too, differ among themselves? I would sooner cut off my right hand than debar a convert under such circumstances. I would teach a young convert as well as I could in the time before he made his application, and I would examine him candidly as to his views, and after he was in the Church I would endeavour to make him grow in knowledge as he grows in grace. And by just as much confidence as I have that my own doctrines are the doctrines of God, I should expect to make him adopt them, if I could have a fair hearing before his mind. But I never would bid one whom I charitably believed to be a child of God, to stay away from his Father's table, because he did not see all I see, or believe all I believe, through the whole system of divinity. The thing is utterly irrational, ridiculous, and wicked.

4. Sometimes persons who are known to entertain a hope *dare not make a profession of religion* for fear they should be deceived. I would always deal decidedly with such cases. A hope that will not warrant a profession of religion is manifestly worse than no hope, and the sooner it is torn away the better. Shall a man hope he loves God, and yet not obey Jesus Christ? Preposterous! Such a hope had better be given up at once.

5. Sometimes persons professing to be converts will make an excuse for not joining the Church, that they can *enjoy religion just as well* without it. This is always suspicious. I should look out for such characters. It is almost certain they have no religion. Ordinarily, if a person does not desire to be associated with the people of God, he is rotten at the foundation. It is because he wants to keep out of the responsibilities of a public profession. He has a feeling within him that he had rather be free, so that he can, by and by, go back to the world again, if he likes, without the reproach of instability of hypocrisy. Enjoy religion just as well without obeying Jesus Christ! It is false on the face of it. He overlooks the fact that religion consists in obeying Jesus Christ.

III. *THE IMPORTANCE OF GIVING RIGHT INSTRUCTION.*
Ordinarily, the Christian character of converts throughout life is moulded and fashioned according to the manner in which they are dealt with when first converted. There are many who have been poorly taught at first, but have been afterwards *re-converted*, and if they are *then* properly dealt with, they may be made something of. But the *proper* time to do this is when they are first brought in, when their minds are soft and tender, and easily yield to the truth. Then they may be led with a hair, if they think it is the truth of God. And

whatever notions in religion they then get, they are apt to cleave to for ever afterwards. It is almost impossible to get a man away from the notions he acquires when he is a young convert. You may reason him down, but he cleaves to them. How often is it the case where persons have been taught certain things when first converted, that if they afterwards get a new minister who teaches somewhat differently, they will rise up against him as if he were going to subvert the faith, carry away the Church into error, and throw everything into confusion. Thus you see that young converts are thworn in the hands of the Church, and it devolves upon the Church to mould them, and form them into Christians of the right stamp. To a large extent, their future comfort and usefulness depend on the manner in which they are instructed at the outset. The future character of the Church, the progress of revivals, the coming of the millennium, depend on right instruction being imparted, and a right direction of thought and life given, to those who are young converts.

IV. *THINGS WHICH SHOULD NOT BE TAUGHT.*

1. "You will not always feel as you do now." When the young convert is rejoicing in his Saviour, and calculating to live for the glory of God and the good of mankind, how often is he met with this reply: " *You will not always feel so.*" Thus, his mind is prepared to expect that he shall backslide, and not to be much surprised when he does. This is just the way the devil wants young converts dealt with, to have old Christians tell them: "Your feelings will not last, but, by and by, you will be as cold as we are." It has made my heart bleed to see it. When the young convert has been pouring out his warm heart to some old professor, and expecting the warm burstings of a kindred spirit responding to his own, what does he meet with? This cold answer, coming like a northern blast over his soul: "You will not always feel so." SHAME! Just preparing the young convert to expect that he shall backslide as a matter of course; so that when he begins to decline, as under the very influences of this instruction it is most likely he will, it produces no surprise or alarm in his mind, but he looks at it just as a thing of course, doing as eveybody else does.

I have heard it preached as well as expressed in prayer, that seasons of backsliding are "necessary to test the Church." They say: "When it rains, you can find water anywhere: it is only in seasons of drought that you can tell where the deep springs are." Wonderful logic! And so you would teach that Christians must get cold and stupid, and backslide from God—and for what reason? Why, forsooth, to show that they are not hypocrites. Amazing! You would prove that they *are* hypocrites in order to show that they are not.

Such doctrine as this is the very last that should be taught to young converts. They should be told that they have only begun the Christian life, and that their religion is to consist in *going on in it*. They should be taught to go forward all the time, and "grow in grace" continually. Do not teach them to taper off their religion—to let it grow smaller and smaller till it comes to a point. God says: "The path of the just is as the shining light, that shineth more and more unto the perfect day" (Prov. 4. 18).[1] Now, whose path is that which grows dimmer and dimmer unto the perfect night? They should be brought to such a state of mind that the first indications of decay in spirituality or zeal will alarm them and spur them up to duty. There is no need that young converts should backslide as they do. Paul did not backslide. And I do not doubt that this very doctrine: "You will not always feel so," is one of the grand devices of Satan to bring about the result which it predicts.

2. "Learn to walk by faith and not by sight." This is sometimes said to young converts in reference to their continuing to exhibit the power of religion, and is a manifest perversion of Scripture. If they begin to lose their faith and

---

[1] This text seems peculiarly appropriate in relation to Finney himself. His long and exhausting labours notwithstanding, he retained his connection with Oberlin College to the end. He had resigned the pastorate of the First Church, Oberlin, in 1872, but he continued to preach occasionally. "His last day on earth," says a note to his "Memoirs," "was on a quiet Sabbath, which he enjoyed in the midst of his family, walking out with his wife, at sunset, to listen to the music, at the opening of the evening service in the church near by. Upon retiring he was seized with pains which seemed to indicate some affection of the heart, and as the morning dawned he died, August 16, 1875, lacking two weeks of completing his eighty-third year."

zeal, and get into darkness, some old professor will tell them: "Ah, *you cannot expect to have the Saviour always with you,* you have been walking by sight; you must learn to walk by faith and not by sight." That is, you must learn to get as cold as death, and then hang on to the doctrine of the Saints' Perseverance, as your only ground of hope that you shall be saved. And that is walking by faith! *Cease to persevere, and then hold on to the doctrine of Perseverance!* "One of guilt's blunders, and the loudest laugh of hell." Living in the enjoyment of God's favour and the comforts of the Holy Ghost is what they call "walking by sight"! Do you suppose young converts *see* the Saviour at the time they believe on Him? When they are so full of the enjoyments of heaven, do you suppose they see heaven, and so walk by sight? It is absurd on the face of it. It is not faith, it is *presumption,* that makes the backslider hold on to the doctrine of Perseverance, as if that would save him, without any sensible excuses of godliness in his soul. Those who attempt to walk by faith in this way had better take care, or they will walk into hell with their "faith." Faith indeed! "Faith without works is dead" (Jas. 2. 20). Can dead faith make the soul live?

3. "Wait till you see whether you can hold out." When a young convert feels zealous and warm-hearted, and wants to lay himself out for God, some *prudent* old professor will caution him not to go too fast. "You had *better not be too forward* in religion, till you see whether you can hold out; for if you take this high ground and then fall, you will disgrace religion." That is, in plain English: "Do not do anything that *constitutes* religion, till you see whether you have religion." Religion consists in obeying God. Now, these wise teachers tell a young convert: "Do not obey God till you see"—what?— till you see whether you have obeyed Him—or, till you see whether you have obtained that substance, that mysterious thing which they imagine is created and put into man, like a lump of new flesh, and called "religion." This waiting system is all wrong. There is no Scripture warrant for telling a person to wait, when the command of God is upon him, and the path of duty is before him. Let him go ahead.

Young converts should be fully taught that this is the only consistent way to find out whether they have any religion, to find that they are heartily engaged in *doing* the will of God. To tell the convert to wait, therefore, *before* he does these things, till he first gets his evidence, is reversing the matter, and is absurd.

4. *"Wait till you get strength, before you take up the cross."* This is applied to various religious duties. Sometimes it is applied to prayer: just as if prayer were a cross. I have known young converts advised not to attempt to pray in their families, or "not to attempt quite yet" to pray in meetings and social circles. "Wait till you get strength." Just as if they could get strength without exercise. Strength comes by exercise. You cannot get strength by lying still. Let a child lie in a cradle continually, and he would never have any strength; he might grow in size, but he never could be anything more than a great baby. This is a law of nature. There is no substitute for exercise in producing strength. It is so in the body; and it is just so with the mind. It is so with the affections; so with the judgment; so with conscience. All the powers of the soul are strengthened by exercise. I need not now enter into the philosophy of this. Everybody knows it is so. If the mind is not exercised, the brain will not grow, and the man will become an idiot. If the affections are not exercised, he will become a stoic. To talk to a convert about neglecting Christian action till he gets strength, is absurd. If he wants to gain strength, let him go to work.

5. Young converts *should not be made sectarian* in their feelings. They should not be taught to dwell upon sectarian distinctions, or to be sticklish about sectarian points. They ought to examine these points, according to their importance, at a proper time, and in a proper way, and make up their minds for themselves. But they should not be taught to dwell upon them, or to make much of them at the outset of their religious life. Otherwise there is great danger that their whole religion will run into sectarianism. I have seen most sad and melancholy exhibitions of the effects of this upon young converts. And whenever I see professed converts taking a strong hold of sectarian peculiarities, no matter of what denomination of Christians, I always feel in doubt about them. When I hear them asking: "Do you believe in the doctrine of Election?" or: "Do you believe in sprinkling?" or: "Do you believe in immersing?" I feel sad. I never knew such converts

to be worth much. Their sectarian zeal soon sours their feelings, eats out all the heart of their religion, and moulds their whole character into sinful, sectarian bigotry. They generally become mighty zealous for the traditions of the elders, and very little concerned for the starvation of souls.

V. THINGS WHICH IT IS IMPORTANT SHOULD BE TAUGHT.

1. One of the first things young converts should be taught is to distinguish between emotion and principle in religion. I want you to get hold of the words, and have them fixed in your mind; to have you distinguish between *emotion* and *principle*.

By emotion, I mean that state of mind of which we are conscious, and which we call *feeling*—an involuntary state of mind, that arises, of course, when we are in certain circumstances or under certain influences. There may be high-wrought feelings, or they may subside into tranquility, or disappear entirely. But these emotions should be carefully distinguished from religious principle. By principle, I do not mean any substance or root or seed or sprout implanted in the soul. But I mean the voluntary decision of the mind, the firm determination to fulfil duty and to obey the will of God, by which a Christian should always be governed.

When a man is fully determined to obey God, because it is RIGHT that he should obey God, I call that principle. Whether he feels any lively religious emotion at the time or not, he will do his duty cheerfully, readily, and heartily, whatever may be the state of his feelings. This is acting upon principle, and not from emotion. Many young converts hold mistaken views upon this subject, and depend almost entirely on the state of their feelings to go forward in duty. Some will not lead a prayer-meeting, unless they *feel* as if they could make an eloquent prayer. Multitudes are influenced almost entirely by their emotions, and they give way to this, as if they thought themselves under no obligation to duty, unless urged on by some strong emotion. They will be very zealous in religion when they feel like it, when their emotions are warm and lively, but they will not act out religion consistently, and carry it into all the concerns of life. They are religious only as they are impelled by a gush of feeling. But this is not true religion.

Young converts should be carefully taught that when duty is before them they are to *do it*. However dull their feelings may be, if duty calls, DO IT. Do not wait for feeling, but DO IT. Most likely the very emotions for which you would wait will be called into exercise when you begin to do your duty. If the duty be prayer, for instance, and you have not the feelings you would wish, do not wait for emotions before you pray, but pray, and "open thy mouth wide" (Psa. 81. 10); and in doing it, you are most likely to have the emotions for which you were inclined to wait, and which constitute the conscious happiness of religion.

2. Young converts should be taught that they have *renounced the ownership of all their possessions, and of themselves, and that if they have not done this they are not Christians.* They should not be left to think that anything is their own; their time, property, influence, faculties, body or soul. "Ye are not your own" (1 Cor. 6. 19); they belong to God; and when they submitted to God they made a free surrender of all to Him, to be ruled and disposed of at His pleasure. They have no right to go anywhere, or do anything, for themselves, but should hold all at the disposal of God, and employ all for the glory of God. If they do not, they ought not to call themselves Christians, for the very idea of being a Christian is to renounce self and become entirely consecrated to God. A man has no more right to withhold anything from God than he has to rob or steal. It is robbery in the highest sense of the term. It is an infinitely higher crime than it would be for a clerk in a store to go and take the money of his employer, and spend it on his own lusts and pleasures. I mean, that for a man to withhold from God is a higher crime against HIM than a man can commit against his fellow-man, inasmuch as God is the Owner of all things in an infinitely higher sense than man can be the owner of anything. If God calls on them to employ anything they have, their money, or their time, or to give their children, or to dedicate themselves in advancing His Kingdom, and they refuse, because they want to use them in their own way, or prefer to do something else, it is vastly more blameable than for a clerk or an agent to go and embezzle the money that is entrusted him by his employer.

God is, in an infinitely higher sense, the *Owner of all*, than any employer can be said to be the owner of what he has. And the Church of Christ never will take high ground, never will be disentangled from the world, never will be able to go forward without these continual declensions and backslidings, until Christians, and the Churches generally, take the ground, and hold to it, that it is just as much a matter of discipline for a Church member practically to deny his stewardship as to deny the Deity of Christ; and that covetousness, fairly proved, shall just as soon exclude a man from the Communion as adultery.

The Church is mighty orthodox in *notions*, but very heretical in practice; but the time must come when the Church will be just as vigilant in guarding orthodoxy in practice as orthodoxy in doctrine, and just as prompt to turn out heretics in practice, as heretics that corrupt the doctrines of the Gospel. In fact, it is vastly more important. The only design of doctrine is to produce practice, and it does not seem to be understood by the Church that *true faith* "works by love and purifies the heart," that heresy in *practice* is proof conclusive of heresy in sentiment. The Church is very sticklish for correct doctrine, but very careless about correct living. This is preposterous. Has it come to this, that the Church of Jesus Christ is to be satisfied with correct notions on some abstract points, and never reduce her orthodoxy to practice? Let it be so no longer.

It is high time these matters were set right. And the only way to set them right is to begin with those who are just entering upon religion. Young converts must be told that they are just as worthy of condemnation (and that the Church can hold no fellowship with them), if they show a covetous spirit, and turn a deaf ear when the whole world is calling for help, as if they were living in adultery, or in the daily worship of idols.

3. Teach them *how to cultivate a tender conscience*. I am often amazed to find how little conscience there is even among those whom we hope are Christians. And here we see the reason of it. Their consciences were never cultivated. They never were taught how to cultivate a tender conscience. They have not even a natural conscience. They have dealt so rudely with their conscience, and resisted it so often, that it has got blunted, and does not act. The usefulness of a Christian greatly depends on his knowing how to cultivate his conscience. Young converts should be taught to keep their conscience just

as tender as the apple of the eye. They should watch their conduct and their motives, and let their motives be so pure and their conduct so disinterested as not to offend, or injure, or stifle conscience. They should maintain such a habit of listening to conscience, that it will always be ready to give forth a stern verdict on all occasions.

It is astonishing to see how much the conscience may be cultivated by a proper course. If rightly attended to, it may be made so pure, and so powerful, that it will always respond exactly to the Word of God. Present any duty to such a Christian, or any self-denial, or suffering, and only show him the Word of God, and he will do it without a word of objection. In a few months, if properly taught, young converts may have a conscience so delicately poised that the weight of a feather will turn them. Only bring a "Thus saith the Lord," and they will be always ready to do that, be it what it may.

4. Young converts should be taught *to pray without ceasing*. That is, they should always keep a watch over their minds, and be all the time in a prayerful spirit. They should be taught to pray always, whatever may take place. For the want of right instruction on this point many young converts suffer loss and get far away from God. For instance, sometimes it happens that a young convert will fall into some sin, and then he feels as if he could not pray, and instead of overcoming this he feels so distressed that he waits for the keen edge of his distress to pass away. Instead of going right to Jesus Christ in the midst of his agony, and confessing his sin out of the fulness of his heart, and getting a renewed pardon, and peace restored, he waits till all the keenness of his feelings has subsided; and then his repentance, if he does repent, is cold and half-hearted. Let me tell you, beloved, never to do this; but when your conscience presses you, go then to Christ, confess your sin fully, and pour out your heart to God.

Sometimes people will neglect to pray because they are in the dark, and feel no desire to pray. That is the very reason why they ought to pray. You should go right to God and confess your coldness and darkness of mind. Tell Him just how you feel. Tell Him: "O Lord, I have no desire to pray, but I know I ought to pray." And immediately the Spirit may come and lead your heart out in prayer, and all the dark clouds will pass away.

5. Young converts should be faithfully warned against adopting *a false standard in religion*. They shoul not be left to fall in behind old professors, or keep such before their minds as a standard of holy living. They should always look at Christ as their model. Not aim at being as good Christians as the old Church members, and not think they are doing pretty well because they are as much awake as the old members of the Church; but they should aim at being holy. The Church has been greatly injured for the want of attention to this matter. Young converts have come forward, and their hearts were warm, and their zeal ardent enough to aim at a high standard, but they were not directed properly, and so they soon settled down into the notion that what was good enough for others was good enough for them, and therefore they ceased to aim higher than those who were before them. And in this way the Church, instead of rising, with every revival, higher and higher in holiness, is kept nearly stationary.

6. Young converts should be taught to *do all their duty*. They should never make a compromise with duty, nor think of saying: "I will do *this* as an offset for neglecting *that*." They should never rest satisfied till they have done their duties of every kind, in relation to their families, the Church, Sabbath Schools, the impenitent around them, the disposal of their property, and the conversion of the world. Let them do their duty, as they feel it when their hearts are warm; and never attempt to pick and choose among the commandments of God.

7. They should be made to feel that they have *no separate interest*. It is time Christians were made actually to feel that they have no interest whatever, separate from the interests of Jesus Christ and His Kingdom. They should understand that they are incorporated into the family of Jesus Christ, as members in full, so that their whole interest is identified with His. They are embarked with Him, they have gone on board, and taken their all; and henceforth they have nothing to do, nor anything to say, except as it is connected with this interest, and bearing on the cause and Kingdom of Christ.

8. They should be taught to *maintain singleness of motive*. Young converts should not begin to have a double mind on any subject, nor let selfish motives mingle with good motives in anything they do. But this can never be so long as Christians

are allowed to hold a separate interest of their own, distinct from the interest of Jesus Christ. If they feel that they *have* a separate interest, it is impossible to keep them from *regarding* it, and having an eye to it as well as to Christ's interest, in many things that they do. It is only by becoming entirely consecrated to God, and giving up all to His service, that they can ever keep their eye single and their motives pure.

9. They should set out with a determination to *aim at being useful in the highest degree possible*. They should not rest satisfied merely with being useful, or remaining in a situation where they can do some good. But if they see an opportunity where they can do more good, they must embrace it, whatever may be the sacrifice to themselves. No matter what it may cost them; no matter what danger or what suffering may be involved; no matter what change in their outward circumstances, or habits, or employments, it may lead to; if they are satisfied that they will on the whole do more good, they should not even hesitate. How else can they be like God? How can they think to bear the image of Jesus Christ, if they are not prepared to do all the good that is in their power? When a man is converted he comes into a new world, and should consider himself as a new man. If he finds he can do most good by remaining in his old employment, let it be so; but if he can do more good in some other way, he is bound to change. It is for the want of attention to this subject, at the outset, that Christians have got such low ideas on the subject of duty; and that is the reason why there are so many useless members in our Churches.

10. They must be taught, *not to aim at comfort but usefulness, in religion*. There are a great many spiritual epicures in the Churches, who are all the while seeking to be happy in religion, while they are taking very little pains to be useful. They had much rather spend their time in singing joyful hymns, and pouring out their happy feelings in a gushing tide of exultation and triumph, than in an agonising prayer for sinners, or in going about pulling dying men out of the fire. They seem to feel as if they were born to enjoy themselves. But I do not think such Christians show such fruits as to make their example one to be imitated. Such was not the temper of the apostles; they travailed for souls; they laboured

in weariness and painfulness, and were "in deaths oft," to save sinners" (2 Cor. 11. 23). Ordinarily, Christians are not qualified to drink deep at the fountain of joy. In ordinary cases, a deep agony of prayer for souls is more profitable than high flights of joy. Let young converts be taught plainly not to calculate upon a life of joy and triumph. They may be called to go through fiery trials; Satan may sift them like wheat. But they must go forward, not calculating so much to be happy as to be useful; not talking about comfort but duty; not desiring flights of joy and triumph, but hungering and thirsting after righteousness; not studying how to create new flights of rapture, but how to know the will of God and do it. They will be happy enough in heaven. There they may sing the song of Moses and the Lamb. And they will in fact enjoy a more solid and rational happiness here, by thinking nothing about it, but patiently devoting themselves to do the will of God.

11. They should be taught *to have moral courage*, and not to be afraid of going forward in duty. The Bible insists fully on Christian boldness and courage in action, as a duty. I do not mean that they should indulge in bravado, like Peter, telling what they will do, and boasting of their courage. The boaster is generally a coward at heart. But I mean moral courage—a humble and fixed decision of purpose, that will go forward in any duty, unangered and unawed, with the meekness and firmness of the Son of God.

12. They should be so instructed as to be *sound in the faith*. That is, they should be early made, as far as possible, complete and correct in regard to their doctrinal belief. As soon as may be, without turning their minds off from their practical duties in promoting the glory of God and the salvation of men, they should be taught fully and plainly all the leading doctrines of the Bible. Doctrinal knowledge is indispensable to growth in grace. Knowledge is the food of the mind. "That the soul be without knowledge," says the wise man, "it is not good" (Prov. 19. 2). The mind cannot grow without knowledge any more than the body without food. And therefore it is important that young converts should be thoroughly indoctrinated, and made to understand the Bible. By "indoctrinating," I do not mean teaching them the catechism, but teaching them to draw knowledge from the fountain-head. Create in their minds such

an appetite for knowledge that they will eat the Bible up—will devour it—will love it, and love it all. "*All* Scripture... is profitable,... that the man of God may be perfect, throughly furnished unto all good works" (2 Tim. 3. 16, 17).

13. Great pains should be taken to *guard young converts against censoriousness.* Young converts, when they first come out on the Lord's side, and are all warm and zealous, sometimes find old professors so cold and dead, that they are strongly tempted to be censorious. This should be corrected immediately, otherwise the habit will poison their minds and destroy their religion.

14. They must *learn to say "NO."* This is a very difficult lesson to many. See that young woman. Formerly she loved the gay circle, and took delight in its pleasures; she joined the Church, and then found herself aloof from all her old associates. They do not ask her now to their balls and parties, because they know she will not join them; and perhaps they keep entirely away from a time, for fear she should converse with them about their souls. But, by and by, they grow a little bold, and some of them venture to ask her just to take a ride with a few friends. She does not like to say "No." They are her old friends, only a few of them are going, and surely a ride is so innocent a recreation that she may accept the invitation. But, now she has begun to comply, the ice is broken, and they have her again as one of them. It goes on, and she begins to attend their social visits—"only a few friends, you know,"—till, by and by, the carpet is taken up for a dance; and the next thing, perhaps, she has gone for a sleigh ride on Saturday night, coming home after midnight, and then sleeping all the forenoon on the Sabbath to make up for it—perhaps Communion Sabbath, too. All for the want of learning to say "No."

See that young man. For a time he was always in his place in the Sabbath School and in the prayer-meeting. But, by and by, his old friends began to treat him with attention again, and they draw him along, step by step. He reasons that if he refuses to go with them in things that are innocent, he will lose his influence with them. And so he goes on, till prayer-meeting, Bible class, and even private Bible reading and prayer are neglected. Ah, young man, stop there! If you do not wish to expose the cause of Christ to scorn and contempt, learn to resist the beginnings of temptation.

15. They should be taught, *what is, and what is not, Christian experience*. It is necessary, both for their comfort and their usefulness, that they should understand this, so that they need not run themselves into needless distress for the want of that which is by no means essential to Christian experience, nor flatter themselves that they have more religion than they really exercise.

16. Teach them not to count anything *a sacrifice which they do for God*. Some persons are always telling about the sacrifices they make in religion. I have no confidece in such piety. Why keep telling about their sacrifices, as if everything they do for God is a sacrifice? If they *loved* God they would not talk so. If they considered their own interests and the interest of Christ identical, they would not talk of making sacrifices for Christ: it would be like talking of making sacrifices for *themselves*.

17. It is of great importance that young converts should be taught *to be strictly honest*. I mean more by this than perhaps you would think. It is a great thing to be strictly honest. It is being very different from the world at large, and different even from the great body of professors of religion. The holiest man I ever knew, and one who had been many years a Christian and a minister, once made the remark to me: "Brother, it is a great thing to be strictly honest and straight in everything, so that God's pure eye can see that the mind is perfectly upright."

It is of great importance that young converts should understand what it is to be strictly honest *in everything*, so that they can maintain "a conscience void of offence toward God, and toward men" (Acts 24. 16). Alas, alas, how little conscience there is! How little of that real honesty, that pure, simple uprightness, which ought to mark the life of a child of God.[1] How little do many regard even an express promise. I

---

[1]   Finney also dealt with this subject in "Lectures to Professing Christians." In Lecture X., on "Dishonesty in Small Matters Inconsistent with Honesty in Anything," he sums up: "You say these are little things. I know they are little things, and because they

heard the other day that of a number of individuals who subscribed to the Anti-Slavery Society, not half will pay their subscriptions. The plea is, that they signed when they were under excitement, and do not choose to pay. Just as if their being excited released them from the obligation to keep their promise. Why, it is just as dishonest as it would be to refuse payment of a note of hand. They promised, signed their names, and now will not pay? And they call that honesty!

I have heard that a number of men signed for hundreds of dollars for the Oneida Institute, promising to pay the money when called on; and when they were called on, they refused to pay the money. And the reason is that all in the Institute have turned Abolitionists! Very well. Suppose they have. Does that alter your promise? Did you sign on the condition that if abolitionism were introduced you should be clear? If you did, then you are clear. But if you gave your promise without any condition, it is just as dishonest to refuse as if you had given a note of hand. And yet some of you might be almost angry if anybody were to charge you with refusing to pay money that you had promised.

Look at this seriously. Who does God say will go to heaven? Read the fifteenth psalm, and see. "He that sweareth to his own hurt, and *changeth not*." What do you think of that? If a man has promised anything, *except it be to commit sin*, let him keep his promise, if he means to be honest and to go to heaven. But these people will make promises, and because they cannot be prosecuted, will break them as if they were nothing. They would not let a cheque of theirs be returned

---

are little things I mention them. It is because they are little things, that they show the character so clearly...Oh, how much would be gained if professors of religion would evince that entire purity and honesty on all occasions and to all persons, and do what is just right, so as to commend religion to the ungodly! How often do sinners fix their eye on some petty delinquencies of professors of religion, and look with amazement at such things in persons who profess the fear of God. What an everlasting reproach to religion, that so many of its professors are guilty of these little, mean, paltry knaveries. The wicked have cause enough to see that such professors cannot have any principle of honesty, and that such religion as they exhibit is good for nothing, and is not worth having."

from the bank. Why? Because they would lose credit, and would be sued. But the Oneida Institute, and the Anti-Slavery Society, and other societies, will not sue for the money, and therefore these people take offence at something, and refuse to pay. Is this honest? Will such honesty as this get them admitted to heaven? What? Break your promises, and go up and carry a lie in your hand before God? If you refuse or neglect to fulfil your promise you are a *liar*; and if you persist in this, you shall have your part in the lake that burns with fire and brimstone. I would not for ten thousand worlds die with money in my hands that I had unrighteously withheld from any object to which I had promised it. Such money will "eat as doth a canker" (2 Tim. 2. 17).

If you are *not able* to pay the money, that is a good excuse. But then, say so. But if you refuse to pay what you have promised, because you have altered your mind, rely upon it, you are guilty. You cannot pray till you pay that money. Will you pray: "O Lord, I promised to give that money, but I altered my mind, and broke my promise; but still, O Lord, I pray Thee to bless me, and forgive my sin, although I keep my money, and make me happy in Thy love"? Will such prayers be heard? Never.

INSTRUCTIONS TO CONVERTS—(*continued*)

Feed My lambs.—John 21. 15.

I propose to continue the subject by: I. Noticing several other points upon which young converts ought to be instructed. II. Showing the manner in which young converts should be treated by the Church. III. Mentioning some of the evils which naturally result from defective instructions given in that stage of Christian experience.

I. *FURTHER INSTRUCTIONS TO YOUNG CONVERTS.*

1. It is of great importance that young converts should early be made to understand *what religion consists in*. Perhaps you will be surprised at my mentioning this. "What! Are they converts, and do not know what religion consists in?" I answer: "They would know, if they had had no instruction but such as was drawn from the Bible." But multitudes of people have imbibed such *notions* about religion, that not only young converts, but a great part of the *Church members* do not know what religion consists in, so as to have a clear and distinct idea of it. There are many ministers who do not. I do not mean to say that they have no religion, for it may be charitably believed they have;[1] but what I mean is, that they cannot give a correct

---

[1] Without suggesting that Finney's candid remarks on the subject of unprepared or unconverted ministers call for apology or

religion.

statement of what does, and what does not, constitute real

It is important that young converts should be taught: Negatively, what religion does not consist in. *(a)* Not in *doctrinal knowledge.* Knowledge is essential to religion, but it is not religion. The devil has doctrinal knowledge, but he has no religion. A man may have doctrinal knowledge to any extent, without a particle of religion. Yet some people have very strange ideas on this subject, as though an increase of doctrinal knowledge indicated an increase of piety. In a certain instance, where some young converts had made rapid progress in doctrinal knowledge, a person who saw it remarked: "How these young converts grow in grace!" Here he confounded improvement in knowledge with improvement in piety. The truth was, that he had no means of judging of their growth in grace, and it was no evidence of it because they were making progress in doctrinal knowledge.

(b) They should be taught that religion is *not a substance.* It is not any root, or sprout, or seed, or anything else, in the mind, as a *part of the mind itself.* Persons often speak of religion as if it were something which is covered up in the mind, just as a spark of fire may be covered up in the ashes, which does not show itself, and which produces no effect, but yet lives, and is ready to act as soon as it is uncovered. And in like manner they think they may have religion, as something remaining *in*

---

explanation, it may be well to remark that the topic had been the groundwork of almost traditional controversy in the Presbyterian Church in America. During the struggles, in the eighteenth century, between the Old Side (Scottish and Irish party) who favoured the adoption of the Westminster Confession as the general Confession of Faith, and the New Side (New England party), who "opposed the imposition of a human creed as a test of orthodoxy," Gilbert Tennent preached a sermon which became famous, on "The Danger of an Unconverted Ministry." Tennent set himself to contravene the widely-held theory that "the ministrations of unconverted men, if neither heretical in doctrine nor scandalous for immorality, are valid." Again, Whitefield, replying to the charge made against him by Dr. Chauncey, that he "seldom preached but he had something to say against unconverted ministers," replied: "Was there any harm in this? Are not unconverted ministers the bane of the Christian Church?"

them, although they do not manifest it by obeying God. But they should be taught that this is not of the nature of religion. It is not part of the mind itself, nor of the body; nor is it a root, or seed, or spark, that can exist, and yet be hid and produce no effects.

(c) Teach them that religion does not consist *in raptures*, or *ecstasies*, or high flights of feeling. There may be a great deal of these where there *is* religion. But it ought to be understood that they are all involuntary emotions, and may exist in full power where there is *no* religion. They may be the mere workings of the imagination, without any truly religious affection at all. Persons may have them to such a degree as actually to swoon away with ecstasy, even on the subject of religion, without having any religion. I have known a person almost carried away with rapture, by a mere view of the natural attributes of God, His power and wisdom, as displayed in the starry heavens, and yet the person had no religion. Religion is obedience to God, the voluntary submission of the soul to His will.

(d) Neither does religion consist in going to services, or reading the Bible, or praying, or any other of what are commonly called *religious duties*. The very phrase, "religious duties," ought to be struck out of the vocabulary of young converts. They should be made to know that these acts are not religion. Many become very strict in performing certain things, which they call "religious duties," and suppose that is being religious; while they are careless about the ordinary duties of life, which, in fact, constitute A LIFE OF PIETY. Prayer may be an expression and an act of piety, or it may not be. Going to church or to a prayer-meeting, may be considered either as a means, an act, or an expression of pious sentiment; but the performance of these does not constitute a man a Christian; and there may be great strictness and zeal in these, without a particle of religion. If young converts are not taught to discriminate, they may be led to think there is something peculiar in what are called religious duties, and to imagine they have a great deal of religion because they abound in certain actions that are commonly called "religious duties," although they may at the same time be very deficient in honesty, or faithfulness, or punctuality, or temperance, or any other of

what they choose to call their common duties. They may be very punctilious in some things, may "pay tithe of mint and anise and cummin" (Matt. 23. 23), and yet neglect "the weightier matters of the law"; justice and the love of God.

(e) Religion does not consist in *desires to do good actions*. Desires that do not result in choice and action are not virtuous. Nor are such desires necessarily vicious. They may arise involuntarily in the mind, in view of certain objects; but while they produce no voluntary act, they are no more virtuous or vicious than the beating of the pulse, except in cases where we have indirectly willed them into existence, by voluntarily putting ourselves under circumstances calculated to excite them. The wickedest man on earth may have strong desires after holiness. Did you ever think of that? He may see clearly that holiness is the only and indispensable means of happiness. And the moment he apprehends holiness as a means of happiness, he naturally desires it. It is to be feared that multitudes are deceiving themselves with the supposition that a desire for holiness, as a means of happiness, is religion. Many, doubtless, give themselves great credit for desires that never result in *choosing* right. They feel desires to do their duty, but do not choose to do it, because, upon the whole, they have still stronger desires not to do it. In such desires there is no virtue. An action or desire, to be virtuous in the sight of God, must be an act of the will. People often talk most absurdly on this subject, as though their desires had anything good, while they remain mere desires. "I think I desire to do so-and-so." But do you do it? "Oh, no, but I often feel a desire to do it." This is practical atheism.

Whatever desires a person may have, if they are not carried out into actual *choice* and action, they are not virtuous. And no degree of desire is itself virtuous. If this idea could be made prominent, and fully riveted in the minds of men, it would probably annihilate the hopes of half the members of the Churches, who are living on their good desires, while doing nothing for God.

(f) They should be made to understand that *nothing which is selfish, is religion*. Whatever desires they may have, and whatever choices and actions they may put forth, if, after all, the reason of them is selfish, there is no religion in them. A

man may just as much commit sin in praying, or reading the Bible, or going to a religious service, as in anything else, if his motive is selfish. Suppose a man prays simply with a view to promote his own happiness. Is that religion? What is it but attempting to make God his Almighty Servant? It is nothing else but to attempt a great speculation, and to put the universe, God and all, under contribution to make him happy. It is the sublime degree of wickedness. It is so far some being piety that it is in fact superlative wickedness.

(g) Nothing is acceptable to God, as religion, unless it is performed heartily, *to please God*. No outward action has anything good, or anything that God approves, unless it is performed from right motives and from the heart. Young converts should be taught fully and positively that all religion consists in obeying God from the heart. All religion consists in voluntary action. All that is holy, all that is lovely, in the sight of God, all that is properly called religion, consists in voluntary action, in voluntarily obeying the will of God from the heart.

2. Young converts should be taught that the duty of *self-denial* is one of the leading features of the Gospel. They should understand that they are not pious at all, any further than they are willing to take up their cross daily, and deny themselves for Christ. There is but little self-denial in the Church, and the reason is that the duty is so much lost sight of, in giving instruction to young converts. How seldom are they told that self-denial is the leading feature in Christianity! In pleading for benevolent objects, how often will you find that ministers and agents do not even ask Christians *to deny themselves* for the sake of promoting the object! They only ask them to give what they can spare as well as not; in other words, to offer unto the Lord that which costs them nothing. What an abomination! They only ask for the surplus, for what is not wanted, for what can just as well be given as not.

There is no religion in this kind of giving. A man might give a very large sum to a benevolent object, and there would be no religion in his doing so, if he could give the money as well as not; nor would there be any self-denial in it. Jesus Christ exercised self-denial to save sinners. So has God the Father exercised self-denial in giving His Son to die for us, and in sparing us, and in bearing with our perverseness. The Holy

433

Ghost exercises self-denial, in condescending to strive with such unholy beings to bring them to God. The angels exercise self-denial, in watching over this world. The apostles planted the Christian religion among the nations by the exercise of self-denial. And are we to think of being religious without any self-denial? Are we to call ourselves Christians, the followers of Christ, the "temples of the Holy Ghost" (1 Cor. 6. 19), and to claim fellowship with the apostles, when we have never deprived ourselves of anything that would promote our personal enjoyment for the sake of promoting Christ's kingdom? Young converts should be made to see that unless they are willing to lay themselves out for God, and ready to sacrifice life and everything else for Christ, they "have not the Spirit of Christ, and are none of His" (Rom. 8. 9).

3. They must be taught *what sanctification is*. "What!" you will say, "do not all who are Christians know what sanctification is?" No, many do not. Multitudes would be as much at a loss to tell intelligibly what sanctification is, as they would be to tell what religion is. If the question were asked of every professor of religion in this city: "What is sanctification?" I doubt if one in ten would give a right answer. They would blunder just as they do when they undertake to tell what religion is, and speak of it as something dormant in the soul, something that is put in, and lies there, something that may be practised or not, and still be in them. So they speak of sanctification as if it were a sort of washing off of some defilement, or a purging out of some physical impurity. Or they will speak of it as if the faculties were steeped in sin, and sanctification is taking out the stains. This is the reason why some people will pray for sanctification, and practise sin, evidently supposing the sanctification is something that *precedes* obedience. They should be taught that sanctification is not something that precedes obedience, some change in the nature or the constitution of the soul. But sanctification *is obedience*, and as a progressive thing consists in obeying God more and more perfectly.

4. Young converts should be taught so as to understand *what perseverance is*. It is astonishing how people talk about perseverance. As if the doctrine of perseverance is: "Once in grace, always in grace"; or, "Once converted, sure to go to

heaven." This is not the idea of perseverance. The true idea is, that if a man is truly converted, *he will* CONTINUE *to obey God*; and as a *consequence*, he will surely go to heaven. But if a person gets the idea that because he is "converted," *therefore* he will assuredly go to heaven, that man will almost assuredly go to hell.

5. Young converts should be taught *to be religious in everything*. They should aim to be religious in every department of life, and in all that they do. If they do not *aim* at this, they should understand that they have no religion at all. If they do not intend and aim to keep all the commandments of God, what pretence can they make to piety? "Whosoever shall keep the whole law, and yet offend in one point, he is guilty of all" (Jas. 2. 10). He is justly subject to the whole penalty. If he disobeys God habitually in one particular, he does not, in fact, obey Him in any particular. Obedience to God *consists* in the state of the heart. It is being willing to obey God; willing that God should rule in all things. But if a man habitually disobeys God, in any one particular, he is in a state of mind that renders obedience in anything else impossible. To say that in some things a man obeys God, out of respect to His authority, and that in some other things he refuses obedience, is absurd. The fact is, that obedience to God consists in an obedient state of heart, a preference of God's authority and commandments to everything else. If, therefore, an individual *appears* to obey in some things, and yet perseveringly and knowingly disobeys in any one thing, he is deceived. He offends in one point, and this proves that he is guilty of all; in other words, that he does not, *from the heart*, obey at all. A man may pray half of his time and have no religion; if he does not keep the commandments of God, his very prayer will be hateful to God. "He that turneth away his ear from hearing the law, even *his prayer* shall be abomination" (Prov. 28. 9). Do you hear that? If a man refuses to obey God's law, if he refuses to comply with any one duty, he cannot pray, he has no religion, his very devotions are hateful.

6. Young converts, by proper instructions, are easily brought to be *"temperate in all things"* (1 Cor. 9. 25). Yet this is a subject greatly neglected in regard to young converts, and almost lost sight of in the Churches. There is a vast deal of

intemperance in the Churches. I do not mean intemperate *drinking*, in particular, but intemperance in eating and in living generally. There is, in fact, but little conscience about it in the Churches, and, therefore, the progress of reform in the matter is so slow. Nothing but an enlightened conscience can carry forward a permanent reform. Ten years ago, most ministers used ardent spirit, and kept it in their houses to treat their friends and their ministering brethren with. And the great body of the members in the Churches did the same. Now, there are but few, of either, who are not actual drunkards, that will do so. But still there are many that indulge, without scruple, in the use of wine. Chewing and smoking tobacco, too, ar acts of temperance. If they use these mere stimulants when there is no necessity for them, what is that but intemperance? That is not being "temperate in all things." Until Christians shall have a conscience on this subject, and be made to feel that they have no right to be intemperate in anything, they will make but little progress in religion. It is well known, or ought to be, that tea and coffee have no nutriment in them. They are mere stimulants. They go through the system without being digested. The milk and sugar you put in them are nourishing; and so they would be, just as much so, if you mixed them with rum, and made milk punch; but the tea and coffee afford no nourishment; and yet I dare say, that a majority of the families in this city give more in a year for their tea and coffee than they do to save the world from hell. Probably this is true respecting entire Churches. Even agents of benevolent societies will dare to go through the Churches soliciting funds, for the support of missionary and other institutions, and yet use tea, coffee, and, in some cases, tobacco. Strange! No doubt many are giving *five times* as much for mere intemperance as they give for every effort to save the world.

If professing Christians could be made to realise how much they spend for what are mere poisons, and nothing else, they would be amazed. Many persons will strenuously maintain that they cannot get along without these stimulants, these poisons, and they cannot give them up, no, not to redeem the world from eternal damnation. And very often they will absolutely show anger, if argued with, just as soon as the argument begins to pinch their consciences. Oh, how long shall the Church show her hypocritical face at the missionary meeting, and pray God to save the world, while she is actually *throwing away* five times as much for sheer intemperance, as she will give to save the world! Some of you may think these are little things, and that it is quite beneath the dignity of the pulpit to lecture against tea and coffee. But I tell you it is a great mistake of yours if you think these are little things, when they make the Church odious in the sight of God, by exposing her hypocrisy and lust. Here is an individual who pretends he has given himself up to serve Jesus Christ, and yet he refuses to deny himself any darling lust, and then he will go and pray: "O Lord, save the world; O Lord, Thy Kingdom come!" I tell you it is hypocrisy. Shall such prayers be heard? Unless men are willing to deny themselves, I would not give a groat for the prayers of as many such professors as would cover the whole of the United States.

These things must be taught to young converts. It must come to this point in the Church, that men shall not be called Christians, unless they will cut off the right hand, and pluck out the right eye, and deny themselves for Christ's sake. A little thing? See it poison the spirit of prayer! See it debase and sensualise the soul! Is that a trifle beneath the dignity of the pulpit, when those intemperate indulgences, of one kind and another, cost the Church five times, if not fifty times, more than all she gives for the salvation of the world?

An estimate has recently been made, showing that in the United States seven millions of dollars' worth of coffee is consumed yearly; and who does not know, that a *great* part of this is consumed by the *Church.* And yet grave ministers and members of Christian Churches are not ashamed to be seen countenancing this enormous waste of money; while at the same time the poor heathens are sending upon every wind of heaven their agonising wail for help. Heaven calls from above: "Go...preach the Gospel to every creature" (Mark 16. 15). Hell groans from beneath, and ten thousand voices cry out from heaven, earth, and hell: "*Do something to save the world!*" *Do it now!* Oh, NOW, or millions more are in hell through your neglect. And oh, tell it not in Gath, the Church, the *ministry*, will not deny even their lusts to save a world. Is this Christianity? What business have you to use Christ's money for such a purpose? Are you a steward? Who gave you this liberty? Look to it, lest it should be found at last, that you have preferred self-gratification to obedience, and made a "god of your belly" (Phil. 3. 19).

The time to teach these things with effect is, when the converts are young. If converts are not properly taught then, if they get a wrong habit, and begin with an easy, self-indulgent mode of living, it rarely happens that they become thoroughly reformed. I have conversed with old professors on these subjects, and have been astonished at their pertinacious obstinacy in indulging their lusts. And I am satisfied that the Church never can rise out of this sloth until young converts are faithfully taught, at the outset of their religious course, to be temperate *in all things*.

7. They should be taught to have just as *much religion in all their business* as they have in prayer, or in going to a religious service. They should be just as holy, just as watchful, aim just as singly at the glory of God, be just as sincere and solemn in all their daily employments, as when they come to the Throne of Grace. If they are not, their Sabbath performances will be an abomination.

8. They should be taught that it is necessary for them to be *just as holy as they think ministers ought to be*. There has for a long time been an idea that *ministers* are bound to be holy and practise self-denial. And so they are. But it is strange they should suppose that ministers are bound to be *any more* holy than other people. They would be shocked to see a minister showing levity, or running after the fashions, or getting out of temper, or living in a fine house, or riding in a coach. Oh, that is dreadful! It does not look well in a minister. Indeed! For a minister's wife to wear such a fine bonnet, or such a silk shawl—oh no, it will never do! But they think nothing of these things in a layman, or a layman's wife! *That* is no offence at all! I am not saying that these things do look well in a minister; I know they do not. But they look, in God's eyes, just as well in a minister as they do in a layman. *You* have no more right to indulge in vanity, and folly, and pride, than a minister. Can you go to heaven without being sanctified? Can you be holy without living for God, and doing all that you do to His glory? I have heard professedly good men speak against ministers

having large salaries, and living in an expensive style, when they themselves were actually spending a great deal more money for the support of their families than any minister. What would be thought of a minister living in the style in which many professors of religion and elders of Churches are living in this city? Why, everybody would say they were hypocrites. But it is just as much an evidence of hypocrisy in a layman to spend God's money to gratify his lusts, or to please the world, or his family, as it is for a minister to do so.

It is distressing to hear some of our foremost laymen talk of its being dishonourable to religion, to give ministers a large salary, and let them live in an expensive style, when it is a fact that their own expenses are, for the number of their families, and the company they have to receive, far above those of almost any minister. All this arises out of fundamentally wrong notions imbibed while they were young converts. Young converts have been taught to expect that ministers will have all the religion—especially all the self-denial. So long as this continues there can be no hope that the Church will ever do much for the glory of God, or for the conversion of the world. There is nothing of all this in the Bible. Where has God said: "You *ministers*, love God with all your heart, and soul, and mind, and strength"? Or, "You *ministers*, do all to the glory of God"? No, these things are said to all alike, and he who attempts to excuse himself from any duty or self-denial, from any watchfulness or sobriety, by putting it off upon ministers, or who ventures to adopt a lower scale of holy living for himself than *he thinks* is proper for a minister, is in great danger of proving himself a hypocrite, and paying in hell the forfeit of his foolishness.

Much depends on the instructions given to young converts. If they once get into the habit of supposing that they may indulge in things which they would condemn in a minister, it is extremely unlikely that they will ever get out of it.

9. They should *aim at being perfect*. Every young convert should be taught that if it is not his *purpose* to live without sin, he has not yet begun to be religious. What is religion but a supreme love to God and a supreme purpose of heart or disposition to obey God? If there is not this, there is no religion at all. It is one thing to *profess to be perfect*, and

another thing to profess and feel you *ought to be* perfect. It is one thing to say that men ought to be perfect, and can be, if they are so disposed, and another thing to say that they *are* perfect. If any are prepared to say that they are perfect, all I have to say is: "Let them prove it." If they are so I hope they will show it by their actions, otherwise we can never believe they are perfect.

But it is the duty of all to be perfect, and to purpose entire, perpetual, and universal obedience to God. It should be their constant purpose to live wholly to God, and obey all His commandments. They should live so that if they should sin it would be an inconsistency, and exception, an individual case, in which they act contrary to the fixed and general purpose and tenor of their lives. They *ought not* to sin at all; they are bound to be as holy as God is; and young converts should'be taught to set out in the right course, or they will never be right.[1]

10. They should be taught *to exhibit their light*. If the young convert does not exhibit his light, and hold it up to the world, it will go out. If he does not bestir himself, and go forth and try to enlighten those around him, his light will go out, and his own soul will soon be in darkness. Sometimes young converts seem disposed to sit still and not do anything in public till they get a great deal of light, or a great deal of religion. But this is not the way. Let the convert use what he has; let him hold up his little twinkling rushlight, boldly and honestly, and *then* God will make it like a blazing torch. But God will not take the trouble to keep a light burning that is hid. Why should He? Where is the use?

This is the reason why so many people have so little

---

[1] "A man may believe in what is really a state of entire sanctification," said Finney, "and aim at attaining it, although he may not call it by that name. Mrs. President Edwards, for example, aimed at it, and manifestly attained it, and yet, such were her views of constitutional depravity, that she did not call her state one of entire sanctification. I care not what this state is called, if the thing be fully explained and insisted upon, together with the conditions of attaining it. Call it what you please: Christian perfection, heavenly-mindedness, the full assurance of faith or hope, or a state of entire consecration; by all these I understand the same thing" (Finney's "Systematic Theology," Lecture 60—"Sanctification").

enjoyment in religion. They do not exert themselves to honour God. They keep what little they do enjoy so entirely to themselves, that there is no good reason why God should bestow blessings and benefits on them.

11. They should be taught *how to win souls to Christ*. Young converts should be taught particularly *what* to do to accomplish this, and *how* to do it; and then taught to live for this end as the great leading object of life. How strange has been the course sometimes pursued! These persons have been converted, and—there they are. They get into the Church, and then they are left to go along just as they did before; they do nothing, and are taught to do nothing, for Christ; and the only change is that they go more regularly to church n the Sabbath, and let the minister *feed them*, as it is called. But suppose he does feed them, they do not grow strong, for they cannot digest it, because they take no exercise. They become spiritual dyspetics. Now, the great object for which Christians are converted and left in this world is, to pull sinners out of the fire. If they do not effect this, they had better be dead. And young converts should be taught this as soon as they are born into the Kingdom. The first thing they do should be to go to work for this end—to save sinners.

II. *HOW THE CHURCH SHOULD TREAT YOUNG CONVERTS.*

1. Old professors *ought to be able* to give young converts *a great deal of instruction*, and they ought to give it. The truth is, however, that the great body of professors in the Churches do not know how to give good instruction to young converts; and, if they attempt to do so, they give only that which is false. The Church ought to be able to teach her children; and when she receives them she ought to be as busy in training them to act, as mothers are in teaching their little children such things as they will need to know and do hereafter. But this is far enough from being the case generally. And we can never expect to see young converts habitually taking right hold of duty, and going straight forward without declension and backsliding, until the time comes when all young converts are intelligently trained by the Church.

2. Young converts should *not be kept back* behind the rest of the Church. How often is it found that the old professors

will keep the young converts back behind the rest of the rest of the Church, and prevent them from taking any active part in religion, for fear they should become spiritually proud. Young converts in such Churches are rarely or never called on to take a part in meetings, or set to any active duty, or the like, for fear they should become lifted up with *spiritual pride*. Thus the Church becomes the *modest keeper* of their humility, and teaches them to file in behind the old, stiff, dry, cold members and elders, for fear that if they should be allowed to do anything for Christ, it will make them proud. Whereas, the very way to make young converts humble and keep them so, is to put them to their work and keep them there. That is the way to keep God with them, and as long as God is with them, *He* will take care of their humility. Keep them constantly engaged in religion, and then the Spirit of God will dwell in them, and so they will be kept humble by the most effectual process. But if young converts are left to fall in behind the old professors, where they can never do anything, they will never know what spirit they are of, and this is the very way to run them into the danger of falling into the worst species of spiritual pride.

3. They should be *watched over* by the Church, and warned of their dangers, just as a tender mother watches over her young children. Young converts do not know at all the dangers by which they are surrounded. The devices of the devil, the temptations of the world, the power of their own passions and habits, and the thousand forms of danger, they do not know; and if not properly watched and warned, they will run right into such dangers. The Church should watch over and care for her young children—just as mothers watch their little children in this great city, lest the carts run over them, or they stray away; or as they watch over them while growing up, for fear they may be drawn into the whirlpools of iniquity. The Church should watch over all the interests of her young members, know where they are, and what are their habits, temptations, dangers, privileges—the state of religion in their hearts, and their spirit of prayer. Look at that anxious mother, when she sees paleness gather round the brow of her little child. "What is the matter with you, my child? Have you eaten something improper? Have you taken cold? What ails you?" Oh, how different it is with the children of the Church, the lambs that

the Saviour has committed to the care of His Church! Alas! instead of restraining her children, and taking care of them, the Church lets them go anywhere, and look out for themselves. What should we say of a mother who should knowingly let her children totter along the edge of a precipice? Should we not say she was horribly guilty for doing so, and that if the child should fall and be killed, its blood would rest on the mother's head? What, then, is the guilt of the Church, in knowingly neglecting her young converts? I have known Churches where young converts were totally neglected, and regarded with suspicion and jealousy; nobody went near them to strengthen or encourage or counsel them; nothing was done to lead them to usefulness, to teach them what to do or how to do it, or to open to them a field of labour. And then—what then? Why, when they find that young converts cannot stand everything, when they find them growing cold and backward under such treatment, they just turn round and abuse them, for not holding out!

4. *Be tender in reproving them.* When Christians find it necessary to reprove young converts, they should be exceedingly careful in their manner of doing it. Young converts should be faithfully watched over by the elder members of the Church, and when they begin to lose ground, or to turn aside, they should be promptly admonished, and, if necessary, reproved. But to do it in a wrong manner is worse than not to do it at all. It is sometimes done in a manner which is abrupt, harsh, and apparently censorious, more like scolding then like brotherly admonition. Such a manner, instead of inspiring confidence, or leading to reformation, is just calculated to harden the heart of the young convert, and confirm him in his wrong courses, while, at the same time, it closes his mind against the influence of such censorious guardians. The heart of a young convert is tender, and easily grieved, and sometimes a single unkind look will set him into such a state of mind as will fasten his errors upon him, and make him grow worse and worse.

You who are parents know how important it is when you reprove your children, that they should see that you do it from the best of motives, for their benefit, because you wish them to be good, and not because you are angry. Otherwise they will soon come to regard you as a tyrant, rather than as a friend. Just so with young converts. Kindness and tenderness, even in reproof, will win their confidence, and attach them to you, and give an influence to your brotherly instructions and counsels, so that you can mould them into finished Christians. Instead of this, if you are severe and critical in your manner, that is the way to make them think you wish to lord it over them. Many persons, under pretence of being *faithful*, as they call it, often hurt young converts by such a severe and overbearing manner, as to drive them away, or perhaps crush them into despondency and apathy. Young converts have but little experience, and are easily thrown down. They are just like a little child when it first begins to walk. You see it tottering along, and it stumbles over a straw. You see the mother take everything out of the way, when her little one is going to try to walk. Just so with young converts. The Church ought to take up every stumbling-block, and treat converts in such a way as to make them see that if they are reproved, Christ is in it. Then they will receive it as it is meant, and it will do them good.

5. Kindly *point out things that are faulty* in the young convert, which he does not see. He is but a child, and knows so little about religion, so that there will be many things that he needs to learn, and a great many that he ought to mend. What ever there is wrong in spirit, unlovely in his deportment, or uncultivated in manner, that will impede his usefulness or impair his influence as a Christian, ought to be kindly pointed out and corrected. To do this in the right way, however, requires great wisdom. Christians ought to make it a subject of much prayer and reflection, that they may do it in such a way as not to do more hurt than good. If you rebuke him merely for the things that he did not see, or did not know to be improper, it will grieve and disgust him. Such instruction should be carefully timed. Often, it is well to take the opportunity after you have been praying together, or after a kind conversation on religious subjects which has been calculated to make him feel that you love him, seek his good, and earnestly desire to promote his sanctification, his usefulness, and his happiness. Then, a mere hint will often do the work. Just suggest that "Such a thing in your prayer," or "your conduct in so-and-so, did not strike me pleasantly; had you not better think of it, and

perhaps you will judge it better to avoid a recurrence of it?" Do it rightly, and you will help him and do him good. Do it in the wrong way, and you will do ten times more hurt than good. Often, young converts will err through ignorance; their judgment is unripe, and they need time to think and make up an enlightened judgment on some point that at first appears to them doubtful. In such cases the older members should treat them with great kindness and forbearance; should kindly instruct them, and not denounce them at once for not seeing, at first, what perhaps they themselves did not understand until years after they were converted.

6. Do not *speak of the faults* of young converts behind their backs. This is too common among old professors; and, by and by, the converts hear of it; and what an influence it must exercise to destroy the confidence of young converts in their elder brethren, to grieve their hearts and discourage them, and perhaps to drive them away from the good influence of the Church.

III. *Some of the Evils of Defective Instruction.*

1. If not fully instructed, they will never be fully *grounded in right principles*. If they have right fundamental principles, this will lead them to adopt a right course of conduct in all particular cases. In forming a Christian character a great deal depends on establishing those fundamental principles which are correct on all subjects. If you look at the Bible, you will see there that God teaches right principles which we can carry out, in detail, in right conduct. If the education of young converts is defective, either in kind or degree, you will see the result in their character all their lives. This is the philosophical result— just what might be expected, and just what will always follow. It could be shown that almost all the practical errors that have prevailed in the Church are the natural results of certain false dogmas which have been taught to young converts, and which they have been made to swallow, as the truth of God, at a time when they were so ignorant as not to know any better.

2. If the instruction given to young converts is not *correct and full*, they will not grow in grace, but their religion will dwindle away and decay. Their course, instead of being like the path of the just, growing brighter and brighter unto the

perfect day (Prov. 4. 18), will grow dimmer and dimmer, and finally, perhaps, go out in darkness. Wherever you see young converts let their religion taper off till it comes to nothing, you may understand that it is the natural result of defective instruction. The philosophical result of teaching young converts the truth, and the whole truth, is that they grow stronger and stronger. Truth is the food of the mind—it is what gives the mind strength. And where religious character grows feeble, rely upon it, in nine cases out of ten it is owing to their being neglected, or falsely instructed, when they were young converts.

3. They will be *left in doubt*, justly, as to whether they are Christians. If their early instruction is false, or defective, there will be so much inconsistency in their lives, and so little evidence of real piety, that they themselves will finally doubt whether they have any. Probably they will live and die in doubt. You cannot make a little evidence go a great way. If they do not see clearly, they will not live consistently; if they do not live consistently, they can have but little evidence; and if they have not evidence, they must doubt, or live in presumption.

4. If young converts are rightly instructed and trained, it will generally be seen that they will *take the right side* on all great subjects that come before the Church. Subjects are continually coming up before the Churches, on which they have to take ground, and on many matters there is often no little difficulty in making the members take right ground. Take the subject of tracts, or missions, or Sabbath Schools, or temperance, for instance—what cavils, and objections, and resistance, and opposition, have been encountered from members of the Churches in different places. Go through the Churches, and where you find young converts have been well taught, you never find *them* making difficulty, or raising objections, or putting forth cavils. I do not hesitate to charge it upon pastors and older members of Churches, that there are so many who have to be dragged up to the right ground on all such subjects. If they had been well grounded in the principles of the Gospel at the outset,when they were first converted, they would have seen the application of their principles to all these things. It is curious to see how ready young converts are to take right ground on any subject that may be proposed. See what they are

willing to do for the education of ministers, for missions, moral reform, or for the slaves! If the great body of young converts from the late revivals had been well grounded in Gospel principles, you would have found in them, throughout the Church, but one heart and one soul in regard to every question of duty. Let their early education be right, and you have got a body of Christians that you can depend on. If it had been general in the Church, how much more strength there would have been in all her great movements for the salvation of the world!

5. If young converts are not well instructed, they will *inevitably backslide*. If their instruction is defective, they will probably live in such a way as to disgrace religion. The truth, kept steadily before the mind of a young convert, in proper proportions, has a natural tendency to make him grow "unto a perfect man,unto the measure of the stature of the fulness of Christ" (Eph. 4. 13). If any one point is made too prominent in the instruction given, there will probably be just that disproportion in his character. If he is fully instructed on some points and not on others, you will find a corresponding defect in his life and character.

If the instruction of young converts is greatly defective, they will press on in religion no farther than they are strongly propelled by the first emotions of their conversion. As soon as that is spent they will come to a stand, and then they will decline and backslide. And ever after you will find that they will go forward only when aroused by some powerful excitement. These are your "periodical" Christians, who are so apt to wake up in a time of revival, and bluster about as if they had the zeal of angels, for a few days, and then die away as dead and cold as a northern winter. Oh, how desirable, how infinitely important it is, that young converts should be *so* taught that their religion will not depend on impulses and excitements, but that they will go steadily onward in the Christain course, advancing from strength to strength, and giving forth a clear and safe and steady light all around.

REMARKS.

1. The Church is verily guilty for her past neglect, in regard to the instruction of young converts.

Instead of bringing up their young converts to be working Christians, the Churches have generally acted as if they did not know how to employ young converts, or what use to make of them. They have acted like a mother who has a great family of daughters, but knows not how to set them to work, and so suffers them to grow up idle and untaught, useless and despised, and to be the easy prey of every designing villain.

If the Church had only done her duty in training up young converts to work and labour for Christ, the world would have been converted long ago. But instead of this, how many Churches actually oppose young converts who attempt to set themselves to work for Christ. Multitudes of old professors look with suspicion upon every movement of young converts, and talk against them, saying: "They are too forward, they ought not to put themselves forward, but *wait* for those who are older." There is *waiting* again! Instead of bidding young converts "Godspeed," and cheering them on, very often they hinder them, and perhaps put them down. How often have young converts been stopped from going forward, and turned into rank behind a formal, lazy, inefficient Church, till their spirit has been crushed, and their zeal extinguished; so that after a few ineffectual struggles to throw off the cords, they have concluded to sit down with the rest, and WAIT. In many places young converts cannot even attempt to hold a prayer-meeting by themselves, without being rebuked by the pastor, or by some deacon, for being so forward, and upbraided with spiritual pride. "Oho," it is said, "you are *young converts*, are you? And so you want to get together, and call all the neighbours together to look at you, because you are young converts. You had better turn preachers at once!" A celebrated Doctor of Divinity in New England boasted, at a public table, of his success in keeping all his converts still. He had great difficulty, he said, for they were in a terrible fever to do something, to talk, or pray, or get up meetings, but by the greatest vigilance he had kept it all down, and now his Church was just as quiet as it was before the revival. Wonderful achievement for a minister of Jesus Christ! Was that what the blessed Saviour meant when he told Peter: "Feed My lambs"?

2. Young converts should be *trained to labour* just as carefully as young recruits in an army are trained for war.

Suppose a captain in the army should get his company enlisted, and then take no more pains to teach and train, and discipline them, than are taken by many pastors to train and lead forward their young converts. Why, the enemy would laugh at such an army. Call them soldiers! Why, as to any effective service, they would no know what to do nor how to do it, and if you brought them up to the CHARGE, how would they fare? Such an army would resemble the Church that does not train her young converts. Instead of being trained to stand shoulder to shoulder in the onset, they feel no practical confidence in their leaders, no confidence in their neighbours, and no confidence in themselves; hence they scatter at the first shock of battle. Look at the Church now. Ministers are not agreed as to what shall be done, and many of them will fight against their brethren, quarrelling about "new measures," or something. As to the members, they cannot feel confidence when they see the leaders so divided. And then if they attempt to do anything—alas! what ignorance, what awkwardness, what discord, what weakness we see, and what miserable work they make of it! And so it must continue, until the Church shall train up young converts to be intelligent, single-hearted, self-denying, working Christians. Here is an enterprise now going on in this city, which I rejoice to see. I mean the *tract* enterprise—a blessed work. And the plan is to train up a body of devoted Christians to do—what? Why, to do what all the Church ought to have been trained to do long ago: to know how to pray, and how to converse with people about salvation, and how to act in anxious meetings, and how to deal with inquirers, and how to SAVE SOULS.

3. The Church has entirely mistaken the *manner in which she is to be sanctified*. The experiment has been carried on long enough, of trying to sanctify the Church, without finding anything for the members to do. But holiness consists in obeying God, and sanctification, as a process, means obeying Him more and more perfectly. And the way to promote it in the Church, is to give every one something to do. Look at these great Churches, where they have five hundred or seven hundred members, and have a minister to *feed* them from Sabbath to Sabbath, while there are so many of them together that the greater part have nothing at all to do, and are never

trained to make any direct efforts for the salvation of souls. And in that way they are expecting to be sanctified and prepared for heaven! They never will be sanctified *so*. That is not the way God has appointed. Jesus Christ has made His people co-workers with Him in saving sinners, for this very reason, because sanctification *consists* in doing those things which are required to promote this work. This is one reason why He has not employed angels in the work, or carried it on by direct revelation of truth to the minds of men. It is because it is necessary as a means of sanctification, that the Church should sympathise with Christ in His feelings and His labours for the conversion of sinners. And in this way the entire Church must move, before the world will be converted. When the day comes that the whole body of professing Christians shall realise that they are here on earth as a body of missionaries, and when they shall live and labour accordingly, then will the day of man's redemption draw nigh.

Christian, if you cannot go abroad to labour, why are you not a missionary in your own family? If you are too feeble even to leave your room, be a missionary there in your bedchamber. How many unconverted servants, and your unconverted children, and be a missionary to them. Think of your physician, who, perhaps, is laying himself out to save your body; think that you receive his kindness and never make him the greatest return in your power.

It is necessary that the Church should take hold of her young converts at the outset, and set them to work in the right way. The hope of the Church is in the young converts.

4. We see what a responsibility rests on *ministers and elders*, and on all who have opportunity to assist in training young converts. How distressing is the picture which often forces itself upon the mind, where multitudes are converted, and yet so little pains are taken with young converts, that in a single year you cannot tell the young converts from the rest of the Church. And then we see the old Church members turn round and complain of these young converts, and perhaps slander them, when in truth these old professors themselves are most to blame—oh, it is too bad! This *reaction* that people talk so much about after a revival, as if reaction was the necessary effect of a revival, would never come, and young

converts never would backslide as they do, if the Church would be prompt and faithful in attending to their instruction. If they are truly converted, they *can be made* thorough and energetic Christians. And if they are not made such, Jesus Christ will require it at the hands of the Church.

LECTURE XXI

THE BACKSLIDER IN HEART [1]

The backslider in heart shall be filled with his own ways.—
Prov. 14. 14.

I cannot conclude this course of lectures, without warning
converts against backsliding. In discussing this subject, I will
show: I. What backsliding in heart is not. II. What backsliding
in heart is. III. What are evidences of backsliding heart.
IV. What are consequences of backsliding in heart. V. How to
recover from this state.

I. *WHAT BACKSLIDING IN HEART IS NOT.*

1. It does not consist in the subsidence of highly excited
religious emotions. The subsidence of religious feeling may be
an *evidence* of a backslidden heart, but it does not consist in the
cooling off of religious feeling.

II. *WHAT BACKSLIDING IN HEART IS.*

1. It consists in taking back that consecration to God and His
service, that constitutes true conversion.

---

[1] This Lecture and the succeeding one were, as we have seen,
inserted by Finney, in 1868, in place of those originally delivered,

2. It is the leaving, by a Christian, of his first love.

3. It consists in the Christian withdrawing himself from that state of entire and universal devotion to God, which constitutes true religion, and coming again under the control of a self-pleasing spirit.

4. The text implies that there *may* be a backslidden heart, when the forms of religion and obedience to God are maintained. As we know from consciousness that men perform the same, or similar, acts from widely different, and often from opposite, motives, we are certain that men may keep up all the outward *forms* and appearances of religion, when in fact, they are backslidden in heart. No doubt the most intence selfishness often takes on a religious type, and there are many considerations that might lead a backslider in heart to keep up the *forms*, while he had lost the *power* of godliness in his soul.

III. *WHAT ARE EVIDENCES OF A BACKSLIDDEN HEART.*

1. Manifest *formality in religious exercises*. A stereotyped, formal way of saying and doing things, that is clearly the result of habit, rather than the outgushing of the religious life. This formality will be emotionless and cold as an iceberg, and will evince a total want of earnestness in the performance of religious duty. In prayer and in religious exercises the backslider in heart will pray or praise, or confess, or give thanks with his lips, so that all can *hear* him, perhaps, but in such a way that *no* one can *feel* him. Such a formality would be impossible where there existed a present, living faith and love, and religious zeal.

2. A *want of religious enjoyment* is evidence of a

---

the subjects, however, being practically the same (see foot-note to Lecturer's Preface). The change appears to have originated in a desire to co-ordinate the sub-topics in a clearer sequence. Divers topics which he had dealt with in a final Lecture, on "Growth in Grace," under the headings of "Evidences of Declension" and "How to Escape from a State of Declension," found a more suitable place in the present chapter. The task of revision once commenced, Finney proceeded to marshal fresh thoughts and expand his subject in the light of mature experience.

backslidden heart. We always enjoy the saying and doing of those things that please those whom we most love; furthermore, when the heart is *not* backslidden, communion with God is kept up, and therefore all religious duties are not only performed with pleasure, but the communion with God involved in them is a source of rich and continual enjoyment. If we do not *enjoy* the service of God, it is because we do not truly serve Him. If we *love* Him supremely, it is impossible that we should not enjoy His service at every step. Always remember then, whenever you lose your religious enjoyment, or the enjoyment of serving God, you may know that you are not serving Him aright.

3. Religious *bondage* is another evidence of a backslidden heart. God has no slaves. He does not accept the service of bondmen, who serve Him because they must. He accepts none but a love service. A backslider in heart finds his religious duties a burden to him. He has promised to serve the Lord. He dare not wholly break off from the *form* of service, and he tries to be dutiful, while he has no heart in prayer, in praise, in worship, or in any of those exercises which are so spontaneous and delightful, where there is true love to God. The backslider in heart is often like a *dutiful*, but *unloving* wife. She tries to do her *duty* to her husband, but fails utterly because she does not love him. Her painstaking to please her husband is constrained, not the spontaneous outburst of a loving heart; and her relationship and her duties become the *burden* of her life. She goes about complaining of the weight of *care* that is upon her, and will not be likely to advise young ladies to marry. She is committed for life, and *must* therefore perform the duties of married life, but it is such a bondage! Just so with religious bondage. The professor *must* perform his duty. He drags painfully about it, and you will hear him naturally sing backslider's hymns:

> Reason I hear, her counsels weigh,
> And all her words approve;
> And yet I find it hard to obey,
> And harder still, to *love*.

4. An *ungoverned temper*. While the heart is full of love, the temper will naturally be chastened and sweet, or at any rate,

the *will* will keep it under, and not suffer it to break out in outrageous abuse, or if at any time it should so far escape from the control of the will as to break loose in hateful words, it will soon be brought under, and by no means suffered to take control and manifest itself to the annoyance of others. Especially will a loving heart confess and break down, if at any time bad temper gets the control. Whenever, therefore, there is an irritable, uncontrolled temper allowed to manifest itself to those around, you may know there is a backslidden heart.

5. A *spirit of uncharitableness* is evidence of a backslidden heart. By this, I mean a want of that disposition that puts the best construction upon every one's conduct that can be reasonable—a want of confidence in the good intentions and professions of others. We naturally credit the good professions of those whom we love. We naturally attribute to them right motives, and put the best allowable construction upon their words and deeds. Where there is a want of this there is evidence conclusive of a backslidden or unloving heart.

6. A *censorious spirit* is conclusive evidence of a backslidden heart. This is a spirit of fault-finding, of impugning the motives of others, when their conduct admits of a charitable construction. It is a disposition to fasten blame upon others, and judge them harshly. It is a spirit of distrust of Christian character and profession. It is a state of mind that reveals itself in harsh judgments, harsh sayings, and the manifestation of uncomfortable feelings toward individuals. This state of mind is entirely incompatible with a loving heart, and whenever a censorious spirit is manifested by a professor of religion, you may know there is a backslidden heart.

7. A *want of interest in God's Word*, is also an evidence of a backslidden heart. Perhaps nothing more conclusively proves that a professor has a backslidden heart, than his losing his interest in the Bible. While the heart is full of love, no book in the world is so precious as the Bible. But when the love is gone, the Bible becomes not only uninteresting but often repulsive. There is no faith to accept its promises, but conviction enough left to dread its threatenings. But in general the backslider in heart is apathetic as to the Bible. He does not read it much, and when he does read it, he has not interest enough to understand it. Its pages become dark and

uninteresting, and therefore it is neglected.[1]

8. A want of interest in *secret prayer is* also an evidence of a backslidden heart. Young Christian, if you find yourself losing your interest in the Bible and in secret prayer, stop short, return to God, and give yourself no rest, till you enjoy the light of His countenance. If you feel disinclined to pray, or to read your Bible; if when you pray and read your Bible, you have no heart; if you are inclined to make your secret devotions short, or are easily induced to neglect them; or if your thoughts, affections, and emotions wander, you may know that you are a backslider in heart, and your first business is to be broken down before God, and to see that your love and zeal are renewed.

9. A want of interest in the *conversion of souls* and in efforts to promote revivals of religion. This of course reveals a backslidden heart. There is nothing in which a loving heart takes more interest than in the conversion of souls—in revivals of religion, and in efforts to promote them.[2]

10. A want of interest in published *accounts or narratives of revivals* of religion, is also an evidence of a backslidden heart. While one retains his interest in the conversion of souls, and in revivals of religion he will, of course, be interested in all accounts of revivals of religion anywhere. If you find yourself, therefore, disinclined to read such accounts, or find yourself not interested in them, take it for granted that you are backslidden in heart.

---

[1] In the original Lecture, Finney pungently remarked, upon this subject: "If you do not delight in the Bible more than in other book, if you find you can relish reading any commentary as well as you do the naked text itself, you have begun to backslide. I do not hesitate to say, that the man who finds he can relish the best commentary that ever was written as well as he does the simple Word of God, has begun to backslide. If he has gone still farther, and thinks he has read the Bible about enough, and that now he will take up other things and study, he is far gone."

[2] It would be a profitable task to study the experiences of men who have in large measure realised their personal responsibility, and have striven to fulfil it with apostolic zeal, in the spirit indicated by Finney. Such a man was Walker, curate of Truro, who, after he had been preaching the Gospel there for seven years, recorded that no

11. The same is true of missions, and missionary work and operations. If you lose your interest in the work, and in the conversion of the heathen, and do not delight to read and hear of the *success of missions*, you may know that you are backslidden in heart.

12. The loss of interest in *benevolent enterprises* generally is an evidence of a backslidden heart. I say, "the loss of interest," for surely, if you were ever converted to Christ, you have had an interest in all benevolent enterprises that came within your knowledge. Religion consists in disinterested benevolence. Of course, a converted soul takes the deepest interest in all benevolent efforts to reform and save mankind; in good government, in Christian education, in the cause of temperance, in the abolition of slavery, in provision for the needs of the poor, and in short, in *every* good word and work. Just in proportion as you have lost your interest in these, you have evidence that you are backslidden in heart.

13. The loss of interest in *truly spiritual conversation* is another evidence of a backslidden heart. "Out of the abundance of the heart the mouth speaketh" (Matt. 12. 34). This our Lord Jesus Christ announced as a law of our nature. No conversation is so sweet to a truly loving heart, as that which relates to Christ, and to our living Christian experience. If you find yourself losing interest in conversing on heart religion, and of the various and wonderful experiences of Christians, if you have known what the true love of God is, you have fallen from it, and are a backslider in heart.

---

fewer than eight hundred persons had sought him out, personally, inquiring: "What must I do to be saved?" Of William Grimshaw, the famous incumbent of Haworth, Bishop J. C. Ryle wrote (in "Christian Leaders of England in the Eighteenth Century"): "Wherever he went he spoke plainly to people about their souls. He seldom preached less than twenty times a week, and often nearly thirty. In doing this he would constantly travel scores of miles, content with the humblest fare." Again, Hay Macdowall Grant, of Arndilly, used to make out a sort of "trading account" of his visits among the people. One of these spiritual chronicles records that: "During twenty months, there have been 1,470 persons visited, most of them twice, and many five, six, or ten times. Of these 266 profess to have been converted."

14. A loss of interest in the conversation and society of *highly spiritual people*, is an evidence of a backslidden heart. We take the greatest delight in the society of those who are most interested in the things that are most dear to us. Hence, a loving Christian heart will always seek the society of those who are most spiritually-minded, and whose conversation is most evangelical and spiritual. If you find yourself wanting in this respect, then know for certain that you are backslidden in heart.

15. The loss of interest in the question of *sanctification* is an evidence of a backslidden heart. I say again, *the loss of interest*, for, if you ever truly knew the love of God, you must have had a great interest in the question of entire consecration to God, or of entire sanctification. If you are a Christian, you have felt that sin was an abomination to your soul. You have had inexpressible longings to be rid of it forever, and everything that could throw light upon that question of agonising importance was most intensely interesting to you. If this question has been dismissed, and you no longer take an interest in it, it is because you are backslidden in heart.

16. The loss of interest in *those newly converted*, is also an evidence of a backslidden heart. The Psalmist says: "They that fear Thee will be glad when they see me; because I have hoped in Thy word" (Psa. 119. 74). This he puts into the mouth of a convert, and who does not know that this is true? There is joy in the presence of the angels of God, over one sinner that repenteth, and is there not joy among the saints on earth, over those that come to Christ, and are as babes newly born into the Kingdom? Show me a professor of religion who does not manifest an absorbing interest in converts to Christ, and I will show you a backslider in heart, and a hypocrite; he professes religion, but has none.

17. An *uncharitable state of mind* in regard to professed converts, is also an evidence of a backslidden heart. Charity, or love, "believeth all things, hopeth all things" (I Cor. 13. 7), is very ready to judge kindly and favourably of those who profess to be converted to Christ, and will naturally watch over them with interest, pray for them, instruct them, and have as much confidence in them as it is reasonable to have. A disposition, therefore, to pick at, criticise, and censure them, is an evidence

of a backslidden heart.

18. The *want of the spirit of prayer* is evidence of a backslidden heart. While the love of Christ remains fresh in the soul, the indwelling Spirit of God will reveal Himself as the Spirit of grace and supplication. He will beget strong desires in the soul for the salvation of sinners and the sanctification of saints. He will often make intercessions in them, with great longings, strong crying and tears, and with groanings that cannot be uttered in words, for those things that are according to the will of God. Or, to express it in Scripture language, according to Paul: "Likewise the Spirit also helpeth our infirmities: for we know not what we should pray for as we ought: but the Spirit itself maketh intercession for us with groanings which cannot be uttered. And He that searcheth the hearts knoweth what is the mind of the Spirit, because He maketh intercession for the saints according to the will of God" (Rom. 8. 26, 27). If the spirit of prayer departs, it is a sure indication of a backslidden heart, for while the first love of a Christian continues he is sure to be drawn by the Holy Spirit to wrestle much in prayer.

19. A backslidden heart often reveals itself by the *manner* in which people pray. For example, praying as if in a state of self-condemnation, or very much like a convicted sinner, is an evidence of a backslidden heart. Such a person will reveal the fact, that he is not at peace with God. His confessions and self-accusations will show to others what perhaps he does not well understand himself. His manner of praying will reveal the fact that he has not communion with God; that instead of being filled with faith and love, he is more or less convicted of sin, and conscious that he is not in a state of acceptance with God. He will naturally pray more like a convicted sinner than like a Christian. It will be seen by his prayer that he is not in a state of Christian liberty—that he is having a Seventh of Romans experience, instead of that which is described in the Eighth.

20. A backslidden heart will further reveal itself in praying almost exclusively for *self,* and for those friends that are regarded almost as parts of self. It is often very striking and even shocking to attend a backsliders' prayer-meeting, and I am very sorry to say that many prayer-meetings of the Church

are little else. Their prayers are timid and hesitating, and reveal the fact that they have little or no faith. Instead of surrounding the throne of Grace and pouring their hearts out for a blessing on those around them, they have to be urged up to duty, to "take up their cross." Their hearts do not, will not, spontaneously gush out to God in prayer. They have very little concern for others, and when they do, as they say, "take up their cross and do their duty," and pretent to lead in prayer, it will be observed that they pray just like a company of convicted sinners, almost altogether for themselves. They will pray for that which, should they obtain it, would be religion, just as a convicted sinner would pray for a new heart; and the fact that they pray for religion as they do, manifests that they have none, in their present state of mind. Ask them to pray for the conversion of sinners, and they will either wholly forget to do so, or just mention sinners in such a way as will show that they have no heart to pray for them.

I have known professed Christian parents to get into such a state that they had no heart to pray for the conversion of their own children, even when those children were under conviction. They would keep up family prayer, and attend a weekly prayer-meeting, but would never get out of the rut of praying round and round for themselves. A few years since I was labouring in a revival in a Presbyterian Church. At the close of the evening sermon I found that the daughter of one of the elders of the Church was in great distress of mind. I observed that her convictions were very deep. We had been holding a meeting with inquirers in the vestry, and I had just dismissed the inquirers, when this young lady came to me in great agitation and begged me to pray for her. The people had mostly gone, except a few who were waiting in the body of the church for those friends who had attended the meeting of inquiry. I called the father of this young lady into the vestry that he might see the very anxious state of his daughter's mind. After a short personal conversation with her in the presence of her father, I called on him to pray for her, and said that I would follow him, and I urged her to give her heart to Christ. We all knelt, and he went through with his prayer, kneeling by the side of his sobbing daughter, without ever mentioning her case. His prayer revealed that he had no more religion than she had, and that he was very much in her state of mind—under an awful sense of condemnation. He had kept up the appearance of religion. As an elder of the Church, he was obliged to keep up appearances. He had gone round and round upon the treadmill of his duties, while his heart was utterly backslidden. It is often almost nauseating to attend a prayer-meeting of the backslidden in heart. They will go round, round, one after the other, in reality praying for their own conversion. They do not so express it, but that is the real import of their prayer. They could not render it more evident that they are backsliders in heart.

21. *Absence from state prayer-meetings* for slight reasons, is a sure indication of a backslidden heart. No meeting is more interesting to Christians than the prayer-meeting, and while they have any heart to pray, they will not be absent from prayer-meeting unless prevented from attending by the providence of God. If a call from a friend at the hour of meeting can prevent their attendance, unless the call is made under very peculiar circumstances, it is strong evidence that they do not *wish* to attend, and hence, that they are backsliders in heart. A call at such a time would not prevent their attending a wedding, a party, a picnic, or an amusing lecture. The fact is, it is hypocrisy for them to pretend that they really *want* to go, while they can be kept away for slight reasons.

22. The same is true of the *neglect of family prayer*, for slight reasons. While the heart is engaged in religion, Christians will not readily omit family devotions, and whenever they are ready to find an excuse for the omission, it is a sure evidence that they are backslidden in heart.

23. When secret prayer is regarded more as a *duty* than as a privilege, it is because the heart is backslidden. It has always appeared to me almost ridiculous, to hear Christians speak of prayer as a "duty." It is one of the greatest earthly privileges. What should we think of a child coming to its parent for its dinner, not because it is hungry, but as a *duty*. How would it strike us to hear a beggar speak of the "duty" of asking alms of us. It is an infinite privilege to be allowed to come to God, and ask for the supply of all our wants. But to pray because we *must*, rather than because we *may*, seems unnatural. To ask for what we want, and because we want it, and because God has

encouraged us to ask, and has promised to answer our request, is natural and reasonable. But to pray as a duty and as if we were obliging God by our prayer, is quite ridiculous, and is a certain indication of a backslidden heart.

24. *Pleading for worldly amusements* is also an indication of a backslidden heart. The most grateful amusements possible, to a truly spiritual mind, are those engagements that bring the soul into the most direct communion with God. While the heart is full of love and faith, an hour, or an evening, spent alone in communion with God, is more delightful than all the amusements which the world can offer. A loving heart is jealous of everything that will break up or interfere with its communion with God. For mere worldly amusements it has no relish. When the soul does not find more delight in God than in all worldly things, the heart is sadly backslidden.

25. *Spiritual blindness* is another evidence of a backslidden heart. While the eye is single the whole body will be full of spiritual light, but if the eye be evil (which means a backslidden heart) the whole body will be full of darkness.

Spiritual blindness reveals itself in a want of interest in God's Word, and in religious truth generally. It will also manifest a want of spiritual discrimination, and will be easily imposed upon by the insinuations of Satan. A backslidden heart will lead to the adoption of lax principles of morality. It does not discern the spirituality of God's law, and of His requirements generally. When this spiritual blindness is manifest it is a sure indication that the heart is backslidden.

26. *Religious apathy*, with *worldly* wakefulness and sensibility, is a sure indication of a backslidden heart. We sometimes see persons who feel deeply and quickly on worldly subjects, but who cannot be made to feel deeply on religious subjects. This clearly indicates a backslidden state of mind.

27. A *self-indulgent spirit* is a sure indication of a backslidden heart. By self-indulgence, I mean a disposition to gratify the appetites, passions, and propensities, to "fulfil the desires of the flesh and of the mind" (Eph. 2. 3).

This, in the Bible, is represented as a state of spiritual death. I am satisfied that the most common occasion of backsliding in heart is to be found in the clamour for indulgence of the various appetites and propensities. The appetite for food is frequently, and perhaps more frequently than any other, the occasion of backsliding. Few Christians, I fear, apprehend any danger in this direction. God's injunction is: "Whether therefore ye eat, or drink, or whatsoever ye do, do all to the glory of God" (I Cor. 10. 31). Christians forget this, and eat and drink to please themselves, consulting their appetites instead of the laws of life and health. More persons are ensnared by their tables than the Church is aware of. The table is a snare of death to multitudes that no man can number. A great many people who avoid alcoholic drinks altogether, will indulge in tea and coffee, and even tobacco, and in food that, both in quantity and quality, violates every law of health. They seem to have no other law than that of appetite, and this they so deprave by abuse that, to indulge it, is to ruin body and soul together. Show me a gluttonous professor, and I will show you a backslider.

28. A *seared conscience* is also an evidence of a backslidden heart. While the soul is wakeful and loving, the conscience is as tender as the apple of the eye. But when the heart is backslidden, the conscience is silent and seared, on many subjects. Such a person will tell you that he is not violating his conscience, in eating or drinking, or in self-indulgence of any kind. You will find a backslider has but little conscience. The same will very generally be true in regard to sins of omission. Multitudes of duties may be neglected and a seared conscience will remain silent. Where conscience is not awake, the heart is surely backslidden.

29. *Loose moral principles* are a sure indication of a backslidden heart. A backslider in heart will write letters on the Sabbath, engage in secular reading, and in much worldly conversation. In business, such a person will take little advantages, play off business tricks, and conform to the habits of worldly business men in the transaction of business; he will be guilty of deception and misrepresentation in making bargains, will demand exorbitant interest, and take advantage of the necessities of his fellow-men.

30. Prevalence of *the fear of man is* an evidence of a backslidden heart. While the heart is full of the love of God, God is feared, and not man. A desire for the applause of men is

kept down, and it is enough to please God, whether men are pleased or displeased. But when the love of God is abated, "the fear of man," that "bringeth a snare" (Prov. 29. 25), gets possession of the backslider. To please man rather than God, is then his aim. In such a state he will sooner offend God than man.

31. A *sticklishness about forms*, ceremonies, and nonessentials, gives evidence of a backslidden heart. A loving heart is particular only about the substance and power of religion, and will not stickle about its forms.

32. A *captiousness about measures* in promoting revivals of religion, is a sure evidence of a backslidden heart. Where the heart is fully set upon the conversion of sinners and the sanctification of believers, it will naturally approach the subject in the most direct manner, and by means in the highest degree calculated to accomplish the end. It will not object to, nor stumble at, measures that are evidently blessed of god, but will exert the utmost sagacity in devising the most suitable means to accomplish the great end on which the heart is set.

IV. *THE CONSEQUENCES OF BACKSLIDING IN HEART.*

The text says, that "the backslider in heart shall be filled with his own ways."

1. He shall be filled with his own *works*. But these are dead works, they are not works of faith and love, which are acceptable to God, but are the filthy rags of his own righteousness. If they are performed as religious services, they are but loathsome hypocrisy, and an abomination to God; there is no heart in them. To such a person God says: "Who hath required this at your hand?" (Isa. 1. 12). "Ye are they which justify yourselves before men; but God knoweth your

1. He shall be filled with his own *works*. But these are dead works, they are not works of faith and love, which are acceptable to God, but are the filthy rags of his own righteousnes. If they are performed as religious services, they are but loathsome hypocrisy, and an abomination to God; there is no heart in them. To such a person God says: "Who hath required this at your hand?" (Isa. 1. 12). "Ye are they which justify yourselves before men; but God knoweth your

hearts: for that which is highly esteemed among men is abomination in the sight of God" (Luke 16. 15). "I know you, that ye have not the love of God in you" (John 5. 42).

2. He shall be filled with his own *feelings*. Instead of that sweet peace and rest, and joy in the Holy Ghost, that he once experienced, he will find himself in a state of unrest, dissatisfied with himself and everybody else, his feelings often painful, humiliating, and as unpleasant and unlovely as can be well conceived. It is often very trying to live with backsliders. They are often peevish, censorious, and irritating, in all their ways. They have forsaken God, and in their feelings there is more of hell than of heaven.

3. They will be filled with their own *prejudices*. Their willingness to know and do the truth has gone. They will very naturally commit themselves against any truth that bears hardly upon a self-indulgent spirit. They will endeavour to justify themselves, will neither read nor hear that which will rebuke their backslidden state, and they will become deeply prejudiced against every one that shall cross their path, who shall reprove them, accounting him as an enemy. They hedge themselves in, and shut their eyes against the light; stand on the defensive, and criticise everything that would search them out.

4. A backslider in heart will be filled with his own *enmities*. He will chafe in almost evry relation of life, will allow himself to be vexed, and to get into such relations with some persons, and perhaps with many, that he cannot pray for them honestly, and can hardly treat them with common civility. This is an almost certain result of a backslidden heart.

5. The backslider in heart will be full of his own *mistakes*. He is not walking with God. He has fallen out of the Divine order. He is not led by the Spirit, but is walking in spiritual darkness. In this state he is sure to fall into many and grievous mistakes, and may get entangled in such a way as to mar his happiness, and, perhaps, destroy his usefulness for life. Mistakes in business, mistakes in forming new relations in life, mistakes in using his time, his tongue, his money, his influence; indeed, all will go wrong with him as long as he remains in a backslidden state.

6. The backslider in heart will be filled with his own

lustings. His appetites and passions, which had been kept under, have now resumed their control, and having been so long suppressed, they will seem to avenge themselves by becoming more clamorous and despotic than ever. The animal appetites and passions will burst forth, to the astonishment of the backslider, and he will probably find himself more under their influence and more enslaved by them than ever before.

7. The backslider in heart will be filled with his own *words*. While in that state, he will not, and cannot, control his tongue. It will prove itself to be an unruly member, full of deadly poison. By his words he will involve himself in many difficulties and perplexities, from which he can never extricate himself until he comes back to God.

8. He will be full of his own *trials*. Instead of keeping out of temptation, he will run right into it. He will bring upon himself multitudes of trials that he never would have had, had he not departed from God. He will complain of his trials, but yet will constantly multiply them. A backslider feels his trials keenly, but, while he complains of being so tried by everything around him, he is constantly aggravating them, and, being the author of them, he seems industrious to bring them upon himself like an avalanche.

9. The backslider in heart shall be full of his own *follies*. Having rejected the Divine guidance, he will evidently fall into the depths of his own foolishness. He will inevitably say and do multitudes of foolish and ridiculous things. Being a professor of religion, these things will be all the more noticed, and of course bring him all the more into ridicule and contempt. A backslider is, indeed, the most foolish person in the world. Having experimental knowledge of the true way of life, he has the infinite folly to abandon it. Knowing the fountain of lifing waters, he has forsaken it, and "hewed out to himself cisterns, broken cisterns, that can hold no water" (Jer. 2. 13). Having been guilty of this infinite folly, the whole course of his backslidden life must be that of a fool, in the Bible sense of the term.

10. The backslider in heart will be full of his own *troubles*. God is against him, and he is against himself. He is not at peace with God, with himself, with the Church, nor with the world. He has no inward rest. Conscience condemns him. God

condemns him. All that know his state condemn him. "There is no peace, saith my God, to the wicked" (Isa. 57. 21). There is no position in time or space in which he can be at rest.

11. The backslider in heart will be full of his own *cares*. He has turned back to selfishness. He counts himself and his possessions as his own. He has everything to care for. He will not hold himself and his possessions as belonging to God, and lay aside the responsibility of taking care of himself and all that he possesses. He does not, *will* not, cast his care upon the Lord, but undertakes to manage everything for himself, and in his own wisdom, and for his own ends. Consequently, his cares will be multiplied, and come upon him like a deluge.

12. The backslider in heart will be full of his own *perplexities*. Having forsaken God, having fallen into the darkness of his own folly, he will be filled with perplexities and doubts in regard to what course he shall pursue to accomplish his selfish ends. He is not walking with, but contrary to God. Hence, the providence of God will constantly cross his path, and baffle all his schemes. God will frown darkness upon his path, and take pains to confound his projects, and blow his schemes to the winds.

13. The backslider in heart will be filled with his own *anxieties*. He will be anxious about himself, about his business, about his reputation, about everything. He has taken all these things out of the hands of God, and claims them and treats them as his own. Hence, having faith in God no longer, and being unable to control events, he must of necessity be filled with anxieties with regard to the future. These anxieties are the inevitable result of his madness and folly in forsaking God.

14. The backslider in heart will be filled with his own *disappointments*. Having forsaken God, and taken the attitude of self-will, God will inevitably disappoint him as he pursues his selfish ends. He will frame his ways to please himself, without consulting God. Of course God will frame his ways so as to disappoint him. Determined to have his own way, he will be greatly disappointed if his plans are frustrated; yet the certain course of events under the government of God must of necessity bring him a series of disappointments.

15. The backslider in heart must be full of his own *losses*.

He regards his possessions as his own, his time as his own, his influence as his own, his reputation as his own. The loss of any of these he accounts as his own loss. Having forsaken God, and being unable to control the events upon which the continuance of those things is conditioned, he will find himself suffering losses on every side. He loses his peace. He loses his property. He loses much of his time. He loses his Christian reputation. He loses his Christian influence, and if he persists he loses his soul.

16. The backslider in heart will be full of his own *crosses*. All religious duty will be irksome, and, therefore,a cross to him. His state of mind will make multitudes of things crosses that in a Christian state of mind would have been pleasant in a high degree. Having lost all heart in religion, the performance of all religious duty is a cross to his feelings. There is no help for him, unless he returns to God. The whole course of Divine providence will run across his path, and his whole life will be a series of crosses and trials. he cannot have his own way. he cannot gratify himself by accomplishing his own wishes and desires. He may beat and dash himself against the everlasting rocks of God's will and God's way, but break through and carry all before him he cannot. He must be crossed and recrossed, and crossed again, until he will fall into the Divine order, and sink into the will of God.

17. The backslider in heart will be filled with his own *tempers*. Having forsaken God, he will be sure to have much to irritate him. In a backslidden state, he cannot possess his soul in patience. The vexations of his backslidden life will make him nervous and irritable; his temper will become explosive and uncontrollable.

18. The backslider in heart will be full of his own *disgraces*. He is a professor of religion. The eyes of the world are upon him, and all his inconsistencies, worldly-mindedness, follies, bad tempers, and hateful words and deeds, disgrace him in the estimation of all men who know him.

19. The backslider in heart will be full of his own *delusions*. Having an evil eye, his whole body will be full of darkness. He will almost certainly fall into delusions in regard to doctrines and in regard to practices. Wandering on in darkness, as he does, he will, very likely, swallow the grossest delusions.

Spiritism, Mormonism, Universalism, and every other *ism* that is wide from the truth, will be very likely to gain possession of him. Who has not observed this of backsliders in heart?

20. The backslider in heart will be filled with his own *bondage*. His profession of religion brings him into bondage to the Chruch. He has no heart to consult the interests of the Church, or to labour for its up-building, and yet he is under convenant obligation to do so, and his reputation is at stake. he must do something to sustain religious institutions, but to do so is a bondage. If he does it, it is because he *must* and not because he *may*. Again, he is in bondage to God. If he performs any duty that he calls religious, it is rather as a slave than as a freeman. He serves from fear or hope, just like a slave, and not from love. Again, he is in bondage to his own conscience. To avoid conviction and remorse, he will do or omit many things, but it is all with reluctance, and not at all of his own cordial goodwill.

21. The backslider in heart is full of his own *self-condemnation*. Having enjoyed the love of God, and forsaken Him, he feels condemned for everything. If he attempts religious duty, he knows there is no heart in it, and hence condemns himself. If he neglects religious duty, he of course condemns himself. If he reads his Bible, it condemns him. If he does not read it, he feels condemned. If he goes to religious meetings, they condemn him; and if he stays away, he is condemned also. If he prays in secret, in his family, or in public, he knows he is not sincere, and feels condemned. If he neglects or refuses to pray, he feels condemned. Everything condemns him. His conscience is up in arms against him, and the thunders and lightnings of condemnation follow him, whithersoever he goes.

V. *HOW TO RECOVER FROM A STATE OF BACKSLIDING.*

1. Remember whence you are fallen. Take up the question at once, and deliberately contrast your present state with that in which you walked with God.

2. Take home the conviction of your true position. No longer delay to understand the exact situation between God

and your soul.

3. Repent at once, and do your first works over again.

4. Do not attempt to get back, by reforming your mere outside conduct. Begin with your heart, and at once set yourself right with God.

5. Do not act like a mere convicted sinner, and attempt to recommend yourself to God by any impenitent works or prayers. Do not think that you must "reform, and make yourself better" before you can come to Christ, but understand distinctly, that coming to Christ, alone, can make you better. However much distressed you may feel, know for a certainty that until you repent and accept His will, unconditionally, you are no better, but are constantly growing worse. Until you throw yourself upon His sovereign mercy, and thus return to God, He will accept nothing at your hands.

6. Do not imagine yourself to be in a justified state, for you know you are not. your conscience condemns you, and you know that God ought to condemn you, and if He is justified you in your present state, your conscience could not justify Him. Come, then, to Christ at once, like a guilty, condemned sinner, as you are; own up, and take all the shame and blame to yourself, and believe that notwithstanding all your wanderings from God, He loves you still—that He has loved you with an everlasting love, and, therefore, with loving kindness is drawing you.

LECTURE XXII

GROWTH IN GRACE

But grow in grace, and in the knowledge of our Lord and Saviour
Jesus Christ.—2 Pet. 3. 18.

I must conclude this Course of Lectures by giving converts
instructions on the subject of Growth in Grace. I shall pursue
the following method, showing: I. What *grace* is, as the term
is here used. II. What the injunction to "grow in grace" does
not mean. III What it *does* mean. IV. The conditions of
growth in grace. V. What is *not* proof of growth in grace. VI.
What *is* proof of growth in grace. VII. How to grow in grace.

I. *WHAT GRACE IS.*

1. Grace is favour. The word is often used in the Bible to
signify a free gift. The grace of God is the *favour* of God.

II. *WHAT TO "GROW IN GRACE" DOES NOT MEAN.*

1. It does not enjoin the *gradual* giving up of sin. Strange to
tell, it would seem that some have so understood it; but we are
nowhere in the Bible commanded to give up sin gradually, we
are everywhere commanded to give it up instantly and wholly.

III. *WHAT IT DOES MEAN.*

1. It enjoins upon us the duty of growing in the favour of

God, of growing in His esteem—in a worthiness of His favour.

IV. CONDITIONS OF GROWTH IN GRACE.

1. Growth or increase in anything implies a beginning. Growth in the favour of God implies that we have *already found favor* in His sight, that we are already indebted for grace received, and that we are already in grace, in the sense of having a place among His favoured ones.

2. Consequently, growth in grace implies that we have already repented of our sin, have actually and practically *abandoned all known sin.* It cannot be that we are in favour with God if we are still indulging in known sin against Him. Being in favour with God implies, of course, that we are pardoned and favoured by Him, for the sake of our Lord and Saviour Jesus Christ. Pardon is favour, and implies the renunciation of rebellion against God. The conditions of the Divine favour, as revealed in the Bible, are repentance and abandonment of all known sin, and faith in our Lord Jesus Christ. I said, as a condition of growth in grace we must have the commencement of grace; in other words, we must be already Christians, must be in a state of acceptance with God, must have accepted Christ, so far as He is understood, must be in a state of obedience to all the recognised will of God. Without this, we cannot be in a state of grace, or in the favour of God. But being in this state, there is room for everlasting growth. As we know more of God, we shall be capable of loving Him more, of having a more universal and implicit confidence in Him. And there can be no end to this while we have any being, either in this or any other world. Our love and confidence in Him may be complete, so far as we know Him. This love and confidence will secure His favour; but there will be no end to our growth in knowledge of Him, and, consequently, there is room for eternal growth in grace. The more we love God, the more we believe, the more we know of Him, if we conform to this knowledge, the more God must be pleased with us, the higher shall we stand in his favour, and more and greater gifts he will continue to bestow upon us.

3. Of course, growth in the *knowledge of God* is a condition of growth in His favour. We might grow in knowledge,

without growing in His favour, because we might not love and trust Him in accordance with this increased knowledge. But we cannot love and trust Him more perfectly, unless we become more perfectly acquainted with Him. If our love and faith keep pace with our growing knowledge, we must grow in His favour. But growth in knowledge must be a condition of growth in love and faith.

4. Growth in the knowledge of God, as *revealed in Christ Jesus*, must be a condition of growth in His favour. It is in and through Christ Jesus that God reveals Himself to man. It is in Christ Jesus that we get the true idea of the personality of the infinite God. Hence, the text says: "Grow in grace, and in the knowledge of our Lord and Saviour Jesus Christ."

5. Growth in grace is conditioned on increased knowledge of what is involved in *entire consecration* to God.

True conversion to God involves the consecration of ourselves and of all that we have to Him, so far as we understand what is implied in this. But, at first, converts are by no means aware of all that is involved in the highest forms of consecration. They will soon learn that there are certain things that they did not think of, and that they did not give up to God. At first, perhaps, all that was in their thought was, to lay their naked soul upon the altar, and give up their whole heart to God. But soon they may learn that they did not think of all their possessions, of everything that was dear to them; they did not surrender all, leaving "not an hoof behind" (Ex. 10. 26). They surrendered all of which they thought, but they were not fully enlightened, they did not think, nor could they think, at the time, of every appetite, passion, propensity, of every desire and affection, and of everything dear to them, in the whole creation, to make a thorough surrender and delivery of these to God.

To gain such knowledge is a work of time; and growth in the favour of God is conditioned on making a full surrender and consecration to God of everything we are, and have, and desire, and love, as fast as these objects are presented to thought. As long as we exist, and knowledge increases, there is no doubt that we shall be called upon to grow in grace, by consecrating to God every new object of knowledge, of desire, and of affection, that we may come to know, and desire, and love, to all eternity. As you get new light, you must enlarge your consecration from day to day, and from hour to hour, or you will cease to grow in grace. Whenever you stop short, and do not lay and leave everything that you are, that you possess, or that you love, upon the altar of consecration, that moment you cease to grow in grace. I pray you to let this saying sink deep into your hearts.

6. Another condition of growth in grace is intense earnestness and constancy in seeking *increased religious light*, by the illumination of the Holy Spirit.[1] You will gain no effectual religious light except by the inward showing and teaching of the Holy Spirit. This you will not obtain unless you continue in the true attitude of a disciple of Christ. Remember, He says: "Whosoever he be of you that forsaketh not all that he hath, he cannot be My disciple" (Luke 14. 33). He will not, by His Holy Spirit, be your Divine Teacher unless you renounce self, and live in a state of continual consecration to Him. To obtain and preserve the teachings of Christ, by the Holy Spirit, you must continually and earnestly pray for this Divine teaching of the Spirit, and watch against resisting and grieving Him.

7. Another condition of growth in grace is a constant *conformity to all the teachings* of the Holy Spirit, keeping up with our convictions of duty and with our growing knowledge of the will of God.

8. A more and more implicit *faith in God* is a condition of growth in grace. By implicit, I mean an unreasoning faith, a confidence in God's character so profound that we trust Him

---

[1] Finney's counsels regarding prayer, thoroughgoing as they were, are by no means to be regarded as mere theoretical advice. He lived in an atmosphere of fervency practically all his life subsequent to his conversion. In regard to his own experience as a preacher his words were: "Unless I had the spirit of prayer I could do nothing. If even for a day or an hour I lost the spirit of grace and supplication, I found myself unable to preach with efficiency or to win souls by personal conversation...I found myself so borne down with the weight of immortal souls that I was constrained to pray without ceasing....I cannot tell how certain it was in my mind that God would answer those prayers which I found myself offering in such agony and faith. My impression was that the answer was near, even at the door."

in the dark as well as in the light, as well when we do not understand the reasons of His dealings with us, or of His requirements, as when we do; a faith like that of Abraham, who "staggered not at the promise of God through unbelief" (Rom. 4. 20), though the thing promised seemed irrational and impossible. An implicit faith is an unwavering, unquestioning faith, a state of mind that will rest in God, in His promises, in His faithfulness, in His love, whatever appearances may be and however trying and apparently unreasonable His commands or providential dealings may be. Abraham's faith is often commended in the Bible. God had promised him a son, but did not give him the promised seed until he was a hundred years old, and Sarah was ninety. But notwithstanding Sarah was past age, and he as good as dead, he believed that God was able to fulfil His promise. Then, when he had received his beloved son, with the assurance that this was to be his heir, and that through him the promise was to be fulfilled through all generations, God tried his faith severely, by commanding him to offer his Isaac as a burnt sacrifice. Yet he obeyed, without the least hesitation, believing "that God was able to raise him up, even from the dead" (Heb. 11. 19). He made all his arrangements to obey this trying command, with such calmness that neither Sarah nor Isaac suspected that nay such thing was in contemplation. This was an instance of the exercise of implicit faith. Growth in grace, or in the favour of God, is conditioned upon growth in implicit confidence in Him.

9. A more thoroughly *sanctified sensibility* is a condition of growth in the favour of God. By the sensibility, I mean that department of our nature that feels and desires, to which belongs all that we call desire, affection, emotion, feeling, appetite, passion, propensity, lust. The sensibility is an involuntary power, and moral actions and qualities cannot, with strict propriety, be predicated of it. The states of the sensibility have moral character only as they derive it, directly or indirectly, from the action of the will. The nature of man, as a whole, in his depraved condition, is in a very unlovely state, and although the will may be given up to God, the sensibility may be in such a state as to be very unlovely in the sight of One that looks directly upon it, and knows perfectly every excited

desire, passion, propensity, lust. It is through the sensibility, mainly, that we are assailed with temptations. It is through this that the Christian warfare is kept up. The Christian warfare consists in the battle of the will with these various appetites, passions, propensities, and lusts, to keep them in subjection to the will of God. If the will maintains its integrity, and cleaves to the will of God, the soul does not sin in its battle with the excited states of the sensibility. But these rebellious propensities embarrass the will in the service it renders to God. To keep them under occupies much time, and thought, and strength. Hence the soul cannot render to God so complete a service, while exerting the full strength of the will to subjugate these propensities, as it otherwise might and would render.

These appetites, passions, and propensities, although not sinful in themselves, have been regarded and spoken of as indwelling sin. Strictly, they cannot be sin, because they are involuntary. But they are often a great hindrance to our growth in the favour of God. "For the flesh lusteth against the Spirit, and the Spirit against the flesh: and these are contrary the one to the other: so that ye cannot do the things that ye would" (Gal. 5. 17). This means that we cannot do for God what we otherwise would, because we have to battle so much with the states of the sensibility, to keep them under. As the sensibility becomes more and more subdued and in harmony with the will's devotion to God, we are left free to render to God a more unembarrassed service. Therefore, the more thorough the sanctification of the sensibility, the more thoroughly we are in favour with God.

10. A growing *thoroughness and universality of conse-cration*, of spirit, soul, and body, is the condition of more and more growth in the favour of God. It is common, at first, for the steadfastness of the will's devotion to God to be overcome by the clamour of the excited appetites, passions, and propensities, or by the various states of the sensibility. Whenever the will yields to these excited states, you sin. But, in such cases, the sin is not wilful, in the sense of being deliberate and intentional; it is rather a slip, an inadvertency, a momentary yielding under the pressure of highly excited feeling. Nevertheless, this yielding is sin. However excited

the states of the sensibility may be, if the will does not yield, there is strictly no sin. Still, while the will is steadfast, maintaining its consecration and obedience to God, the appetites originating in the body, and the various propensities of the soul, which inhere in the sensibility, may be so ajar, in such confusion, and in such a state of morbid development, that the soul may be unfitted for the employments and enjoyments of heaven.

11. Hence, the taking on of a *greater fulness of the Divine nature* is a condition of growth in the favour of God. Both the will and the sensibility of God must be in a state of utmost perfection and accord. All of His desires and feelings must be in perfect harmony with His intelligence and His will. Not so with us, in our state of physical depravity. The depravity of sensibility must be physical, because it is involuntary. Still, it is depravity, it is a lapsed or fallen state of the sensibility. This lapsed department of our nature must be recovered, sanctified, or completely restored to harmony with a consecrated will, and an enlightened intelligence, or we are never fitted for heaven. As we become more and more the partakers of the Divine nature, and of the Divine holiness, we are more fully sanctified in spirit, soul, and body, and of course grow more and more in the favour of God.

12. A greater and *more all-pervading fulness of the Holy Spirit's residence* is another condition of growth in the favour of God. You cannot have it too thoroughly impressed upon you that every step in the Christian life is to be taken under the influence of the Holy Spirit. The thing to be attained is the universal teaching and guidance of the Holy Spirit, so that in *all* things you shall be led by the Spirit of God. "Walk in the Spirit, and ye shall not fulfil the lust of the flesh" (Gal. 5. 16). "If ye through the Spirit do mortify the deeds of the body, ye shall live" (Rom. 8. 13). "To be carnally minded is death; but to be spiritually minded is life and peace" (Rom. 8. 6). Always remember, therefore, that to grow in grace, you must grow in the possession of the fullness of the Holy Ghost in your heart.

13. A deeper personal *acquaintance with the Lord Jesus Christ*, in all His official work and relations, is a condition of growth in grace. His nature, work, and relations are the theme of the Bible. The Bible presents Him to us in a great variety of

relations. In my "Systematic Theology" [1] I have considered some sixty or more of these official relations of Christ to the human race, and these are presented rather as specimens and illustrations than as covering the whole ground of His relations to us. Now, it is one thing to know Christ simply on paper, and as spoken of in the Bible, by reading or hearing of Him, and quite another thing to know Him personally, in these relations. The Bible is the medium of introduction to Him personally. What is there said of Him is designed to lead us to seek after a personal acquaintance with Him. It is by this personal acquaintance with Him that we are made like Him. It is by direct, personal intercourse with His Divine mind that we take on His image. "We all, with open face beholding as in a glass the glory of the Lord, are changed into the same image

---

[1] The "Systematic Theology," the largest of Finney's literary works, is an exhaustive volume of Lectures delivered at Oberlin College. It involved its author in considerable controversy. By the advice of Dr. George Redford, of Worcester, to whom he had been introduced by John Angell James, the book was revised, enlarged, and partly rewritten—during Finney's first visit to Great Britain (1849-51). His labours during this visit were not only literary, for his sermons produced awakenings of a remarkable character, first at Houghton (a village in Huntingdonshire), then at Birmingham and Worcester, and, more particularly, because his stay was longer, at the historic Whitefield Tabernacle, Moorfields. Dr. Campbell, the pastor, laughed at Finney's proposal to hold a meeting solely for the anxious (following a certain Sunday night service), saying: "You might get the people to come in America, but not here." Finney replied that the Gospel was the same in England as in America, and secured Dr. Campbell's reluctant consent. To the pastor's amazement a vast crowd followed Finney to the appointed place of meeting, some distance away. "There was sobbing and weeping everywhere," and in the end Finney remained nine months at the Tabernacle, preaching to huge congregations and conversing with great numbers of people. "That thousands were converted there is no reason to doubt," he said. Moreover, a new impetus was given to revival—among Churchmen as well as Nonconformists. Eventually the call of duty took him back to Oberlin, and when he sailed from England an enormous crowd remained on the wharf for hours, while the vessel waited for the tide, signifying their lively interest in his welfare.

from glory to glory, even as by the Spirit of the Lord" (2 Cor. 3. 18). "Faith cometh by hearing" (Rom. 10. 17) and faith secures for us a personal acquaintance with Christ. Christ has promised to manifest Himself personally to those who love and obey Him. Do not stop short of securing this personal manifestation of Christ to your souls. Your growth in grace will depend upon this. Think not of stopping short of personally knowing Christ, not only in all these relations, but in the fulness of these relations. Do not overlook the fact that the appropriation of Christ, in each of these relations, is a personal act of faith. It is a putting on of the Lord Jesus Christ, a taking of Him as yours, in each of these relations, as your wisdom, righteousness, sanctification, and redemption; as your Prophet, to teach you, your King, to govern you, your High Priest, to atone for you, your Mediator, your Advocate, your Strength, your Saviour, your Hiding-place, your High Tower, your Captain and Leader, your Shield, your Defence, your Exceeding Great Reward. In each of these relations, and in all other of His official relations, you need to appropriate Him by faith so as to secure to you personal intercourse with Him in these relations. Growing in a personal acquaintance with Him, in these relations, is an indispensable condition of growth in His favour.

V. *SOME THINGS THAT ARE NOT PROOF OF GROWTH.*

1. Growth in *knowledge* is not *conclusive* evidence of growth in *grace*. Some *degree* of knowledge is indispensable to our being in favour with God; and growth in knowledge, as I have shown, is a *condition* of growth in grace; but *knowledge* is not grace, and *growth* in *knowledge* does not constitute growth in grace. A person may grow ever so much in knowledge, and have no grace at all. In hell, they cannot but grow in knowledge, as they grow in experience, and in the knowledge of God's justice. But there, their growth in knowledge but aggravates the guilt and misery of hell. They know more and more of God and His law, and their own guilt, and the more they know, the more wretched they are. From their increased knowledge they never learn piety.

2. It is not certain evidence that an individual grows in

grace, because he grows in *gifts*. A professor of religion may increase in gifts, that is, he may become more fluent in prayer, and more eloquent in preaching, or more pathetic in exhortation, without being any more holy. We naturally increase in that in which we exercise ourselves. And if any person often exercises himself in exhortation, he will naturally, if he makes any effort or lays himself out, increase in fluency and pungency. But he may do all this, and yet have no grace at all. He may pray ever so engagedly, and increase in fluency and apparent pathos, and yet have no grace. People who have no grace often do so. It is true, if he has grace, and exercises himself in these things, as he grows in grace, he will grow in gifts. No person can exercise himself in obeying God without improving in those exercises. If he *does not* improve in gifts, it is a true sign he *does not* grow in grace. But, on the other hand, it is not sure evidence that he grows in grace because he improves in certain exercises, for he will naturally improve by practice, whether he is a Christian or a hypocrite.

3. It is not proof that a person grows in grace because *he thinks he is doing so*. One may be very favourably impressed with regard to his own progress in religion, when it is evident to others that he is not only making no progress, but is, in fact, declining. An individual who is growing worse and worse, is not ordinarily well aware of the fact. It is not uncommon for both impenitent sinners and Christians to think they are growing better, when they are growing no better.

This results from the very nature of the case. If any person is growing worse, his conscience will, for the time being, become more and more seared, and his mind more and more dark, as he stifles conscience and resists the light. Then he may imagine he is growing better, just because he has less sense of sin; and while his conscience continues to sleep he may continue under the fatal delusion. A man will judge of his own spiritual state as he compares himself with a high or low standard. If he keeps Christ before him, in His fulness, as his standard, he will doubtless always, at least in this state of existence, have but a low estimate of his own attainments. While at the same time, if he sets before himself the Church, or any member of the Church, as a standard, he will be very likely to form a high estimate of his progress in religion, and be very well satisfied with himself. This is the reason why there is such a difference in people's views of their own state and of the state of the Church. They compare themselves and the state of the Church with different standards. Hence, one takes a very humbling view of his own state, and complains of that of the Church; another thinks such complaints of the Church censorious, for to him the Church appears to be doing very well. The reason why he does not think the Church cold, and in a low state, is that Christ is not his standard of comparison. If a man shuts his eyes, he will not see the defilement on him, and may think he is clean, while to all around he appears loathsome.

VI. *WHAT IS PROOF OF GROWTH.*

1. The manifestation of more *implicit and universal trust* in God is an evidence of growth in grace. The exercise of greater and more implicit confidence, as I have said, is the condition of growing in the favour of God. The manifestation of this implicit and universal confidence is proof that this growing confidence exists, and is, therefore, satisfactory evidence of growth in the favour of God. If you are conscious in your own soul that you do exercise more implicit and universal confidence in God, this is conclusive proof to you that you are growing in grace, and as you manifest in your life, and temper, and spirit, this growing confidence, you prove to yourself and to others that you are growing in the favour of God. For as you grow in implicit confidence in Him you must grow in His favour.

2. Another evidence of growth in grace, is an increasing *weanedness from the world.* The will may be in an attitude of devotion to God, while the world's seductive charms very much embarrass the healthy action of the Christian life. As the soul becomes crucified and dead to the world, it grows in the favour of God.

3. *Less reluctance of feeling*, when called to the exercise of self-denial, is an evidence of growth in grace. It shows that the feelings are becoming less and less despotic, that the will is getting more the mastery of them, that the sensibility is getting more into harmony with the devotion of the will and

the dictates of the intelligence.

4. *Less temptation to sins of omission*, is another evidence of growth in grace, *e.g.,* less temptation to shun the cross, to neglect unpleasant duties; less temptation to indolence, to the shirking of responsibility, to neglect of prayer, to reading the Scriptures, and to private and family devotions; in short, less and less temptation to shun the performance of any duty is evidence of growth in grace. These temptations consist in the excited states of the sensibility. As these become less in strength and frequency, we learn that our sensibility is becoming more completely subjugated to the law of the intelligence and the decisions of the will, and consequently, that the work of the sanctification of the spirit, soul, and body is progressing, and that therefore we are growing in the favour of God.

5. A growing *intensity and steadiness* of zeal in promoting the cause of God, is evidence of growth in the favour of God. Sometimes Christian zeal is comparatively cool, at other times deep and intense; sometimes it will be steady, at other times fitful and evanescent. As Christians grow in piety, their zeal becomes deep, intense, and steady, and as you are conscious of this, and in your life and spirit give evidence of it to others, you have, and give, proof that you are growing in the favour of God.

6. Losing more and more the *consciousness of self*, and respect to self, in every action of life, is an evidence of growth in the favour of God. Some have so much consciousness of self in everything, and so much respect to self in everything they say and do, as to be embarrassed in all their Christian life, whenever they attempt to act or speak in the presence of others. As they lose this self-consciousness, and have less respect to self, their service of God becomes more free and unembarrassed, and they are all the better servants by how much less they think of self. Sometimes young converts cannot speak or pray, or perform any public duty, without being either proud or ashamed, as they think themselves to have performed their duties with more or less acceptance to those around them. While this is so, their piety is in a feeble state. They must lose sight of their own glory, and have a single eye to the glory of God, to find acceptance with Him.

But as they lose sight of self and set God always before them, having an eye single to His glory they grow more and more in His favour.

7. Consequently, a growing *deadness to the flattery or censure of men*, is an evidence of growth in grace. Paul had grown in grace so much the he counted it a light thing to be judged of man, he only sought to commend himself to God (1 Cor. 4. 3, 4). As you find yourself growing in this state of deadness to the flatteries or censures of men, you have evidence that you grow in grace.

8. A growing cordiality in the *acceptance of the whole will of God* is evidence of growth in His favour. Some rebel against His will as revealed in His Word and in His providence. Others, under trying circumstances, will barely tolerate His will; but those who are growing in grace find it more natural to them to embrace his whole revealed will with greater and greater cordiality.

9. Growing *calmness* and quietness under great afflictions give an evidence of growth in the favour of God. There is evinced a more explicit faith, a fuller and more cordial acceptance of the will of God, as revealed in these afflictions; the soul is shown to be more steadily and firmly at anchor upon its rock, Christ.

10. A growing *tranquillity* under sudden and crushing disasters and bereavements, is an evidence of growth in grace. The more tranquil the soul can remain, when sudden storms of providence come upon it, sweeping away loved ones, and blighting earthly hopes, the greater is its evidence of being under the particular favour of God. The tranquillity is both a result and an evidence of the favour of God.

11. Growing *patience* under much provocation, is an evidence of growth in the favour of God.

12. "*Longsuffering with joyfulness*" (Col. 1. 11) is an evidence of growing in favour with God. When you can not only tolerate, but accept, the will of God, as revealed in calling you to suffer; and especially when you can accept these sufferings, and endure them long and with joyfulness, you have evidence that you are growing in the favour of God.

13. A growing *cordiality and joyfulness* under crosses and disappointments and severe pain, is evidence of growth in the

favour of God.

14. An increasing *deadness* to all that the world has to offer, or to threaten, is an evidence of growth in the favour of God.

15. A growing *repose* in, and satisfaction with, all the allotments of Providence, is evidence of growth in grace.

16. Less temptation to *murmur* or repine at any allotment of Providence, is evidence of growth in grace.

17. Less temptation to *fret*, when we are crossed or disappointed in any respect, is an evidence of growth in grace.

18. Less and less temptation to *resentment*, and the spirit of retaliation, when we are in anywise insulted or abused, is evidence that the sensibility is becoming more and more thoroughly subdued, and consequently, that we are growing in favour with God.

19. Less temptation to *dwell upon*, and to *magnify* our trials and troubles, to think of them, and speak of them to others, is evidence that we think less and less of self, and accept our trials and troubles with more and more complacency in God. It is sad to hear some professedly good people, dwelling ever upon, and magnifying, their own troubles and trials. But, if they grow in grace, they will think less and less of these, and be more inclined to think of them as "light afflictions." The more we grow in grace, the less stress we lay upon the evils we meet with in the way. Said a good man to me once, who was really passing through what the world would call very severe trials and afflictions (he had lost a beloved wife, and his children had died one after another): "I have many mercies, and few afflictions." When, under such circumstances, a man can say, "The lines are fallen unto me in pleasant places; yea, I have a goodly heritage" (Psa. 16. 6) he has the most satisfactory evidence that he is growing in the favour of God. For this state of mind is both a result and an evidence of the favour of God.

20. A growing disposition to *make light of our trials* and to magnify our blessings, is an evidence that we are growing in the favour of God.

21. Less and less *anxiety* and carefulness about the events of Providence, and especialy about the things that nearly and deeply affect ourselves, is evidence of growth in grace. This is an evidence of a broader and more implicit faith, of a more submissive will, and of a diminishing tendency to self-

seeking; and is, therefore, an evidence of growing favour with God.

22. Being less and less *disturbed* and troubled by the events of life, especially those that go counter to our own plans, and hopes, and expectations, and desires, and that thwart our most cherished aims, is an evidence of growth in grace.

23. A growing and realising *confidence* in the wisdom, benevolence, and universality of the providence of God, a state of mind that sees God in everything, is evidence of growth in race. Some minds become so spiritual that they hardly seem to reside in the body, but appear continually to perceive the presence of God in every event, almost as if they were disembodied, and beheld God face to face. They seem to dwell, live, move, and have their being, rather in the spiritual than in the natural world. They are continually under such a sense of the Divine presence, agency, and protection, as hardly to appear like inhabitants of earth. They are a living, walking mystery to those in the midst of whom they dwell. The springs of their activity are so Divine, their life is so much hidden in God, they act under influences so far above the world, that they cannot be judged by the same standards as other men. Carnal minds cannot understand them. Their hidden life is so unknown and so unknowable to those who are far below them in their spiritual life, that they are necessarily regarded as quite eccentric, as being mystics or monomaniacs, as having very peculiar religious views, as being enthusiasts, and perhaps fanatics. These persons are in the world, but they live above the world. They have so far escaped from the pollutions that are in the world, that they can truly and understandingly say, with Paul: "But God forbid that I should glory, save in the cross of our Lord Jesus Christ, by whom the world is crucified unto me, and I unto the world" (Gal. 6. 14). Such persons are evidently growing in the grace of God.

24. Being less and less disposed to *dwell upon the faults* and foibles of others, is an evidence of growth in grace.

25. Being less and less disposed to *speak severely*, or to judge uncharitably of others. A growing delicacy, or tenderness, in speaking of their real or supposed faults, behind their back, is an evidence of growth in grace.

26. An increasing reluctance to regard or *treat any one as an*

enemy, and an increasing ease and naturalness in treating them kindly, in praying for them heartily, and in efforts to do them good, is an evidence of growth in grace.

27. Less and less temptation to *remember an injury*, and the abatement of all desire to retaliate when injured, is an evidence of growth in grace.

28. A growing readiness and cordiality in *forgiving* and burying an injury out of sight, and a kind of moral inability to do otherwise than seek the highest good of those who have injured us most deeply, is an evidence of growth in grace.

29. When we find in our own experience, and manifest to others, that it is more and more natural to *regard all men as our brethren*, especially to drop out of view all sectarian discriminations, all ideas and prejudices of caste, and of colour, of poverty, and of riches, of blood relation, and of natural, rather than of spiritual ties, and to make common cause with God, in aiming to do good to all men, to enemies and friends alike, we have then ourselves, and give to others, the highest evidence of our growing in the favour of God.

30. Especially is it true, when we find ourselves very cordial and full-hearted in *making great sacrifices* for those that hate us, and having a willingness to lay down our lives for the promotion of their eternal salvation, that we have evidence of growth in grace.

31. Still more especially, when we find ourselves less and less inclined to *account anything a sacrifice* that we can do for God, or for the souls of men. When we can account our lives not dear unto us, if called to lay them down to save the souls of enemies; when, for the joy of saving them, we can "endure the cross, and despise the shame," or any sacrifice that we are called to make, we have evidence that we are growing in favour with God.

32. Again, when we find ourselves more and more inclined to "*count it all joy* when we fall into divers temptations" (Jas. 1. 2), and when we are disposed to look upon our trials, vexations, losses, and crosses in such a light as to lay less and less stress upon them, we have evidence that we are growing in patience, and therefore in favour with God.

33. When we find less and less reluctance to *making full confession* to those whom we have injured, when with

increasing readiness we lay our hearts open to be searched, when we take home conviction of wrong-doing, when, in such cases, we cannot rest till we have made the fullest confession and reparation within our power, and when to "own up," and confess, and make the fullest satisfaction, is a luxury to us, rather than a trial and a cross, we have evidence that we are growing in the favour of God.

34. When we are more and more impressed and affected by *the mercies of God*, and by the kindnesses of our fellow-men and those around us, when we more deeply and thoroughly appreciate manifestations of kindness in God, or in any one else, when we are more and more humbled and affected by these kindnesses, and find it more and more natural "to do justly, and to love mercy, and to walk humbly" (Mic. 6. 8), and live gratefully, we have evidence that we are growing in favour with God.

35. When we find ourselves drawn, with increasing earnestness, to follow on to *know more of the Lord*, we have evidence of growth in grace.

36. When we find ourselves more and more readily *impressed and affected, quickened and stimulated by religious truth*, and when we find an increasing harmony in the action of all our powers, intellectual, voluntary, and sensitive, in accepting, and resting in, the whole will and providence of God, however afflictive they may at present be, we have evidence that we are growing in grace.

37. A growing *jealousy for the honour of God*, for the purity and honour of His Church, for the rights of God, and for the rights of all men, is evidence of growing in conformity to God, and, of course, of growing in His favour.

VII. *HOW TO GROW IN GRACE.*

1. Fulfil the conditions noticed under the fourth head of this Lecture.

2. Remember that every step of progress must be made by faith, and not by works. The mistake that some good men have made upon this subject is truly amazing. The custom has been almost universal, to represent growth in grace as consisting in the formation of habits of obedience to God.

Now, it is quite surprising that so many good men have fallen into this mistake. The fact is, that every step of progress in the Christian life is taken by a fresh and fuller appropriation of Christ by faith, a fuller baptism of the Holy Spirit. As our weaknesses, infirmities, besetting sins, and necessities are revealed to us, by the circumstances of temptation through which we pass, our only efficient help is found in Christ, and we grow only as we step by step more fully appropriate Him, in one relation or another, and more fully "put Him on" (Rom. 13. 14). As we are more and more emptied of selfdependence, as we more and more renounce all expectation of forming holy habits by any obedience of ours, and as by faith we secure deeper and deeper baptisms of the Holy Ghost, and put on the Lord Jesus Christ, more and more thoroughly, and in more of His official relations, by just so much the faster do we grow in the favour of God. Nothing can be more erroneous and dangerous than the commonly received idea of growing in grace by the formation of holy habits. By acts of faith alone, we appropriate Christ, and we are as truly sanctified by faith as we are justified by faith. In my "Systematic Theology," in pointing out the conditions of entire or permanent sanctification, I have noticed some sixty of the official relations of Christ, as I have before said, and have there insisted, as I here insist, that growth in holiness, and consequently, in the favour of God, is secured only by fresh, fuller, and more thorough appropriation of Christ, in all these official relations. If you would grow in grace you must do it through faith. You must pray in faith for the Holy Spirit. You must appropriate and put on Christ through the Holy Spirit. At every forward step in your progress, you must have a fresh anointing of the Holy Spirit through faith.

REMARKS.

1. We see, from this subject, the vast importance of rightly instructing young converts. In many cases, they have very little instruction suited to their experience and degree of Christian intelligence. By some, such views are taken of the Perseverance of the Saints, that it is assumed that babes in Christ will grow without nursing, and without that sincere milk of the Word, by means of which they must grow. Some, taking it for

granted that they need instruction, unwittingly give them *false* instruction, and set them to work outwardly and zealously, without paying much regard to the strengthening and developing of the inward life. They do not teach them how to appropriate and live on Christ as their life, but continually press them to "do their duty, to labour for God, and labour for souls," while not sufficiently impressing upon them the idea that their doing is of no account, unless it proceeds from the life of God in their own souls. The result of this is a bustling, outward activity, while the inward spiritual life is decaying. This must end in disgust at one's own want of heart, and a settling back into apathy and neglect.

2. Sometimes there is a mistake made in the opposite direction. They are taught to rest in Christ, in such a sense as to take on a type of quietism and antinomian inactivity. They are exhorted to exercise faith, but they are not earnestly impressed with the conviction that it must be a faith that works, and works by love, that purifies the heart, and overcomes the world. The result is, they do nothing in religion. Sinners are allowed to sleep on in their midst, and go to hell, and they make no effort to save them.

3. We see the importance of a Holy Ghost anointed ministry. The great want of the Church is a ministry so thoroughly anointed by the Holy Ghost as to know how to lead the Church onward and upward, to the fullest development of Christian piety. In order to instruct converts, and keep the Church progressing in holiness, the minister must progress himself. He must be a truly living, growing Christian. I have good reason to know that the Churches in many places are deeply pained by the want of living piety and growth in their ministers. Their ministers are intellectual, literary, philosophical, theological, in their teaching, but they are sadly deficient in unction. They have but little power with God or with man. They instruct the intellect to a certain extent, but they do not meet the wants of the heart. Converts starve under their preaching. They preach an intellectual, rather than a spiritual Gospel. They preach religion as a theory, a doctrine, a philosophy, and not as a real living experience. It is often exceedingly painful to hear ministers preach who manifestly do not know what they say, or whereof they affirm. They speak

of religion as an inward sentiment, instead of heart devotion to God; as an emotion, a feeling, instead of an all-embracing and efficient love, a voluntary state and attitude of the mind, from which necessarily proceeds a holy life. They speak of faith as a mere intellectual state or conviction, and not as an act of trust, and of committal of the whole being, to do and suffer all the will of God. They speak of repentance as if it were a mere involuntary sorrow for sin. They do not teach that repentance is a change of mind toward God, a renunciation of the self-seeking spirit, and a turning of the whole mind to God. They speak of holiness as if it were a state utterly unattainable in this life. Indeed, I say it with sorrow, but I must say it, the teaching of a great many ministers is but a stumbling-block to the Church. Under their instruction, converts do not, and cannot get so established in grace as to be greatly useful, or to live lives that are honourable to Christ. Just think that in the Nineteenth Century ministers preach to converts that they must grow in grace by works. Be heaven and earth amazed at this! Such teachers do not know how to grow in grace themselves. Shall I be accounted harsh if I say: "They be blind leaders of the blind"?

4. We see the reason of so much backsliding. Converts will of course backslide who are led by false instruction. If, on the one hand, they are set to work out sanctification by works, their works will soon become dead works, and not be the result of that faith that works by love. If, on the other hand, they are crammed with abstract notions and doctrines, and taught to rest in an antinomian faith, they will sink into supineness and inactivity. I fully believe that in nearly all cases where there has been disastrous reaction after a revival, it has been owing to the want of timely and proper instruction. But to be timely and proper, it must be anointed instruction.

5. The Theological Seminaries need to pay vastly more attention to the growth in grace of their students. They need a professor of experimental religion, who has experience and power enough to press them along into those higher regions of Christian experience which are essential to their being able to lead the Church on to victory. It is amazing to see how little effort is made to cultivate the heart of young men studying for

the ministry.[1] We must have a change in this respect. A much higher standard of Christian experience must be required as a condition of ordination. It is painful to see how carefully men will be examined in regard to their intellectual attainments, while the accounts they give of their Christian experience will barely allow us to hope that they have been converted. How sad it is to set such young men to feed the Church of God. How do old Christians mourn, when they see the appointed leaders in the Church of God but spiritual babes.

6. I have never been present at the examination of a candidate for ordination where anything more than simple evidence of conversion was required of him. I never heard them questioned touching their progress in Christian experience, and regarding their spiritual ability to lead the flock of God into green pastures and beside still waters. I never

---

[1] In view of the fact that the idea of "revival," as advocated and explained by Finney, is in our own time, seldom associated primarily with colleges and seminaries, it is well to remember that Finney would recall very different conditions, and was urging a return to first principles rather than advocating a new departure. For example, Samuel Davies (regarding whom, see footnote, p. 20) cited (June 3, 1757) a letter (dated April 16th of the same year) from a friend (Mr. Samuel Finley, minister of Nottingham, Penn., one of the trustees of the College of New Jersey, and, like Davies himself, afterwards a President of the Institution): "Our glorious Redeemer has poured out His Holy Spirit upon the students at our College. The whole house was a Bochim. Mr. William Tennent, who was on the spot, says that there never was, he believes, more genuine sorrow for sin and longing after Jesus, that this glorious work spread like the increasing light of the morning, that there were no public outcries, but a decorous, silent solemnity." Again, in 1832 Dr. Ashbel Green wrote, regarding Princeton: "While I was a member of College, there were but two professors of religion among the students, and not more than five or six who scrupled the use of profane language in common conversation. When I was called to the Presidency of the College (1812), it was with a firm purpose that I would either work a reformation or sink under the attempt. In January, 1815, without any extraordinary preaching, in about four weeks there were very few individuals who were not deeply impressed. It seemed as if the whole of our charge was pressing into the Kingdom of God. The fruits of this revival were happy and

heard them questioned in a manner that manifested the slightest conception of what are the indispensable spiritual qualifications of a man who is to stand forth as the leader and spiritual instructor of the Church of God. More *hours* are spent in ascertaining the intellectual attainments of a candidate than *minutes* to ascertain his spiritual and experimental attainments. The whole examination will plainly indicate that the ordaining body lay very little stress on this part of a minister's education. Is it any wonder that the Church of God is so feeble and inefficient, while the leaders and teachers are, many of them, mere children in spiritual knowledge, while a ripe Christian experience is made no part of the indispensable education of a minister? Why, this is infinitely more dangerous and ridiculous than to entrust men to lead an army in the field, while they merely understand

---

lasting." (An account of this movement, issued in pamphlet form, was reprinted in Great Britain; and a "short system of questions and counsel," drawn up for the occasion by Dr. Green, was subsequently widely distributed as a tract.) In 1815, at Dartmouth College, Hanover, N.H., "while the College was beginning to be agitated by difficulties (between the President and the Trustees), without a premonition the Spirit of God evidently descended, and saved the whole body of students. A general and almost instantaneous solemnity prevailed. The chapel, the recitation-room—every place of meeting, became a scene of weeping, and presently of rejoicing. A revival of such rapidity and power has rarely been known." So testified (March 12, 1832) the President of the College (Dr. Nathan Lord), who also added particulars of subsequent revivals. Dr. Jeremiah Day (President of Yale) wrote (March 2, 1832): "The College Church was constituted in June, 1757. Since that time there have been several seasons of earnest attention to the great interest of religion, on the part of students, three of which, at least, were during the administration of President Dwight. . . . The fruits have been seen in the turning of numbers from the dominion of sin to a life devoted to the service of God. (See, more especially, Gillies' "Historical Collections" (appendix), and the Appendix to Sprague's "Lectures on Revivals of Religion.") In connection with revivals in seats of learning and education, the reader will inevitably recall the influence of the Wesleys and Whitefield at Oxford, of Simeon at Cambridge, and of the meetings at both Oxford and Cambridge conducted by D. L. Moody.

mathematics, and never have had any training or experience in military matters.

In this respect, too, there must be a great change. Churches should refuse to ordain and receive pastors, unless they are fully satisfied of their having made much progress in Christian experience, so as to be able to lead on, and keep the Church awake.

They should insist upon the education of his *heart* as well as his *head*; upon his ability to take young converts, and conduct them on to those deep experiences that will make them stable and efficient workers in the cause of God. Think of Theological Seminaries, where the leaders of the Church of God are taught that sanctification or growth in grace is attained by works and not by faith! Tell it not in Gath! Alas for Zion, when her great and good men fall into such mistakes![1]

---

[1] In the final Lecture, as originally delivered, Finney ended, as he began, with a general appeal to the Church at large. "Growth in grace" was to end in no self-satisfied introspection, but was to find its natural and glorious consequence in the spreading of the Redeemer's Kingdom. "When there is a revival, and Christians are awake, and get to a certain point, and then are carried no farther, the revival will of course cease. If the Church is kept advancing, the revival will not cease. If the instructions given, and the measures pursued, keep the Church going ahead, and the young converts growing in grace, the revival will go on. Let the minister keep pouring in the truth, let him know fully, from time to time, the state of the Church, and find out just what the people need, and treat them thoroughly, and not suffer them to stand still for the want of being searched, and probed, and urged along in their course; then the revival may gain strength and power all the time. If the means could be made whereby to bring influence to bear upon the Church, and upon the young converts—to keep them out of the way of sinners, and keep them continually advancing in holiness—the revival would never cease."